Governing the Workplace

Governing the Workplace

The Future of Labor and Employment Law

Paul C. Weiler

Harvard University Press
Cambridge, Massachusetts
London, England
1990

Library of Congress Cataloging-in-Publication Data

Weiler, Paul C.
  Governing the workplace : the future of labor and employment law / Paul
  C. Weiler.
    p. cm.
  ISBN 0-674-35765-5 (alk. paper)
    1. Labor laws and legislation—United States.   2. Trade-unions—
  Law and legislation—United States.   I. Title.
KF3369.W397   1990
344.73'01—dc20   89-26969
[347.3041]   CIP

To Florrie

Preface

I set out in these pages to cover much of the vast terrain encompassed within the law of the workplace. The story of how this book came to be written will, I hope, orient the reader to the particular trail that my argument will follow.

Four years ago I began work on what I expected would be a law review article about wrongful dismissal, in which I wanted to examine both the theoretical question of why wrongful dismissal might be considered a significant problem in the labor market, and the kinds of solutions that might be forthcoming from corporate management, common law litigation, administrative regulation, or collective bargaining. The article was to be the latest in a series of detailed analyses I had already published, dealing with workplace topics such as the union representation campaign, comparable worth, affirmative action, and occupational injuries. The issue of wrongful dismissal forced me to confront head-on the fundamental challenge to contemporary labor and employment law, launched in the eighties by Richard Epstein, which proclaims employment at will as the legal apotheosis of a free and competitive labor market. Eventually, my treatment of employment at will and wrongful dismissal evolved into Chapter 2 of this book.

I soon realized that a fully adequate treatment of these topics required a much broader analysis of the comparative advantages of the market and its institutional competitors. In tandem with Epstein's distinctive approach, Richard Posner had led his law and economics confrères in a serious and critical look at the ways that our labor laws foster and shape a system of collective bargaining to effect an unfortunate—in his eyes—cartelization of the market. In the labor and employment field, at least, the brand of economics espoused by the law and economics movement has been of the neoclassical price/auction persuasion usually associated with the University of Chicago. My response to their critique drew heavily on the rather different understanding of the contemporary labor market that has its deepest roots at Harvard and M.I.T. My depiction of and response to the law and economics analysis of labor law and labor unions is contained in Chapters 3 and 4 of this book.

Even before law and economics entered the scholarly debates about the law of the workplace, an equally potent challenge had been launched in the seventies by the Critical Legal Studies (CLS) group, whose most prominent exponent in the labor field is Karl Klare. Because CLS is the legal offspring of the New Left movement of the sixties, one would expect its adherents to judge that present-day labor law and collective bargaining has systematically attenuated any serious role for direct participation by employees, not simply in the bargaining process, but also in making decisions that would affect their daily life on the job.

Ironically, a similar criticism of the organization of work in America has come in this decade from within the establishment, propounded by a number of teachers and scholars of human resource management in the business schools at Harvard, M.I.T., and elsewhere—people who argue that much greater employee involvement and commitment is indispensable for American industry if it is to compete effectively in the new international marketplace. Chapter 5 of this book analyzes the reasons for concern about the standard *modus operandi* of American managers and American unions, describes innovative modes of direct employee involvement now emerging in both union and nonunion contexts, and critically appraises the legal treatment of "participatory management" by our labor jurisprudence, which may be traced back to the Wagner Act model of the thirties.

As I reflected on this range of scholarly perspectives on the law at work, it became evident that the stark decline of private-sector unionism in this country has left a serious vacuum in effective representation of the interests of employees in a world of work that has been undergoing a fundamental economic, demographic, technological, and cultural transformation. And for reasons that I spell out in detail in this book, I am convinced that this representation gap will not effectively be filled even by more sophisticated human resource management or more ambitious government regulation.

In my early work on American labor law, I explained why the National Labor Relations Act made it far too easy for nonunion employers to frustrate any desire among their employees for representation by independent unions of their own choosing. Building on my personal experience of helping reshape Canadian labor law, I spelled out a program of labor law reform that would do a better job of protecting the ability of American employees to exercise their rights to self-organization and collective dealing with their employers, rights that the federal government had promised them a half-century earlier. But although I believe that a program of labor law reform is still necessary—even more necessary—in the nineties, I am now convinced that it would not be sufficient. If we do want to guarantee to employees in a firm anything like the kind of representation now enjoyed as a matter of course by the firm's shareholders, we will have to take seriously the European experience in the workplace (as Clyde Summers has been arguing for the last decade). In particular, we shall have to establish a new basic employment right that will guarantee meaningful participation and representation for employees in every sizable office and plant in this country. Chapter 6 describes the nature, rationale, and prospects for such wide-ranging legal reforms both within and beyond our current labor law model.

In a project that involved not only writing this book over the last four years, but also publishing related law review articles in the previous half-dozen years, I have incurred scholarly and personal debts to a great many people, far too many to mention all of them individually. There are some, though, whom I must explicitly thank here. First are my intrepid research assistants in the labor area, Glen Fine, Brian Boyle, Jonathan Wiener, and Chip Brannen. Next are those who were kind enough to read and comment on my manuscript: among my colleagues at the Harvard Law School, Lance Liebman, David Charny, Lou Kaplow, Lucian Bebchuck, and Charles Fried; among visitors to the Law School, Cass Sunstein, Bill Simon, and Oliver Williamson; among those who work in the labor field around Cambridge and elsewhere, John Dunlop, Richard Freeman, Tom Kochan, Charles Heckscher, Sanford Jacoby, David Beatty and Karl Klare; and finally, Richard Posner, who, as a reader of the manuscript for Harvard University Press, offered a host of cogent observations to which I attempt to respond in this final version. I also want to express appreciation to my colleagues on the Public Review Board of the United Auto Workers, with whom I have had the pleasure for the last ten years of meeting and discussing what is happening in the world of work: George Higgins, Frank McCulloch, Jean McKelvey, James Jones, Ben Aaron, Ted St. Antoine, Eleanor Holmes Norton, and David Klein—as well as Larry Gold, General Counsel of the AFL-CIO.

Needless to say, the actual production of a work such as this entails the efforts and contributions of many more people than the author and his scholarly colleagues. My hard-working secretaries, Joann Beserdetsky and her predecessors, endured innumerable dictation tapes and turned them into a readable manuscript. The invaluable word processing team at the Harvard Law School—especially Cheryl Frost, Susan Salvato, and Deborah Soares—were unfailingly cooperative with the many additions and revisions I made in this manuscript from start to finish. Dennis Myers rendered valuable assistance in checking the numerous citations throughout the book. Finally, I express my appreciation to Michael Aronson and the staff at Harvard University Press for turning the manuscript into this published volume.

But my greatest debt by far is owed to my wife, Florrie. She has been part of this project for a decade, not only providing encouragement and moral support at home, but also serving occasionally as a researcher and consistently as my most valuable editorial critic and adviser, from my first *Harvard Law Review* article to the last chapter in this book. For better or for worse, then, this book is dedicated to Florrie.

Contents

Governing the Workplace

1 · The Transformation of Labor and Employment Law

The Workplace Setting

Late in 1987 a San Francisco jury awarded nearly half a million dollars to one Barbara Luck after she had been fired for refusing to undergo a drug test at work.[1] For six years Luck had been a computer programmer with the Southern Pacific Transportation Company. As have a great number of employers in recent years, Southern Pacific instituted in 1985 a mandatory program of random drug testing of all its employees. Luck was one of the first in the engineering department to be asked to provide a urine sample for chemical testing: when she refused to do so, she was fired. All her fellow employees complied with the employer's directive. The jury found that Southern Pacific's action was illegal, and the size of its monetary award vividly conveyed the jury's displeasure with the company's actions.

So far as I know, the Luck ruling is the first occasion on which the legality of mandatory drug testing has been scrutinized in the context of a wrongful dismissal suit by the aggrieved employee. As such, the case presents a number of hotly contested issues raised by such programs. Is drug testing really an effective mechanism through which employers can reduce the use of drugs by their employees and thereby enhance the safety and productivity of their operations? Does the application of such a program on a random basis to the entire work force, regardless of particular assignments and responsibilities and of past employment records and problems, constitute excessive and undue invasion of the personal privacy of the employees?

1. The Barbara Luck wrongful dismissal case was described in a brief note in 5 *BNA Employee Relations Weekly* 1384 (1987). I learned more about the factual background of the case in a telephone conversation with Luck's attorney, Mark Rudy, on May 24, 1988.

These are crucial issues, indeed, and they are being canvassed in a variety of constitutional challenges to mandatory drug testing by public employers and in debates about legislation which would control this practice in the privately owned workplace.[2] However, the problem of drug abuse is not my focus here. My concern, instead, is with the institutional question lurking beneath the surface of this and every other contemporary dispute in the workplace—disputes over, for example, employer use of lie detector tests as well as drug tests, the pursuit of pay equity by women in traditionally "female jobs," affirmative action for minority workers, or plant closings and mass layoffs affecting all employees. What is the appropriate procedure for resolving such conflicts on the job? Should a problem such as drug testing simply be relegated to voluntary resolution by the employer and the employees directly affected? Or, if we believe individual employees like Barbara Luck need some external help to constrain the power of management in large enterprises like Southern Pacific, what is the mechanism appropriate for that purpose? Should we applaud the burgeoning growth of private litigation, which brings employer practices under the scrutiny and verdict of lay juries, or should we explore other devices? The theme of this book, then, is how the American workplace should be governed, and the comparative advantages—from the perspective of workers, employers, and the general community—of alternative institutions which are or should be available for this purpose.

One finds little popular or political preoccupation with this theme. For example, the problem of how best to organize and govern the workplace was conspicuous by its absence from the debates in the last (1988) presidential race, which went on for over two years, in stark contrast to the often detailed attention the candidates paid to policies for agriculture, energy, trade, capital formation, and the like. However, if the recent surge of scholarly analysis of work and employment is any harbinger, this strangely invisible quality is likely to change.

2. The U.S. Supreme Court finally weighed in with its view of the constitutional dimensions of drug testing in a pair of decisions in the spring of 1989, holding that the Fourth Amendment does not preclude the federal government from mandatory testing of certain categories of its employees with special responsibilities. See Skinner v. Railway Labor Executives Association, 109 S.Ct. 1402 (1989), and National Treasury Employees Union v. Von Raab, 109 S.Ct. 1384 (1989). In the fast growing legal literature on the broader topic of drug testing of all employees, private as well as public, the best review I have seen of the issues and developments is the Report of the Committee on Labor and Employment Law, "Drug Testing in the Workplace," 43 *The Record of the Association of the Bar of the City of New York* 447 (1988).

Throughout the eighties writers from a variety of intellectual perspectives underscored the pervasive importance of the world of work, the vital and often conflicting interests of employees and firms in decisions which must be made on or about the job, and the major changes in the socioeconomic environment which undermine our traditional arrangements for producing and legitimizing such decisions.[3]

Why are work and employment so important—vastly more so than other areas of import such as agriculture, for example, however much we feel compelled to fashion and debate a national farm policy? More than one hundred million Americans are employed at any time. Wages and salaries paid to employees to support themselves and their families amount to three-quarters of the gross national income. In the American political economy, the job rather than the state has become the source of most of the social safety net on which people must rely when they are not employed—that is, when they are sick, disabled, or retired. And the plants and offices in which we work are the places where we spend much of our adult lives, where we develop important aspects of our personalities and our relationships, and where we may be exposed to a variety of physical or psychological traumas.

These several dimensions of work make it clear how vital employment is to the personal and financial aspirations of workers.[4] The flip side of the coin is that for employers, payments of worker salaries and benefits constitute the bulk of the financial cost of production in the economy (and are also, of course, the major source of consumer purchasing power for goods and services produced by the employers' firms). Equally important, we now appreciate that labor is a peculiarly challenging factor of production. However rich its natural resources, however costly and sophisticated the capital technology, a firm or an economy which does not have a skilled and committed work force will not be able to transform these physical assets into efficient and productive enterprises.[5]

At the same time, while both employers and employees, labor and capital, need each other's contribution and cooperation for the success

3. References to the most important recent writing on the subject will be provided at different points in this opening chapter and again where relevant to my argument in the main body of the book.

4. For a more extended discussion, see the introductory chapter in the Report of the Special Task Force to the Secretary of HEW, *Work in America* 1 (Cambridge, Mass.: MIT Press, 1973).

5. For a book-length treatment of this theme, see F. Ray Marshall, *Unheard Voices: Labor and Economic Policy in a Competitive World* (New York: Basic Books, 1987).

of their joint enterprise, these parties are constantly at risk of conflict over the terms of their relationship and how to share the fruits of their venture. It is not surprising, then, that we have a vast and complex system of law to settle many of these issues in the employment relationship. This body of law has two aspects. The immediately visible task is to make and enforce judgments about how to deal with particular substantive problems, such as reducing exposure to toxic substances on the job. But there is a further latent function of this law: the allocation of authority for making and implementing policies such as the prevention of industrial disease. In that respect, labor and employment law both controls and empowers workers and employers (and the administrative apparatus of the state) in a manner analogous to the way in which corporate and securities law functions for suppliers of capital to the firm.

However, the underpinnings of traditional authority relationships on the job have been eroded by a number of profound changes in the socioeconomic environment of the workplace. Consider this very brief synopsis of some of these trends.[6]

Product Markets. In less than two decades we have moved from a comparatively sheltered and sometimes closely regulated domestic economy in which American firms were readily able to sell the goods and services produced by their employees, into a world of much sharper internal and international competition, at levels which regularly threaten the economic viability of some of our largest corporations. If we hope to provide "good jobs at good wages" to our citizens, American enterprise is going to have to exhibit much more creativity and flexibility in producing high-value products that cannot readily be duplicated by low-wage mass producers in third world economies.

---

6. The trends that I will be sketching in the next few pages have been the subject of a vast outpouring of recent writing. Among the books written from the perspective which assumes that the governance of the workplace and the contribution and fate of the employee are important dimensions in these broader socioeconomic trends are Marshall, *Unheard Voices;* Robert B. Reich, *The Next American Frontier* (New York: Times Books, 1983); Michael J. Piore and Charles F. Sabel, *The Second Industrial Divide: Possibilities for Prosperity* (New York: Basic Books, 1984); Robert Kuttner, *The Economic Illusion: False Choices Between Prosperity and Social Justice* (Boston: Houghton Mifflin, 1984); Lester C. Thurow, *The Zero-Sum Solution: Building a World Class American Economy* (New York: Simon and Schuster, 1985); Frank Levy, *Dollars and Dreams: The Changing American Income Distribution* (New York: Russell Sage, 1987); Stephen S. Cohen and John Zysman, *Manufacturing Matters: The Myth of the Post-Industrial Economy* (New York: Basic Books, 1987); Bennett Harrison and Barry Bluestone, *The Great U-Turn: Corporate Restructuring and the Polarizing of America* (New York: Basic Books, 1988); and the Cuomo Commission Report, *A New American Formula for a Strong Economy* (New York: Simon and Schuster, 1988).

Capital Markets. At the same time, developments in our capital markets have facilitated a far higher incidence of corporate raids and hostile takeovers, which have removed much of the comfortable insulation hitherto enjoyed by senior management from the consequences of less than optimal financial performance for the firm's shareholders. The typical aftermath (indeed, increasingly often the prelude) for such a raid is a major restructuring of corporate strategy and operations aimed at enhancing the value of the shareholders' equity, but frequently with much less salubrious consequences for other stakeholders in the firm—in particular, its employees.[7]

Technological Innovation. Such pressures from the product and capital markets have spurred the development and introduction of computer technology to American industry, thereby helping to transform the plant and the office for better and for worse. Like labor-saving technology introduced over the last century, computer automation has a two-edged impact on the work force. Typically it produces cleaner, safer, less physically demanding, and often more lucrative jobs for those who fill them, while imposing considerable burdens of adjustment on those who are displaced and must find new jobs or new careers. What some consider distinctive about the computer—about what has been termed "the age of the smart machine"[8]—is the dramatically different vantage point it offers on the entire enterprise. The computer's capacity for collecting and recalling the sweep and the detail of the firm's operations may be bringing us to a fork in the road of workplace governance from which we can choose to proceed either toward much closer managerial monitoring and control, or toward greater worker autonomy in and influence on the enterprise.

Work Force. That choice will be made by and for the most heterogeneous work force that has ever existed in this country.[9] In the fifties, the

7. For a rather skeptical review of the supposedly benign consequences of the new era in American capitalism, see David J. Ravenscraft and F. M. Scherer, *Mergers, Sell-Offs and Economic Efficiency* (Washington, D.C.: Brookings Institution, 1987). For essays expressing a variety of viewpoints on this phenomenon, see John Coffee, Jr., Louis Lowenstein, and Susan Rose-Ackerman, eds., *Knights, Raiders, and Targets: The Impact of Hostile Takeovers* (New York: Oxford University Press, 1988).

8. This is the title of the provocative book by Shoshana Zuboff, *In the Age of the Smart Machine: The Future of Work and Power* (New York: Basic Books, 1988), describing and speculating about the potential effects of computerization on the distribution of authority at work.

9. Levy, *Dollars and Dreams,* provides a detailed statistical picture of the evolution of the American labor force since World War II; and William B. Johnston et al., *Work Force 2000: Work and Workers for the 21st Century* (Indianapolis: Hudson Institute, 1987), projects the likely trends in the composition of the work force by the year 2000. Perhaps the most

standard image of the worker was a white male wearing a blue collar, working in a manufacturing plant to earn a wage to support himself, his wife, and his family at home. As we near the nineties, such a composite image accurately reflects only a small fraction of the hundred million employed Americans. A worker today is far more likely than ever to be a female or minority employee in a white-collar office job, and only one of two or more wage earners in the family. The average age of the work force has gradually declined at the same time as the average length of workers' schooling (though not necessarily the quality of their education) has been increasing. More subtle but equally significant is the fact that many entrants into the labor force over the last two decades were part of or heirs to the cultural revolution of the sixties, which called into question the expectation that deference to established authority was part of the natural order of things—whether the authority was the parent in the home, the teacher in the classroom, or the manager on the job.

This is just a brief sketch of some of the important trends which are reshaping the present-day employment relationship. My aim in this book is not so much to document these socioeconomic changes as to trace their connection to an equally striking transformation in the governance of the workplace.

In the next chapter I shall use the issue of wrongful dismissal as an extended case study of the meaning and implication of these trends. It is intuitively obvious that the way we handle the firing of an employee is vitally important to the workers and firms affected. As we shall see, reflection on why this has become a serious challenge for public policy also provides an illuminating angle of vision on the nature of the employment relationship itself. But my overriding theme in this book is the question, who will represent the interests of workers in decisions about how and when employees will be fired, or hired and retired, or dealt with in the innumerable situations which arise while they are actually employed and on the job? Should such representation come from the lawyer in the courtroom, or the government official in charge of an administrative program, or the personnel manager devising the firm's human resource policies in the executive suite, or the union leader engaged in collective bargaining with the employer, or perhaps

eye-catching figure from *Work Force 2000* is the estimate (pp. xx-xxi) that five out of six (or about 84 percent) net additions to the labor force between 1985 and 2000 will be women, nonwhite minority group members, or immigrants (versus their 50 percent share of the present work force).

from employees themselves participating in a committee structure that exercises real influence inside the firm? Before undertaking a systematic appraisal of each of these options and then developing a program of legal reform to facilitate the ones I favor, I shall review in this opening part of the book the rise and decline of these several contenders for the crucial role of governing the workplace.

The Rise and Decline of Collective Bargaining

Unquestionably, thirty years ago one would not have dreamed of settling such a contentious issue as drug testing through the use of legal authority in the civil jury process. The favored instrument, instead, would have been direct voluntary negotiation between the employer and a union which the employees had selected for purposes of collective bargaining. Sometimes such problems were explicitly addressed by the parties, which would negotiate detailed programs to deal with them. Alternatively, the matters might first have arisen under the umbrella of the general contract protection against unjust discipline and discharge, and been taken through the grievance arbitration procedure for resolution. Even that process was ultimately subject to the control of the immediate parties, who could select and remove their arbitrators as well as revise arbitration rulings for future cases.

In the eyes of its proponents[10] the institution of collective bargaining had several important virtues. First, while a solitary employee—a Barbara Luck, for example—would probably have little realistic chance of avoiding either invasion of privacy by a drug test or loss of her job if she refused to provide a urine sample, her prospects would be much better if she were to band together with all her fellow employees in pursuit of that goal. At a minimum, such an association would provide a forum in which the employees could discuss and formulate their concerns, then use a skilled representative to voice their position to a management team representing the employer, and in all likelihood exert considerable influence on the design, if not the existence, of any drug testing program.

At the same time, any restraints on management prerogatives would be those that had been mutually accepted by the parties themselves, given their respective needs and priorities. In other employment relationships in which the participants had different views about what was

10. The major recent work reviewing the evidence about the positive values as well as the negative consequences of collective bargaining is Richard B. Freeman and James L. Medoff, *What Do Unions Do?* (New York: Basic Books, 1984).

important, they were free to go their own way on this and other issues. Indeed, the initial judgments made in the original setting were equally open to renegotiation as experience seemed to dictate. Nor is this just an imaginary scenario with respect to the drug issue itself. Inveterate readers of the sports pages will have observed essentially that scenario unfolding as collective bargaining in the several professional sports has grappled in a variety of ways with the common problem of drugs and testing throughout the eighties.

In sum, collective bargaining was and is a governance mechanism which offers employees a blend of *protection* and *participation* through private, local, and voluntary settlement of workplace problems. However, the existence and shape of the institution itself is assumed to be a matter of public concern and is thus the object of substantial legal support and influence. A half century ago the National Labor Relations Act (NLRA) was enacted to encourage the organization of employees for purposes of collective bargaining whenever employees in a work unit favored that option; to protect the employees in question from coercion and restraint in making their choice; and to require the employer to recognize and deal with any union that might be selected by a majority of the employees. Since the mid-thirties, then, our federal labor policy has been to facilitate the *reconstruction* of the unfettered individualistic labor market so as to give employees greater group leverage in dealing with what were often large, powerful corporate employers. But the actual terms and conditions of employment which flowed from the bargaining process were, with rare exceptions, determined by the mutual agreement of the parties. The content of their agreement would reflect the parties' respective needs and resources, shaped both by the state of the labor market and by the external product and capital markets in which the firm and its employees had to operate.

For the first twenty years of its life, this New Deal labor policy was highly successful in its own terms.[11] The scope of union representation

11. The figures following in the text regarding trends in union representation of the private sector work force are drawn from earlier research which is distilled in my essay, "Milestone or Tombstone: The Wagner Act at Fifty," 23 *Harvard Journal on Legislation* 1 (1986). While there is considerable variation in the precise numbers for union density reported by different authors (the ratio varying widely depending on how the numerator and the denominator are defined), there is no doubt about the basic phenomenon, that private sector unionization experienced a steep rise and fall over the last fifty years. For recent brief but careful analyses of the trends and causes, see Henry S. Farber, "The Recent Decline of Unionization in the United States," 238 *Science* 915 (Nov. 13, 1987); and Richard B. Freeman, "Contraction and Expansion: The Divergence of Private Sector and Public Sector Unionism in the United States," 2 *Journal of Economic Perspectives* 63 (Spring 1988).

in collective bargaining, which had been roughly 15 percent of the private sector labor force just before enactment of the NLRA, soared to nearly 40 percent by the mid-fifties; all indications were that this figure would rise to 45 or even 50 percent some time thereafter. Indeed, the influence of the union movement was actually much broader than the direct measures of "union density" might indicate. The core of union membership was male, blue-collar production workers in manufacturing industries, many of whom were employed by the larger, more successful firms—such as General Motors, U.S. Steel, and General Electric—which were pacesetters in sophisticated management techniques. Thus the human resource innovations developed in collective bargaining between these firms and their unions soon set a pattern which was imitated by unionized firms for their nonunion white-collar workers, and by nonunion firms for both their blue-collar and white-collar labor force.

In the mid-fifties there began a remarkable turnaround in the fortunes of collective bargaining, and the institution started on a long and inexorable downhill slide. Associated with the decline was an equally marked change in the composition of the work force. The pendulum swung from manufacturing to service industries, from blue-collar to white-collar jobs, from an almost exclusively male work force to a high percentage of female workers, and from the northern to the southern regions of the country. The established unions found that they could not put down substantial roots among the new and growing segments of the labor force (at least in the private if not the public sector); therefore, even if these unions had been able to maintain their existing positions in their traditional constituencies, their proportionate statistical share of the overall labor force would decrease.

But starting in the early seventies, union coverage began to fall even in its traditional bastions. Union representation typically suffers significant attrition when already organized plants are closed and firms go out of business. That trend was even more pronounced in the early eighties, when the "rust belt" reeled under the pressures of intensified foreign competition and a deep recession. Just to stay even, unions annually had to organize their proportionate share of the workers in the new plants and firms which opened to supply new markets. But the dominant industrial unions such as the United Auto Workers, the Steel Workers, the Electrical Workers, the Teamsters, and the construction building trades were not able to secure bargaining rights in many of the new units, either in the fast-growing "sun belt" or even in the north. By the mid-eighties, then, private sector union coverage had fallen from its 40 percent share in the mid-fifties to just over 15 percent only three decades later. Recall that the latter was roughly the same percentage as had obtained a half-century earlier, when the Wagner Act was enacted in order to expand the prospects for collective employee action. Moreover, there is no reason to suppose that the 15 percent figure is a bottom point in the slide. Unless the next decade witnesses a change as far-reaching as the one that occurred in the fifties, simple extrapolation of existing trends indicates that union density will be down to less than 10 percent by the turn of the century.

But these empirical trends are not by themselves an index of the failure of the legal policy of the NLRA. Such a value judgment must ultimately rest on a diagnosis of the reasons fewer and fewer American workers are securing collective bargaining under the auspices of the Act.

For our purposes, the multitude of specific explanations for this phenomenon can be divided into two categories—a decline in the demand for collective bargaining and a decline in the supply of this institution. On the demand side, one explanation emphasizes that to many of the new breed of white-collar and often female workers (exemplified by Barbara Luck, our computer programmer), joining a union has had little appeal.[12] Note that this demographic and attitudinal story could hold true for only private sector employees, because one predominantly female, white-collar occupational category, the school teachers, has actually been the fastest-growing segment of the unionized work force for the last quarter-century. But in this view, to the extent that this account is generally valid for the private sector covered by the NLRA, the decline in union representation represents only a failure of the unions, not of the labor laws. After all, the object of the law is simply to give workers the right to collective bargaining if they want it, not to foist it upon worker groups who would rather not have it.

The contrary prescription would follow if the "supply side" diagnosis were valid—that the source of a considerable share of union decline is sustained employer resistance, making collective bargaining less readily available to employees. From this point of view the problem is

12. Among labor law scholars the major exponent of this position is Jack Getman. For a recent distillation of his views, see Julius G. Getman, "Ruminations on Union Organizing in the Private Sector," 53 *University of Chicago Law Review* 45 (1986). I am probably Getman's opposite number in the debate regarding the need, if any, for labor law reform, as is clear from my essay "Milestone or Tombstone." Later I shall delve more deeply into the debate, giving the evidence and arguments on both sides, with references both to our own writing and to the major contributions of several other legal scholars and social scientists.

that more and more American employers, wanting to remain or to become nonunion, are utilizing a variety of antiunion measures which make it ever more difficult for employees interested in collective bargaining to actually exercise their statutory rights to join a union, at least at a price most workers might reasonably be expected to pay. If and to the extent this second account is valid, there is clearly much better reason to believe that something in our labor law needs fixing.

Later in this book I present the evidence for the two competing explanations for the downward trend in union membership, and consider the implications for the future design of our national labor policy. For the moment it is more interesting to speculate on the reasons why a shift might have occurred in either or both the demand for or supply of union representation.

With respect to the apparent decline in employee demand, two factors seem to be operating side by side. One is that human resource management by many American employers has become more professional, more sophisticated, and more attuned to the needs and interests of the employees.[13] Increasingly sustained efforts are being made to provide decent wages and benefits, to eliminate unfair treatment of individual employees, and to produce a secure and congenial workplace environment. Part of the reason for the improvement in personnel practice is the expectation that it will attract and retain a high-quality, well-motivated work force. Needless to say, another powerful factor is the employer's hope that such measures will head off any felt need among the employees to explore an alternative instrument—unionization—to secure favorable conditions on the job.

At the same time there has been a gradual alteration in the character of unionism itself.[14] From one perspective, unionization has been and can be viewed as an *activity* of the employees themselves, whereby they participate as a group in the improvement of their own working conditions. In its current image, though, the union is usually perceived as an *entity* external to the employees: as a large, bureaucratic organization whose full-term officials periodically negotiate a long-term contract behind closed doors with the employer, and then represent a

---

13. See Michael Beer, Bert Spector, Paul R. Lawrence, D. Quinn Mills, and Richard E. Walton, *Managing Human Assets* (New York: Free Press, 1984), for a presentation of the current lore of human resource management as developed and taught by the case studies at the Harvard Business School.

14. This is one theme of the important book by Charles C. Heckscher, *The New Unionism: Employee Involvement in the Changing Corporation* (New York: Basic Books, 1988).

fairly small number of employees who are aggrieved by the way management administers the contract during its lifetime.

Of course, the main reason unionism and collective bargaining have evolved this way is that a large and sophisticated organization and professional staff were needed to deal effectively with even larger and more sophisticated corporations, and to establish the kinds of protection employees want without having to pay an unacceptable price for it. But whatever the reason for its evolution, the resulting brand of unionism displayed certain negative attributes.

First, even if larger, more highly bureaucratized unions do produce a higher level of employment protection, at least within the standard compass of the labor contract, there is little participation by the employees in the effort.[15] And, until recently at least, little or no attention has been paid to the felt need of workers to have a positive personal influence on the daily character of their jobs and the productive operation of which they are a part.

Even worse, as the union appears increasingly to be an entity separate and apart from the employees—a professional organization analogous in function if not in constituency to the company personnel department—concerns naturally arise about how to protect the employees, individually and collectively, from the union itself and its management. That need will be felt even when the union's leadership ethos is benign, because it is desirable to reduce the incidence of ineffective and inadequate representation. But the unhappy reality is that occasionally the attitude of union officialdom is not benign; union leaders' actions are sometimes motivated by the desire to perpetuate their tenure and to enhance their financial rewards, a situation that may result in an undemocratic and corrupt union organization. Perhaps the ultimate testimony to this human and organizational failing is the recent spate of trusteeships imposed on local unions by courts acting under the auspices of RICO, a piece of criminal legislation which the Congress enacted to fight organized crime.

If the trends I have just described were widespread enough, the

---

15. The sense of alienation of the ordinary employee from the union and the bargaining process is a major theme in the critique from the left of the American industrial relations system. In the world of labor law scholarship, the most prominent critic of conventional unionism and labor law (albeit a strong defender of the principle of collective bargaining for workers) is Karl E. Klare, whose recent piece, "Workplace Democracy and Market Reconstruction: An Agenda for Legal Reform," 38 *Catholic University Law Review* 1 (1988), distills much of his writing and analysis over the last decade.

combination of a more appealing work situation provided by the employer and a less attractive union alternative could have been sufficient to produce much if not all the decline in union representation observable in the aggregate statistics. But American employers have not been content to allow these forces to play themselves out, with whatever impact they might have on the employees' own sentiments. American business has adopted, instead, a posture of sustained and active resistance to collective bargaining for its employees.

Within the longer-term historical perspective, that posture is not surprising.[16] For the last century management in the United States has been vigorously opposed to union representation, as much if not more so than management in any other industrialized nation. True, in the mid-fifties an *entente cordiale* was seemingly reached with organized labor, but with hindsight that appears to have been merely a temporary lull in the struggle. A number of maverick nonunion employers continued to develop and to demonstrate the effectiveness of a variety of tactics for frustrating union organizing. By the early seventies, more and more supposed business statesmen were beginning to utilize these and other tactics as part of a corporate strategy to achieve as low a level of unionization as possible. The result is that whatever wavering affections American workers might have as between their employer and a union, they now recognize that it will be an arduous, stressful, and risky journey to proceed from an initial interest in collective bargaining, through the representation campaign, and eventually to a first contract with a union representative firmly inside the plant or office. Unsurprisingly, whatever their personal inclinations, fewer and fewer workers are prepared to undertake that journey.

My aim at this point, though, is not to appraise the legitimacy and the effectiveness of such employer resistance, but rather to understand the motivation behind it. A standard management refrain is that however necessary or even helpful collective bargaining might have been for the workplace and economy fifty years ago, the institution has become unsuited for the present economic climate. It simply cannot

16. For a historical account of the highly distinctive response of American business to unionism, see Sanford M. Jacoby, "American Exceptionalism Revisited: The Importance of Management," in Sanford M. Jacoby, ed., *Masters to Managers: Historical and Comparative Perspectives on American Employers* (forthcoming; New York: Columbia University Press, 1990). In an earlier article, "Reflections on the Distinctive Character of American Labor Laws," 84 *Harvard Law Review* 1394 (1971), Derek Bok shows how the long-existing phenomenon of vigorous employer resistance to union representation of employees has shaped the peculiar features of American labor law.

accommodate the pronounced changes in product and capital markets and in the nature of the work force and the new technology to which I alluded earlier.[17]

There is a particular failing to which collective bargaining is said to be especially prone. Although the wages and other contract terms developed by unions and employers may well have been suitable for the situations for which they were first devised, the political dynamic in large, industry-wide unions impels their leadership to use their leverage to expand each of such terms far beyond what they were in the original setting, and then to fight vigorously against any "concessions" which employers find they need to accommodate changing market conditions, new technology, or even the aspirations of a different work force. The consequence of this inertial force to the labor agreement is that a unionized auto worker or steel worker or construction worker ends up being paid wages and benefits that are far higher than the going rate among their competitors, and a network of contract restrictions—"featherbedding," as these are often called—hamstrings management in adjusting its production process to the firm's fast-changing environment. In sum, while the proponents of collective bargaining have celebrated its capacity for voluntary, decentralized problem solving, American business has persuaded itself that the institution is far too ossified a mechanism with which to burden the enterprise in the more testing climate of the eighties and nineties.

In sketching the managers' refrain, I do not mean to endorse its general accuracy. Enough anecdotal evidence exists to give their story some verisimilitude,[18] but whether it is systematically valid is a matter I shall take up later on. I should also underline that this account is not a *refutation* of the employer resistance explanation for the decline in

17. For a brief and comparatively balanced statement of the management point of view by the president of the National Association of Manufacturers, see Alexander Trowbridge, "A Management Look at Labor Relations," in Seymour M. Lipset, ed., *Unions in Transition: Entering the Second Century,* p. 405 (San Francisco: ICS Press, 1986).

18. That there is in fact substance to that concern is evidenced by recent accounts of the performance of collective bargaining in the auto and steel industries over the last several decades, by authors who are fundamentally sympathetic to the institution of union representation. See Harry C. Katz, *Shifting Gears: Changing Labor Relations in the U.S. Automobile Industry* (Cambridge, Mass.: MIT Press, 1985); and John P. Hoerr, *And the Wolf Finally Came: The Decline of the American Steel Industry* (Pittsburgh: University of Pittsburgh Press, 1988). There is no question that the union-nonunion pay differential rose sharply in the sixties and seventies in tandem with employer resistance to collective bargaining. See Robert J. Flanagan, *Labor Relations and the Litigation Explosion* (Washington, D.C.: Brookings Institution, 1987).

union representation; rather, it is an attempted *justification* for that management strategy. But the bottom-line implication is the same as the conclusion to be drawn from the worker resistance hypothesis: whatever might have been the case in the thirties, collective bargaining is felt to be an outmoded form of governance for the contemporary workplace; thus we should applaud rather than lament its apparent demise.

Institutional Alternatives

The Uses and Limits of the Market

Even among those who recognize the awkward fit of traditional union representation with many of the developing features of modern employment, most would be loath to cheer its passing unless they knew of some alternative institution capable of performing the roles for which collective bargaining was designed—providing workers a decent level of protection against management power and affording employees a meaningful level of participation in the affairs of the enterprise. In the last two decades a number of contenders have come on the scene to try to fill the vacuum left by the sharply reduced availability of union representation. I will sketch the apparent uses and limits of each of these models, beginning with the market itself.

There are two aspects to the market alternative. The first consists in the external product and capital markets which exert certain demands and constraints on the operation of the labor market. I have alluded already to the marked changes in the product market: the shifts in consumer demand from tangible goods to services of various types; the sharp increases in international competition for the domestic suppliers of most goods and some services; the rapid deregulation in the supply of transportation, communication, and financial services. As a result, American firms now face strong pressure to streamline their operations, to cut costs, and to increase productivity in order to make themselves more competitive in the more intense market environment. At the same time, changing capital markets have put much greater pressure on incumbent managers to initiate necessary changes in operations, because if the visible rate of return to their shareholders dips appreciably below what someone else believes is feasible with the existing assets, an outside raider may threaten to dislodge management on the promise that he can do better.

The unleashing of these market forces has certainly been to the advantage of the shareholders whose equity in the firm increases in value, to the executives who have been able to deliver that capital premium, and to the consumers in the economy who benefit from lower costs and prices. At the same time, the result has been to place much greater pressure on the labor market, if only because wages and benefits paid to employees make up the bulk of the firm's costs of production, and an even higher share of the costs which management can realistically seek to influence from inside. That is why a standard feature of a corporate raid, successful or unsuccessful, is the dismissal of significant numbers of "surplus" employees, the reduction of wages (sometimes only for new employees) to "competitive" levels, and the elimination or revision of unduly "generous" benefit plans. Understandably, management feels much better off when it is free of the restraints of a collective agreement or the threat of a union reaction as it undertakes the "restructuring" of the firm in this manner. But can one really believe that workers are also left better off without such protection against the bracing winds of an unreconstructed marketplace?

In fact, one major branch of neoclassical economics has long argued that workers would be generally better off without unions or other forms of external regulation of their employers.[19] Recently this intellectual persuasion has penetrated the law schools as the "law and economics" wing has turned its attention to issues of labor and employment law.[20] More important, the scholarly assumptions and policy prescriptions of that school of thought found an influential position in the Reagan administration, which had been in charge of our federal labor policy for nearly a decade.

From such a market perspective it is a fundamental fallacy to view the employment relationship as marked by a serious imbalance of

19. For a short popularized version of this viewpoint on the labor market by two of the leading economists of this persuasion, see Chapter 7 of Milton Friedman and Rose Friedman, *Free to Choose: A Personal Statement*, pp. 218–236 (New York: Harcourt Brace Jovanovich, 1979).

20. The most vigorous and interesting exponent of this critical perspective on contemporary labor and employment law is Richard Epstein, although his conclusions rest on a (happily congruent) combination of economic efficiency and moral libertarianism. See Richard A. Epstein, "A Common Law for Labor Relations: A Critique of the New Deal Labor Legislation," 92 *Yale Law Journal* 1357 (1983) (arguing for the dismantling of virtually the entire body of labor law protecting and encouraging union representation and collective bargaining); and Richard A. Epstein, "In Defense of the Contract at Will," 51 *University of Chicago Law* 947 (1984) (contending that any legal regulation of the employer's decision to dismiss is economically and socially misguided).

power between the lone employee and the large corporate employer, an imbalance which can be cured only by the countervailing power of a union organization or other external agency. Rather, workers in the labor market are said to be in a position analogous to that of consumers in the product market. We would not ordinarily say that even a lone consumer has no power in dealing with a large supermarket chain, because we realize that this individual relationship is located amidst a host of supermarkets or other grocery stores competing for the patronage of a large number of customers. Thus if a particular shopper does not like the products, services, or prices in one store, he can go elsewhere. While the customer loses the opportunity to shop at what might be a convenient location, the store also experiences the loss of his business. It takes only a limited number of comparison shoppers with the same tastes and resources of this customer to impose the discipline of the marketplace on the decisions made by the store about the mix of product quality and price that will be offered to each and every one of its customers. By the same token, in almost any occupation or locality the individual employee knows that there is and will be a variety of job openings among a number of alternative employers that provide some measure of choice if the employee does not like the specific features of the job he now has.

Return for a moment to our drug testing case. If Barbara Luck objected to the mandatory, random drug testing program initiated by Southern Pacific, it is not true that there was nothing that she could do about it: she was free to take a computer programming job with another employer that did not engage in drug testing. It is true that Luck probably did not want to take such action, because she would have had to give up her present job, which she presumably liked and preferred to retain. But Southern Pacific also would have been a loser from her decision had she chosen to leave. At a minimum, the firm would have been deprived of the services of a valuable employee in whom it had invested considerable training and experience in its own operations. Worse, the termination of Luck's employment over drug testing would send a message to other employees about Southern Pacific's personnel policies. If the message were distasteful to the other employees, it would be costly to the firm's reputation and hamper its ability to recruit, retain, and motivate its work force.

Of course, such factors are no guarantee against mandatory drug testing of employees. Presumably Southern Pacific felt that drugs were a grave enough problem in its type of operations to warrant such a program, and it was satisfied that the work force generally would not be seriously concerned about the invasion of privacy that drug testing entails. Given such a blend of employer need and employee acceptance, random drug testing would be conducted at Southern Pacific. But that was hardly true of all firms in the economy, so individual employees who felt strongly about this attribute of their jobs were able to gravitate toward firms without a drug testing program. Again, this process of selection is similar to the one engaged in by customers who may have to— and are able to—pay more for certain kinds of specialized services and quality than are available in the standard supermarket.

From the point of view of the neoclassical economic model, then, there really is no governance gap in the contemporary workplace— even given the sharp decline in collective bargaining—because there is actually no significant measure of management power over the employees. An unstructured competitive labor market trains sufficient strong incentives on the firm to offer the kinds of benefits and treatment that the typical employee wants in a job. Thus, instead of a union that would tend to obstruct management's ability to adjust to changing economic conditions, a more effective source of worker protection is the presence of a good many other employers bidding for the services of those employees who are discontented with their present lot.[21] Needless to say, such competition will be greatly reduced in periods of high unemployment, when many workers are bidding for scarce jobs. But even such a qualification to the case for benignly competitive labor markets only constitutes an argument for the kinds of macroeconomic policies which would eliminate such slack in the labor market and its associated increase in management power, rather than an argument for constructing an elaborate mechanism such as collective bargaining to protect employees against the occasional abuse of such employer power.

That, in essence, is the pro-market position. To my mind, its claim that market incentives (for a safer workplace, for example) place significant restraints on management's personnel policies is much more plausible than is commonly conceded by the left-liberal critique of the exercise of corporate power over the worker. However, for reasons I shall outline shortly, there are significant limits on the impact of economic incentives within the labor market, such that wholehearted re-

21. As the Friedmans put it in *Free to Choose*, pp. 235–236, the best protection for the worker against his current employer ultimately comes not from a union, or a lawyer, or a government official, but from *other employers*.

liance on that instrument alone would be an unwise public policy. But when the Reagan administration came to Washington at the beginning of the eighties, it did so with its eyes fixed solely on the promise rather than on the limits of the marketplace, and with the determination to roll back many of the regulatory constraints which had been placed on managerial authority—either by unions through collective bargaining, or, more recently, by government administrators applying direct legal controls to the employment relationship.

Perhaps the most graphic illustration of the administration's ideological bent was the appointment of Donald Dotson as Chairman of the Reagan National Labor Relations Board (NLRB). Sometime before his appointment, Dotson had characterized collective bargaining in print as frequently entailing "labor monopoly, the destruction of individual freedom, and the destruction of the marketplace as the mechanism for determining of labor. . . . The price we have paid is the loss of entire industries and the crippling of others."[22] Nor was this merely idle rhetoric on his part. In a lengthy series of decisions, the Dotson-led Reagan board overturned some forty NLRB doctrines and developed a number of novel positions of its own, almost invariably antithetical to the union position.[23] Most of these rulings removed legal constraints on management power that had been established earlier. Lifting such constraints might have been justified as no more than an antiregulation, laissez-faire stance toward labor law, except that the same Reagan Board was simultaneously developing and expanding a number of intrusive regulatory constraints on union action under the same NLRA.[24]

Much the same ideological persuasion also marked such Reagan

22. See Dotson's letter to the editor in 66 *American Bar Association Journal* 938 (1980). Another key Reagan appointee to the NLRB was Robert Hunter, formerly senior legislative assistant to Senator Orrin Hatch, and principal author of the chapter in *Mandate for Leadership: Policy Management in a Conservative Administration,* pp. 453–501 (Washington, D.C.: Heritage Foundation, 1981) which recommended wholesale policy changes in the Department of Labor (including the NLRB). The book was written under the auspices of the right-wing Heritage Foundation.

23. For a critical review of these decisions, see Paul A. Levy, "The Unidimensional Perspective of the Reagan Labor Board," 16 *Rutgers Law Review* 269 (1985).

24. The most important of these decisions is Machinists, Local 1414 (Neufeld Porsche-Audi), 270 NLRB 1330 (1984). This decision sought to prohibit unions from disciplining members who resigned from the union during a strike, but outside the resignation period designated in the union constitution, in order to be free to cross the picket line and go back to work. Whatever the pros and cons of this specific issue, it is significant that on this as on several other occasions the Reagan Board came down in favor of expanding rather than contracting the scope of labor law regulation, but only when to do so would contain *union* and not management power.

appointments as Thorne Auchter, in charge of occupational safety and health policy, and Bradford Reynolds, a key official in the development of antidiscrimination policy in employment and elsewhere. The actions of the President himself left little doubt about his own predisposition. Early in his administration President Reagan dismissed almost the entire corps of striking air traffic controllers and successfully disestablished their union, PATCO, thereby setting an example which was regularly followed by a number of private sector firms in breaking legal strikes. And near the end of his term, the President vetoed a massive trade bill simply because it contained a modest legal requirement that management give early warning to its workers of impending plant closings and mass layoffs. All in all, in the eighties the free market in employment enjoyed a favored rhetorical position in a national administration that it had not occupied since the twenties.

There are, however, key differences, both analytical and political, between the labor market and the consumer market. The combined force of such differences made it impossible to roll back real national policies to anything close to what they had been in the twenties.

The most obvious factor is that even if an unfettered labor market might maximize the productivity and efficiency of the overall economy in the longer run, it can and does inflict immediate and severe distress upon individual workers and their families. In fact, since the early seventies the real earnings of the average full-time worker have declined, and family living standards have been maintained only because more and more family members (especially wives) have stayed at work or returned to jobs outside the home. Worse, this slide in productivity per worker for the last twenty years (which coincided with the steepest segment of the decline in union representation) has been marked by a sharply increased degree of inequality in the distribution of earnings. Thus college-educated professional and technical workers have generally fared quite well in the new marketplace, but more and more high school-educated, blue-collar craftsmen and production workers have fallen out of the middle-class economic (and social) position originally secured for them by collective bargaining.[25]

25. Detailed accounts of these recent trends appear in Levy, *Dollars and Dreams*, especially pp. 75–78; and Harrison and Bluestone, *The Great U-Turn*, especially pp. 112–128. The emphases and explanations in these two works differ, however, particularly regarding the significance of the shift from manufacturing to service employment. Even strong defenders of Reaganomics who challenge the assertion that there has been a generally shrinking middle class (see, for example, the essay of that title by Marvin H. Kosters and

There are further reasons why even the better endowed professional worker ought not to be exposed to the consequences of an entirely untrammeled labor market. After all, what is being purchased and sold in the labor market is control over the time and activities of a human being. Thus, despite the apparent economic soundness of a voluntary transaction between employer and worker—such as an employee's consenting to random drug testing—the American polity often judges such a practice to be an affront to the employee's personal privacy and dignity, and concludes that workers must be secured against any temptation to agree to such measures, even in return for immediate job opportunities and benefits. Indeed, such a protective ethical stance of the law operates within the consumer market as well, as evidenced, ironically, by the public policy that seeks to protect people from purchase and use of these same drugs. In fact it is this very community antidrug stance that has in turn sparked much of the present employer inclination to test for prohibited drugs such as marijuana, and not for other equally if not more harmful substances such as alcohol.

Finally, a more profound economic analysis confirms the soundness of our intuitive impression that the large corporate firm exercises much greater power over its employees than it could possibly exercise over its customers. The difference arises from the fact that contemporary employment typically takes the form of an enduring career relationship. After an initial period of casual experimentation with a variety of jobs and firms, most employees eventually settle down to work for a particular firm (although not necessarily in the same job) for an indefinite and extended period. As he invests more and more years of work in his firm, the employee in turn obtains a variety of service-related advantages—higher pay on the salary scale, more generous and more secure fringe benefits, more promising promotional opportunities, and more attractive perquisites and amenities on the job. Much of this flavor of modern personnel policy has been deliberately designed by human resource managers precisely in order to solicit the employee's tie and commitment to the firm. But the consequent balkanization of the labor market has significantly weakened the direct impact of competitive forces in that setting.

Often that phenomenon works to the advantage of the longer-service employee, who is ordinarily protected from cuts in wages and benefits

---

Murray N. Ross in 90 *The Public Interest* 3 (1988)) admit that there has been a significant decline in the economic prospects of the key group of blue-collar workers who were the bastion of the American union movement in its heyday (see Kosters and Ross, pp. 19–22).

that might have been the result of having to bid against a pool of unemployed workers for his own job. But the other side of that coin is the existence of considerable managerial power over this employee. Recall my suggestion that an employee like Barbara Luck, with her six years of service with Southern Pacific, has the choice of submitting to a drug test or finding a job elsewhere. Even when there are many available jobs for computer programmers, this employee will lose her investment in that extended period of service with her present firm and will have to start much farther down the ladder with the new employer. Understandably, most employees with any appreciable tenure at their current firm will be very reluctant to leave at that price. And while it is true, as a market proponent would point out, that the employer also suffers some tangible loss when an employee leaves because of dissatisfaction with working conditions, the senior employee loses the only job she has, while the firm loses only one of what may be a work force composed of thousands of such employees.

In sum, while the presence of other employers competing for workers does fix some outer boundaries to the terms and conditions that can be offered by any one firm in the market, ample room remains for the exercise of managerial power in establishing and designing its own employment package. The consequence of the imbalance of power between the firm and those employees who gradually become locked into their present jobs means that we do have a problem of how the American workplace is to be governed, a challenge that we must confront rather than just assume away. And the problem of who will represent the workers in those decisions has become much more urgent in recent years, as collective bargaining has become less and less accessible to more and more nonunion workers.

The Emergence of Government Regulation

There is a sound analytical footing, then, for the feeling of the average career employee that an unfettered labor market will not deliver sufficient protection of the vital interests in adequate wages, benefits, and employment security, a safe and healthy workplace, and fair treatment on the job. As we saw in an earlier section, American workers have been unwilling or unable to utilize the instrument of collective bargaining in order to achieve these goals, and naturally enough they have wanted to try something else. In our political democracy, the votes of some one hundred million American workers and their families were likely to elicit some response from the political system. That is why we have observed over the last two decades the emergence of a third institutional contender for the role of workplace governance: direct legal regulation of the employment relationship.

Of course, employment regulation has been around for a much longer time than that. One of the earliest pieces of social insurance legislation was the requirement by the states early in this century that employers provide workers' compensation for much of the financial consequence of job-related injuries. Shortly after the enactment of the NLRA, Congress also passed the Fair Labor Standards Act (FLSA) to regulate minimum wages and maximum hours of work. But both state workers' compensation law and federal minimum wage law operated a long distance from those employment conditions and personnel policies which preoccupied most firms and workers. Indeed, perhaps a more intrusive and controversial measure was the restriction imposed by the NLRA itself upon the core employment prerogative of hiring and firing, at least in situations where such power was used to discriminate against union supporters.[26]

Needless to say, the present-day legal environment for the employment relationship is worlds apart from what it was then. A vast array of legal rules now dictates to employers what they can and cannot do with their employees. What initially opened the regulatory floodgates was the enactment in 1964 of Title VII of the Civil Rights Act, which expanded the scope of the antidiscrimination principle to encompass race, gender, religion, and alien status.[27] Three years later age was added to these protected categories by the Age Discrmination in Employment Act. But at the outset this body of law was viewed less as employment regulation than as part of the emerging civil rights jurisprudence, designed to eradicate demeaning and disparaging treatment of blacks and other groups in public accommodations, schools, voting, or housing, as well as in the workplace.

To my mind the logjam was really broken at the start of the seventies, when the Supreme Court decided the famous *Griggs* case,[28] hold-

26. Indeed, only when a narrow 5–4 majority of the U.S. Supreme Court (in NLRB v. Jones and Laughlin Corp., 301 U.S. 1 (1937)) upheld the validity of Section 8(a)(3) of the NLRA against a constitutional challenge based on the liberty of employer and employee to agree to an employment-at-will contract, was the *Lochner* roadblock removed from the path of any systematic government regulation of the labor market of either the NLRA or the FLSA type.

27. The next two paragraphs draw on a more detailed account of the unfolding of the antidiscrimination principle in Richard H. Fallon and Paul C. Weiler, "*Firefighters v. Stotts*: Conflicting Models of Racial Justice," 1984 *Supreme Court Review* 1, 10–26.

28. Griggs v. Duke Power Co., 401 U.S. 424 (1971).

ing that employer practices would violate Title VII if they had a disparate impact on blacks, unless the employer could demonstrate that there was a business necessity for the practice in question. For the first time the substance of personnel policies—in *Griggs* itself, the use of tests in hiring and promotion—was to be subjected to legal scrutiny to determine whether the benefits to the employer actually justified the burden on the employee group. Associated with *Griggs* was the development by the Johnson and Nixon administrations of Executive Order 11,246, which required the vast number of firms doing business with the government to initiate and document affirmative steps to improve the real position of women and minorities in the work force. Following a trail blazed by these programs, in the early seventies Congress enacted several pieces of employment legislation of the same interventionist genre. The Rehabilitation Act required many employers to do what was feasible to accommodate greater employment opportunities for the handicapped. The Occupational Safety and Health Act (OSHA) directed most employers to provide a safer and healthier workplace. The Employee Retirement Income Security Act (ERISA) sought to enhance the fairness and security of pensions and other similar retirement benefits. During the remainder of the seventies, the Ford and Carter administrations substantially expanded the scope, precision, and sophistication of these initially rather vague congressional mandates.

As I noted in the prior section, with the election of President Reagan the political pendulum swung back the other way at the federal level. Many of his senior officials were determined to roll back the newfangled social legislation designed to protect the quality not just of the workplace but also of consumer products, the environment, and so on. But even in the Reagan years such an effort was not politically sustainable. Both Dotson at the NLRB[29] and Auchter at the Occupational Safety and Health Administration were eventually replaced by more moderate Republicans, and Reynolds's civil rights ambitions were largely frustrated both by new Secretary of Labor William Brock under the Executive Order and by the Supreme Court under Title VII.[30]

---

29. For early evidence of somewhat different attitudes on the part of the second group of Reagan appointees to the NLRB, see Douglas E. Ray, "The 1986–87 Labor Board: Has the Pendulum Slowed?" 29 *Boston College Law Review* 1 (1987).

30. It was not until after President Reagan and Mr. Reynolds had left office that the Reagan Court began to unravel some of the legal threads in the Title VII fabric, most conspicuously in Wards Cove Packing Co. v. Atonio, 109 S.Ct. 2115 (1989), a decision

When the Democrats finally regained control of the Senate in 1986, the pent-up demand for even more employment regulation began to surface. A dozen or so new bills were introduced in the 100th Congress to deal with perceived problems and abuses in different aspects of the employment relationship. An unlikely bipartisan coalition of senators Ted Kennedy and Orrin Hatch secured the enactment of restraints on employer use of polygraph tests (perhaps a harbinger of analogous controls on urine testing to detect drug use). Although an initial plant closing law which passed in both houses of Congress was vetoed by the President, the Worker Adjustment and Retraining Notification Act (WARNA) went back through the legislative mills with so much numerical support that the President simply let the measure become law. With any degree of receptivity or even acquiescence from President George Bush, we are likely to see another burst of federal regulatory activity in the nineties (with pay equity for women in female-dominated jobs probably high on the political agenda).[31]

Even more important, throughout the seventies and eighties major regulatory activity was occurring at the state level. Some of the action took place inside a number of state legislatures whose efforts eventually became the models for national laws. But the more prominent players at the state level were state court judges, who tend to be less responsive than legislators to arguments about the supposedly unfavorable business climate produced by regulatory lawmaking within their state. Such state court action occurred primarily in the context of litigation challenging what discharged employees claimed was wrongful dismissal.

I shall focus below on the legal details of common law developments in this area. For the moment, suffice it to say that the new body of common law restraints on employer dismissal action developed in two stages. The first, the so-called "public policy" doctrine, consisted of cases in which employers had fired workers for not violating their legal

---

that reduced employer exposure to *Griggs*-type suits by reason of disparate minority representation in their work force; and in City of Richmond v. J. A. Croson Co., 109 S.Ct. 706 (1989), which increased public employer exposure to suits by whites in cases in which the employer had voluntarily adopted affirmative preferences for minorities in order to remove such disparities. The broader political struggle within and against the Reagan administration about the meaning of the antidiscrimination principle in employment and elsewhere is recounted in Norman C. Amaker, *Civil Rights and the Reagan Administration* (Washington, D.C.: Urban Institute Press, 1988).

31. For the background of this issue see Paul C. Weiler, "The Wages of Sex: The Limits and Uses of Comparable Worth," 99 *Harvard Law Review* 1728 (1986).

obligations—price fixing, for example—or for exercising their right to enjoy certain legal benefits, such as workers' compensation. The theory behind these cases was in somewhat the same vein as the antidiscrimination principle that had recently been established in the civil rights arena. In a sense the rubric of "public policy" was really a generic expression of the legal principle that employees should not be discriminated against for asserting or complying with any established public policy, whatever its source.

The second wave of cases, those akin to Barbara Luck's claim, was quite different. Although there is as yet no legislatively or judicially proclaimed public policy against drug testing, a jury was nonetheless authorized to scrutinize Southern Pacific's drug problem and implicitly to decide whether there was sufficient business need for it to outweigh its adverse effects on employee privacy. Perhaps, then, we are inching toward state court adoption of something like the *Griggs* principle, although now in the form of a common law right available to all workers to challenge the validity of objectionable personnel practices, at least those that are enforced by the threat of dismissal.

To its proponents, the major strength of this body of employment law is that its protection is afforded to workers as a matter of legal (and usually moral) principle rather than on the footing of disparate market power. Not just in the individualist labor market but also under collective bargaining, the distribution of favorable employment conditions ultimately turns on the economic resources enjoyed by different groups of employees. Although collective bargaining is designed to enhance the prospects of employees generally vis-à-vis their employers, the ability of different units of workers to translate their collective organization into improvements in their working lives still depends on a constellation of labor, product, and capital market forces. The aim of the FLSA, OSHA, and wrongful dismissal laws is to remove from the vagaries of the marketplace these crucial issues in the employee's life. Instead, the community proclaims that simple respect for the humanity of the worker requires a modicum of decent treatment on the job, and that this right is to be enjoyed equally by all workers, whatever their personal resources.

This stance seems feasible because the source and definition of these legal rights is an outside governmental authority, one which is not directly affected by the varying resources and bargaining power of the immediate protagonists (although that aura of detachment and impartiality varies somewhat as among legislature, court, and administrative agency). At the same time, there are disadvantages in having to act from this external vantage point, in both the definition and the implementation of these rights.

From the perspective of American businessmen, the deficiency they lament is the often procrustean fit of a single legal requirement imposed by a remote government agency on the varying needs of millions of workplaces. It is only too easy for lawmakers to persuade themselves that certain abstract principles or values are absolute and must be uniformly respected—for example, that all employees are entitled to have a safe workplace provided by their employer. The difficulty from the employer's point of view is that such a goal is not feasibly attainable in practice:[32] for instance, every year thousands of workers are killed or injured while driving on highways which it has not yet been possible to render safe for any group, workers or managers.

The judgment about whether a particular hazard is avoidable at a reasonable cost—reasonable not simply to the firm but also to its employees, whose own wages, benefits, and job security depend on the revenues and costs of their employer—hinges on the particular setting. Ideally such a judgment would be made by the people who are intimately involved in and acquainted with the relevant circumstances. But because we have shifted the power of decision-making to distant lawmakers in order to overcome the problem of disparity in local bargaining power, we thereby sacrifice the necessary appreciation of what precautions would actually be most sensible in a particular setting.

The preceding line of objection has been advanced most forcefully in connection with the particular mode of government intervention represented by OSHA, an agency that must formulate fairly specific rules that will cover entire industries and regions. Inevitably OSHA's standards seem to fit awkwardly, even foolishly, in many of the workplaces under its aegis: less than reasonable safety will be the consequence in one setting, more than reasonable precautions in another.

The common law mode exemplified by wrongful dismissal avoids this particular pitfall by expressing its prescriptions in vague legal standards, leaving the specifics to be worked out case by case. Courts thus

---

32. See W. Kip Viscusi, *Risk by Choice: Regulating Health and Safety in the Workplace* (Cambridge, Mass.: Harvard University Press, 1983), for a readable and cogent analysis of the limitations as well as the uses of direct legal regulation in improving workplace safety, as compared with market incentives that are themselves shaped and defined by such background institutions as workers' compensation and collective bargaining.

have the comparative advantage of being able to review a great deal of evidence concerning the specific needs and costs in each employment situation. But while the resulting common law judgments may be more sensitive and sounder than those that follow from a bright-line legal rule, there is a significant price to be paid for that. Part of the price is the substantial expense of gathering and presenting a mass of evidence to a civil jury. But the deeper problem of relying on case-by-case litigation to elucidate the meaning of a legal principle is that the affected parties will not know until long after they acted whether or not they acted properly. And since, as we saw in the case of Southern Pacific Transportation, the price of guessing wrong may be an adverse jury award of a half million dollars (and occasionally a lawyer's bill that may be just as high), a not unlikely consequence is that many employers may choose to adopt defensive personnel practices which are quite different and much less sensible than anything the court had in mind (as we are told has been happening in the analogous sphere of tort regulation of safe medical practice).

But although the representatives of the business community express vociferous objections about the formulation of new legal standards, employees encounter equally apparent flaws at the implementation stage. Whatever laws are adopted by the legislature or the courts, management remains in charge of the firm, making the decisions about what are to be its employment policies (subject to the loose boundaries set by the labor market). The presence of a new law on the books will alter management's own inclination only if there is real bite in the legal program, that is, a reasonable level of frequency and severity in the sanctions meted out for violations. But such an enforcement process is heavily dependent on the initiative of the employees and their representatives. The problem is that the capacity of the employees to discern and complain about the employers' violations of their rights is in turn dependent on their widely varying intellectual, financial, and organizational resources. That is why successful wrongful dismissal claims, for example, are far more likely to be filed by managerial or professional employees than by the less skilled, less well paid workers whose plight usually precipitates the original call for such protective laws. Unfortunately, the initial promise of legal regulation—that it would insulate the fundamental and equal rights of workers from disparities in their resources (which clearly influence the outcomes of the market and of collective bargaining)—turns out in great part to be mythical.

Having noted these oft expressed reservations about legal regulation, I do not mean to stake out an *a priori* position against this model of governance. There are very good reasons for maintaining a basic social safety net for the workplace. Often these potential defects in government controls are not that weighty in particular cases, and where they are, we may be able to devise measures to alleviate the problem (as I shall develop in detail later when considering the wrongful dismissal problem). Having said that, I think we should be more conscious than we usually are about the limited uses and value of the law in the workplace. The mere fact that we often observe and decry instances of arbitrary treatment in the workplace is not itself proof that government intervention can generally improve the situation at a reasonable price.

The Quest For Direct Employee Involvement

There is a further aspect to these characteristic limits of external regulation. That governance instrument does nothing to repair the representation gap left inside the firm by the decline of union organization of the employees for purposes of collective bargaining. One reason those responsible for the administration of OSHA, for example, have been loath to adopt vague but flexible performance standards in the campaign for a safer workplace is because they could not rely on any kind of organized worker base in the firms to deal with management in fashioning acceptable safety specifications tailored to each setting.[33] And that also explains why the ordinary unorganized employee finds it so difficult in particular cases to take advantage of general legal norms such as the right to sue for wrongful dismissal.

For these reasons, the representation gap considerably reduces the potential of external legal regulation for providing effective protection to the intended employee beneficiaries. Recall, moreover, that there are two vital social functions to be performed by any instrument for workplace governance: protection *of* workers as well as participation *by* workers. Therefore an equally important reservation about the gradual substitution of legal regulation for collective bargaining is that the former model entirely ignores that second participatory value.

Through collective bargaining employees themselves take consider-

---

33. See Joseph V. Rees, *Reforming the Workplace: A Study of Self-Regulation in Occupational Safety* (Philadelphia: University of Pennsylvania Press, 1988), for an illuminating case study of the dependence of flexible regulation on meaningful employee organization and representation.

able responsibility for establishing and enforcing any such protective restraints on management power. Whatever the precise content of the standards thus produced, there is an additional intrinsic value simply in having the employees play a major role in developing and designing, say, a program for controlling their own drug abuse, even though such a program may, to a certain extent, infringe their privacy through random drug testing. Granted, there are significant inequalities in the distribution of the fruits of collective action by workers, because some units of employees can deploy much greater bargaining power than can others, and, of course, very few nonunion employees have any realistic access to this process in their present firm. But the more we utilize legal regulation as our response to that problem, the more we ask distant legislatures or courts to write the standards and bureaucrats or lawyers to enforce them. At best, the employees are passive beneficiaries of these governmental efforts on their behalf.

Although one should not be unduly romantic about the participatory value of collective bargaining, the workers do play a more active role than is conceded by many popular critics, who, as I observed earlier, tend to dismiss the process as consisting only of a remote union bureaucracy negotiating a complicated contract with management, then hiring lawyers to fight grievances in front of professional arbitrators.[34] In most of the unions with which I am very familiar (the United Auto Workers [UAW] being the one I know best), there is a substantial degree of worker involvement in union elections, especially at the local level: the employees' views are taken into account in framing the bargaining agenda, the members vote on whether to strike or to ratify a settlement, and once the contract is in effect the local membership plays a major role in deciding whether particular cases are worth pursuing up the grievance arbitration ladder. Indeed, I believe that most unionized workers take a good deal more personal responsibility for their representation in and the results of their collective bargaining process than they do as citizens in the outside political process (one index being a simple comparison of the voting turnouts in these respective arenas).

There is, however, a restricted focus to the kind of worker participation that occurs through the collective bargaining process. The aim of the process is to develop and enforce a network of contract standards that will specify what management must do in paying wages and

---

34. See, e.g., Stanley Aronowitz, *False Promises: The Shaping of American Working Class Consciousness* (New York: McGraw-Hill, 1974); in particular, Chapter 4, "Trade Unions: The Illusion and Reality," pp. 214–263.

benefits, allocating favored job opportunities, and avoiding unfair treatment by supervisors. Unquestionably such contractual rights have been a valuable achievement in protecting ordinary workers from the arbitrary exercise of managerial authority and insuring them a fair share of the fruits of the enterprise. But the participatory values of collective bargaining are a byproduct of this rather narrow concentration on the defense of employees from the firm and its management. We now appreciate that workers have broader needs and aspirations on the job, that they want to be challenged to become active participants in the production process, and, indeed, even to play some role in certain decisions which have hitherto been the sole prerogative of management.[35] In fact, one of the reasons unionism has fallen from favor is that it has historically downplayed this vision of the positive contribution that employees themselves can make to the productivity and success of the enterprise of which they are a part.

But this kind of employee aspiration has not been ignored by certain influential firms and their executives. Roughly two decades ago a number of nonunion firms began to develop what has by now become an extensive array of employee involvement programs.

At first these programs consisted of limited efforts at job rotation and enrichment to give employees more breadth and variety in their daily work experience. The "quality circle" idea was imported from Japan to tap the insights and contributions of the work force toward the improvement of the firm's production quality and efficiency. At the same time, quality-of-working-life (QWL) committees were set up with a view to improving the attractiveness of the work environment for the employees. A more far-reaching innovation was the adoption by some firms of the team system of production. Small groups of employees, led by a coordinator rather than controlled by a supervisor, were given responsibility for distinct segments of the production process, with a high degree of autonomy in scheduling, assignments, hiring, and even dismissal from the group, and in some cases the authority to deal directly with suppliers of materials and purchasers of the product. The ultimate stage in the progressive enlargement of the employee role in a few firms has been worker ownership and effective representation on the board of directors, enabling the employees to influence the overall strategy of the enterprise.

This unfolding pattern in human resource management is a testimo-

---

35. An influential early statement of that viewpoint is the Report of the Special Task Force, *Work in America*.

nial to the real benefits that the free market can provide to workers. In the earlier decades the more generous wages and benefits and the formal procedures for job assignment and discipline that were pioneered in collective bargaining were forced upon nonunion firms in order to preserve their nonunion status. But most of the pioneers in the new modes of employee involvement (EI), firms such as IBM and Hewlett-Packard, were actually in no real danger of union organization; the aim of their leaders was rather to move away from the traditional style of "scientific" management with its close monitoring of a work force in which each employee played a small routinized role on the assembly line.[36] This older management style was considered to be much less effective for the new work force, the new technology, and the new product markets which together were requiring major adjustments on the part of American business. Because the human capital embodied in the work force was certainly more expensive, and perhaps more indispensable, than the firm's physical and financial capital, it was more important than ever before to elicit from the employees the kind of motivation, cooperation, and commitment necessary to compete in the new international economy. The assumption of this novel style of participatory management was that such a response would be more forthcoming from workers if management was prepared to elicit from its employees the kind of involvement and collaboration that characterize the programs described above.[37]

The new EI model did not fit comfortably with the tenor of traditional labor policy as embodied in the NLRA. The premise of the authors of the Wagner Act was that a basic conflict of interest exists between the firm and its employees; that a management team selected by and accountable to the shareholder owners of the firm would rep-

36. Ironically, these business leaders were echoing (unconsciously, I am sure) the thoroughgoing critique of this mode of work organization from the left, expressed by Harry Braverman in *Labor and Monopoly Capital: The Degradation of Work in the Twentieth Century* (New York: Monthly Review Press, 1974). For a more extended historical account, see Daniel Nelson, *Frederick W. Taylor and the Rise of Scientific Management* (Madison: University of Wisconsin Press, 1980).

37. And as we shall see later, a key corollary of the new style of human resource management is that the firm also guarantees to the majority of its work force the kind of employment security and status that was traditionally offered to a small core of key salaried employees. On the nature and dimensions of the transition from the *industrial*-style employment relationship, with its emphasis on "job control," to the more flexible, participatory, but still secure *salaried* model, see Paul Osterman, *Employment Futures: Reorganization, Dislocation and Public Policy* (New York: Oxford University Press, 1988), especially Chapter 4, "Reorganization of Work Within Firms," pp. 60–91.

resent the latter's position, and that employees therefore needed to be able to organize their own association, a union, to defend their interests. Management was assumed to have the responsibility of running the enterprise, both on the shop floor and in the executive suite, whereas the union's role was to secure for the employees more generous rewards and more decent treatment. Given this division in responsibility and in constituency, it seemed important to ensure that there be no blurring of the line between management and worker representation. The specific legal expressions of that philosophy were embodied in Section 8(a)(2) of the NLRA, which prohibits employer involvement in any organization or committee representing the workers in the firm (the prohibition against "company unions"), and in the exclusion of anyone who performs a discretionary managerial function from union representation and collective bargaining under the Act. Unfortunately, in many of its manifestations the contemporary participatory management movement appears to run afoul of both the letter and the original intent of this provision in the NLRA.[38]

Regardless of the judgment made by the authors of the Wagner Act, I believe that the new model of employee involvement meets a genuine need in the contemporary workplace, and that our laws will have to be revised to accommodate it.[39] At the end of this book I shall develop my own views about how such revision would mesh with a general overhaul of labor law. But we must recognize that the concern behind the Wagner Act's distaste for company unions is still valid. While the modern version of EI does provide nonunion employees with varying levels of participation in the enterprise, it is participation without real power.

Within the standard EI program workers are asked for their views and are encouraged to make suggestions—returning to our ongoing case, for example, about how to deal with drug use. If management is persuaded that a recommendation from the employees is a good idea, it will be adopted. But if management does not like the recommendation, it holds the trump cards and its views will prevail. Thus a QWL committee of employees has no independent power base from which

38. The most persuasive demonstration of this legal conclusion is offered by Thomas C. Kohler in "Models of Worker Participation: The Uncertain Significance of Section 8(a)(2)," 27 *Boston College Law Review* 499 (1986).

39. See Karl E. Klare, "The Labor-Management Cooperation Debate: A Workplace Democracy Perspective, 23 *Harvard Civil Rights–Civil Liberties Law Review* 39 (1988), for a careful statement of why we need more direct employee involvement, written by a legal scholar who appreciates the values of the traditional industrial relations/labor law model as expounded by Kohler, "Models of Worker Participation."

to challenge management's action—to insist, for example, that there will be drug testing only when there is reasonable suspicion that a particular employee is using drugs, and to tie management down to such a position in a written contract.

Indeed, the very existence as well as the operation of a nonunion EI program are dependent on management judgment. It is management that decides whether the advantages of such an employee role will outweigh the costs (including the impact on the morale of supervisors), and, if so, how far the firm should go in this direction—for example, whether to move from the rather modest version of the quality circle to a full-blown system of autonomous production teams. Even the most far-reaching system of worker participation, one which involves substantial employee ownership of the firm, may be jettisoned if the marketplace results are unfavorable and the leadership of the firm changes hands. Perhaps the most graphic illustration of this phenomenon is the fate of the widely heralded People Express Airline version of employee involvement. For years People Express and its head, Donald Burr, were the darlings of the human resources group at the Harvard Business School for having shown how worker participation could be built into the structure of the firm from bottom to top. But it was Donald Burr and a few key advisors who alone made the fateful expansion decisions that eventually led to People's bankruptcy, the loss of the employees' entire ownership stake, and eventually the takeover of the airline's assets and work force by Texas Air, with Frank Lorenzo's very different ideas about human resource management.

In short, then, nonunion employee involvement often gives workers meaningful participation in the enterprise but without any serious protection from management—indeed, even without any guarantee that the employees will continue to enjoy the kind of influence to which they may have become accustomed. In this respect employee involvement as a model of workplace governance is the reverse image of the model of external legal regulation described in the previous section, which can give employees significant protection from the firm but grants them only minimal participation.

The contrasting deficiencies in the regulatory and employee involvement models stem from the same underlying source: the absence within the firm of a cohesive worker organization capable of effective representation of employee interests. It was the presence of such a *union* of the work force that made it possible for the traditional governance model of collective bargaining to achieve some blending of the protective and participatory functions which are both necessary for the modern workplace. But the crucial failing of traditional collective bargaining is that it narrowed the scope of worker participation to merely securing a network of protective constraints on management action, and thus did not sufficiently satisfy the desire of present-day workers for broader influence on their jobs and on the enterprise.

Yet although this deficiency is characteristic of much of the existing pattern of industry bargaining by large national unions, representation by independent unions is by no means inherently incompatible with significant involvement in the firm by employees.[40] Indeed, one would expect to have seen some evolutionary expansion of the aims of collective bargaining. Initially, the focus of the union was on securing more generous wages and benefits and formal procedures for supervisory action in dismissals, layoffs, and the like. These achievements responded to the immediate tangible needs of the workers for decent living standards and job security. But as these economic goals were achieved, it was only natural that workers would want more attention paid to their psychological need for a fulfilling work experience, one that would challenge their mind and creativity on the job. And indeed, in the early seventies, collective bargaining began to respond to this felt aspiration of its constituents with the gradual development of QWL, team production, and other EI programs for unionized workers.

In fact, one might anticipate that collective bargaining would produce an even stronger form of employee involvement, if only because a jointly developed program is more likely to reflect the true wishes of the average career employee than one which is unilaterally formulated by the employer. Moreover, union-negotiated EI is able to penetrate more deeply into the exercise of management prerogatives, especially in the area of broader corporate strategy, because unionized employees can have more professional representation on the corporate board, and their ownership stake (under an employee stock ownership plan, ESOP, for example) is more likely to carry with it effective voting rights. At the same time, collectively bargained EI rests on a firmer contractual footing, protected from unilateral alteration or revocation by the employer, and with clearer demarcation lines between existing contract rights and the agenda for direct employee collaboration with management.

That said, it is also true that there is marked ambivalence about EI in

40. The successful blending of collective bargaining and worker participation is a theme in the general treatment of this subject by Thomas A. Kochan, Harry C. Katz, and Robert B. McKersie, *The Transformation of American Industrial Relations* (New York: Basic Books, 1986); and Heckscher, *The New Unionism;* and in studies of the auto industry by Katz, "Shifting Gears," and the steel industry by Hoerr, *And the Wolf Finally Came.*

much of the union movement.[41] Serious and sustained activity in the EI domain has been limited to a number of union settings, most prominently the UAW in the auto industry, the United Steel Workers of America (USWA) in the steel industry, and the Communications Workers of America (CWA) in the telecommunications industry. In these sectors there has been both a special industry need for and union leadership receptivity to trying out this rather different mode of labor-management relations. But in turn these experiments have evoked strong objections from both sides of the union political spectrum. On the one hand, leaders of the "business unionism" persuasion believe that their members are interested primarily in traditional bread-and-butter issues, and that the union's bargaining leverage should therefore not be frittered away on intangible job enrichment and worker participation schemes. On the other hand, those unionists who continue to be concerned about the fundamental conflict of interest between labor and capital are wary about trusting management in such a collaborative relationship.

It is clear that trust is a central ingredient to the new EI venture. Once employees begin to deal directly with managers about a variety of immediate concerns in the production process and the workplace, it is virtually impossible to insulate the terms of the union contract and the prerogatives of union leadership from their purview. One reason for this is that the EI model evolved not simply from the need to reduce the sense of alienation in the worker's psyche, but also from the serious problems which arise in adjusting the enterprise to the demands of the new technology and the new marketplace. It did not take very long for participants in joint worker-manager consultation at the local level to realize that a significant part of that adjustment problem resulted from obstacles imposed by nationally negotiated, industry-wide contracts which, in up to 500 printed pages, meticulously spelled out what management could or could not do.

The future of this novel style of EI unionism may well be visible in the controversial Saturn project agreement between General Motors and the UAW, a contract which runs for only 20 pages. This document consists primarily of the formulation of the mutual goals of the parties

---

41. See Thomas A. Kochan, Harry C. Katz, and Nancy R. Mower, *Worker Participation and American Unions: Threat or Opportunity?* (Kalamazoo: W. E. Upjohn Institute, 1984). Perhaps the most vigorous critique of the entire concept is Michael Parker's *Inside the Circle: A Union Guide to QWL* (Boston: South End Press, 1985). Parker's argument reflects a significant current of opinion within American unions.

and the institution of a bilateral committee structure from the top to the bottom of the operation. The role of the joint committees is to work out the implications of the goals as problems arise and must be solved on a day-to-day basis in the plant. Understandably, then, a good many union leaders feel essentially the same sense of vertigo as do their management counterparts about having to give up the security blanket of a lengthy, tightly drafted collective agreement supplemented by thousands of additional pages of letters of understanding and arbitration awards recording what had been decided in the past.

Even more unsettling in this brave new world is the likely shift in the locus of power within the union, from the national to the local level and from local officers to local members. Instead of a vertical relation between national officer, local officer, and local member, with the ultimate authority resting with those at the top of the union ladder who deal with senior management of the company, much more emphasis will be placed on horizontal relations between local members and local managers in each plant and firm. Indeed, we may be about to witness a transformation of *industrial* into *enterprise* unionism, as far-reaching a shift as that which took place from craft to industrial unionism a half-century ago. The future shape of the national union will be a rather loose confederation of enterprise-specific organizations. While the national union office would provide a variety of resources and professional services which could most effectively be delivered in that fashion, the real decision-making power would reside at the local level, where the parties could devise measures specially tailored to the needs of a particular segment of the firm and its work force.

A Path for the Future

The Need for Labor Law Reform

If, as I suspect is the case, this new brand of enterprise unionism is better attuned to the growing worker need for personal involvement and to the employer need for flexible adjustment, the leadership of the union movement will have to start down that path if unions hope to have any real chance of improving their current bleak prospects. And it is at least possible that such a sharply altered style of collective bargaining could reduce the degree of resistance to this institution among American workers, if not American managers, thereby expand the quality of worker influence inside the firm, and perhaps even lessen the political and judicial incentive to proliferate external legal regulation to fill the present vacuum in workplace governance.

Unhappily, a dilemma remains to be faced on the way toward this hoped-for happy ending. However unsuited it may be in other respects, the large, bureaucratic union organization does fill a central need in the present labor relations climate: overcoming management's opposition to any concerted action by employees through an independent union. Even if the new unionism were to be significantly more decentralized in structure and more responsive to the specific needs of a particular enterprise, the fact that the employees would have a measure of group cohesion and leverage still poses a significant threat to the interests of the firm and its management. Such worker organization would likely win for employees a somewhat greater share of the employer's revenues, particularly any "rents" secured by the firm in protected market niches. It would also threaten traditional managerial prerogatives as employee influence expanded in scope and became more secure. While the currently unionized segment of American management, which often feels hamstrung by traditional pattern bargaining, would likely applaud the kind of evolution I have just sketched, firms which now have no union are likely to fight hard to fend off even this new brand of worker representation. As occurs now under the NLRA, such employer resistance would be mounted on a variety of fronts and last for months, even years: from the initial organizing drive through the representation campaign, and even after the union has been certified by the NLRB, during the negotiation of a first contract that might for the first time make collective employee action a presence inside the firm.

Rarely if ever does the group of employees over which such a fierce struggle is waged have the wherewithal to combat this sort of resistance on their own. The necessary finances, experience, and staying power can only be the product of, not the predecessor to, a successful organizing effort. Thus a major role for the national union is to provide the backing and the resources which are necessary at the crucial start-up phase of unionization. But the catch is that the large union organization needed to contend with the employer at this stage may be precisely the kind of external, hierarchical entity that more and more American workers find is *not* the instrument they have in mind to enhance their own influence on their employer.

Recognition of this dilemma brings me finally to the structure and reform of labor law—especially its central core, which establishes and defines the fundamental right of workers to organize and take concerted action for their mutual aid and protection, primarily though not exclusively through union representation and collective bargaining. The design of the legal machinery through which this right is to be exercised makes it a difficult and obstacle-laden undertaking, thus requiring the presence of a big union which can afford to pour huge sums into a single major campaign—even as much as a million dollars, as the American Federation of State, County, and Municipal Employees, for example, has done for the last two years for the 3,500 clerical and technical employees at Harvard University. In the last section of this book I shall delve deeply into these features of our labor law and develop three models for its reform.[42] Here I shall merely sketch my position in broad strokes and indicate how such a solution squares with the overall course of my argument up to this point.

What is wrong with the present legal regime? Section 7 of the NLRA confers upon American workers the right to organize themselves into a union through which they can collectively bargain with their employer. However, the transformation from their "natural" nonunion status is by no means an easy and routine matter. Even if the bulk of the employees have joined a union, the unit must formally vote for such representation in a secret ballot election before the employer need recognize and deal with their union. The employees must then secure a first collective agreement from the employer before their concerted action can have any real significance in the plant or office. NLRB jurisprudence and rhetoric basically assumes that at each of these stages there will be a heated contest between union and employer. During the pre-election campaign the employer will exercise its protected right of free speech to paint a dark picture of life with a union. Even if the employer loses the election battle, it is still entitled to resist any meaningful contractual restraints on its prerogative to set wages, benefits, and working conditions at whatever level the free market will permit. The limited role of the Labor Board is simply to act as the referee for this contest, to prohibit unlawful "threats" (as opposed to legal "predictions") about the consequences of union representation, and to ban "surface" (as opposed to "hard") bargaining over the terms of the contract under negotiation.

---

42. Much of the chapter will present and update arguments originally developed in detail in Paul C. Weiler, "Promises to Keep: Securing Workers' Rights to Self-Organization Under the NLRA," 96 *Harvard Law Review* 1769 (1983); and in Paul C. Weiler, "Striking a New Balance: Freedom of Contract and the Prospects for Union Representation," 98 *Harvard Law Review* 351 (1984).

The one fact about which there is little dispute in the entire debate about labor law reform is that the current legal framework now generates very few new union members. Although the NLRA process is set in motion only after a union has already established a significant showing of interest among the work force, something less than 40 percent of these employees now end up in Board-certified units, and not much more than half of these units secure first contracts. This bottom-line yield rate of roughly 20 percent produces far fewer new members than are needed just to match natural union attrition as currently organized work sites close and are replaced by new plants or offices—which, recall, all start up nonunion.

The crucial and hotly debated question, of course, is what is the cause of this union decline? The assumption of those who favor labor law reform is that a prime culprit is illegitimate employee resistance to collective bargaining (although this account by no means excludes the likelihood that the hidebound attitudes of many union leaders also bear a substantial share of the responsibility for the current union plight). Later in this book I shall review the evidence for and against this key premise in the case for labor law reform. Here I wish only to sketch three different strategies through which the law might tackle that employer posture as and where it does manifest itself.

Strategies for Labor Law Reform

The Regulatory Model. The first regulatory strategy accepts the assumption of the current law that there is and should be a vigorous contest between employer and union for the hearts and minds of the employees, but seeks to provide more effective legal sanctions against the growing employer inclination to flout the rules of that contest. Even ignoring the problem of employer threats and bad faith bargaining maneuvers, when the employer uses the crudest tactic of all, firing union supporters in the midst of a representation campaign, the legal response is picayune. If the employer chooses to contest the case up until the first legally enforceable order is issued, that order will not be forthcoming for about a thousand days. In practice, given a delay of even a few months before voluntary settlement of their charges, only a minority of employees actually exercise any right won for them by the NLRB to return to their jobs, and the majority of these returnees leave soon thereafter. At the same time, the monetary penalty faced by the employer for depriving any union supporters of their job is an award of no more than the net back pay lost by the fired employee; such awards now average only about $2,000 a case. Small wonder, then, that the incidence of such illegal firings has spiraled from under 1,000 a year in the late fifties to over 10,000 in the mid-eighties.

In the last part of this book I shall develop the case for two reform proposals designed to respond to the delay and the weakness of such regulatory remedies. One proposal is for *interim injunctions* from the federal courts directing the reinstatement of apparently illegally fired employees pending the ultimate disposition of the case in the administrative process. The other proposal would give employees fired in violation of the public policy embodied in the NLRA the same right to sue for *general damages* as was exercised by Barbara Luck. Such an award to the fired employee would include front pay as well as back pay, compensation for the consequential economic and emotional harm, and even punitive damages if the employer's behavior was particularly egregious. The combination of these two new remedies would provide more adequate relief to the actual victims of employer unfair labor practices and more effective deterrence against other firms tempted to follow that example. Interestingly, these reforms would give injured employees no more than the same kind of judicial relief—injunctions and damages—now afforded by the NLRA to employers who are injured by union unfair labor practices.

The Reconstructive Model. The second reform strategy springs from the same skepticism about the sufficiency of NLRA regulation that motivates employment regulation generally. The problem is that the NLRA first structures a contest between union and employer in which the employer experiences strong economic temptation to use its managerial prerogative to win this struggle; then the law responds with costly, cumbersome, and only partially effective legal disincentives to such employer behavior. An alternative strategy would attempt to reconstruct the framework of the representation contest itself so as to reduce the employer's initial opportunity and incentive to contravene the rules of the representation battle.

There are several reform proposals in that vein. One is for *instant elections*. This idea presumes that it is the protracted election campaign—lasting for several weeks and even months—which provides the setting in which employers are tempted to use dirty tactics to try to win the election. One could drastically alter that setting by conducting immediate elections within five days or so of the certification petition; presumably requiring these union petitions to be based on a significant majority (perhaps 60 percent) of the employees' having signed up as union members and paid a minimum membership fee, say $5.00. The unmistakable lesson from the use in Canadian labor law of this alternative certification model is it does remarkably well in reducing the number of discriminatory discharges and increasing the number of union certifications. Whether the price of such "success" is unacceptable erosion of the employer's legitimate role in the representation campaign is a subject I shall address in detail later in this book.

But even if union certification were the outcome of an instant election, such an NLRB verdict in reality gives the union little more than a legal license to bargain with the employer. The acid test of employee sentiment occurs when the union goes back to the bargaining unit to elicit a credible strike mandate, which it will then use to try to extract an attractive contract offer from the employer. At present, however, fewer and fewer such strike efforts succeed—and consequently fewer and fewer first contracts follow certifications, because increasingly employers are exercising their legal right to continue operating with strike replacements, a right that employers are granted in any strike not precipitated or prolonged by their own unfair labor practices. Addressing the problem of the diminishing value of the strike as a union tool will require significant changes in the legal framework in which that economic contest is carried on.

The most prominent reform candidate for enhancing and protecting the right to strike is to limit the employer's right to hire *permanent replacements* in the strikers' jobs, at least for some minimum strike period, such as three or six months. Typically, employers do not need to guarantee such permanent priority in order to recruit strike replacements; on the rare occasion that there is such need, it is hardly vital enough to warrant depriving incumbent workers of their jobs simply because they have exercised their statutory right to strike for better working conditions.

But the assumption of this particular proposal is that employers would and should be entitled to use temporary replacements to operate during a strike and thereby resist the union's bargaining demands. That means that we should also re-examine the reciprocal right of strikers to call for a boycott of their employer's struck product. Under the current law, if the union asks the customers of a retailer not to buy the struck product, this would be labeled a legal *primary* boycott, but if the request is made to the retailer's employees not to handle or stock that product, this is an illegal *secondary* boycott. On its face, this distinction seems strangely arbitrary, unless one assumes that the law's aim here is simply to grant employees a right to bring economic pressure to bear on struck employers wherever the pressure is *least* likely to be effective. Even worse, in practice such legal intervention on behalf of the employer has an especially disparate impact on the prospects of less skilled and poorly paid workers. These are the people who comprise the bulk of newly organized units in which the employer will bargain hard to avoid any first contract and thereby precipitate a strike, during which strike replacements eventually free the firm of the unwanted union. Thus an extension of the legal scope for *primary boycotts* of the struck employer is an essential tool for strengthening the ability of workers themselves to secure and protect their Section 7 rights to self-organization and concerted action.

The Constitutive Model. The regulatory model for labor law reform basically accepts the current framework for the representation contest, then tries to do better at enforcing the legal ground rules for legitimate employer resistance to unionism. The reconstructive model would revise some of the key ground rules in order to provide a more even balance between employer action and employee reaction during the struggle. A third *constitutive* strategy challenges the very idea that there should be such a contest between employer and union regarding the majority employee verdict, because it would eliminate any such choice by workers themselves about whether there will be organized employee participation in the affairs of the enterprise.

Even if my entire package of far-reaching reforms of the NLRA were enacted—which it will not be—and even if the reforms which were adopted were fully and successfully implemented—which they will not be—only a minority of American workers would ever have union representation and collective bargaining. There are simply too many inhibiting factors: the deeply felt aversion of American employers to any union intrusion in their operations; the inevitable limits imposed on any labor law reform out of deference to such time-honored values as free speech, free markets, and due process; the prospect that securing union representation will always be a tension-filled and stressful experience for the employees involved; and thence their need to rely on the resources of a large, bureaucratic union organization in order to overcome daunting employer resistance, even though what many workers really want is a more direct, indigenous procedure of their own. In the face of these obstacles, natural human inertia will ensure that in most instances the nonunion starting point will remain the stopping point. Employees who are strongly dissatisfied with existing conditions will exit, one by one, for other jobs rather than struggle fruitlessly for a more comfortable voice in and influence over their present workplace.

Assume, though, that some form of employee participation in the governance of the workplace is a good thing—both for the employees immediately affected and for the broader political economy. Should the existence of such a procedure be left to the vagaries of employee choice, affected as it inevitably is by resistance from employers? True fifty years of the Wagner Act model make it difficult to imagine a regime under which the issue of employee participation would be settled as a matter of general public policy, rather than through ad hoc majority verdicts by different units of employees. That possibility might appear in a somewhat different light, however, if one recalls that in 1988 alone it was decided that such issues as the use of lie detectors or notice of plant closings are too vital to be left to employee choice, either individual or collective; instead, these subjects are now controlled by legislative regulation.

I do not suggest that we should consider mandating employee representation through national unions engaged in full-fledged collective bargaining. There is no doubt that a large number of American workers, let alone employers, feel that such a step would be quite contrary to their interests. But I shall argue for a policy that establishes an indigenous worker voice in the firm through elected *employee participation committees.* I suspect that such a committee structure would turn out to be more propitious soil in which full-scale collective bargaining could put down roots (at least within the more inviting legal environment achieved through my reconstructive and regulatory strategies for labor law reform). But whether or not my prediction is accurate is not the main point. The aim of this new public policy would not be to enroll workers in large national unions, but rather to guarantee employees a mode of direct immediate organization—*union* in a more generic sense of the term—that is necessary to help fill the yawning representation gap which has been ever widening in the American workplace.

A Road Map of My Argument

In this first chapter of the book I have sketched the socioeconomic trends which are transforming the employment relationship and the alternative paths from among which we must choose for the future governance of the American workplace. The main body of the work will provide detailed evidence and analysis for the claims and proposals I have made in this initial overview. However, in the rest of the book I shall pursue a rather different line of argument in order to address directly some of the key developments and debates in both the law and legal scholarship. Thus it is useful to provide a road map of the course this account will take.

Chapter 2 consists of an in-depth analysis of the problem of wrongful dismissal. I shall focus on the legal principles and public policies rather than the doctrinal detail reflected in discharge cases and conclude the chapter with a proposed program about how best to handle them. But although wrongful dismissal is sufficiently challenging in its own right to warrant even more extended treatment, I have a broader aim in mind. I want to display the kind of stake that career employees have in their present job, a stake that requires protection against not only wrongful dismissal but also a variety of other harms that might befall employees in the workplace. I shall argue that the peculiar character of this career nexus obstructs the ideal operation of both competitive markets and governmental enforcement of legal rights. This is one case where collective bargaining through union representation has done a much better job, by addressing the problem of the unjust discharge of ordinary workers without imposing unnecessary costs on the employer and the economy.

With the stage set by this case study, Chapter 3 portrays the frontal challenge which has been mounted against collective bargaining as a general mode of workplace governance. Unions have faced not only sustained employer opposition to their very existence, but also an intellectual formulation which provides legitimacy and responsibility to the quest by American business for a union-free environment. Scholars, especially in law and economics, depict the union as a cartel which obstructs the ideal operation of the labor market in a variety of ways that are both unproductive for business and unfair to many workers and consumers. To the extent that politicians and pundits are influenced by this viewpoint, they may privately applaud employers' evasion of the principles of our labor laws, preferring to weaken rather than to strengthen enforcement of the NLRA. My response to that position will show that even within this neoclassical frame of reference, the antiunion case badly overstates the contrast between one labor market populated by unions and corporations, and another which consists simply of corporate organizations; and that, moreover, to the extent that the two regimes do differ, the world of collective bargaining may well be more efficient and is certainly more equitable than one dominated by business enterprise alone.

But my assumption, as developed in Chapter 4, is that the problems of the contemporary workplace are more complicated than the issue of whether or not employees will be represented by a union. Present-day employment relations, nonunion as well as union, are characterized by a variety of special features, both financial and personal, which cannot be accounted for by the standard economic paradigm. Real product and labor markets leave ample room for the exercise of discretion about how to settle vital issues in the employment relationship; what the law does (at least implicitly) is allocate the authority to make these decisions. A number of major contenders now vie for this preferred role in the governance of the workplace—managerialism, government regulation, worker control, and collective bargaining. I shall argue that collective bargaining between management representatives of the shareholders and union representatives of the work force actually stands up surprisingly well as an instrument for resolving a host of workplace issues besides wrongful dismissal.

But the argument in Chapter 4 is more analytical than contextual: admittedly it does not fully address the felt discontent about the actual performance of American unions. To many people, including myself, this institution seems to impose too much protective regulation on employers while eliciting too little participatory involvement by employees themselves. Chapter 5 will consider the extent to which and the reasons why contemporary unionism has not sufficiently responded to the changing needs of the firm and the aspirations of employees; and will do so by placing this institution side by side with the burgeoning trend toward employee involvement programs.

In contrast to the traditional independent unionism encouraged by the NLRA, management-sponsored EI smacks strongly of the "company union" supposedly banned by Section 8(a)(2) of the Act. EI programs provide employees with greater or lesser degrees of participation in the operation of the enterprise, but with little real power to protect their interests, even interest in greater participation, when they conflict with the interests of the employer. Still, more and more firms and employees now feel a strong need for worker autonomy, responsibility, and cooperation with management on the job. This aspiration is equally visible in the many innovative EI programs being developed in the context of collective bargaining itself. I see no reason why our labor laws should (at least formally) send to nonunion employees the message that they can participate in workplace decision-making only if they opt for unionism as well. Consequently I believe that it is time to begin dismantling Section 8(a)(2) and much of the other extraneous legal regulation that has grown up under the NLRA, with the caveat that any such legislative steps should be undertaken only as part of a broader reform effort which would give all workers an independent base of their own from which to influence the operation of their workplace, through either full-fledged collective bargaining or more limited in-plant initiatives and programs.

Chapter 6 develops in detail the legal program and the political strategy which are needed to finally make good on that promise to American workers.

2 · The Case of Wrongful Dismissal

Legal Inroads on Employment at Will

Turning now to the case of wrongful dismissal, I shall not rehearse here the oft-told tale of the rise and decline of employment at will.[1] Suffice it to say that this legal regime emerged rather suddenly in the late nineteenth century.[2] The employment relationship, termination of which by either party had been closely regulated for centuries, was transformed into one in which the employer was entitled to dismiss its employees (and the employees were entitled to quit their jobs) "at will . . . for good cause, no cause or even for cause morally wrong, without thereby being guilty of legal wrong." In theory, this legal doctrine was simply a background presumption of contract law, one which the parties were perfectly free to alter by explicit agreement. In practice, judges erected high barriers against any jury's concluding that the parties had agreed to enforceable guarantees. Indeed, the courts considered such freedom of action in employment to be so valuable that they regularly struck down as unconstitutional any federal[3] or state[4] legislative intrusion on the prerogative of employers to terminate the relationship. Even when these rigid constitutional constraints were relaxed in order to uphold the prohibition in the Wagner Act against the discharge of

1. Three valuable accounts of this history are Jay M. Feinman, "The Development of the Employment at Will Rule," 20 *American Journal of Legal History* 118 (1976); Sanford M. Jacoby, "The Duration of Indefinite Employment Contracts in the United States and England: An Historical Analysis," 5 *Comparative Labor Law* 85 (1982); and Gary Minda, "The Common Law of Employment at Will in New York," 36 *Syracuse Law Review* 939, 966–990 (1985).

2. See Jacoby, "The Duration of Indefinite Employment Contracts," pp. 113–116, and Feinman, "The Development of the Employment at Will Rule," pp. 127–129.

3. Adair v. United States, 208 U.S. 161 (1908).

4. Coppage v. Kansas, 236 U.S. 1 (1915).

union supporters,[5] this limitation on employment at will remained very much the exception to the general rule (just as did the enactment in the sixties of a broader version of the antidiscrimination principle in the Civil Rights Act and the Age Discrimination in Employment Act).

Not until the late sixties and the early seventies was the argument seriously advanced in the law reviews that there should be a general protection against *any* unfair dismissal rather than only specific categories of discriminatory discharge. The argument for this proposition, which by the eighties was well on the way to becoming the conventional wisdom, can be broken down into several components:[6]

1. Experience has shown that the employer's prerogative to dismiss workers at will is regularly abused. In particular, such power can be wielded to pressure employees into violating the law on behalf of their employer, or into sacrificing their own entitlements to a variety of legal benefits. Therefore, the exercise of this kind of economic power by private management warrants much the same kind of scrutiny as does the exercise of public governmental power.

2. An employer's legal freedom to fire employees at will carries so much actual power—that is, so much ability to pressure workers to act in ways which frustrate the public policies referred to above—simply because the employee places so much value on his present job and will take extreme measures to avoid losing it. His job is valuable both because it generates the earnings which probably constitute the major financial support for the worker and his family, and because work is so important to the personal identity and sense of self-worth of the employee. In a real sense, then, a worker's job is the asset about which he cares most in modern life, even more important to him than the various other forms of property which the law now says that he "owns."

5. NLRB v. Jones and Laughlin Steel Corp., 301 U.S. 1 (1937).

6. These strands in the argument are drawn from my reading of the major pieces in this scholarly literature; e.g., Lawrence E. Blades, "Employment at Will vs. Individual Freedom: On Limiting the Abusive Exercise of Employer Power," 67 *Columbia Law Review* 1404 (1967); Clyde W. Summers, "Individual Protection Against Unjust Dismissal: Time for a Statute," 62 *Virginia Law Review* 481 (1976); Cornelius J. Peck, "Unjust Discharge from Employment: A Necessary Change in the Law," 40 *Ohio State Law Journal* 1 (1979); Mary Ann Glendon and Edward R. Lev, "Changes in the Bonding of the Employment Relationship: An Essay on the New Property," 20 *Boston College Law Review* 458 (1979); Peter Linzner, "The Decline of Assent: At-Will Employment as a Case Study of the Breakdown of Private Law Theory," 20 *Georgia Law Review* 323 (1986). Lest there be any misunderstanding, I want to emphasize that this section sketches my interpretation of the standard liberal case for legal regulation of employer discharge decisions. As is also true of the account in the next section of the market critique of legal intervention, the arguments in this portion of the text do *not* constitute a statement of my own position, which will be elaborated later in this chapter.

3. A freely negotiated agreement between an individual employee and his employer is not an effective means for establishing the employee's entitlement to his job and protecting both workers and the community from management's abusing its power of dismissal. This conclusion flows from the fact that holding a job with the employer is typically much more important to the employee than retaining any individual worker is to the employer. The consequence of this pronounced tilt in the balance of bargaining power between the two parties is that very few workers would ever be able to use their apparent legal freedom to alter the at-will presumption embedded in the employment contract.

4. In contrast with this regime of individual employment contracts is the situation of the unionized employee who works under a collective agreement negotiated under the auspices of the NLRA. The unionized worker almost always enjoys a broad right to keep his job until and unless he gives his employer just cause to fire him. That right (with its standard remedy of reinstatement in the former position) is readily enforceable through the accessible procedure of grievance arbitration.[7] Thus, in addition to the substantive claims about the intrinsic importance of the job and the injustice of denying legal protection against its loss, there is the additional unfairness of so treating only nonunion, private-sector workers, when their counterparts who belong to a union or work for the government enjoy the right to protection against unjust dismissal as a matter of course.

Because it has been made and reiterated by so many judges and scholars for the last decade, the case for protection against unjust dismissal now seems virtually self-evident to many sophisticated commentators.[8] It is one thing, though, to state the argument for legal protection at this high a level of abstraction; it is quite another to

7. Many public employees also enjoy comparable protection under civil service legislation, typically enforceable through administrative procedures.

8. For example, Theodore J. St. Antoine, in his piece on "Protection Against Unjust Discipline: An Idea Whose Time Has Long Since Come," in James L. Stern and Barbara D. Dennis, eds., *Arbitration Issues for the 1980s* (Washington, D.C.: Bureau of National Affairs, 1983), writes (p. 49): "At this late date, I take it as a given that employees, generally, should be protected, generally, against unjust discipline." Given this apparent consensus about the objective, the only policy issue he deems worth debating concerns the appropriate legal technique for affording such protection. Indeed, Professor St. Antoine is the reporter for a committee that is drafting a model Employment Termination Act (referred to hereinafter as "Model Employment Termination Act") on behalf of the National Conference of Commissioners on Uniform State Laws. Later in this chapter I shall refer to certain provisions of their working draft in my discussion of a program for the dismissal problem.

translate the broad principle into an enforceable legal right. Suppose we agree that employment at will in all its rigor—empowering the employer to fire its workers "for good reason, bad reason or no reason at all"—is no longer tolerable in a civilized society. How far are we prepared to go in restricting this employer prerogative?

The relatively easy cases—which were the focus of the initial scholarly writing and favorable judicial decisions in the seventies—are those in which the employer fires a worker for a *bad* reason: for refusing to perjure himself in testimony which might endanger the employer,[9] for example, or for claiming a workers' compensation benefit that would ultimately affect the employer's insurance rating.[10] By and large, state courts are now prepared to prohibit discharge for illegitimate reasons such as these, under the rubric of the public policy exception to employment at will. Considerable debate continues about the nature and scope of the public policies that employers may be charged with offending through use of their dismissal prerogative.[11] But the underlying principle in these cases is modest in scope (in a sense consisting only of a judicial prerogative to build by analogy on the long-established antidiscrimination principle under legislation such as the NLRA and the Civil Rights Act); moreover, this principle does not encroach on the proper domain of freedom of contract. If perjury or price-fixing is justifiably deemed illegal when perpetrated by the firm itself, it is hard to dispute the legitimacy of putting legal constraints on the employer's power to coerce employees to do the dirty work for it.

Assuming that a legal ban on dismissal for *bad* reasons is fairly easy to accept, and assuming also (for reasons that I shall elaborate below) that a legal power to dismiss for *good* reasons is justifiable, that leaves the hard cases, the ones that fall in between these poles. How should the law treat the firing of a worker for *no* apparent reason or, more likely, for a not demonstrably *good enough* reason?

Consider the following example. An employee has worked for his employer for several years, doing a perfectly acceptable job. However, a new applicant appears on the scene with strong credentials and rave

9. As in Peterman v. Teamsters Local 396, 174 Cal. App. 2d 184 (1959).

10. As in Frampton v. Central Indiana Gas Company, 297 N.E.2d 425 (Ind. 1973).

11. Illustrative of the recent extension of the concept of "public policy" concerns that extend beyond clearly applicable legal rights and obligations are cases such as Wagenseller v. Scottsdale Memorial Hospital, 710 P.2d 1025 (Ariz. 1985) (nurse fired for refusing to "moon" in a campfire skit with colleagues and supervisors during a friendly rafting trip), and Novosel v. Nationwide Insurance Co., 721 F.2d 894 (3d Cir. 1984) (insurer's department head fired for refusing to support employer's lobbying efforts against no-fault auto reform).

references for his performance in previous positions. Should the employer be free to dismiss the merely satisfactory incumbent and replace him with the apparently better qualified and more productive newcomer?

It would be difficult to label such a discharge as dismissal for a *bad* reason in the sense of an abuse of management power in conflict with some public policy. The employer would say that it is doing no more than enhancing the efficiency of its operations by replacing a good performer with a better one. Indeed, there are settings in which such behavior is common and considered perfectly acceptable. In professional sports, for example, veteran athletes are regularly displaced by younger, faster (and usually less expensive) rookies. On reflection, however, the sports example is very much the exception which proves how different is the rule in modern employment. Very few workers ever experience the equivalent of an annual training camp in which they must repeatedly prove themselves superior to competitors in order to retain their job. The standard expectation in the real world of work is that the employee will keep his job unless he does something wrong—in the sense of some specific misconduct or a general pattern of poor performance—and as a consequence forfeits the position. Indeed, a further feature of the social mores at work is that even if an employee does something wrong—for example, if he takes a day off without a legitimate reason—it will not cost him his job immediately; he will be dismissed only if the bad act is part of a broader pattern of unsuitable behavior which has not been corrected by the employer with less severe disciplinary measures.

As I observed earlier, the easy case for reform of employment at will is one which seeks only to restrict dismissals in the presence of a bad reason for the firing—that is, some form of *employer* fault. The much harder case is the one which would restrict dismissals in the absence of a good (enough) reason; in other words, some form of serious *employee* default. That type of case is the standard grist for the mill of grievance arbitration under the "just cause" provision in collective agreements.[12] Notwithstanding the preoccupation so far in the law reports and the

---

12. Comprehensive accounts of the legal principles fashioned by labor arbitrators for the appraisal of discharge cases appear in Frank Elkouri and Edna A. Elkouri, *How Arbitration Works*, 4th ed. (Washington, D.C.: Bureau of National Affairs, 1985), in particular in Chapter 15 on "Discharge and Discipline"; and in Roger I. Abrams and Dennis R. Nolan, "Towards a Theory of 'Just Cause' in Employee Discipline Cases," 1985 *Duke Law Journal* 594.

law journals, such cases would surely constitute the vast majority of the estimated 150,000 claims a year of unfair dismissal of private-sector nonunion workers if some such "just cause" standard were adopted in that sphere.[13] The challenge, then, to those who would advocate such a standard, is to justify not simply prohibiting abuses of power by employers that frustrate the policies of the community, but also conferring upon workers (at least once they have served a suitable probation period) a form of legal *tenure* in their jobs.[14]

The second generation of discharge litigation in the early eighties presented this tougher challenge to the courts. Typically these cases involved firms that had developed procedures and criteria for limiting dismissal decisions by lower-echelon managers, where the firm had communicated these standards to its employees in written handbooks or oral representations, but it was alleged that the system had miscarried in connection with the individual litigant. Under the traditional at-will approach, the claim that a binding obligation had been created and violated would likely fail on the grounds either that the commitment was not explicit enough, or that it had not been written down, or that it had not been paid for by a specific reciprocal commitment from the employee. The second significant step in the evolution of the law, then, was to relax those somewhat artificial limits on the normal approach of contract law, and to find that an enforceable agreement had actually been made.[15] If an employer had presented itself to its workers as one which did not wield the authority to fire employees at will—whether these representations were made to recruit better workers, to enhance morale and productivity, or even to avoid a union contract—the employer should be required by the law to live up to those assurances on later occasions when it was tempted to ignore them.

Such a development is not only compatible with, but even support-

13. This figure was calculated by Jack Steiber and Michael Murray in "Protection Against Unjust Discharge: The Need for a Federal Statute," 16 *University of Michigan Journal of Law Reform* 319, 322–324 (1983).

14. In characterizing the right under examination as "tenure," I do not mean to imply that an employee should have an absolute right to retain his present job. The proposal is simply that the incumbent employee should have a defeasible right to retain his job unless he gives the employer good reason—just cause—for dismissal. In principle this is the same kind of protection that is now standard for university professors, although in practice the grounds for dismissal in the case of professors are interpreted more tightly and utilized more rarely than they are for, say, factory workers under collective agreements.

15. Among the important early decisions on this issue were Toussaint v. Blue Cross and Blue Shield of Michigan, 292 N.W.2d 880 (Mich. 1980), and Pugh v. See's Candies, Inc., 116 Cal. App. 3d 311 (1981).

ive of, the values of free contract in employment. Moreover, this doctrine will likely be a significant benefit to those workers who happen to be in a position to take advantage of this area of the law in transition. In the longer run, though, even this evolution is probably not a sufficient and satisfactory response to the strong version of the case against employment at will.

The reason is that once employers learn from the courts that there is a real chance that their arrangements might be held contractually binding, they will take the steps necessary to remove any suggestion that their practices are intended to be legally enforceable. The employer may still give its employees a handbook that informs them of the internal procedure for reviewing dismissal decisions, a procedure that is designed to avoid unfair firings. However, the firm's lawyers will carefully draft disclaimer clauses which make it explicit that no binding undertaking is being given to maintain such practices, nor that the procedures will be foolproof, nor that the handbook (or other representations) can serve as the legal basis for a lawsuit if the system does miscarry.[16]

A judiciary determined to implement its new policies against unfair dismissals might be tempted to strike down any such disclaimer of liability as oppressive and unconscionable.[17] However, that reaction would seem rather perverse if it were confined to cases where employers had developed these special protective procedures. In effect, a more onerous legal liability would thus be imposed on firms which had

16. Illustrations of scholarly legal advice to employers on reducing their exposure to unjust dismissal claims through, *inter alia*, appropriately drafted disclaimers are Sam Estreicher, "Unjust Dismissal: Preventive Measures," in *Unjust Dismissal* 783 (New York: Practicing Law Institute, 1984); and Kenneth T. Lopatka, "The Emerging Law of Wrongful Discharge: A Quadrennial Assessment of the Labor Law Issue of the 80's," 40 *Business Lawyer* 1, 26–32 (1984). Indeed, the American Society of Personnel Administration Foundation has drafted and announced a model disclaimer clause which reads as follows: "This is not a contract of employment. Any individual may voluntarily leave employment upon proper notice, and may be terminated by the employer at any time and for any reason. Any oral or written statements or promises to the contrary are hereby expressly disavowed and should not be relied upon by any prospective or existing employee. The contents of this handbook are subject to change any time at the discretion of the employer." (Quoted in Matthew W. Finkin, "The Bureaucratization of Work: Employer Policies and Contract Law," 1986 *Wisconsin Law Review* 733, 748–749.)

17. An apt analogy upon which judges might draw would be the principle that a doctor or hospital is not permitted to secure from a patient a legally valid waiver of liability for injuries negligently inflicted in the course of their relationship; see, e.g., Tunkl v. The Regents of the University of California, 383 P.2d 441 (Cal. 1963). For contrasting views of *Tunkl* and its progeny, see Randall Bovbjerg and Clark C. Havighurst, "Medical Malpractice: Can the Private Sector Find Relief?" 49 *Law and Contemporary Problems* 1 (Spring 1986).

voluntarily taken steps to try to reduce the incidence of unfair dismissals inside their operations, while leaving with the luxury of at-will the less conscientious employers that made no effort to provide their workers with reasonable protection against arbitrary treatment by their managers. In any event, for this or other reasons, so far no court has been prepared to invalidate such contractual waivers of legal liability.[18]

Quite a different view of such disclaimers would be appropriate if the social judgment were made that *all* employers should be held to a mandatory legal standard of just cause as the precondition for discharge, whether or not representations to this effect had been made to the employees. In fact, that is the logical implication of the broad array of arguments sketched earlier against employment at will: the claims

18. Although the major decisions which developed the contractual theory for unjust dismissal litigation typically stated that the employer could exclude such liability through appropriate language and action (see *Toussaint,* 292 N.W.2d 890–891; Thompson v. St. Regis Paper Co., 685 P.2d 1081, 1088 (Wash. 1984); and Wooley v. Hoffmann-LaRoche, 491 A.2d 1257, 1271 (N.J. 1985)), several commentators have expressed doubts that such disclaimers would be legally effective in the courts; see Finkin, "The Bureaucratization," pp. 748–750, and Julius M. Steiner and Allan M. Dabrow, "The Questionable Value of Inclusion of Language Confirming Employment-at-Will Status in Company Personnel Documents," 37 *Labor Law Journal* 639 (1986). However, in recent cases courts have almost uniformly refused to permit employee suits (even past a motion for summary dismissal) if the employer had developed appropriate language for its employment application forms, handbooks, and the like. See Reid v. Sears Roebuck, 790 F.2d 453 (6th Cir. 1986); Dell v. Montgomery Ward and Co., 811 F.2d 970 (6th Cir. 1987); Hughlett v. Sperry Corp., 650 F. Supp. 312 (D.C. Minn. 1986); Bailey v. Perkins Restaurant, Inc., 398 N.W.2d 120 (N.D.S.C. 1986); Castiglione v. Johns Hopkins Hospitals, 517 A.2d 786 (Md. App. 1986); Arnold v. Diet Center Inc., 746 P.2d 1040 (Idaho App. 1987); and Nork v. Fetter Printing Co., 738 S.W.2d 824 (Ky. App. 1987). This will be the result at least as long as the employer's wording is clear and unambiguous and has been adequately communicated to the employee; see, e.g., Schipani v. Ford Motor Company, 302 N.W.2d 307 (Mich. App. 1981); Ferrara v. Koelsch 368 N.W.2d 666 (Wis. 1985); and Morriss v. Coleman Co., 738 P.2d 841 (Kan. 1987).

A possible exception to this contractual logic regarding disclaimers might be the third basis for limiting the at-will doctrine, the implied-in-law covenant of good faith and fair dealing; see Cleary v. American Airlines, Inc., 111 Cal. App. 3d 443 (1980). Both the nonconsensual, tort-like flavor of this covenant and its use in the analogous insurance context (see Koehrer v. Superior Court, 181 Cal. App. 3d 1155, 1169–71 (1986)) suggest that the covenant should not be waivable by employees who are meant to enjoy its protection. However, subsequent cases, even in California, have ordered summary dismissal of implied good faith claims where there was explicit at-will language in the employment contract documents. See Shapiro v. Wells Fargo Realty Advisors, 152 Cal. App. 3d 467 (1984); and Crain v. Burrough, 560 F. Supp. 849 (C.D. Cal. 1983). The only case of which I am aware in which a court ignored such an express disclaimer was decided by a divided panel of the Fifth Circuit, purporting to apply Texas law, but without any reasons or citations on this point; see Aiello v. United Airlines, Inc., 818 F.2d 1196, 1200 (5th Cir. 1987).

not just about the possible abuse of employer power, but also about the substantive value to the worker of his job, the lack of meaningful bargaining power of the individual employee to win such protection on his own, and the inequitable situation of the nonunion worker relative to his unionized counterpart. However, scholars who draw that strong conclusion from these arguments tend typically to propose legislative rather than judicial adoption of the just cause standard, and to favor the administration of this standard (and the award of reinstatement as the normal remedy) by labor arbitrators, who are usually the same people who now deal with the nuances of just cause under collective agreements.[19] Until very recently, no American legislature has been prepared to take that step, and no court has proposed to do it for them.[20] However, the case for such reform has filtered north of the border and borne fruit in statutes enacted in several jurisdictions in Canada, which provide some useful evidence of how such a program might operate in practice.[21]

The Intellectual Debate

A Critique of the Critique of At-Will Status

I shall reserve for later my discussion about alternative legal instruments for implementing any mandatory right to tenure in employment. At this point I merely want to emphasize that such a right is the natural outcome of the standard critique of employment at will. When

19. See, e.g., Summers, "Protection Against Unjust Dismissal"; Steiber and Murray, "Protection Against Unjust Discharge"; St. Antoine, "Protection Against Unjust Discipline"; William B. Gould, "Reflections on Wrongful Discharge Litigation and Legislation," in Walter J. Gershenfeld, ed., *Arbitration 1984*, (Washington, D.C.: Bureau of National Affairs, 1985); and Report of the California State Bar Adhoc Committee on Termination at Will and Wrongful Discharge, "To Strike a New Balance," *Labor and Employment Law News* (Special Edition, Feb. 8, 1984).

20. Clyde W. Summers, "The Contract of Employment and the Rights of Individual Employees: Fair Representation and Employment at Will," 52 *Fordham Law Review* 1082, 1109 (1984), lists several of the states where such bills have been introduced but not passed. Finally, in mid-1987 the state of Montana enacted the first comprehensive statutory protection against wrongful dismissal: see BNA, "Montana's At-Will Employment Law," 126 *Labor Relations Reporter* 19 (1987). I shall describe and evaluate the rather different Montana approach at pp. 96–99 in the text.

21. For a comprehensive description of the law, practice, and impact of the Canadian legislation, both in the provinces of Nova Scotia and Quebec and at the federal level, see Gilles Trudeau, "Statutory Protection Against Unjust Dismissal for Unorganized Workers" (S.J.D. diss., Harvard Law School, 1985).

that stronger version of the new legal regime is spelled out in these terms, it becomes easier to appreciate the vigorous criticism it has recently provoked from the defenders of employment at will: from those who believe that the historic virtues of mutual freedom in the standard employment contract, the mutual freedom about how to make and remake that employment contract, have much more contemporary value than is supposed in the conventional argument for liberal reform.[22]

There are two lines of defense of employment at will. The first and more traditional one, the defense of *mutuality*,[23] can be stated as follows. Employment at will actually replaced a legal regime which strictly regulated the power of both employer and employee to terminate their relationship.[24] Such a regime would now be quite distasteful to Amer-

22. The most forthright defense of employment at will and critique of the recent legal constraints on dismissal has been mounted by Richard A. Epstein in two articles, "In Defense of the Contract at Will," 51 *University of Chicago Law Review* 947 (1984), and "Agency Costs, Employment Contracts, and Labor Unions," in John W. Pratt and Richard J. Zeckhauser, eds., *Principals and Agents: The Structure of Business* (Boston, Mass.: Harvard Business School Press, 1985). To much the same effect is Richard W. Power, "A Defense of the Employment at Will Rule," 27 *Saint Louis University Law Journal* 881 (1983). Another important article which is skeptical of the relative costs and benefits of judicial intervention, although less emphatically critical of the legal trend, is Jeffrey L. Harrison, "The 'New' Terminable-at-Will Employment Contract: An Interest and Cost Incidence Analysis," 69 *Iowa Law Review* 327 (1984).

23. A review of the historic use by courts of the mutuality argument is contained in Jacoby, "The Duration of Indefinite Employment," pp. 122–126. A succinct statement of the reasons why this is no longer a persuasive argument as a matter of modern contract doctrine appears in Summers, "The Contract of Employment," pp. 1098–99. However, the continuing intuitive feeling that it is in fact fair to equate employer and employee in this respect is evidenced by the fact that most contemporary disclaimer clauses begin by stating that just as the employee has the freedom to terminate the job relationship at will, so also does the employer; see the authorities cited in notes 16 and 18. And Epstein, in "In Defense," relies strongly on the mutual advantage of an easily terminable contract to support his case against legal intervention.

24. Indeed, as Jacoby pointed out in "The Duration of Indefinite Employment," pp. 105–107, the employment contract as administered by American courts in the mid-nineteenth century gave employers the freedom to dismiss their employees at will, but penalized workers if they quit their job without sufficient cause; see also Wythe Holt, "Recovery by the Worker Who Quits: A Comparison of the Mainstream, Legal Realist, and Critical Legal Studies Approaches to a Problem of Nineteenth Century Contract Law," 1986 *Wisconsin Law Review* 677. In that respect, the adoption of a mutual at-will legal doctrine in fact improved the legal situation of workers. Of course, a modern contract which permits employees to quit at will while limiting the employer's power of dismissal to just cause (which is the standard arrangement under collective agreements) is quite likely to be even more beneficial for workers, especially since (as I indicate later in the text) the employer can protect itself from indiscriminate worker quits through a variety of service-related benefits in its overall employment package.

ican workers. Even ignoring the variety of idiosyncratic reasons why they might want to quit their current job, the fact is that before they actually start a job, very few workers are in a position to experience and learn of its conditions and thence to judge if they really like it. So they need the freedom to be able to leave for any reason they want, without having to justify their actions to an outside adjudicator. But if employees are to be given that freedom, so also should employers. The latter have the same practical need to observe new workers on the job before deciding whether to keep them. More fundamentally, the contract of employment consists in a bilateral arrangement between the employee, the owner of the labor, and the employer, the owner of the capital. If freedom of one side to terminate the relationship at will is necessary to protect its interests, then it is only fair to provide a similar freedom for protection of the interests of the other side.

While that argument was the traditional underpinning of the legal doctrine, it is no longer very compelling. And the basic philosophical claim that the owners of labor and of capital are each deserving of equal concern here assumes precisely the point at issue in the debate.[25] When one looks more closely at the actual state of the employment relationship, what one finds is a complex structure that does not involve a mutual exchange of *identical* promises by the two sides. Typically the employer reserves a probation period (of several weeks, months, or even years) during which to appraise new hires. And as I shall describe shortly, the employer also deploys a variety of economic carrots to induce its longer-service employees to remain in their jobs: thus it is by no means evident that the employer also needs a legal stick to prevent its employees from quitting.[26]

A more plausible defense of a broad employer prerogative to terminate the employment relationship (one which would concededly be subject to the new and relatively narrow ban on *bad* reasons) is that this is necessary for the *efficient* operation of the labor market. That argument can be put in terms of the following four steps:[27]

25. In any event, it is implausible to assume that employer and worker are in the identical situation. It is almost unheard of, for example, that an employee abuses his power to quit at will by using it to coerce his employer to violate its legal obligations or forfeit its statutory rights.

26. Even in those relatively rare circumstances where an employer might appear to need some device to prevent the defection of an employee—the entertainer or the athlete again serve as examples—employers can and do negotiate such protection for themselves.

27. This is my distillation of the arguments spelled out in the articles by Richard A. Epstein, Jeffrey L. Harrison, and Richard W. Power, cited in note 22.

1. Employers need the freedom to dismiss employees for *good* reasons; that is, because an employee has not been meeting the minimum standards of performance and behavior required for the productive operation of the enterprise. Such a prerogative is not an aspect of capitalist domination or management hierarchy: it would be required in a firm owned and operated by the workers themselves. In a market economy which gives the consumers the freedom to choose the type, quality, and price of the goods and services they will buy, each firm has to be able to operate within a reasonable margin of efficiency with its competitors. That means that all firms, even worker-managed firms, must have the authority to insure that an individual employee who is not doing his job as well as can be reasonably demanded is dismissed and replaced by someone else who will.

2. Employers do not want to fire employees for *no* reason, because to do so would inflict a loss not only on the employee-victim but also on the firm itself. The employer immediately loses the investment in "human capital" that it made in training the dismissed worker to become an effective part of its production team. More important, perhaps, a pattern of such arbitrary management action will damage the firm's good reputation, which it requires in order to recruit and retain other valuable employees. A broader implication of this point is that it is a mistake to focus, as so often happens, on the apparent disparity in resources between an individual worker and the large corporate firm for which he works, and to assume that there is an obvious and inherent inequality of bargaining power between the two. With rare exceptions (one thinks, for example, of the air traffic controllers) many large employers are looking for the services of different types of employees (just as many employees are looking for these jobs), and this competition in the labor market provides a real incentive to the firm not to fire employees unless it has good and apparent reasons for doing so.[28]

28. For explicit judicial recognition of this economic constraint, see the opinion of Judge Richard A. Posner in Jordan v. Duff and Phelps, Inc., 815 F.2d 429, 447–450 (7th Cir. 1987), dissenting, ironically, from the majority judgment authored by his law and economics confrère, Judge Frank Easterbrook. Easterbrook concluded that in this particular context, at least, such labor market forces were insufficient to control the "opportunistic" behavior by the employer.

I should note that to the free market devotee, the analysis in the text does not apply to cases in which the employer has fired an employee for a *bad* reason, that is, for a reason that flouts some public policy. Whether the policy in question is banning price-fixing or mandating workers' compensation, it was embodied in a law in the first place because employers appeared to need additional legal incentive to serve that particular public interest. If employers do require such incentives, then it is not unlikely that some

3. One response to the last point is that if it is true that employers do not need—indeed, do not even want—to fire employees without good reason, then they should have no tangible objection to a law that prohibits such action. The immediate rejoinder is that there is a vast difference between management's exercising the authority to distinguish between good and not-so-good reasons for dismissal, and a law that empowers juries to second-guess the decision initially made by the firm. Not only is there the ever-present risk of jury error, but given that these cases usually involve a contest between an employee who is without a job and an employer with a deep pocket, the likelihood is that the jury will systematically err on the side of finding the discharge to be improper, even where it really was not. When one adds the fact that the price of such a "false positive" can be a six- or even seven-figure damage award,[29] the real long-term risk of such a legal regime is defensive personnel practice: an unwillingness on the part of the firm to exercise its apparent right of dismissal for good reasons, at least unless the grounds are truly egregious and readily demonstrable at trial. Thus the ultimate consequence of a law which says that it is up to the courts rather than management to distinguish between good and not-so-good reasons for dismissal will be a less productive enterprise and less efficient economy.

4. If this concern were to materialize, the creation by the law of this form of tenure in employment (defeasible only by proof in court of good reasons for its termination) might well be a benefit to workers, but it would impose a significant cost burden on employers. That cost would have to be distributed somewhere among the constituencies of

of them would be tempted to use their power of dismissal to coerce employees into cooperating in covert avoidance of the legal requirement. Therefore, a further prohibition on this particular type of wrongful dismissal would be a useful legal buttress for the underlying public policy. The point of the argument sketched in the text is that in the far more numerous cases in which the firing is a consequence of the private relationship between employer and employee, the employer has a strong economic incentive to use its dismissal prerogative only for good reasons, to maximize the performance of its employees. As a result, any added legal incentive would be superfluous, perhaps even harmful. This line of argument is ultimately not compelling, as I shall argue later, at pp. 63–67 and 71–78.

29. William B. Gould, "The Idea of the Job as Property in Contemporary America: The Legal and Collective Bargaining Framework," 1986 *Brigham Young University Law Review* 885, 905, reports the results of a study of jury verdicts in California from 1982 through 1986. Plaintiffs in that state have been winning nearly three-quarters of these unjust dismissal trials and receiving awards which average more than $650,000—nearly twice as much as the final settlement amount proposed by the *plaintiffs*. For further data and analysis of this aspect of the problem, see pp. 79–83 and 101, n. 99.

the enterprise. Assuming relatively competitive consumer and capital markets, the cost would likely be borne by the work force in the form of somewhat lower wages or benefits.[30] Indeed, there might well be a rather unattractive tilt to the distribution of these benefits and burdens within the work force itself. The more likely beneficiaries of such legal protection would be the mediocre workers, those on the borderline between dismissal and retention, whereas the cost of providing the benefit would come out of wages and benefits that typically are paid according to general criteria applicable to all employees, the good and the not-so-good alike.

The thrust of the foregoing argument is not that protecting workers against unjust firings is socially undesirable. On the contrary, the premise is that because this objective is affirmatively desirable for both workers and employers, the free and competitive labor market can be relied on to provide a substantial degree of protection on its own. What is asserted to be undesirable is the use of the law to force and enforce that protection, because the modest additional weight the law would add to natural market incentives is outweighed by the sizeable economic costs, immediate and long-term, of legal intervention.

One need not assume, though, that the costs of an enforceable right to be dismissed only for good reasons always outweigh the benefits. Since employment at will is a waivable rather than a mandatory contract doctrine, the parties are free to negotiate a higher degree of job tenure if that benefit is worth more to particular employees than the at-will prerogative is worth to the firm. However, the fact that such special contractual guarantees are so exceptional in the real world is felt to be strong corroboration of the critic's thesis that adding legal constraints to the market's influence on management authority is rarely to the mutual advantage of the parties.

Even if one accepts each of the steps in this argument (and I shall consider later whether and to what extent they are valid), they merely establish the proposition that workers as a whole may be somewhat better off if their employers cannot be sued by individual employees who contend that they were unjustly fired. Such an abstract proposition will not satisfy the concerns of those who believe that the task of the law here is to protect the individual worker from the severe con-

30. If the justification for legal intervention here is that workers do not have enough bargaining power on their own to secure this kind of job tenure from their employers, it is quite likely that the employer will simply redeploy its greater bargaining power to recoup the cost of the new benefit from savings in other aspects of its labor costs.

sequences of an injustice which may in fact have been done to him.[31]

A further feature of the argument, then, is that the conventional liberal critique of employment at will badly overestimates the severity of the loss of one's job. Such an event, it is said, is not at all akin to losing one's life or a limb in a workplace accident, with the irreversible harm such an event inflicts on the individual and society. By contrast, discharging a worker from his present job leaves a vacancy that will be filled by another worker while the previous incumbent finds a new job.[32] Of course, there will be an interim period when the dismissed worker has no earnings from work. However, a better way to respond to this potential hardship is through a full-employment policy that would make it easy for the worker dismissed from one job to find another job quickly, and through unemployment insurance benefits that cushion the transition, rather than through establishing a mandatory legal entitlement to retain the first job (one side effect of which would be a reduced willingness of firms to hire as many workers in the first place).

Implicit in this line of argument, then, is that one job is very much like

31. A telling illustration of this issue is the case of Rulon-Miller v. International Business Machines, 162 Cal. App. 3d 241 (1984). In the eyes of the business community and business scholars, IBM is the paragon of a nonunion firm with a sophisticated and benevolent human resources management program. IBM designed elaborate policies to protect the rights and interests of its employees—such as their right of privacy—by issuing instructions for and reviewing its managers' personnel decisions. So if it is possible at any firm, it must surely be at IBM that the work force as a whole would be better off with the protection afforded by such informal internal mechanisms, which entail much lower legal and transaction costs to the employer and thereby make more money available for compensating the employees.

However, the case of Virginia Rulon-Miller is an example of what can happen to the victim of a purely voluntary, nonlegal mechanism. She was fired for dating an employee of a smaller competitor of IBM: the relationship, according to Rulon-Miller's superior, constituted a conflict of interest for someone in her lower management position. However, the California Court of Appeals made clear in its close analysis of the positions and functions of both Rulon-Miller and her friend that there was no valid basis for presuming the existence of a conflict of interest in this case. Unfortunately, IBM's review procedures simply had not picked up and corrected this invasion of the employee's right to privacy, which was supposed to be protected by the firm's formal policy. Although the employees of IBM taken as a group and viewed *ex ante* arguably might be better off without the right to mount a legal challenge to their possible discharge, the same could certainly not be said about Rulon-Miller herself, the actual victim of the illegitimate firing. The *raison d'être* of a mandatory law protecting against wrongful dismissal is to insure that extra protection is made available to employees who really need it in the event they are injured when internal firm processes have miscarried.

32. Thus Epstein writes (in "Agency Costs," p. 140): "When one employee is wrongfully discharged, another will typically be hired in his place, so that the personal hardship of one is offset by the benefits that are conferred upon another." To the same effect, see Power, "A Defense," pp. 891–892.

another. It is important to have a job (or other source of income when one is without a job); it is much less important to remain in one's old job rather than to find a new one. The image of work and employment implicit in this traditional common law doctrine is that employment not only can be but regularly is terminated at will—by employees as well as by employers—with some initial dislocation but no serious long-term losses. And this legal image accords with a broader vision of a labor market composed of fluid, casual relationships that are readily and flexibly adjusted to changing economic forces, both internal and external.

The Special Value of One's Own Job

The foregoing critique presents a coherent and powerful thesis about the appropriate roles of the law and the labor market, one which should awaken liberal reformers from a rather dogmatic slumber. In appraising this position, I shall begin with the last crucial assumption—that dismissal from one's job is not so significant an event that the law should worry about it, because the loss of one job will soon be remedied by securing another comparable position, something which is happening all the time in an ever-changing economy marked by casual, episodic, at-will employment relationships.

To the extent that the defense of employment at will rests on this premise it is in difficulty, because that description simply does not square with what we know about contemporary employment life. The fact is that most workers now enjoy long-term, if not lifetime jobs. [33]

Actually, the picture is somewhat more complicated than the last

33. The most prominent empirical demonstrations of this phenomenon in the modern American labor market appear in Robert E. Hall, "The Importance of Lifetime Jobs in the U.S. Economy," 72 *American Economic Review* 716 (1982), and George A. Akerlof and Brian G. M. Main, "An Experience-Weighted Measure of Employment and Unemployment Durations," 71 *American Economic Review* 1003 (1981). Of course, the degree to which employment relationships are stable and enduring varies considerably from one historical era to another. See Sanford M. Jacoby, "Industrial Labor Mobility in Historical Perspective," 22 *Industrial Relations* 261 (1983), showing that there was much more employee turnover early in the century than now. Employment stability also depends on union status; see John T. Addison and Alberto C. Castro, "The Importance of Lifetime Jobs: Differences Between Union and Nonunion Workers," 40 *Industrial and Labor Relations Review* 393 (1987) (union members enjoy greater tenure on average than nonunion workers). The durability of employment relationships also varies among different national economies. See, e.g., Masanori Hashimoto and John Raisian, "Employment Tenure and Earnings Profiles in Japan and the United States," 75 *American Economic Review* 721 (1985) (the typical employee-firm relationship endures longer in Japan than it does even in the contemporary U.S. labor market).

simple statement implies. New, younger entrants to the work force typically try out a number of jobs on a relatively short-term basis; many women drop out of the labor force for the birth and infancy of their children. But those workers who stay at (or come back to) work for the long run eventually settle into a position with a single employer which lasts for one, two, or three decades. If the law is to be responsive to real life, then, it must rest on the footing that employment predominantly takes the form of a *career* rather than a *casual* relationship.[34]

It is easy to appreciate why this kind of relationship becomes attractive to most workers. The type, the place, and the responsibilities of one's job exert an important influence on one's home life, friendships, routines, and sense of identity. Since most people, after a period of initial adventure and exploration, want stability in their lives, they will also want and need stability in their employment.

Employers also have a tangible interest in long-term career relationships with their employees. For reasons I will develop in Chapter 4, such an enduring relationship with its employees provides the firm with much more productivity and efficiency than does the flexibility to make constant adjustments in the size, composition, and treatment of its work force. Interestingly, such stability is so valuable to most employers that they have not been prepared to trust the natural inclinations of their workers to stay on of their own accord. A number of key features in the structure of the employment relationship are designed to provide a tangible economic incentive to workers to stay on with the firm even if their personal feelings might have taken them elsewhere.

Wages. Typically a firm will have a wage structure that pays employees more money the longer they remain in its employ. The progression of an employee up the salary schedule (a scale which itself rises in tandem with inflation and economic growth) is not a reward for greater experience and productivity. Not only are such step increases typically paid for years of service in the *firm* rather than for years in the occupation or industry, but empirical investigation has shown that after a fairly brief initial period in the job, individual productivity does not increase nearly as fast as do relative wages.[35] Thus this standard fea-

34. These terms were used by Arthur M. Okun in his *Prices and Quantities: A Macroeconomic Analysis* 81, 83 (Washington, D.C.: Brookings Institution, 1981). Chapters 2 and 3 of that important work (pp. 26–133) contain an in-depth analysis of the importance of this labor market phenomenon for the macroeconomic performance of the United States.

35. For empirical demonstrations of this claim see James L. Medoff and Katherine G. Abraham, "Experience, Performance, and Earnings," 95 *Quarterly Journal of Economics*

ture of pay systems in modern industry is designed to reward individual longevity rather than productivity in employment.

Benefits. A variety of fringe benefits are also explicitly linked to length of service: the number of weeks of paid vacation, for example, is commonly based on the number of years with the employer. The most valuable of these benefits is usually the pension plan. Pension plans typically provide an initial period before benefits vest, so an employee who leaves before the vesting period is complete forfeits any entitlement to pension credits for the time already worked. This kind of forfeiture provision has long been a subject of legal regulation; the vesting period can now be no longer than five years. However, a subtle feature of most pension plans continues to generate a powerful incentive to an employee to remain with his current employer even after the vesting date has passed. The standard defined benefit pension plan promises to pay upon retirement (say, at age sixty-five) a pension that is calculated as a percentage of the earnings in the last year (or the last several years) with the firm. This means that if the worker leaves the firm sometime earlier (say, at age fifty) and wages continue to increase with inflation and economic growth, the pension credits earned even for previous years of service (say, from ages thirty-five to fifty) will be much less valuable than if the worker had remained at his job until he was eligible to retire on a pension based on the last and highest wage level. Economic analysis has shown that the worker himself actually paid for the earlier pension credits by receiving less take-home pay during the years of earlier service (from ages thirty-five to fifty), so a substantial financial penalty in future pension benefits is a significant consequence of leaving one's job early.[36]

Job Opportunities. Most workers are interested not only in the wages and benefits they earn from their immediate job, but also in the opportunity to move to better, higher-paid jobs and to enjoy job security when the available number of jobs shrinks in a layoff, even if that

---

703 (1980), and James L. Medoff and Katherine G. Abraham, "Are Those Paid More Really More Productive?: The Case of Experience," 16 *Journal of Human Resources* 186 (1981). Edward P. Lazear, "Why Is There Mandatory Retirement?" 87 *Journal of Political Economy* 1261 (1979), focuses on the explanation and significance of this phenomenon.

36. An elaborate empirical proof of this feature of the standard defined benefit pension plan is presented in Richard A. Ippolito, "The Labor Contract and True Economic Pension Liabilities," 75 *American Economic Review* 1031 (1985). See also Richard A. Ippolito, *Pensions, Economics and Public Policies* (Homewood, Ill.: Dow Jones-Irwin, 1986), in particular Chapter 3, "Pension Liabilities," (pp. 36–62), for an analysis of the implications of this phenomenon for the operation and regulation of private pension plans.

protection takes the form of a right to bump into a lower-paying position. These opportunities are typically awarded, in whole or in part, on the basis of seniority, which is usually the dominant factor in layoffs and a significant factor in promotions. That means that for each year spent with the firm, the worker banks an entitlement to a preferential claim in future competition for job opportunities as they may arise.[37] This valuable in-kind benefit is explicitly tied to longevity with the firm, and is therefore also forfeited by the worker in the event of early termination.

A number of more general observations are implied by these specific features of the typical employment relationship. First, while such heavy reliance on the seniority principle—on length of service with the firm as a key determinant of the worker's wages, benefits, and job opportunities—originated in and is still accentuated in unionized firms, it pervades nonunion employment as well.[38] Next, this aspect of the employment relationship provides the answer to the *mutuality* problem alluded to earlier. While the employer may not have a legal right to force a recalcitrant employee to stay when he wants to leave (a right that would be of little value for a firm and virtually impossible to enforce), there is an elaborate set of financial incentives for employees to stay and penalties if they quit, a system that is quite sufficient to secure the employer's side of the career employment bargain.

More pertinent to our purposes here, it is now clear why a new job is not fungible with an old job even if the jobs are virtually the same in type, pay, and conditions. An employee who has worked his way up the seniority ladder with one firm and now enjoys all the perquisites that long service provides loses this major advantage when he leaves his current job. The loss cannot be repaired even if he were to find an otherwise identical job the very next day, because in the new position he would have to begin at or near the bottom of the seniority ladder, with all the disadvantages that entails.

Suppose, then, that the employee was fired by the employer for no

37. See generally Richard B. Freeman and James L. Medoff *What Do Unions Do?* (New York: Basic Books, 1984) particularly Chapter 8, "Respect Your Elders: The Role of Seniority," pp. 122–135.

38. See Katherine G. Abraham and James L. Medoff, "Length of Service and Layoffs in Union and Nonunion Work Groups," 38 *Industrial and Labor Relations Review* 87 (1984); Fred K. Foulkes, *Personnel Policies in Large Nonunion Companies* (Englewood Cliffs, N.J.: Prentice-Hall, 1980), in particular Chapter 7, "Promotion Systems," pp. 123–145; and Philip Selznick and Howard Vollmer, "The Rule of Law in Industry: Seniority Rights," 1 *Industrial Relations* 97 (May 1962).

good reason. The unfairness of such an action can be appreciated by comparing it with the situation in Fortune v. National Cash Register,[39] one of the noteworthy early cases in the judicial erosion of employ- ment at will. Fortune, a salesman, was fired shortly before he was to receive a substantial commission from an earlier sale under a firm program that made commissions payable to employees at the time of delivery of the equipment they had sold. Though the case raised no issue of public policy and there had been no representation by the employer about any limits on its power of dismissal, the Massachusetts court found that the firing was a violation of an implied obligation of good faith in the employer relationship. The firm's bad faith consisted in its denial to the employee of the fruits of his earlier work and efforts.

Now consider the standard employment relationship in the light of *Fortune*. New employees come to work under a regime in which they initially earn less in pay and benefits than they produce, and they enjoy less favorable jobs, shifts, and security than their senior fellow workers. This system has been designed by the firm to induce workers to remain in its employ, because the employees realize that eventually they will reap the benefits of the system when they have put in suffi- cient time under it. The commission scheme in *Fortune* is simply a more visible, more dramatic example of this implicit contract at the heart of the modern employment relationship. If an employer suddenly exer- cises its unilateral prerogative to terminate that contract when the em- ployee has obtained more senior status (and, by the way, has thereby become more expensive), the employee is deprived of what he ex- pected would be the return on his bargain with the firm: he suffers the irreversible loss of his investment of a significant part of his working life making his way up the ladder in this job rather than somewhere else. All in all, a rather compelling claim for judicial intervention![40]

39. 364 N.E.2d 1251 (Mass. 1977).

40. A recent decision, Metz v. Transit Mix, Inc., 828 F.2d 1202 (7th Cir. 1987), illus- trates this point well in an analogous context. Metz was a manager who had worked for Transit Mix for twenty-seven years, and the regular annual salary increases that he had received during this period had pushed his salary to a significantly higher level than the salary paid to a younger man, a junior manager at another location. The Seventh Circuit panel concluded as a matter of fact that Transit had dismissed Metz and replaced him with his younger and equally productive colleague because the younger employee was less expensive. The court then concluded as a matter of law that in this case the salary disparity served as a proxy for Metz's age, making his dismissal therefore a violation of the Age Discrimination in Employment Act. The majority judgment elicited a spirited dissent from Judge Easterbrook, especially with regard to the legal ruling. Irrespective of the legal debate, however, *Metz* is a revealing case study of the direct connection be-

Practical Qualifications on the Moral Claim

My argument, then, is that as modern employment has evolved from a casual to a career relationship between worker and firm, the traditional at-will legal concept has become morally untenable. Employees can rightfully assume that they have some entitlement to retain their position as long as they are performing their jobs reasonably well. But we must immediately incorporate certain important refinements and qualifications into that moral claim.

First, in a variety of contexts employees typically have no such expectation of tenure in their present job. Earlier I used the example of the professional athlete who knows that his position is at risk every year in training camp. So also do the holders of high-level government jobs realize that their appointment will end when the political pendulum swings. Blue-collar construction workers who constantly move from a relatively short assignment with a particular contractor on one project to a new job with a different contractor on another project can lodge no serious claim to being retained by the second firm when that job is complete.[41] Essentially the same is true of the top-flight professionals and executives in such industries as high technology in the Silicon Valley, who readily jump from one firm to another as better opportunities open up for them—perhaps even starting their own firms.

When such patterns of worker mobility develop, the system of compensation and job prerequisites will itself be designed so as to accommodate such routine separations. Within that context, then, an employee cannot reasonably claim that he will suffer serious and unanticipated losses when the firm also elects to terminate the relationship for its own reasons. I do not mean to suggest, even as to these kinds of workers, that they have no significant interest in protection against at least some kinds of wrongful dismissal. Consider, for example, the athlete who is released for alleged drug abuse, or the high-tech executive who is fired for supposed dishonesty. Such employer action will stigmatize the employee's reputation and as a result his ability to

---

tween longer length of service on the job and greater employment benefits; and of the consequent financial temptation employers may feel to dismiss older, senior employees in order to reduce labor costs, absent a legal disincentive to do so (which could derive as easily from a general wrongful dismissal law as from the ADEA).

41. Jan Stiglitz, "Union Representation in Construction: Who Makes the Choice?" 18 *San Diego Law Review* 583, 585–593 (1981), provides a useful sketch (with references to some of the literature) of the special character of the construction industry and its distinctive transient employment relationships.

continue working in the occupational community in which he has been making his career. My point is that the stronger claim to some form of entitlement to one's present job (given reasonably good performance) seems unsuitable for people who themselves are wont to leave for better jobs as these open up, and thus who do not and should not expect to hold on to their present job when the employer sees a preferable replacement.

But these cases are exceptions for the large majority of workers, or at least of workers committed to full-time, long-term employment. Contemporary personnel systems induce such employees to plan on an indefinite career with a particular firm and consequently inflict a considerable cost on the employee if he must leave, at either the firm's behest or his own.

But one must not assume that even these employees should thereby be entitled to retain the particular job that they have been accustomed to performing. Otherwise, the employer's decision to institute major changes in the employee's work assignments, pay, and location might be said to be a "constructive" discharge insofar as it puts to the employee an unacceptable choice between taking the new and less attractive job, or leaving apparently on his own decision. Such a notion of *job* tenure, as opposed to *employment* tenure, might have been appropriate for work in standardized mass production operations for stable markets, in which each employee would be hired and trained for a particular job ladder which he could call his own unless he sought transfer or promotion. But in the modern world of fast-changing markets and technology, any such "right" would place unacceptable constraints on the firm's ability to respond quickly and flexibly to a continually shifting environment. Thus in companies like IBM or countries like Japan, which promise lifetime employment to at least their core work force, the reciprocal expectation is that employees may face significant changes in their training, assignments, compensation, and even geographic location in order that the firm be able to make good on its promise of an enduring relationship.[42]

42. Paul Osterman, *Employment Futures: Reorganization, Dislocation and Public Policy* (New York: Oxford University Press, 1988), particularly Chapter 4, offers an illuminating analysis of the differences and the trends in two distinct models of the employment relationship. One system, which he calls the *industrial model* and which has been the norm for blue-collar workers in the manufacturing sector, gives individual employees certain rights in and control over the particular job in which they are the senior incumbent, but offers no guarantees to the work force as a whole of long-term employment security with the firm. The other system, the *salaried model*, initially developed for upper

However, few firms have the economic resources of an IBM to be able to make such an unqualified guarantee of lifetime employment, come what may. Even in Japan, the Nenko system applies in practice only to a core of employees working for the key firm, leaving a large group of "contingent" workers, many employed by satellite contractors in the broader business federation, to serve as buffers against substantial dislocation in the enterprise's markets. As a general matter, then, it is necessary to draw a distinction between *dismissal*, in the sense of termination of employment for the personal misconduct or poor performance of the individual employee, and the permanent *layoff* of a group of employees because of lack of work for them to do. The financial and human consequences of such a layoff may be as severe for the employee who must try to find another job starting at the bottom of the ladder[43] (though without the stigma of a disciplinary firing); however, these consequences are perceived as the product of unfavorable changes in the firm's own market or technological environment rather than of the employer's voluntary initiative to fire a particular employee no longer considered to be suitable.

---

level, white-collar positions, affords the firm considerable flexibility in the manner in which it deploys this sector of the work force, but only in return for an (at least implicit) undertaking of employment security and tenure with the firm. Harry C. Katz and Charles F. Sabel, "Industrial Relations and Industrial Adjustment in the Car Industry," 24 *Industrial Relations* 295 (1985), and Michael J. Piore, "Perspectives on Labor Market Flexibility," 25 *Industrial Relations* 146 (1986), show how for some of America's competitors, particularly in Japan and West Germany, the trend in work organization and the employment relationship has been away from the industrial model and toward the salaried model for the majority of blue-collar production workers in the auto industry and elsewhere. I shall return to this theme in Chapter 5. My point here is simply that a guarantee of some kind of employment security with the firm by no means entails a further right to retain one's current job. Indeed, employment security may be much harder to achieve if the mores of the firm and of the economy embody the latter, more restrictive practice.

43. Thus, Paul Osterman, *Employment Futures*, pp. 21–25, reports a study of the consequences of layoffs (*not* disciplinary discharges) which found that a year or more after they had lost their previous job, more than a quarter of these prime-age (26- to 55-year-old) male workers had not obtained new jobs; and of those who had found work, one third were earning at least 25 percent less than in the previous job. This means not only that roughly 45 percent of the victims of such layoffs were long-term financial losers as a result, but also that they suffered from a host of personal and family traumas, described by Barry Bluestone and Bennett Harrison in *The Deindustrialization of America: Plant Closings, Community Abandonment, and the Dismantling of Basic Industry*, pp. 61–66 (New York: Basic Books, 1982). In a very modest response to this human and economic problem, the federal government recently enacted the Worker Adjustment and Retraining Notification Act (WARNA), which requires that the employer give, where feasible, at least 60 days' notice of a plant closing or mass layoff to the workers and the community. For a brief description of the content of that law, see Neil N. Bernstein, "The 'Plant Closing' Bill Creates a New Set of Legal Restrictions," *National Law Journal*, Oct. 31, 1988; p. 15, col. 1.

That is why one regularly finds both in union contracts and in popular parlance a distinction between dismissal and layoff, with any guarantees extending only to the former decision. However, it is generally recognized that in an impending layoff the career employee needs some protection of his investment of years of service with his firm. That protection is secured through a different technique, the principle of *seniority*. In selecting workers who are going to lose their jobs, the employer is required to retain the longer-service employees if they are able to perform in the remaining jobs at a reasonable level of ability.

In practice, the seniority principle is honored in layoffs by nonunion employers on a noncontractual basis nearly as often as by unionized firms governed by collective agreements.[44] This principle trumps not only management's interest in retaining its younger, cheaper, and sometimes more productive employees, but also the community's interest in pursuing its policy of affirmative action on behalf of minority and female workers. Thus in a series of decisions in the mid-eighties, in which the Supreme Court re-endorsed the legality and legitimacy of affirmative preferences in recruiting and hiring, the Court also decided that even so vital a national aim must not be permitted to override the rights of senior employees in a layoff.[45] The Court believed that to require the individual white male worker to sacrifice his most valuable economic asset, a protected job—a position earned through years of irretrievable service with an employer—was simply unfair, even if done to preserve the gains that had been achieved in the nation's quest for an integrated work force.[46]

Imperfections in the Market for Nonunion Labor

The defenders of employment at will would respond that while individual cases of dismissal from an existing job often do present very

44. See the references in note 38.

45. See Wygant v. Jackson Board of Education, 476 U.S. 267 (1986), quoting (at 283) Richard H. Fallon and Paul C. Weiler, "*Firefighters v. Stotts:* Conflicting Models of Racial Justice," 1984 *Supreme Court Review* 1, 58, on why affirmative preferences for blacks, although necessary and legitimate at the hiring stage, should not be used to require the layoff of senior white workers: "The rights and expectations surrounding seniority make up what is probably the most valuable asset that the worker 'owns,' worth even more than the current equity in his home."

46. Fortunately, though surprisingly, it turns out that with the help of affirmative action in hiring, black workers have accumulated lengths of service comparable to those of whites with their respective employers. The May 1979 Current Population Survey asked a representative national sample of 29,000 workers how many years they had worked for their current employer. The answer was an average of 6.8 years of service for blacks and 6.6 years for whites: see Fallon and Weiler, "*Firefighters v. Stotts*," p. 65, n. 238.

appealing cases for judicial relief *ex post*, workers generally might prefer to bear this risk *ex ante*, because the gains to employers from being free of judicial scrutiny outweigh the benefits to employees from obtaining more protection, and the economic surplus generated by this feature to their bargain would likely be shared in other parts of the employment relationship.

This is not a purely speculative hypothesis. It appears to find ample corroboration in the almost total absence of voluntary agreements between employers and individual workers which would provide a contractual guarantee of tenure in the job. Although a considerable number of large and sophisticated firms have developed internal open-door procedures for reviewing lower-echelon dismissal decisions,[47] such procedures rarely permit appeal of the decision by the personnel director or chief executive officer (CEO) to an outside adjudicator; and never permit, as far as I know, an appeal over the substantive policy involved in the dismissal. Given the apparent absence of any vigorous worker demand for broader guarantees than has thus far developed in the labor market, one should be skeptical, or so it is argued, about the government's imposing such a "benefit" on the employment relationship.

There is a discordant note against this argument, however. Contractual guarantees against dismissal without just cause are an almost universal fact of life under collective agreements between unionized firms and their workers.[48] A fundamental difference between a union and a nonunion firm is that in the former, management's decision is ulti-

---

47. Recent descriptions and analyses of a variety of approaches adopted by different nonunion firms include David W. Ewing, *"Do It My Way or You're Fired!": Employee Rights and the Changing Role of Management Prerogatives* (New York: Wiley, 1983); Foulkes, *Personnel Polices*, in particular Chapter 15, "Grievance Procedures," pp. 299–322; Ronald Berenboim, *Nonunion Complaint Systems: A Corporate Appraisal* (New York: Conference Board, 1980); David Lewin, "Dispute Resolution in the Nonunion Firm: A Theoretical and Empirical Analysis" (unpublished, 1987); Alan Balfour, "Five Types of Non-Union Grievance Systems," *Personnel* 67 (March–April 1984); Lawrence R. Littrell, "Grievance Procedures and Arbitration in a Nonunion Environment: The Northrup Experience," in James L. Stern and Barbara D. Dennis, eds., *Arbitration Issues for the 1980's* 35 (Washington, D.C.: Bureau of National Affairs, 1982); and, most recently and most extensively, Alan F. Westin and Alfred G. Feliu, *Resolving Employment Disputes Without Litigation* (Washington, D.C.: Bureau of National Affairs, 1988).

48. See Mark A. Rothstein, Andria S. Knapp, and Lance Liebman, eds., *Cases and Materials on Employment Law* 749 (Mineola, N.Y.: Foundation Press, 1987). In my experience the exceptions to this largely uniform pattern in collective bargaining usually occur in industries like construction, in which employment relationships are inherently episodic and short-term in any event, and where there is consequently little or no point in developing procedures for protecting employees against unjust dismissal; see Stiglitz, "Union Representation in Construction."

mately challengeable by the employee in a neutral arbitral forum, which will appraise the facts, the process, the proportionality of the penalty, and even the substance of the alleged offense itself (such as the refusal to submit to a random drug test unilaterally adopted as company policy).[49] This collective bargaining experience provides strong evidence both that workers would really like to have such broad protection if they had a union representative able to secure it, and also that employers can and do readily concede this right without thereby increasing their labor costs and depressing employee compensation. There is little reason to suppose that workers who happen to be employed in a union shop have qualitatively different preferences than those employed in a nonunion shop.[50] One would infer, instead, that a number of features of the nonunion labor market obstruct the satisfaction of this worker preference for contractual guarantees against unjust dismissal, and that these features can be remedied by collective bargaining.

There is considerable evidence that the labor market is a rather imperfect realization of the competitive ideal. Most workers do not know very much about the range of job openings and comparative employment conditions across different firms, and they are unwilling to invest a lot of effort and resources in finding this information. The result is a remarkable range in wages and benefits paid for the same occupations in the same local labor markets.[51] However, many similar imperfections and disparities are also observable in local product markets, without detracting unduly from the ability of consumers to exert meaningful control over the price, terms, and quality of the goods they are offered. It

49. For a useful review of the growing body of arbitral jurisprudence scrutinizing employer drug testing programs and practices, see the Report of the Committee on Labor and Employment Law, "Drug Testing in the Workplace," 43 *The Record of the Association of the Bar of the City of New York* 447, 462–464 and nn. 74–86 (1988).

50. Because the vast majority of currently unionized operations were already unionized by the early sixties, the determining factor in the individual worker's status is not whether he would vote for a union if he had the opportunity, but simply whether or not he happened to be hired into and remain in a union plant. Indeed, it is estimated that roughly 27 million present employees of nonunion firms previously worked under union contracts in jobs which they had to leave for one reason or other.

51. See, e.g., John T. Dunlop, "The Task of Contemporary Wage Theory," in John T. Dunlop, ed., *The Theory of Wage Determination* 3, 21–22 (New York: St. Martin's Press, 1957); Richard A. Lester, "Wage Diversity and Its Theoretical Implications," 28 *Review of Economic Statistics* 152 (1946); Alan B. Krueger and Lawrence H. Summers, "Efficiency Wages and the Inter-Industry Wage Structure," 56 *Econometrica* 259 (1988); and William T. Dickens and Lawrence F. Katz, "Inter-Industry Wage Differences and Industry Characteristics," in Kevin Lang and Jonathan S. Leonard, eds., *Unemployment and the Structure of Labor Markets* 49 (New York: B. Blackwell, 1987). See Chapter 4 for additional idiosyncratic features of the labor market and the broader significance of these phenomena.

takes only a small critical mass of comparison shoppers to generate a satisfactory degree of market control over product sales by a business.[52] One might surmise that essentially the same phenomenon would be true in the purchase of labor by that business, with only a small number of workers needing to become informed and concerned about any particular working condition to make that condition a meaningful option for workers who would like to have it and to pay a price for it.

To make the case for public policy intervention, then, one has to suppose that there are systemic flaws in the private labor market (as contrasted with the consumer product market) which lead to the supply of less than the optimal amount of a particular benefit—in this case a guarantee against dismissal without just cause. The plausible candidates for that role are the following.

Information. There is reason to doubt that workers are actually making an informed sacrifice of any such guarantee, even if they do obtain somewhat higher wages and benefits in return for giving their employer a free hand in making dismissal decisions. The incidence of unjust discharge is low and varies considerably across firms, but the worker who is shopping for a job will find it very difficult to learn (and certainly will not want to ask) about the actual dismissal risks in the firms being interviewed. Worse, even if accurate comparative statistics were made broadly available, people have a psychological tendency to discount unduly the present risk value of low incidence/high severity events in choosing whether to trade these off for immediate tangible benefits or costs.[53] For the same reasons the community has concluded

52. The most elegant demonstration of this proposition with respect to consumer product markets can be found in Alan Schwartz and Louis L. Wilde, "Intervening in Markets on the Basis of Imperfect Information: A Legal and Economic Analysis," 127 *University of Pennsylvania Law Review* 630, 662–666 (1979), and Alan Schwartz and Louis L. Wilde, "Imperfect Information in Markets for Contract Terms: The Examples of Warranties and Security Interests," 69 *Virginia Law Review* 1387, 1402–20 (1983).

53. To some extent this is because the experience of being fired is such a rare event that we are simply unable to estimate realistically the odds that it will happen to us. An obvious rejoinder to this explanation is that the absence of accurate information makes us as prone to overestimate as to underestimate the true odds. However, what is special about dismissal (as compared, say, to a natural mishap) is that one's own behavior and job performance are likely to play a role in the employer's decision. If people believe—as I assume most do—that they can and do perform acceptably in their jobs, the phenomenon of cognitive dissonance is likely to make workers discount rather than inflate the chances that they (rather than others) will be singled out for dismissal. For reviews by legal scholars of the psychological literature on this subject and its implications for the choice between market and legal protection, see Thomas H. Jackson, "The Fresh-Start Policy in Bankruptcy Law," 98 *Harvard Law Review* 1393, 1410–14 (1985); and Cass R. Sunstein, "Legal Interference with Private Preferences," 53 *University of Chicago Law Review* 1129, 1166–69 (1986).

that workers may underinvest in insurance against severely disabling physical injuries and thus mandates workers' compensation benefits,[54] it could also support a law which requires protection against the rather unlikely occurrence of an unfair firing of a long-service employee, which does severe harm to the individual victim when it does occur.

Public Good. Even the unusual well-informed individual who believes it worthwhile to trade a modicum of present compensation for protection against the future possibility of unfair dismissal from a valuable job may find it hard to persuade his employer to make that kind of exchange. One difficulty is that protection against unfair firings cannot be secured by a simple undertaking in a contract of employment; it requires the development of an elaborate program of progressive discipline, personnel documentation and record-keeping, and some procedure for appeal and even adjudication. Development and maintenance of such a program involves a considerable investment by the employer, and once it is in place the program would almost certainly be made available to all employees. This produces the classic problem of the public good in an individualistic market. Even though all the employees might prefer to make this exchange, and even though the employer might be prepared to incur these costs if all the employees were to agree to whatever sacrifice in compensation might be needed to pay for it, each individual employee lacks the full incentive to make the investment to secure the desired guarantee, because he can hope that some of his fellow employees will do this for him.[55]

Employee Power. The problem of coordinating employee action is likely to be a major factor only in smaller firms. In larger enterprises with sophisticated personnel departments management could take the initiative on behalf of all its employees if it believed that the bulk of them would like such a program and were willing to pay the price for it. The package would then be instituted as part of standard working conditions for all workers, whether or not any might have been tempted to be free riders. The information gap alluded to above is likely to be much less a problem for incumbent employees than for new hires. The longer-service worker will have some sense of the incidence of arbitrary firings, will not be as likely to downplay the consequences when he sees them inflicted on his colleagues, and will develop greater

54. See Paul C. Weiler, "Legal Policy for Workplace Injuries" (American Law Institute Working Paper, 1986).

55. The classic treatment of this issue in the labor market and other contexts is Mancur Olson, *The Logic of Collective Action: Public Goods and the Theory of Groups* (Cambridge, Mass.: Harvard University Press, 1965).

interest in the issue as his personal investment in his job increases with time. The problem is that the labor market tends to undervalue these concerns of the *average* long-service employee, and instead to focus the firm's attention on the interests of the *marginal* employee, the one who is being newly recruited (or who is likely to leave and have to be replaced).[56] Because the latter has much less knowledge and concern about the risk of discharge, his comparison shopping will not serve as an adequate surrogate for the wishes and priorities of the majority of the incumbent employees. Not only does the employer have less economic incentive, then, to fashion this kind of guarantee as a prominent part of its employment package, but the long-term employee has less ability to deploy the standard market lever to revise the employer's incentives by exiting from his job and finding another one (or mounting a credible threat to do so). Because any new job will be considerably less valuable to this worker than his present position, even though longer service with his firm enhances the employee's knowledge of and interest in the subject of unjust discharge, the "equity" he would lose by changing jobs correspondingly reduces his bargaining power to do something about it.

56. The importance of this tendency of the labor market is at the heart of the research program of my colleagues Richard Freeman and James Medoff, building on the more general analysis of Albert O. Hirschman, *Exit, Voice, and Loyalty: Responses to Decline in Firms, Organizations, and States* (Cambridge, Mass.: Harvard University Press, 1970). See Freeman and Medoff, *What Do Unions Do?*, and Richard B. Freeman and James L. Medoff, "The Two Faces of Unionism," 57 *The Public Interest* 69 (1979); and Richard B. Freeman, "Individual Mobility and Union Voice in the Labor Market," 66 *American Economic Review Papers and Proceedings* 361 (1976).

I acknowledge that merely because a competitive labor market tends to emphasize the interests of the marginal employee rather than the average worker does not, in and of itself, indicate that the market is socially malfunctioning. Indeed, it is arguable that younger junior workers, many of whom are minority group members or women, deserve more consideration than do senior, better paid, white male incumbents who are protected in their jobs by the various job security arrangements (including "just cause") that are likely features of unionized operations.

The response to this argument rests on two premises. First, the long-service employee's losing his job with his current employer, in which he has irretrievably invested much of his working career, is considerably more devastating in its personal impact than is the young recruit's loss of an opportunity to obtain a particular job or retain a new job to which he likely has a relatively casual attachment. Second, the development of social arrangements to protect the average longer-service employee will ultimately redound to the benefit of presently junior workers (including minorities). When they commit themselves to a career with a particular firm, they can expect to work their way up the seniority ladder and eventually to enjoy the security and perquisites that seniority entails. For an elaboration of this argument in the context of the conflict between affirmative action for junior minorities and seniority rights of white males when layoffs are necessary, see Fallon and Weiler, "*Firefighters v. Stotts,*" pp. 54–67.

Management Power. Up to this point I have treated the job issue as though it involved an inherent conflict between the worker's interest in fair treatment and the employer's interest in efficient and lower-cost labor. The true conflict is more complicated than that. In any sizable firm, the "employer" actually consists of both the shareholders and the management of the firm. While the management theoretically is an agent whose responsibility it is to run the business on behalf of its principal, the shareholder-owners, in practice management has and will pursue certain personal and institutional interests of its own. Although the capital markets deploy a variety of techniques for the alignment of management's interests with those of the shareholders, inevitably these techniques leave managers with significant slack for making self-regarding decisions on behalf of the firm. Recognition of this fact is crucial in this context, because although any mutual advantage from a contractual undertaking about unjust dismissal would be shared between workers and shareholders, the tangible and immediate costs would be borne by managers. They would have to take much greater care in investigating and documenting the case for dismissal, they would have to defend their decisions and policies against challenges in an outside forum, and they would lose the felt benefit that comes from wielding unreviewable power over their subordinates. As I observed earlier, senior managers in an increasing number of firms have become more receptive to the idea of entertaining appeals by employees from the decisions of lower management; so far as I know, however, no senior management in a nonunion firm allows external appeals about its own dismissal *policies.* This phenomenon is much more easily explained by certain elementary facts of human psychology than by the assumption that it is the product of an optimally functioning labor market.[57]

The foregoing are the imperfections most likely to occur in the functioning of the labor market with respect to dismissal, especially given that these factors operate cumulatively, not singly. Admittedly, my argument here has been conceptual in nature. I have speculated about the probable explanation for an assumedly imperfect labor market, rather than documented the actual incidence and sources of such flaws. In that respect, my analysis mirrors the equally conceptual flavor of the argument that the free market does operate optimally in this area.

However, one can point to certain phenomena to establish the rel-

57. For a detailed treatment of this "agency" problem in the labor and employment law area, see Douglas L. Leslie, "Labor Bargaining Units," 70 *Virginia Law Review* 353, 373–374 (1984).

ative validity of my underlying premise. The first is the total absence of explicit contract guarantees against the wrongful discharge of ordinary workers in the world of nonunion employment. To my mind, this constitutes much stronger evidence of something wrong in the way the free market functions on this issue than of something inherently unappealing in such protection. Especially now that thousands of court cases have made it clear how often American management arbitrarily wields its authority to fire long-service employees, it stretches the imagination beyond belief to suppose that there is no context in which such a guarantee would be worth more to nonunion workers than it would cost their employers to provide it to them.

We are not left just to speculation on that score. The fact that this kind of protection is provided as a matter of course under collective agreements is a much better index of the mutual advantage that exists on this issue. Whatever the other deficiencies of union representation (and I shall address these later on), it is designed to repairing each of the flaws noted earlier in the way the nonunion relationship responds to dismissal. Union representation provides the institutional memory to secure a true understanding of the dimensions of the discharge problem in different firms and industries; collective bargaining gives much more emphatic voice to the needs and priorities of the longer-service employee who has invested much of his working life with his firm; the collective agreement erects a broad structure of rules and procedures into which the just cause guarantee can be fitted; and the organization of the employees into a cohesive bargaining unit gives them the leverage necessary to extract such an undertaking from recalcitrant management, insistent on the maintenance of its unilateral prerogatives. If "just cause" is nearly always the product of such a process, then it does stake out a fair claim for enactment and enforcement by protective employment legislation.

The Institutional Dimension

Alternative Forms of Legal Intervention

The case for legal intervention is still some distance from being made. Suppose that one is persuaded by my arguments that the nonunion labor market has significant flaws that lead it to supply less protection than is optimal for this valuable "asset" of workers. This premise does not necessarily imply that the legal process will do better. There is

enough distance between the abstract promise and the concrete realization of any legal reform to warrant considerable skepticism about the
easy assumption that where the market is not perfect, the law will be an
improvement. Sometimes the law can actually make things worse.
Which of these it will be must be settled on empirical, not *a priori*
grounds. With respect to the dismissal issue we have been reviewing
here, we now have a growing body of experience and some systematic
investigation of different forms of legal intervention[58] that should enable us to make a somewhat more informed judgment on this score.

Common Law Litigation. To this point at least, the standard American
response has been through the judicial process: lawsuits are brought
by discharged workers against their former employers, and, if successful, they produce monetary awards. As we have seen, the substantive
scope of the law is still quite narrow. Most states now agree that discharges for bad reasons—that is, for reasons that contravene public
policy—are actionable in tort. A growing number of states will entertain contract suits for dismissals in violation of some representation or
undertaking to the employee. However, in the reported cases there is
as yet only a bare hint of a mandatory requirement of good reason for
the dismissal of any long-service employee (as an aspect, perhaps, of
a nonwaivable duty of good faith in the employment relationship). The
third generation of cases to emerge in the next decade will face the last
crucial test of how far the law will go in constraining the employer's
dismissal prerogative.

There are significant advantages to private litigation as the vehicle
for such sociolegal reform. The most important virtue is that the individual victim can serve as a one-person lobby seeking redress for injury
done to him and requiring an agency of government (the courts) to
confront and deal with his claim on its merits—if necessary, by rethinking the prevailing legal standard when it appears to be out of
touch with community sentiments. This process is initially likely to be
more responsive to the individual and unorganized victims of wrong-
doing than is a legislature, which must overcome both natural inertia

58. The most important empirical study of wrongful dismissal litigation in the United
States is James N. Dertouzas, Elaine Holland, and Patricia Ebener, *The Legal and Economic
Consequences of Wrongful Termination* (Santa Monica: Rand Institute for Civil Justice, 1988),
produced under the auspices of the Rand Institute for Civil Justice (referred to below as
the Rand Study). This study systematically reviewed all of the wrongful dismissal jury
trials and verdicts that could be located in California from 1980 to 1986 (120 cases in all).
I shall report the key findings of the Rand Study as they are relevant to the discussion
in the text.

and the vigorous resistance of determined employers before it will come to grips with such a low-visibility problem.[59] Furthermore, litigation is an instrument with bite. The conflict will be aired in front of a jury of ordinary people, who will hear and decide whether injustice was done to someone, and who can then respond with large damage awards (one reported to be as high as $19 million[60]) which will likely galvanize other employers into taking corrective action to avoid having such a verdict strike them. In this context, as for personal injuries generally, the judicial model may well be the necessary prelude to (if not the ideal version of) a humanitarian social response to the way business treats individuals.[61]

I am nevertheless skeptical that in the longer run litigation in court will prove to be the best way to handle the dismissal problem. These are some of the characteristic vices of that process.

Risk of Error. The initial successful claims of unjust discharge (as in most cases of judicial innovation) are the egregious cases, those in which it does not take much expertise to judge that someone was fired for entirely unacceptable reasons, and in which it appears fair to permit a damage award that comprises a variety of possible losses and penalties, with sizable amounts in each category. Once this legal bridgehead is established, though, the next cases coming through the system will be the less obvious ones, in which there is a much more even balance between the claims of employer and employee, and where it is not at all clear that an ad hoc jury is appropriate for deciding the grounds for termination of employment in a particular industry, occupation, and firm. The risk of error here is aggravated by the fact that the principles which allowed huge damage awards in the early cases will now be available to juries, without anyone having seriously thought through the question of whether the role of the law in this situation is compensation, prevention, or retribution, and which of these functions is actually pertinent to awards against large bureaucratic organizations for decisions often made by lower-echelon managers.[62]

---

59. See generally Robert E. Keeton, *Venturing to Do Justice: Reforming Private Law* (Cambridge, Mass.: Harvard University Press, 1969).

60. See Rothstein et al., *Employment Law*, p. 764.

61. For an argument in favor of this premise see Fred C. Zacharias, "The Politics of Torts," 95 *Yale Law Journal* 698 (1986).

62. For example, in Rulon-Miller v. IBM, 162 Cal. App. 3d 241 (1984), the court upheld a punitive damages award of $200,000 against the company (over and above an award of $100,000 in compensatory damages) by reason of the wrongful behavior of a particular manager, without even addressing the question of whether and how such a verdict might in fact improve IBM's overall performance as an employer. IBM was actually rather

Transaction Costs. This forensic lottery, as it has been labeled in the personal injury area, is an expensive process to run. Even assuming there is no social loss from forcing defendant employers to transfer large sums of money to plaintiff workers, the problem is that each party in this high-stakes contest has to hire a lawyer, and society has to provide them with a court in which to do battle. In complex civil litigation of this type, one can expect that for every three dollars that the defendants and the community must pay out, not much more than one dollar of redress will end up in the pockets of the victims, with the remainder expended on resolving the legal conflict.[63] In any individual case one might conclude that all these resources were well spent in ensuring that the correct answers were arrived at under the governing legal doctrines. But when one asks whether the overall gains to workers from such a legal right really do outweigh the aggregate costs to employers and to society of providing it, the need to expend these resources must become a major factor in that inquiry.

Maldistribution of the Right. The aim of the law here, as is true of protective employment standards generally, is to insure that all workers enjoy certain basic entitlements without regard to the inadequacies and the disparities in their relative abilities to secure these rights on their own. But the shape of the legal model through which this right is to be secured can exert a powerful influence on who gets to enjoy the

---

fortunate. The Rand Study found that fully half (40 out of 81) of the successful plaintiffs in California wrongful dismissal trials were awarded punitive damages averaging more than $500,000. I should note, however, that since the time period covered by the Rand Study (1980–1986) the California Supreme Court has confined punitive damage awards to the "public policy" category of wrongful dismissal litigation; see, e.g., Foley v. Interactive Data Corp., 765 P.2d 373 (Cal. 1988).

63. The Rand Study (pp. 39–40) found that in the 120 trials analyzed, the defendants as a group ended up spending an average of $293,000, of which the lawyers received $165,000 ($81,000 for the plaintiff's lawyer and $84,000 for the defendant's lawyer), whereas the fired employees as a group received on average $128,000 (or 44 percent of the total). From an additional survey of wrongful dismissal cases that were settled out of court (comprising 19 out of every 20 claims initiated), it appeared that the lawyers received an average of $37,000 per case and the fired employees only $18,000 or about 30 percent of the total (see p. 48). Moreover, these figures merely represent a breakdown of the amount spent on lawyers and victims, with no allowance for either the proportionate share these trials consumed of public expenditures on the court system or the overhead costs of the insurers who provided coverage against such litigation risks (insurance was carried by over 60 percent of the defendants whose insurance status was known; see p. 24). In sum, the ratio of victim recovery to transaction costs for wrongful dismissal litigation is in the same general range as has been found for most tort litigation—for medical malpractice, for example. See Paul C. Weiler, "Legal Policy for Medical Injuries" 99–102 (American Legal Institute Working Paper 1987), for estimates of the medical malpractice ratio.

right in practice. With respect to common law protection against unjust dismissal, studies in both the United States[64] and Canada[65] have shown that the successful claimants in the reported cases are drawn disproportionately from the ranks of upper-level employees—managers and professionals—with very little representation of factory or clerical workers.

To some extent this distributional pattern is a function of the legal doctrines: only certain types of workers are likely to fit within the public policy exception or to receive representations about job security. To a larger extent, I believe, the pattern is due to the litigation model and the substantial expenditures it entails. To mount private litigation for discharge claims is an expensive undertaking. Almost invariably the plaintiff's lawyer funds the lawsuit through a contingent fee arrangement. As a result, cases that tend to be selected for suit are those which promise a high damage award if successful; which means that there must have been high losses suffered; which implies that there was a high salary in the job the claimant lost. All this is a natural implication of a litigation-financing arrangement that nevertheless has significant virtues as a means of enforcing private rights in a variety of contexts. Again, though, if we step back from these details and ask why the law should mandate such a protective term in the employment relationship, we would hardly suppose that the imperfections we identified earlier in the labor market primarily affect executives rather than their secretaries—although that seems to be the latent message of the law in action.

The judgment whether these costs of litigation outweigh the benefits of seeing that the legal rule is enforced will turn to a considerable extent on the type of regulation one has in mind. If the object of concern is dismissal for bad reasons, the abuse of employer power that undermines important community values, a good case can be made that private tort litigation is the best vehicle for policing and deterring such antisocial behavior. But if one wants to penetrate more deeply into the employment relationship and establish an employee right to be fired only for good and sufficient reason—a right which is assumed to be optimal for the parties but obstructed by the operation of the nonunion labor market—there are real grounds for concern that enforcing such a

64. The Rand Study (p. 21) found that 54 percent of the claimants in the California cases were from middle or top management, which corroborates the findings in a survey of reported cases described in Note, "Protecting Employees At Will Against Wrongful Discharge: The Public Policy Exception," 96 *Harvard Law Review* 1931 (1983).

65. Steven L. McShane, "Reasonable Notice Criteria in Common Law Wrongful Dismissal Cases," 38 *Relations Industrielles* 618 (1983).

right in the courts may do more harm to the employer (and thence to the general economy) than good for its individual beneficiaries.

Statutory Administration. We would probably feel somewhat easier about this verdict if we could imagine alternative policy instruments for implementing the desired right, rather than simply retreat to the inadequate protection of the free labor market. There are in fact two available alternatives to the *judicial* model: the *administrative* model and the *arbitral* model. I shall proceed to sketch briefly what we know about these two options.

Enforcement of discharge rights through an administrative tribunal is the mechanism used in the United Kingdom and most of Europe.[66] This variation in the procedure is part and parcel of a larger difference in the administrative model's version of the right and remedy. The legislation provides broad protection against any discharge without just cause, though sometimes with narrow exclusions of certain types of positions (executives, for example) or periods of service (in the range of one year or less). On the other hand, the available remedy is quite limited, typically only a modest amount of back pay which is often calculated according to a formula that awards a certain number of weeks' pay for previous years worked, with a deduction for earnings received in other jobs.[67] This regime stands in marked contrast to the current American pattern of a narrow substantive right for workers that can produce huge damage awards if violated by the employer. Because the stakes are much smaller in dismissal cases in Europe, enforcement of the legislation can be entrusted to a specialized industrial tribunal. Such a tribunal develops considerable experience through its continuing involvement with the problem and is much cheaper and more accessible to ordinary workers, because the informality of the process makes it feasible for workers to present their claims without a lawyer (or at least without a lawyer who must charge a large fee).

That administrative model could readily be worked into American

66. Useful introductory descriptions of the European laws and experiences in this domain are contained in Sam Estreicher, "Unjust Dismissal Laws: Some Cautionary Notes," 33 *American Journal of Comparative Law* 310 (1985), and Janice R. Bellace, "A Right of Fair Dismissal: Enforcing a Statutory Guarantee," 16 *University of Michigan Journal of Law Reform* 207, 208–231 (1983).

67. Research in Great Britain indicates that the average dismissal award there is for little more than 1,000 pounds (or roughly $1,500), in a program moreover which rarely grants reinstatement to the victimized employee without the employer's consent. See Linda Dickens, Moira Hart, Michael Jones, and Brian Weekes, "The British Experience Under a Statute Prohibiting Unfair Dismissal," 37 *Industrial and Labor Relations Review* 497 (1984); and Leonard Rico, "Legislating Against Unfair Dismissal: Implications from British Experience," 8 *Industrial Relations Law Journal* 547 (1986).

law through a fairly simple modification of the present unemployment insurance (UI) system.[68] The states administer the UI program through tribunals which deny benefits to workers who have been dismissed for good reasons. Since employers have an incentive to see that such benefits are not paid to their discharged workers—because the firm's UI premium varies with its claims experience—these state tribunals annually hear and decide thousands of disputes about the propriety of individual dismissals. At the moment, though, all that rides on a tribunal's decision is denial of a UI benefit if the employee gave the employer good reason for the discharge, and payment of the standard benefit if there was no good reason. Thus the improperly discharged employee is left in no better position than if he had lost his job for any valid reason (lack of work, for example). Suppose one wanted both to add a special disincentive against unjust dismissals and to give the employee some redress for the loss of his job, with all the perquisites that he enjoyed from long service with the firm. One easy way to do this would be to establish a standard schedule of monetary compensation—perhaps a multiple of the employee's weekly wage (or UI benefits) for each year of service—and leave this schedule to be administered by the same state tribunal that has to deal with the case in any event, when the discharged worker claims UI benefits while he is out of a job and the employer objects on the grounds of its discharge decision.

While this step would solve the problem of *how* to design an economical procedure for administering protection against unjust discharge, it raises anew the question of *why* we should establish such a right. The easy answer, that we want to reduce the incidence of unwarranted dismissals, will not do. The proponents of at-will also endorse that aim: they assert that the labor market already contains sufficient incentives to employers to avoid the self-inflicted loss of experienced workers for no good reason.[69] The assumption of the case for a mandatory legal right has to be that the loss of one's present job is such a serious and unfair deprivation that we must provide enforceable legal guarantees, rather than rely simply on the rather loose in-

68. This idea is nicely developed in Janice R. Bellace, "A Right of Fair Dismissal," pp. 231–247.

69. Indeed, the current UI program establishes an additional financial incentive, because the employee discharged without good cause is entitled to collect UI benefits until he finds another job, and these payments will increase the experience-rated UI premium charged to the firm that fired the employee.

centives generated by the market to protect this valuable asset of the individual worker. However, if this is the premise of the proposed legal right, then a legal remedy that pays only modest amounts of lost wages seems to trivialize the argument, to undermine the claim that this is such an important priority for employment law reform. Yet if the proponent of job tenure responds to this argument by agreeing to escalate the size of the remedy (that is, by valuing the lost job at tens or even hundreds of thousands of dollars), the risk of erroneous awards against employers becomes too significant (at least in the American constitutional culture) for these cases to be entrusted to an administrative tribunal rather than to a court, notwithstanding the substantial cost of providing due process in the court system. This is the apparently insoluble dilemma of the discharge issue.

Arbitral Reinstatement. There is a possible solution to this dilemma: the law would make the standard remedy for improper dismissal reinstatement in the job, rather than monetary compensation for loss of the job. That path has been followed in those jurisdictions in Canada (such as Quebec) which have taken action in this area in the last decade. Again, reinstatement must be seen as part of a broader arbitral model, one which attempts to provide nonunion workers with the very same just cause protection now enjoyed by unionized workers, by giving the nonunion employees an appeal procedure that utilizes the same labor arbitrators who have developed and applied the jurisprudence of just cause under collective agreements.[70] Not only is the reinstatement remedy a natural part of this larger package, but it also responds to the policy concern with which we have been wrestling. On the one hand, the worker is protected for the full value of his investment in his current job; however, this is accomplished by restoring him to the job itself, rather than by replacing the job with a sum of money. On the other hand, reinstatement avoids the deadweight loss to the firm and to the economy of fighting over and then having to pay for the substantial value of jobs that have been lost by long-service employees.

While this regime seems to accord most closely with the principle of

70. Gilles Trudeau, "Statutory Protection," in Chapter 2, "The Arbitral Review of Dismissal Cases" (pp. 136–222), describes in detail how Canadian arbitrators have utilized with only slight modifications the standards applied to unionized employees in appraising the dismissal of nonunion workers under this new employment standards legislation. The preliminary draft of a Model Employment Termination Act, prepared for the National Conference of Commissioners on Uniform State Laws ("Model Termination Act"), contemplates arbitration as the standard procedure in its current version (see Sections 4 and 5 of the Act).

the proposed reform, unfortunately it encounters grave difficulties in realization.[71] It is one thing for an outside adjudicator to calculate and order the payment of a fixed sum of money: the standard mechanisms of law enforcement can readily assure that the money does change hands. It is quite another thing to try to reinstate a worker in his old job in the plant and expect the relationship to be restored as though no serious rupture had occurred. The reality is that the employee must return to work under the same manager who dismissed him in the first place, a manager who likely feels aggrieved at losing face by having his authority and judgment successfully challenged, and who still wields enough power over the employee to make life on the job very uncomfortable for him—and even, if he is determined, to force the employee out of the job, whatever the law might have ordained.

Study of the experience with reinstatement under a collective agreement reveals a high (70 to 80 percent) "success rate"—defined as actual return to work for an appreciable period.[72] By contrast, the experience of workers reinstated after discriminatory discharges in violation of the NLRA has been a dismal 10 percent rate of return for an entire year.[73] One might speculate that the latter situation is not a fair test of what would happen under a general just cause protection, because in the discriminatory discharge cases the nonunion employer had a special incentive to get rid of the union supporters in order to fend off the union itself. However, the one existing empirical study of the reinstatement remedy in Quebec—a law that applies only to workers with at least five years' service, and thus with a much higher commitment to their previous jobs than the groups of workers in the above two

71. See Julius G. Getman, "Labor Arbitration and Dispute Resolution," 88 *Yale Law Journal* 916, 934–938 (1979), for a sophisticated review of why labor arbitration cannot readily be transplanted into the nonunion context.

72. See Thomas J. McDermott and Thomas H. Newhams, "Discharge-Reinstatement: What Happens Thereafter," 24 *Industrial and Labor Relations Review* 526 (1971); Arthur A. Malinowski, "An Empirical Analysis of Discharge Cases and the Work History of Employees Reinstated by Labor Arbitrators," 36 *Arbitration Journal* 31 (1981); and for the most extensive treatment, George W. Adams, *Grievance Arbitration of Discharge Cases: A Study of the Concepts of Industrial Discipline and Their Results*, pp. 52–96 (Kingston, Ont.: Industrial Relations Centre, Queen's University, 1978).

73. The two in-depth studies of this experience under the NLRA include one by Leslie Aspin of New England workers in the early sixties, summarized in *Hearings on H.R. 11725 Before the Special Subcomm. on Labor of the Comm. on Education and Labor*, 90th Cong., Sess. 3–12 (1967); and one of Texas workers in the early seventies; see Elvis C. Stephens and Warren Chaney, "A Study of the Reinstatement Remedy under the National Labor Relations Act," 25 *Labor Law Journal* 31 (1974); and Warren Chaney, "The Reinstatement Remedy Revisited," 32 *Labor Law Journal* 357 (1981).

studies—also reveals rather pessimistic results, with much the same pattern of employer resistance and harassment reducing the successful level of reinstatement to only 30 percent or so.[74]

The explanation for these disparate results is easy to understand when we compare life under a collective agreement with life under employment legislation. Though the same outside arbitrator may make the same reinstatement order, in the former case the employee returns to work under the umbrella of a well-defined set of contract rights that limit management's authority and possible reprisals (in work assignments, wage or benefit cuts, or generally unpleasant conditions); and these rights are enforceable with the assistance of union stewards, shop committees, and fellow workers who all have an interest in insuring that the contract rights they have fought for as a group are actually honored in this individual case. Since none of these resources are available to the nonunion worker, one should not be surprised to learn that the legal efforts to transplant the bare reinstatement remedy from the union to the nonunion setting have met with much less success in practice.

Collective Bargaining over Dismissal

The major reason a collective bargaining regime is more successful in the implementation of the right of reinstatement after an unjust discharge is that the workers and their union structure are inside the firm. From that vantage point they are far better able than an outside adjudicator (arbitrator, administrator, or judge) to deal with the variety of subtle tactics that a supervisor might use to try to achieve a constructive discharge of a disfavored employee. The presence of the workers inside the plant or office is part of the basic reality that they are an integral part of the enterprise. These workers and their union are in a position, then, to negotiate directly with their employer over the substantive content of the protection against unjust dismissal.

As I noted earlier, this right is much more complex than it might appear on the surface. Judgments have to be made about a multitude of contingent issues. Should the workers in a particular occupation and industry enjoy any such general protection? (Recall my earlier example of the veteran athlete released by his team because someone else is better and/or cheaper.) What length of probation period should be

74. See Gilles Trudeau, "Statutory Protection," 247–298.

available to the employer to determine the suitability of a new worker before he comes under the umbrella of just cause? There are vast differences in the length of time considered necessary for appraising factory workers and university teachers, for example. What kinds of behavior might be especially deemed to warrant dismissal in a particular industry? For example, should this category include drug use by workers in hazardous jobs or intimations of dishonesty among workers handling the funds of the employer or the public? What type of due process must be observed in establishing and communicating the rules of the workplace and in investigating cases of suspected infractions? What kinds of rehabilitation programs (for alcoholism, say) or progressive discipline (for persistent lateness and absenteeism, for example) must first be tried before the ultimate sanction of discharge can be meted out?[75] Rather than having everyone governed by a single set of rules laid down by an external agency of government, collective bargaining enables the immediate parties to set their own standards for these and a host of other issues, standards that are tailor-made for their own business and occupations and that reflect the relative needs and priorities of a particular firm and group of workers.

Unlike other features of the employment relationship (such as the design of the fringe benefit package), the discharge issue is rarely dealt with through a detailed blueprint written into the collective agreement. Instead, a general provision is inserted in the contract—no discharge without just cause—and the parties gradually give content to this principle through its application to individual cases within the grievance procedure. Judgments about a few especially significant, recurring problems will be recorded in letters of understanding or perhaps even reflected in specific sections of the contract. However, mutual understandings about the bulk of the problems will be evidenced only in the customary practice of the parties. As new issues arise, management will normally take the initiative in developing its own policy, the union will react either favorably or unfavorably, and if the parties are not able to agree, an arbitrator will be called on to resolve the dispute. The awards of arbitrators also constitute a major component of the common law of discharge in the enterprise.

If one believes, as I do, that there is no single right answer to the numerous and contentious aspects of the dismissal problem, then pri-

---

75. For a general flavor of how such problems are dealt with in union arbitration, see the sources cited in note 12.

vate, decentralized collective bargaining is just as attractive a technique for defining the scope of the right as an inside enforcement procedure is for effectively implementing the right. One would expect, of course, that any sensible public tribunal which had to interpret and apply a statutory just cause standard would be sensitive to the special features of different industries and jobs (though not likely aware of and deferential to the practices peculiar to individual firms within an industry). Ultimately, collective bargaining is qualitatively more pluralistic than external legal regulation, for two reasons. First, adjudication is done not by a tribunal appointed by the government, but by an arbitrator selected by the parties themselves, an arbitrator who must make a special effort to learn and respect their practices and understandings if he is to remain acceptable enough to these parties to be invited back. Second, if the parties do not approve of the standards set in an arbitration award, they are free through subsequent negotiations to alter that standard for their own relationship, rather than try to persuade the government to pass corrective legislation for the community at large.

Leaving the parties free to make their own agreement about the discharge issue does have one significant flaw from the point of view of those who believe that this is a fundamental right which must be guaranteed to everyone: the employees may be too weak to secure -adequate protection on their own. After all, it is the growing perception that nonunion workers simply do not have sufficient leverage to obtain contractual protection from their employers that has made this a more and more inviting area for legal intervention. Moreover, although collective bargaining enables workers to pool their bargaining resources in order to enhance their ability to extract better terms and conditions from their employers, in the final analysis the fruits of union representation also reflect and reinforce disparities in economic power in different employment settings.[76]

It is certainly true that the gains secured by workers through collec-

76. Systematic critiques of the performance of collective bargaining in this regard (although from profoundly different philosophical perspectives) are developed in Charles Fried, "Individual and Collective Rights in Work Relations: Reflections on the Current State of Labor Law and Its Prospects," 51 *University of Chicago Law Review* 1012 (1984); David M. Beatty, "Ideology, Politics and Unionism," in Kenneth P. Swan and Katherine E. Swinton, eds., *Studies in Labour Law*, p. 299 (Toronto: Butterworths, 1983); and Harry J. Glasbeek, "Voluntarism, Liberalism and Grievance Arbitration: Holy Grail, Romance and Real Life," in Geoffrey J. England, ed., in *Essays in Labour Relations Law*, p. 57 (Don Mills, Ont.: CCH Canadian, 1986).

tive bargaining vary with the level of resources they are able to marshall against those of their employer. Some bargaining units will always do significantly better than others in a private, voluntary system.[77] The question remains, though: exactly what is wrong with that?

If the objection is simply to the relative inequality in results produced by collective bargaining, it is unlikely that legal regulation would solve that problem. Presumably the law would simply establish a floor of basic protection on top of which individual firms could still be persuaded by their employees' union to adopt more progressive programs, and to be more civilized in the exercise of their discharge power.[78] In any event, the objection to reliance on collective bargaining on the grounds that some groups of workers will end up with an inadequate level of protection (perhaps none at all), while often a significant problem in collective bargaining about wages and benefits, is of little importance with respect to dismissal. At least in the case of meaningful bargaining relationships in which a union has been able to secure and renew a collective agreement with the employer, protection against unjust dismissal enforceable through arbitration is almost universally present in collective agreements that cover enduring employment relationships (thus excepting industries like construction). That inequities exist in the resources and results of collective bargaining is an important feature of the general appraisal of this instrument for solving problems in the workplace, and one to which I will return later. In the particular context of discharge, though, it is not a terribly significant issue.

There is one important caveat: interestingly, it is an outcome of the relationship not between employee and employer, but between employee and union. The decision whether to enforce the collectively bargained right to protection against unjust dismissal is made by the union representative of the bargaining unit, not by the individual worker who was fired. This is so because under current law individual claims under the collective agreement must be enforced through arbitration (where it is provided for) rather than in the courts. The union

77. For references to some of the empirical research documenting this point, not only for economic benefits but also for noneconomic working conditions, see Paul C. Weiler, "Striking a New Balance: Freedom of Contract and the Prospects for Union Representation," 98 *Harvard Law Review* 351, 382–383 (1984).

78. In the longer run, the achievement of higher levels of protection by the few will probably improve the situation of the many, as new standards adopted by one firm spread to others, whether through the force of example, the pressures of the market, or even enhancing the basic legal guarantee.

almost always retains control over access of the grievance to arbitration, so the union is entitled to drop or settle an individual grievance without the consent of the employee immediately affected. This union prerogative is limited by a duty of fair representation (DFR) owed by the union to the employee. However, the DFR is a rather narrow obligation not to act in an arbitrary, discriminatory, or bad faith manner toward the individual, not a broader duty of the union to be correct in its judgment that there is no merit to a particular claim of unjust discharge.[79]

This well-established position in federal labor law does not persist simply because of its historical and legal roots; it also has a contemporary pragmatic justification. There has to be some process for screening and settling the bulk of employee grievances in order to relieve the otherwise highly accessible arbitration forum of an unacceptable number of cases. Workers as a group benefit from their union's reserving the power to arrive at an authoritative disposition of doubtful employee claims, in spite of how the individual employee may feel about this decision. Higher management then has an incentive to wield a reciprocal authority to alter a supervisor's action where that seems appropriate, rather than force the union into a war of attrition in which it has to adjudicate every little case, thus emptying the union's treasury and clogging the arbitration procedure so that no one can get timely relief in the truly meritorious and pressing cases.

This pragmatic perspective offends some labor law scholars, who find it an unacceptable denial of the individual worker's right to enforce his own claim in front of a neutral adjudicator.[80] Such an arrangement would horrify the trial litigator, who tends to picture wrongful dismissal cases as essentially the same as actions seeking damages for personal injuries. Certainly for personal injury claims it would be unthinkable to empower a union to unilaterally enforce or waive an injured worker's right to secure redress under either tort law or workers'

---

79. See Vaca v. Sipes, 386 U.S. 171 (1967). On the law of fair representation generally, including its application to contract administration, see the various articles in Jean T. McKelvey, ed., *The Changing Law of Fair Representation* (Ithaca, N.Y.: ILR Press, Cornell University, 1985).

80. The most prominent legal critic of the leeway that DFR doctrine gives to a union in settling or dropping discharge (or other) grievances of unionized employees is Clyde Summers, the scholar whose writings did so much to spark the judicial erosion of employment at will for nonunion workers. For his intriguing analysis of how the two evolving bodies of law can and should be woven together, see his article, "Contract of Employment."

compensation, however efficient such a procedure might seem to the employees as a group.

Defending the current method of presenting just cause grievances under the labor contract must be done on a rather different philosophical footing. Unlike workers' compensation or product liability law, for example, it is not a case of simply enforcing a legal protection against unjust discharge that the government has conferred upon employees directly. Rather, the overall unit of employees has itself participated in an effort which included first their organization into a union, then their sharing the risks and burdens of securing the collective agreement that created this right in the first place, and now their financing and operating a grievance arbitration procedure in order to implement these negotiated provisions in the day-to-day life of the workplace. Viewed from that angle, it is not implausible for the national labor law to say, in effect, that it is the unit of employees and their union, not the individual worker, that actually "owns" the right of just cause, and that the unit is therefore entitled to decide whether or not the employer has really violated the right (subject, of course, to fair consideration of the interests of the employee immediately affected).

While I have always found the foregoing combined philosophical and pragmatic case to be persuasive with respect to the general run of collectively negotiated worker rights, the issue of unjust discharge *is* different. To the individual employee the financial and personal consequences of being wrongfully dismissed are as severe when they are the result of a union's mistakenly dropping a meritorious claim as when they are due to management's mistakenly concluding that the employee committed an infraction.[81] Moreover, it seems insufficient to justify this legal position on the grounds that it permits the employee community to decide what is the most sensible interpretation of its just cause provision and what is the most economic use of its arbitration machinery. The unfortunate fact is that the discharged employee whose case is dropped will no longer be a member of the workplace community and consequently able to share in the general advantages of such a process.

An arrangement much to be preferred, it seems to me, is one in

81. Indeed, the irony in the current situation is that whereas unions have almost universally established the principle that under a collective agreement employers must have a valid, substantiated reason for firing a worker, the union can be sued for breach of its DFR for dropping the discharge grievance only if the worker proves that the union had a bad reason for its action, an extremely difficult undertaking for most employees. See Michael J. Goldberg, "The Duty of Fair Representation: What the Courts Do in Fact," 34 *Buffalo Law Review* 89 (1985).

which the union representing the employees is given the authority to drop or settle a case or take it to arbitration if the grievance is believed to be meritorious. However, if the union has not been able to win at least reinstatement of the employee (with or without back pay) and still declines for its own good reasons to go to arbitration, the employee should have the option of taking the case at his own expense to some designated tribunal for a hearing on the merits.[82] That arrangement has functioned quite acceptably in a good many public sector bargaining relationships without eroding the grievance procedure. It also accords much better with all the reasons we have just explored (and unions have long proclaimed) why it is so important to protect the career employee against loss of his valuable job through unfair dismissal by the employer. Ideally, the stronger version of the right not to be discharged without demonstrably good reasons will also become the governing norm with respect to union decisions in dismissal cases (either through voluntary union action, perhaps stimulated by the recently enhanced financial liability of unions,[83] or through the evolution of the legal DFR).

With that one significant (but answerable) caveat, I am satisfied that collective bargaining is the preferred instrument for handling the dismissal issue. Indeed, it should now be clear that there are two distinct aspects to the at-will debate. The first centers on the more appropriate conception of employment: should it be treated as a fluid, easily terminable, casual transaction, or as a structured, quasi-tenured career relationship? Contemporary trends in the real world of work demonstrate that most employers and employees now find the second conception much more to their mutual advantage. This presents a second facet to the problem: is it better to protect individual employees against unfair termination of the career relationship through voluntary contracts or mandatory laws? My conclusion is that the best technique for establishing constraints on management's dismissal prerogative is through collective contracts voluntarily negotiated by employees who have been organized into a unit with a meaningful chance to bargain for such protection. Such a self-made right in a reconstructed market

82. For a more detailed development of this argument see Paul C. Weiler, *Reconcilable Differences: New Directions in Canadian Labour Law*, pp. 137–139 (Toronto: Carswell, 1980).

83. Under the Supreme Court's decision in Bowen v. U.S. Postal Service, 459 U.S. 212 (1983), unions are now presumptively liable for all lost earnings of an improperly discharged employee during the period between the date on which an arbitrator might have reinstated the employee had the union pressed the case, and the date on which the jury actually renders a verdict on the employee's Section 301 claim against the employer.

will be more comprehensive and effective than anything management might be induced to offer by the pressures of an individualist labor market, and more flexible and sensitive than anything a government could hope to provide through a judicial or administrative bureaucracy. To the extent this comparative judgment is valid,[84] it will seem to some that the sustained effort to transplant just cause from its traditional setting in voluntary collective agreements into a new, mandatory legal regime is a mistake. Perhaps workers should be invited, instead, to use union representation to secure that right on their own.[85]

A Program for the Dismissal Problem

Pursuing a Second-Best Solution

There is an immediate practical objection to the last suggestion. As I indicated in the opening chapter of this book, and as I will document in the next chapter, union representation is now available to far too small a fraction of the labor force (less than 15 percent of private-sector workers, and dropping) to make collective bargaining a realistic source of job protection for the vast majority of American workers. The proponent of legal controls would argue in any event that if the individual worker is considered entitled to such protection as a matter of principle, he should not have to join a union, which will negotiate a wide-ranging collective agreement to secure this particular benefit for him.

84. I do not mean to imply that arbitral treatment of unjust discharge claims is unqualifiedly benign. Apt illustration to the contrary is found in James B. Atleson, "Obscenities in the Workplace: A Comment on Fair and Foul Expression and Status Relationships," 34 *Buffalo Law Review* 693 (1986). I do believe, though, that an objective comparison of both the substance and the process of arbitral, judicial, and administrative (such as NLRB) responses to workers who have been fired will show that arbitration clearly functions best in this context.

85. This is the conclusion of Susan L. Catler, "The Case Against Proposals to Eliminate the Employment at Will Rule," 5 *Industrial Relations Law Journal* 471 (1983). The argument would have more force if it were the case, as some fear, that extending the "paper" protection of the law to nonunion workers makes them less eager to embrace collective bargaining, through which they might be able to secure the real thing. For some initial evidence that when states provide the stronger "implied contract" version of protection against unjust dismissal, workers are less apt to vote for unions in representation campaigns, see George R. Neumann and Ellen R. Rissman, "Where Have All the Union Members Gone?" 2 *Journal of Labor Economics* 175 (1984). On the other hand, notwithstanding the possible risks to its own institutional future, the AFL-CIO Executive Council, in a *Policy Statement on the Employment-At-Will Doctrine* (Feb. 20, 1987), described legal protection against unjust dismissal as one of the "basic legal standards that are the hallmark of a decent society," calling upon governments to create procedures and remedies which would be broad in scope, effective in practice, and readily accessible to ordinary workers.

Of course, that claim assumes the answer to the matter at issue: that although collective bargaining may be the ideal mode of protection against unjust discharge, government regulation (through the common law or statute) is the second-best mode. Is that really true, especially if we include among our aims not simply reducing the incidence of wrongful dismissal of employee-victims, but also securing such protection in a manner that does not impose undue costs of litigation and defensive personnel practices on employers and the overall economy?

To my mind, this is a much more difficult question than is uniformly assumed by both sides to the debate. Even granted its shortcomings, the unregulated labor market provides a good deal more protection to workers than is popularly supposed. Employers have a significant economic incentive to develop programs that will avoid the unnecessary termination of employees in whom the firms have a considerable investment, as well as to preserve the firm's employment reputation and employee morale from erosion through a pattern of arbitrary treatment by lower-echelon managers. At the same time, the law actually provides much less satisfactory protection than is hoped for—in terms both of the efficacy and the equity of the relief meted out—while still imposing significant costs on employers who must contend with and worry about the mistakes made in legal proceedings, errors that might inflict multimillion-dollar damage awards.

But while this is a much closer call than might appear from a first glance at the egregious cases of unjust treatment that first brought this problem to the attention of judges and scholars, on balance I believe that there is a sufficient case for government intervention. When a long-service employee loses his job because of wrongful dismissal by a manager, the employee suffers the severe and irretrievable loss of his investment of a significant part of his working life. As the law has gradually and steadily opened its doors to these claims, it has become apparent that they occur in far greater number, and in a broader spectrum of employment life, than anyone might have imagined. It was the immediate threat of litigation and large damage awards, not the impersonal operation of labor market, which primarily moved nonunion employers to devise the growing number of sophisticated internal procedures that now protect not just the worker but also the firm itself from the consequences of such managerial errors and abuses.[86] As I noted,

86. This conclusion emerges incontrovertibly from a survey and from twelve case studies reported by Westin and Feliu, *Resolving Employment Disputes*. Interestingly, however, in only three of the case studies did the nonunion employers establish outside

the trial litigation/jury process is itself prone to damaging mistakes, first in deciding who was right and wrong in a particular firing and then in assessing the compensation appropriate for any such harm done. This is a good reason to tailor a new legal approach that would reduce the burden of such suits on employers and the overall economy, while leaving the individual worker with an adequate safety net against managerial misjudgments which can cost him the only job he has.

A New Tack in Montana

In 1987 the state of Montana enacted a broad statute to address the problem of wrongful dismissal.[87] It was the first time an American legislature had treated the matter, doing so somewhat differently than the judge-made common law. I shall comment briefly on the Montana law as a prelude to presenting my own position.

Rather than prohibit particular categories of wrongful dismissal, Montana enacted a broad ban on any discharge not for "good cause" as defined by the statute. The meaning of discharge has been expanded to include "constructive" dismissals in cases in which employees quit because they were placed in an intolerable employment situation. However, the law correspondingly narrows the remedies available to the victims of this broader protection. Only net lost earnings can be recovered, up to a maximum period of four years, with deduction of all amounts earned (or which should have been earned) in the interim. No other compensatory damages can be awarded for either consequential economic losses or psychological distress, and punitive damages are available only in cases where the employee demonstrated "actual fraud or actual malice."[88] To reduce the use of expensive litigation, the employee is required to exhaust any existing and reasonably expeditious internal appeal procedures. Both parties are prodded to accept offers to arbitrate the dispute by the threat of paying subsequent attorney

---

neutral arbitration as the end-point of their in-house procedure (at Northrop, Michael Reese Hospital, and the Squibb Life Savers plant); and what motivated management to do so was avoiding a serious threat from a union, not avoiding the most recent burst of civil litigation.

87. The Wrongful Discharge From Employment Act, Montana Code Ann. Section 39-2-901 (1987). Some of the background of the Montana bill, including the debate preceding its passage, is recounted in an unpublished paper by Alan B. Krueger, "The Evolution of Unjust Dismissal Legislation in the U.S." 4–6 (1988).

88. The Montana legislature did not indicate, though, whether the corporate employer should be held vicariously liable for the actual malice of its supervisory personnel.

fees to any party who makes such an offer which is refused, if the offering party ultimately is successful in the litigation. Explicitly excluded from this new wrongful discharge statute are employees covered by collective agreements, presumably on the theory that unionized employees will have their discharges remedied by grievance arbitration under the just cause provisions in the labor contract.

In my opinion there are signal virtues to the new Montana approach. Employees are afforded a single simplified cause of action for wrongful dismissal, with a carefully drafted content, procedures, and remedies.[89] Even though nonunion Montana workers will now enjoy essentially the same substantive protection as their unionized counterparts, the legislature has rightly concluded that the reinstatement remedy cannot effectively be transplanted to the nonunion context. Instead, the courts are told to do what we know they can do quite well: force a guilty party to pay monetary damages to its victim, both to compensate for the harm done in previous cases and to prevent their recurrence in the future. In order to protect employers from the possible overkill of litigation before unpredictable juries, the legislature has supplied a specific formula for the calculation and containment of compensatory damages.

The problem, though, is that the Montana wrongful dismissal legislation ignores the lessons which can and should be drawn from the analogous debate about legislative caps on and offsets to tort damages awarded for personal injuries.[90] Such a response to the perceived problem of occasionally excessive jury awards ignores the fact that it is from such a damage award that the victim will get the money to pay for the services of the lawyer who is necessary to assert and enforce the rights supposedly conferred by the law.

Take the case of an ordinary worker who was fired from a job that paid, perhaps, $25,000 in wages and fringe benefits. Both economic necessity and the legal duty to mitigate the harm require the employee to find another job. That new job will probably be less valuable to the fired worker, both in monetary and nonmonetary terms. However, the employer's liability for the firing will be reduced dollar for dollar by the amounts earned by the employee in other jobs, and a four-year ceiling is imposed on the employer's liability for even this net loss of earnings.

89. While the action for dismissals contrary to public policy is expressed (in Section 4(1)) separately and apart from the general ban on discharge without good cause (which appears in Section 4(2)), nothing seems to turn on that characterization.

90. For my own analysis of the problem in the particular context of medical injuries and malpractice litigation, see Weiler, "Legal Policy for Medical Injuries," pp. 85–112.

What about the other side of the coin, the problem the worker faces in finding and paying for a lawyer? Hitherto, most litigators have been willing to take promising dismissal cases on a contingency fee basis.[91] The prospect of receiving one-third or more of a six- or even seven-figure damage award is sufficiently attractive to induce a lawyer to bear the risk that any particular claim might not be established successfully. However, for most lawyers the contingent fee from an award of even $100,000 (which, in my example, assumes the unlikely possibility that the employee will find no work at all in the four-year period) would not warrant doing a significant amount of work on any reasonably difficult claim that is being actively resisted by the employer. That means that the average employee will probably have to agree to pay for the lawyer's time and expenses out of his own assets. Those employees who still assert and then prevail in a wrongful discharge case will therefore receive even less than the strictly limited compensation provided under the Montana statute, since the damages for net lost earnings will be reduced by the legal costs incurred. Worse, most such employees, naturally risk-averse in an alien legal environment, will simply decide not to commit themselves to substantial legal expenses in the pursuit of a chancy and now limited return. And if most employees who were in fact fired without good cause do not sue or do not recover substantial sums even if they do sue, the legal disincentive on the employer to avoid such behavior in the first place will be correspondingly weakened.

As I said earlier, such an analysis is a fairly standard critique in the debate about tort reform and has moved the courts in a number of states to strike down damage caps imposed on personal injury awards. Indeed, this Montana law only narrowly survived such a constitutional challenge.[92] Suppose we picture the problem as how to devise a fairer

91. The Rand Study (p. 38) found that all of the California cases were brought on a contingency fee basis, with 40 percent being the most common percentage for the lawyer's share.

92. See Meech v. Hillhaven West, Inc., and Semingson, 776 P.2d 488 (Mont. 1989), in which the Montana Supreme Court rejected by a bare 4–3 margin the argument that the statute denied the discharged employee the state constitutional right to "full legal redress for every injury." The Montana law and this litigation have sparked a debate not only in that state but also across the country between those who want to expand the legal protection available to discharged workers and those who want to limit the exposure of employers to what are often very large damage awards, such as the award of $1.5 million to a Montana bank teller that sparked the more restrictive statutory remedy. See "Wrongful Dismissal Laws May Feel Effect of Disputes Before Montana's High Court," *Wall Street Journal*, Nov. 8, 1988, p. B1, col. 3. For the developing jurisprudence in all states concerning the constitutionality of personal injury tort reform, see Weiler, "Legal Policy for Medical Injuries," pp. 56–70, and Richard C. Turkington, "Constitutional Limitations on Tort Reform: Have the State Courts Placed Insurmountable Obstacles in the Path of

and more sensible litigation system. Any limitation on the damages awarded to the victim must be combined with a requirement that the employee (or the tort defendant/insurer) pay the reasonable attorney fees charged to the successful plaintiff. After all, the necessary legal cost of enforcing the new statutory right is just as much an economic harm inflicted by the employer on the wrongfully fired employee as are the wages and fringe benefits lost by the employee. And if the legislature is serious about creating a new legal right for unorganized employees who are assumed to be, on their own, unable to secure such protection in the labor market, it must find some such way to finance the representation of such employees by lawyers, who are asked to fill the gap left by the unavailability of union representation.[93]

The Components of a Different Approach

The approach I prefer is somewhat different from either the Montana legislation or the evolving common law in the rest of the country. My program would utilize the resources of tort, contract, and administra-

---

Legislative Responses to the Perceived Liability Insurance Crisis?" 32 *Villanova Law Review* 1299 (1987).

93. Presumably because of its tacit recognition of this problem, the Montana legislature established an incentive for the parties to use the somewhat cheaper arbitration procedure for adjudication of such cases. In practice, though, this option is just advantageous to employers as to employees, if not more so. Sizable firms, at least, are familiar with this nonjudicial procedure from their experience with labor or commercial arbitration. Such employers would probably be regular participants in wrongful dismissal arbitration if it were more generally used and consequently would often be able to select the arbitrators and present their cases themselves, without having to use and pay for an outside attorney. By contrast, the individual employee who has been fired only once would probably have to hire a lawyer to defend his interests. The lawyer would have to invest considerable time and money in investigating and presenting the case in arbitration. Moreover, the employee would also be potentially responsible for the added expense of the arbitrator's fees. The problem remains that the still significant costs of legal services must be recouped from an artificially limited damage award. In sum, while perhaps not as problematic as the reinstatement remedy, this formulation contains significant obstacles to a successful transplant of the arbitration procedure from the union to the nonunion context (see Getman, "Labor Arbitration," pp. 934–938). The Montana legislation may actually aggravate the problem, because the plaintiff's attorney, who is likely most experienced and comfortable resolving matters in the courts, can be confronted with an employer's offer to arbitrate which, if declined, exposes his client to paying the employer's legal bill as well as his own. I note parenthetically that the Montana law requires the employer to pay the arbitrator's costs if the employee prevails, but the employee is not obliged to pay if he loses. Such one-way fee shifting in this context is precisely the analogy I would draw on to make the guilty employer pay the employee's legal fees for a successful wrongful discharge claim in either arbitration or the courtroom. This procedure is proposed in Section 6(6)F of the current version of the Model Termination Act.

tive law, each with its own distinctive substantive and procedural features; the use of each would be tailored to the specific facet of the dismissal problem for which it is best suited.

There should continue to be a mandatory, judicially enforced tort action for those instances of wrongful dismissal that contravene public policy in the stronger sense of that term. This tort action should be available whenever an employer has exercised its contractual prerogative to terminate the worker's employment and in the process has flouted some value that has been authoritatively declared by the legislature or the judiciary to be in the general interest of the community. The best test of that status would be whether the policy in question is implemented through a legal regime that operates outside the dismissal context. If that be so, the individual worker who has been fired should be allowed to sue for substantial tort damages in order to deter such abuses of employer power which threaten to undermine the policies and values of the community as a whole.[94] And because prevention is our primary aim here, we should *not* try to confine the damages awarded with a readily calculable formula which would let even the risk-averse employer know what the price would be if it chose to pursue its illegitimate objectives and were caught.[95]

But when we pose the quite different question of whether the behavior or performance of the employee gave the employer a good enough reason to terminate their private relationship, the common law answer should remain on a voluntary, contractual footing.[96] Judges should be

94. In Chapter 6, I will show how a public policy action for wrongful dismissal would be useful in particular for enforcing our long-standing public policy of protecting and encouraging employee self-organization and union representation.

95. Thus, to the extent that our goal is to prevent dismissals in violation of public policy, there is positive value in the Rand Study finding (p. 26) concerning the distribution of awards in California. While the median jury award to 81 successful plaintiffs was $177,000, the top ten awards averaged $4 million, and the highest was $8 million. In this particular policy setting, we should *want* to make employers who might be contemplating firing an employee in contravention of an established public policy worry about ending up in the high-award group, rather than assure employers that they risk only paying damages of a predictable and much lower median amount.

96. In that respect I agree with the underlying logic of the recent and controversial majority decision of the California Supreme Court in the *Foley* case, 765 P.2d 373 (Cal. 1988). However, the real problem with *Foley* and its primary emphasis on containing at-large damage awards by juries is that the majority opinion ignores the reciprocal problem of the discharged employee—securing and paying for legal representation to pursue his contract action. I think that the simplest and fairest solution to the dilemma (in personal injury claims as well as wrongful dismissal litigation) is a legal regime that protects the employer from open-ended exposure to psychological or retributive damages, but makes reasonable attorney fees incurred by the wrongfully harmed employee

prepared to interpret the representations and exchanges of the parties as producing an enforceable undertaking; that is, some level of seriousness in the employee's offense and some measure of fairness in the employer's process must be required before dismissal is appropriate. The earlier legal barriers to a judicial finding of more than an at-will cast to the employment relationship are simply no longer appropriate in an economy in which employees are typically led to believe that they will have an enduring career with their present firm.[97] Conversely, such a standard expectation in practice should not be transformed by judges into an equally rigid legal barrier against any and all at-will employment contracts—through, for example, a mandatory, nonwaivable, and open-ended requirement of employer good faith in termination actions. While more and more firms are developing internal procedures and policies to try to reduce the incidence of wrongful dismissals, they are also making it clear to their employees that these innovations should not be taken as a contractual undertaking that would expose the employer's reasons and procedures for dismissal to scrutiny by a jury.[98] Those employees who accept and continue in their jobs on such an at-will basis should be held to that arrangement, even if later they come to regret the outcome of such a status.

A prime reason for my belief that employers should be allowed to exclude broad-ranging intervention by the courts is my own skeptical appraisal of the operation of wrongful dismissal litigation. The substantial burden that the experience and the prospect of such lawsuits now imposes on employers (and consequently on their employees and customers, as well as their managers and shareholders) is simply not warranted by the kinds of relief and protection actually obtained by ordinary workers whose lack of bargaining power initially inspired judicial concern.[99]

---

a separate category of compensable pecuniary damages. See Weiler, "Legal Policy for Medical Injuries," pp. 85–112, and John Leubsdorf, "Recovering Attorney Fees as Damages," 38 *Rutgers Law Review* 439 (1986).

97. See Finkin, "The Bureaucratization."

98. See pp. 54–55.

99. The most startling findings of the Rand Study graphically illustrate this conclusion. The median amount of money actually taken home by the plaintiffs in the California cases (including both plaintiffs who won and those who lost) was $30,000 each. Since the money was not paid until an average of five years had elapsed following the discharge, the discounted value as of the date of firing was approximately $18,000 per case. This sum represents only a half year of severance pay on average for this entire group, whose annual salaries prior to dismissal averaged $36,000. But the employers in these cases spent an average of $84,000 per case to defend against the lawsuits which eventually

There is a better legal technique for implementing the moral claim of the worker to some form of tenure in the job, a right which should now be recognized as part of the social safety net that protects employees from especially harmful outcomes of the unfettered labor market. A statute should be drafted which affords such protection only to workers who have a distinctive need for legal help: one would exclude those still mobile employees who invested a relatively short period of service with their employer, and also those people who are sufficiently high in the corporate structure that they can be expected to negotiate a "parachute" of their own. In order to limit the burden on both employer and employee of enforcing this legal guarantee, workers should have ready access to an informal and inexpensive administrative procedure that would award them a scheduled financial remedy (some multiple of their current weekly earnings for each year of past service) in every case where there was no good reason for the dismissal. As I suggested earlier, an obvious candidate for this job would be the present unemployment insurance procedure, which already generates much the same kind of decision in order to award or to withhold UI benefits for the support of the dismissed employee before he has found another job.[100]

The initial reaction of many lawyers to that proposal, I am sure, is that it would be unthinkable to require a worker to accept the rough

---

produced such limited financial returns for the employee-victims (although they did produce handsome returns for the lawyers on both sides).

100. Such a proposal intentionally bears a striking resemblance to the shift earlier in this century from common law litigation to administrative compensation for physical injuries in the workplace. If we were to pursue the workers' compensation analogy in the context of dismissal, we might even consider dealing with dismissal cases on a no-fault basis. By that I mean that if an employee has given no good cause for his dismissal, but the employer terminates him for good and legitimate reasons of its own (such as eliminating the job because of new technology), the employee would be entitled to the same "severance" compensation for the loss of his investment in the job as would be provided to any employee who happened to be fired because of a supervisor's mistaken view of what constitutes good disciplinary practice. Perhaps it is time for the United States to follow the lead of a number of European countries and to take seriously the notion that workers, like shareholders and bondholders, build up a stake in the firm and therefore have some claim on the firm's assets when their jobs are liquidated for any reason. I appreciate that there are real complexities and pitfalls in the idea of compulsory severance benefits: perhaps the prospect of having to pay such compensation whenever they release a superfluous employee would make American employers unduly reluctant to hire workers in the first place. I raise the analogy here simply to underscore the point that when we think carefully about why we might want to provide mandatory protection against all forms of "wrongful" dismissal, the logic of the rationale may well call for such expansion in the scope of protection, just as it calls for retrenchment on the burden of common law litigation as suggested in the text.

justice and limited relief one would expect from an administrative body like the state UI tribunal, instead of being able to assert a claim in the courts for sizable general damages for his wrongful dismissal. But that objection ignores the fact that at issue here is precisely when and on what terms the law should deem a discharge to be "wrongful," even though the dismissal complies with both the public policy of the community and the private agreement of the parties.

I have argued that we should now adopt further legal guarantees against unwarranted dismissal as part of the general network of employment standards legislation. I also believe that most ordinary workers would actually find that a scheme such as this would give them more real protection than they get from the formal legal right to bring a lawsuit, since the right to sue is meaningful only if the workers can surmount the practical barriers that now filter out most of such claims from employees who do not have either managerial/professional status or a particularly eye-catching quality to the circumstances of their dismissal. But it is crucial to remember that such a law would establish only a miminum mandatory guarantee applicable across the entire labor market.

This means that nothing in the law would preclude employees' negotiating additional contract protection enforceable in court (as some highly specialized and talented employees now have the leverage to do). Not only would such a law not prevent, but it should be designed to encourage, the establishment by employers of internal mechanisms for reviewing their dismissal decisions,[101] so as to protect the firm's as well as the employee's investment in their relationship from being dissipated without good reason. And of course employees would still be entitled to bargain collectively to induce their employer to agree to a negotiated just cause provision, enforced by grievances brought by

101. In the specific legal context of claims of sexual harassment in violation of Title VII, the Supreme Court indicated in Meritor Savings Bank v. Vincent, 477 U.S. 57, 69 (1986), that while the availability of an internal grievance procedure would not be dispositive with respect to employer liability, it would certainly be relevant if the procedure were accessible, effective, and fair. The Montana Wrongful Discharge From Employment Act requires (in Section 6) that for at least 90 days the discharged employee first utilize any internal appeal procedure established by the employer; the draft of the Model Employment Termination Act, note 8, provides (in section 4(2)) that the employee must pursue any *reasonable* internal procedure for at least 120 days, and that any subsequent external forum should give *due* or *substantial* deference to the disposition of the case within the internal process. For a recent canvass of the components of a fair internal procedure and its likely effects on common law wrongful dismissal suits, see Westin and Feliu, *Resolving Employment Disputes*, pp. 255–282.

their union representative before a private arbitrator empowered to reinstate the employee in the original job. I recognize that the widespread availability of this negotiated arrangement for unionized workers was the initial inspiration for the recent judicial movement to establish general legal guarantees against the wrongful dismissal of nonunion employees. But the lesson of this chapter has been that in the absence of worker organization and participation inside the firm, there are inherent limits on the protection that the government can effectively and sensibly provide from the outside.

3 · The Declining Fortunes
of Collective Bargaining

Employer Resistance to Collective Bargaining

Wrongful dismissal is only a single illustration of the broader theme of the affinity between meaningful worker participation and effective workplace protection. As I shall observe at other points in this book, essentially the same judgment can be made about a number of other contemporary challenges to the law at work, such as occupational injuries, plant closings, and pay equity for working women. Still, the proponent of more searching legal rights and guarantees will offer two rejoinders. First, if the individual worker is felt to be entitled to such protection as a matter of principle, he should not have to join a union and see that it negotiates a contract in order to secure this benefit. In any event, as a practical matter union representation is now available to too small a fraction of the labor force to be a realistic source of any kind of job protection for the overwhelming majority of American workers.

Back in the mid-fifties the preference for collective bargaining over legal regulation might have been sensible, because that institution covered nearly 40 percent of the private sector, and the percentage was increasing. However, such a policy is simply too remote from the real world of the eighties, in which unionization now covers less than 15 percent of the same sector and is still on the wane.[1] The sharp decline in union success in winning NLRB representation elections and then securing collective agreements for the new units meant that by the

1. See Paul C. Weiler, "Milestone or Tombstone: The Wagner Act at Fifty," 23 *Harvard Journal on Legislation* 1, 3 (1986); and Richard B. Freeman, "Contraction and Expansion: The Divergence of Private Sector and Public Sector Unionism in the United States," 2 *Journal of Economic Perspectives* 63, 64 (1988).

early eighties only about 100,000 nonunion workers a year were achieving a viable collective bargaining relationship with their employers under the NLRA[2]—much fewer than were losing the benefits of such representation as a result of the attrition of unionized plants and firms. Right now for the vast majority of American workers union representation is a matter of inheritance rather than of choice, a result of having gone to work in a place like an auto plant or a steel mill that was organized in the thirties and the forties. Precisely because collective bargaining is almost totally unavailable to workers in computer plants, financial offices, or generally in those spheres of the economy which have emerged and grown in the last two or three decades, legal regulation is more and more relied on to fill the vacuum.

The meaning of these statistical phenomena is not self-evident, however. Is the sharp decline in union representation due to its lack of appeal to American workers, resulting in a drop in the demand for this institution? Or is it due to sustained resistance on the part of American employers, producing a drop in the available supply of collective bargaining, at least at a price which workers are prepared to pay?

The first of these hypotheses is plausible. One can point, for example, to public opinion polls which show that whereas in the fifties unions enjoyed a high level of public approval, it had dropped sharply by the eighties, to the point where unions and their officials are at or near the bottom rank of institutions and occupations in the eyes of the American public.[3] Added to these changes in popular attitude were

2. See Paul C. Weiler, "Promises to Keep: Securing Workers' Rights to Self-Organization Under the NLRA," 96 *Harvard Law Review* 1769, 1775–76 (1983) (significantly fewer than 200,000 workers are included in newly certified bargaining units each year); and Paul C. Weiler, "Striking a New Balance: Freedom of Contract and the Prospects for Union Representation," 98 *Harvard Law Review* 351, 354–355, n. 3 (1984) (nearly 40 percent of newly certified units do not secure a first contract.).

3. A comprehensive review of polling data regarding unions and their leaders is presented in Seymour M. Lipset, "Labor Unions in the Public Mind," in Seymour M. Lipset, ed., *Unions in Transition*, p. 287 (San Francisco: ICS Press, 1986). The most frequently cited polling statistic is the public's answer to the question in the Gallup Poll of whether they approve or disapprove of labor unions. In 1957, 76 percent of the American public answered yes and 14 percent no, for a net union approval rating of 62 percent. In 1987 only 55 percent said yes and 35 percent said no, for a net rating of 20 percent, less than a third of what it had been a quarter-century before. In his later essay in *Unions in Transition*, "North American Labor Movements: A Comparative Perspective," pp. 421, 438–444, Lipset argues that the decline in public approval of unionism is the primary explanation for its shrinking membership rate in this country. Note, however, that 1981 marked the bottom point in labor's slide in the popular mind. By 1988, 61 percent of the Americans polled said they approved of unions, versus only 25 percent who disapproved, for a net positive rating of 36 percent, nearly double what it was at the beginning of the decade. Yet

major changes in the demography of the American work force. Whereas collective bargaining has largely been concentrated among male blue-collar workers employed in a large factory environment, most of the growth in the labor force has taken place among female white-collar workers in office and service jobs, where employees traditionally enjoy a more personal, less structured relationship with their employer. It is not surprising that an institution developed to meet the needs of one kind of worker in the factory would prove unappealing to quite another kind of worker in an office.[4]

Suppose these and other features of this "postindustrial" account do capture the true story of the decline in union representation. What are its implications for public policy? From the point of view of labor law, the answer is quite clear. There is little or no justification for reforming the NLRA to make it easier for unions to win bargaining rights for unorganized workers. Rather, it is up to the union movement to refurbish its own structure, platform, and image in order to make itself more appealing to the new breed of worker whom unions have not thus far been able to interest in collective bargaining.[5] Additionally, the case for reform of employment law for the benefit of nonunion workers is also weakened; particularly to the extent that such a case rests on the premise that it is unfair to deny nonunion workers protection against, say, unjust dismissal, when unionized workers enjoy that protection as a matter of course. If that kind of regulation of management behavior is a textbook illustration of what unions do, and if it is assumed that nonunion workers do not want to have collective bargaining to secure this right on their own, it is not apparent why the law should provide it for them.

This version of the decline in union representation does have considerable validity. It likely holds true especially for the new breed of so-called knowledge workers. These technical, administrative, and professional employees (such as systems analysts or engineers), who comprise a sizable and fast-growing share of the work force, see themselves

---

the slide in union membership in the private sector quickened rather than declined during the same time period. See Freeman, "Contraction and Expansion," p. 64.

4. For variations on this theme see Daniel Bell, *The Coming of Post-Industrial Society: A Venture in Social Forecasting*, pp. 129–142 (New York: Basic Books, 1973); and William J. Moore and Robert J. Newman, "On the Prospects for American Trade Union Growth: A Cross-Section Analysis," 57 *Review of Economics and Statistics* 435 (1975).

5. This position is argued, for example, by Julius G. Getman in "Ruminations on Union Organizing in the Private Sector," 53 *University of Chicago Law Review* 45 (1986); and Stanley Aronowitz in *Working Class Hero: A New Strategy for Labor* (New York: Pilgrim Press, 1983), in particular Chapter 6, "Organizing the New Workers," pp. 125–170.

as different from the standard union member: they appear to want a distinctive type of collective voice in the affairs of their workplace.[6]

Where the story does not ring so true, though, is with respect to large segments of office and service workers—the clerk-typist in an office or the counterperson in a fast food restaurant.[7] Many of these people now work in large impersonal organizations in an assembly-line atmosphere—exactly the environment in which collective bargaining appeared so promising from the thirties to the fifties. Jobs like these have been readily organized in other countries and indeed in the public sector in the United States. Some other explanation must be found to account adequately for the almost total absence of union representation for these workers in the private sector in the United States.

Another possible cause of the decline in unionization is employer resistance to union representation. A closer look at the polling data reveals a more complicated picture of public attitudes than emerged at first glance.[8] Unquestionably, the American public does have a jaun-

---

6. This is one of Charles Heckscher's themes in *The New Unionism: Employee Involvement in the Changing Corporation*, pp. 62–71 (New York: Basic Books, 1988). Heckscher notes (p. 69) that all of the five occupations projected up to the year 2000 to grow most rapidly in percentage terms are white-collar, semi-professional in character: paralegals, computer programmers, systems analysts, medical assistants, and data processing equipment repairers. None of these groups has ever evinced any particular interest in traditional unionism.

7. As Bennett Harrison and Barry Bluestone point out in *The Great U-Turn: Corporate Restructuring and the Polarizing of America*, pp. 69–73 (New York: Basic Books, 1988), while it is true that there will be very high percentage increases in the size of the semi-professional occupations emphasized by Heckscher (*The New Unionism*), the data are slightly deceptive because of the very low current base from which these jobs are now taking off. The occupations that are growing fastest in absolute numbers are, in order, cashier, registered nurse, janitor, truck driver, and waiter and waitress. Of these positions only nursing is professional in character, and it is a profession which is comparatively unionized. Moreover, nothing about the working conditions in the other occupations would suggest that they do not need union representation and collective bargaining, traditional or not. For a provocative description of the situation of many of these expanding occupations and industries, see Robert Howard, *Brave New Workplace* (New York: Viking, 1985).

8. See James L. Medoff, "The Public's Image of Labor and Labor's Response" 3–20 (1984), an unpublished document initially prepared for the AFL-CIO Committee on the Evolution of Work; and Thomas A. Kochan, Harry C. Katz, and Robert B. McKersie, *The Transformation of American Industrial Relations*, pp. 215–220 (New York: Basic Books, 1986). The most recent Gallup Poll, "Public Knowledge and Opinion Concerning the Labor Movement" (1988), disclosed not just a major upturn in the net favorable ratings of the union movement (see note 3), but also that a large majority of the American public agrees that "labor unions are good for the nation as a whole" (60 percent saying yes versus 26 percent saying no); that "the standard of living of many American workers has been seriously undermined by wage reductions and benefit cuts" (70 percent yes versus 23 percent no); that "without union efforts, most laws which benefit employees would be seriously weakened or repealed" (68 percent yes versus 21 percent no); and conse-

diced view of the practice and performance of unions and their leaders. (Interestingly, to a large degree this view derives from the belief that unions wield too much power, particularly in the political arena). However, there remains a strong public commitment to the principle that workers have a right to union representation to improve their conditions at work, a high level of satisfaction expressed by current union members in connection with what their unions do for them vis-à-vis their employers, and a significant segment of the nonunion work force (about one-third) that would vote right now for collective bargaining if they had the chance (and that percentage is higher among female white-collar workers than among male blue-collar workers). The continuing appeal of collective bargaining to the work force was tapped during the dramatic increase in public sector unionism in the sixties and seventies, among workers who were also exposed to the drop in popular approval of unions recorded in Gallup polls.[9] But a major hurdle remains before any such employee demand for union representation in the private sector can be translated into an actual enduring presence for collective bargaining. The "natural" state for any new firm or plant is always a nonunion relationship, and employers typically prefer to keep it that way. American business has repeatedly demonstrated that it is ready to take vigorous action to preserve (or to recreate) a union-free environment in its operations.[10] This attitude of employers may help explain the inability of unions to establish a foothold among the employees in many of the new and growing sectors of the economy ever since the fifties.

---

quently that "existing labor laws should be strengthened to prevent corporations from denying workers rights to organize" (66 percent yes versus 25 percent no). The likely explanation for the rising public support for unions is the perception that union representation has been seriously declining in scope and availability to workers (a fact with which 73 percent of the Gallup respondents agreed), because the major popular concern about unionism has always been the feeling that unions are too big and too powerful. It is intriguing, then, to see how much of that stereotype remains. In the same Gallup poll of people largely favorable to unionism, when they were asked to estimate the current percentage of union membership in the work force, the average response was 45 percent, or nearly three times the actual figure.

9. The significance of the contrasting trend in public sector unionism in the United States is the focus of Freeman's "Contraction and Expansion."

10. On the deeply felt distaste of American business for union representation of employees, see Sanford M. Jacoby, "American Exceptionalism Revisited: The Importance of Management," in Sanford M. Jacoby, ed., *Masters to Managers: Historical and Comparative Perspectives on American Employers* (forthcoming, New York: Columbia University Press, 1990). On the special flavor which this antipathy has given to American labor laws, see Derek C. Bok, "Reflections on the Distinctive Character of American Labor Laws," 84 *Harvard Law Review* 1394 (1971).

The employer aim of union *avoidance* can be pursued through two quite different strategies: union *substitution* or union *suppression*.[11] The former is the tactic of the firm which sets out on its own to provide its employees with the kinds of working conditions that traditionally have been won through collective bargaining: above-market wages and fringe benefits; protection against unjust treatment (not only in firing, but also in discipline, work assignments, promotions, and the like); open-door policies through which employees can appeal to senior management the unfavorable decisions of lower-ranking supervisors; and, most recently, a variety of employee involvement programs that give workers some voice in what is happening around them.[12] The point of this strategy is to make the firm and its atmosphere so attractive to its employees that they will find union representation *unnecessary*. The numerous examples of this style of benign human resource management (IBM and Hewlett-Packard being two of the most widely heralded) make it quite evi-

11. These terms were coined by Thomas A. Kochan, *Collective Bargaining and Industrial Relations: From Theory to Policy and Practice*, p. 183ff. (Homewood, Ill.: R. D. Irwin, 1980).

12. For the full array of personnel management techniques, see Fred K. Foulkes, *Positive Employee Relations: Personnel Policies and Practices of the Large Nonunion Company* (Englewood Cliffs, N.J.: Prentice-Hall, 1980); and Michael Beer, Bert Spector, Paul R. Lawrence, D. Quinn Mills, and Richard E. Walton, *Managing Human Assets* (New York: Free Press, 1984). A regular centerpiece of such a strategy is the development of a systematic program to protect nonunion workers against wrongful dismissal, which it is hoped will serve as an antidote to a union's effort to tap employee discontent over arbitrary management action. See, e.g., Kinoshita v. Canadian Pacific Airlines, Inc., 724 P.2d 110 (Hawaii 1986), in which the firm announced its new guarantees and procedures in the midst of ongoing efforts to organize its employees; and Jeski v. American Express Company, 708 P.2d 110, 110–111 (Ariz. App. 1985), in which the American Express personnel manual stated: "*A Word About Unions*. We feel that a union would not be of advantage to any of us—it would hurt the business which we all depend on for our livelihood. Furthermore, we have enthusiastically accepted our responsibility to provide you good working conditions, good wages, good benefits, fair treatment and the personal respect which is rightfully yours. . . . We are pledged to high standards of individual treatment and respect for all employees. You can be certain that we will constantly strive to maintain your respect for our individual treatment of your welfare and job security." Significantly, although this manual also expressly stated that employment at American Express was on a purely at-will basis, these additional representations by the company precluded a summary judgment against a discharged employee's contract action. Likewise, of the twelve case studies of internal appeal systems in nonunion firms presented in Alan F. Westin and Alfred G. Feliu, *Resolving Employment Disputes Without Litigation* (Washington, D.C.: Bureau of National Affairs, 1988), the only three employers which provided binding neutral arbitration as the endpoint in their procedures were those which had adopted the program to avoid union representation rather than to avoid employment litigation.

dent why there is rarely, if ever, a successful union organizing drive among the employees of such firms. Whether or not this model of workplace governance is a sufficient alternative to collective bargaining is a matter I shall take up later. At present, though, union substitution does not represent the kind of abuse of employer power that calls for a response from labor law or its reform.

Unfortunately quite a different attitude is appropriate in the face of the other type of employer strategy, union suppression. Most employers are not prepared to pay the price of voluntarily extending to their workers all the benefits of collective bargaining.[13] Some of these firms will prove fertile ground for an initially successful union organizing drive and a petition to the NLRB for bargaining rights. At this point, the employer which is determined to remain free of the union will be tempted to utilize a variety of measures designed to make collective bargaining unpalatable to its employees:[14] a vigorous campaign against the union in which management regularly raises the spectre of strikes and job losses, and adds credibility to the threats through selective discriminatory action against key union supporters. If the union wins the election nonetheless, the employer will simply carry on its resistance at the next stage by stonewalling at the bargaining table, forcing the union members out on strike, and hiring permanent replacements to fill their jobs, thus confirming the accuracy of the employer's initial campaign prognostications, but too late for these workers. To the extent this scenario has become anything

13. The price of union substitution rose sharply in the sixties and the seventies as the union wage and benefit premium over the wage/benefit package for nonunion employees nearly doubled, apparently stimulating in nonunion employers a greatly increased tendency to commit unfair labor practices; see Robert J. Flanagan, *Labor Relations and the Litigation Explosion*, pp. 67–71 and 85–94 (Washington, D.C.: Brookings Institution, 1987). This evidence further corroborates the implausibility of lack of employee interest in unionization as a sufficient explanation of the decline in union membership in this period. Although it is true that average union dues were increasing relative to average wage rates, as can be calculated from the tables in Paula Voos, "Trends in Union Organizing Expenditures, 1953–1977," 38 *Industrial and Labor Relations Review* 52 (1984), the absolute size of union dues (typically in the range of $250 to $500 a year) is dwarfed by the roughly $5,000 annual premium in employee compensation under a union contract.

14. For detailed descriptions of the techniques that employers can and do use in the present legal framework through which a collective bargaining relationship is established, see Weiler, "Promises to Keep" (on the organizing/certification process), and Weiler, "Striking a New Balance" (on negotiation of the first contract). In Chapter 6 I shall return to this topic and explain in detail how the current NLRA framework permits such a strategy of union suppression.

like a widespread phenomenon in the last several decades, it would provide an alternative account for at least some of the drop in union representation during that period.[15]

Ample evidence for this account can be found in the remarkable increase in discriminatory discharges and bad faith bargaining by employers during the very thirty-year period in which union election victories and first contracts were consistently declining.[16] Indeed, the increase in employer intimidation had reached the point that for every twenty recorded votes for unions in elections in 1980, and for every *ten* votes in 1985, there was one case of an illegally discharged worker obtaining reinstatement through the offices of the NLRB.[17] A number of econometric studies have demonstrated that this increase in employer unfair labor practices is significantly associated with the decline in union election success, after controlling for the variety of other possible explanatory factors.[18] An interesting recent study in-

15. This is the argument advanced by Richard B. Freeman and James L. Medoff, *What Do Unions Do?* (New York: Basic Books, 1984), in particular, Chapter 15, "The Slow Strangulation of Private-Sector Unionism," pp. 221–245; and by Michael Goldfield, *The Decline of Organized Labor in the United States* (Chicago: University of Chicago Press, 1987), in particular, Chapter 9, "The Continuing Search for the Real Culprits: The Relation of Class Forces," pp. 180–217.

16. See Weiler, "Promises to Keep," pp. 1779–81 (statistics on increases in discriminatory discharges and other unfair labor practices during the representation campaign); and Weiler, "Striking a New Balance," pp. 353–357 (increasing bad faith bargaining by employers during the negotiation of the contract). The figures in these articles span the period 1955 through 1980; I update them to 1985 in Chapter 6 at pp. 236 and 238–240. Since employer infractions and union failures occur among groups of workers whom unions have initially organized in the face of the presumed socioeconomic barriers to their appeal of unionization, these cases furnish a particularly apt test of the "union suppression" hypothesis.

17. Weiler, "Promises to Keep," p. 1716 n. 2. I am aware, of course, that a substantial number of the reinstatees recorded by the NLRB were fired outside the context of any representation campaign in which they might have been voters. At the same time, however, a large number of union supporters in representation campaigns have undoubtedly been fired without later filing charges, or have been unable to substantiate their claims, or have settled for back pay without reinstatement. See the figures in Weiler, "Milestone or Tombstone," p. 8 n. 12, and below in Chapter 6, n. 18. It is not known whether or not these two adjustments to the crude ratio in the text roughly offset each other. As another index of the current dimensions of illegal employer resistance to union representation campaigns, I have calculated that in the early eighties the NLRB was obtaining reinstatement (or preferential hiring) rights for workers fired in fully one-third of the certification elections the Board was conducting (Weiler, "Milestone or Tombstone," p. 11 n. 17).

18. Freeman and Medoff, *What Do Unions Do?* pp. 237–239; and David T. Ellwood and Glen Fine, "The Impact of Right-to-Work Laws on Union Organizing," 95 *Journal of Political Economy* 250 (1987). See also Goldfield, *Decline of Organized Labor*, pp. 201–205,

vestigated firms which were already partially organized, but which opened new plants in the late seventies and early eighties. The study found that those firms which had decided as a matter of company policy to pursue a union-free environment in their new operations were far more likely to win certification elections than were their counterpart firms in this sample, even after controlling for any innovations in benefits and programs for the workers—that is, after taking account of any tangible signs of "union substitution" as between these firms.[19]

There is still considerable scholarly disagreement about whether the specifically illegal forms of employer resistance (coercive speech and discriminatory action) make any real difference in the outcome of representation campaigns.[20] If they do not, there would be much less reason for concern about NLRB procedures and remedies which have proved incapable of stemming the tide of employer unfair labor practices. Even assuming, though, that empirical research has not been able to disentangle and demonstrate the impact of illegal tactics in the context of a firm's broader antiunion campaign,[21] I doubt that this distinction

demonstrating that a significant contributor to dwindling union election success is the sharp drop in employers' willingness to agree to the Board's speedier "consent election" procedure; this unwillingness to agree is likely a proxy for the increasing disposition of employers to wage a vigorous antiunion campaign.

19. Thomas A. Kochan, Robert B. McKersie, and John Chalykoff, "The Effects of Corporate Strategy and Workplace Innovations on Union Representation," 39 *Industrial and Labor Relations Review* 487, 498–499 (1986).

20. The most prominent skeptics about the existence of such a connection are Julius G. Getman, Stephen B. Goldberg, and Jeanne B. Herman, the authors of *Union Representation Elections: Law and Reality* (New York: Russell Sage Foundation, 1976), a detailed empirical study of 31 NLRB elections in the midwestern United States in the early seventies. I question the analysis and conclusions of Getman et al. in "Promises to Keep," pp. 1781–86, relying heavily on William T. Dickens's careful reexamination of their data, summarized in Dickens, "The Effect of Company Campaigns on Certification Elections: *Law and Reality* Once Again," 36 *Industrial and Labor Relations Review* 560 (1983). Getman and his coauthors responded to our empirical and policy misgivings in "The Relationship Between Free Choice and Labor Board Doctrine: Differing Empirical Approaches," 79 *Northwestern University Law Review* 721 (1984). For reasons which are alluded to in Weiler, "Milestone or Tombstone," pp. 10–11 n. 1, and which are developed in further detail in the testimony of Dickens before the Senate Committee on Labor and Human Resources, January 29, 1988, I am not persuaded by the response of Getman et al. However, I do agree with them that as a matter of labor law policy there is too much NLRB regulation of the current representation process, much of which I would (as would they) like to see dismantled (see Chapter 6).

21. This assumption is not obligatory, both for the reasons given in Dickens, "The Effect of Company Campaigns," and because of a study by William N.Cooke, "The Rising Toll of Discrimination Against Union Activities," 24 *Industrial Relations* 421 (1985),

has much policy significance. Given the widespread pattern of illegal dismissals of union supporters, it is likely that the vigorous antiunion campaigns of the "good" employers who do comply with the law (the control group in this research) are now the unwitting beneficiaries of the actions of the "bad" employers who flout the law. Indeed, a 1984 Harris poll of a national sample of nonunion workers found that 43 percent of them believed that *their* employer would fire or otherwise discriminate against union supporters in a campaign.[22] Given the perceived risk that such a significant price might have to be paid in the quest for collective bargaining, it is not surprising that whatever latent employee demand there may be for union representation, it is not often being translated into established bargaining relationships.

I do not mean to deny the importance of changing sentiments among contemporary American workers, most of whom are reasonably satisfied with their current job situation or at least satisfied that collective bargaining would not produce significant improvements in the situation. Any complex social phenomenon such as the decline in union representation over the last thirty years is likely to have a variety of causal explanations, some appropriate for one kind of firm or occupation, others for quite different settings.[23] I am convinced, though, that a substantial share of the responsibility must be attributed to the increasingly no-holds-barred resistance exhibited by American business toward unions, a level of employer opposition that tends to be facilitated rather than foiled by the present NLRA framework for the representation contest.

To test the plausibility of that judgment, let us do a thought experiment in which we shall reverse the current assumptions of our labor laws. These assumptions are, first, that the "natural" pre-labor law

---

which shows that Section 8(a)(3) violations had a substantial effect on the outcome of a sample of NLRB elections in Indiana in 1979.

22. See Weiler, "Milestone or Tombstone," p. 11 n. 18.

23. For a careful examination of the several components and sources of the decline in union representation, see William T. Dickens and Jonathan S. Leonard, "Accounting for the Decline in Union Membership, 1950–1980," 38 *Industrial and Labor Relations Review* 323–334 (1985); Henry S. Farber, "The Extent of Unionization in the United States," in Thomas A. Kochan, ed., *Challenges and Choices Facing American Labor*, p. 16 (Cambridge, Mass.: MIT Press, 1985); and Henry S.Farber, "The Decline of Unionization in the United States: What Can Be Learned From Recent Experience?" (forthcoming, 9 *Journal of Labor Economics*, 1990). Farber concludes that roughly half of the decline in unionization since the early seventies is due to decreased employee demand for union representation, with the other half due to employer efforts to reduce the supply. As I observe in the text, one should not assume that the former trend is wholly independent of the latter.

state of each plant or office is to have no worker organization. Second, before any employees in these firms may be represented by a union for purposes of collective bargaining, the majority must vote by secret ballot to make this change in the status quo; and even before the certification vote a vigorous campaign will take place during which the employer will make clear its distaste for any such change in the employment relationship. Third, even if the employees do vote for union representation, they will still have to fight hard (perhaps to the point of risking their jobs in a strike) in order to win a collective agreement that will establish their union as a meaningful presence on the job. Given such a setting, in which only a minority of initially successful union organizing drives actually bear fruit in the form of certifications and first contracts, it is hardly surprising that fewer and fewer American workers are inclined even to start down that path.

But what could one expect if certain of these key assumptions were changed? Suppose, for example, the law were to presume that employees would have union representation and collective bargaining unless the majority freely voted for a union-free environment. Adding a feature from current NLRA law and practice, the choice against union representation would have to be preceded by the organization of the non-union employees to display sufficient interest in getting rid of the union, followed by a pitched campaign waged by and against the union. Then conduct the nonrepresentation campaign under the watchful eye of *union* officials, who would, in our experiment, wield the standard managerial prerogatives of transfer, promotion, demotion, layoff, discipline, and dismissal. The final and crucial counterfact is that the union officials would retain all these managerial powers over the work force after the election, no matter what the employee verdict was.

Most people would surely believe the foregoing to be an Alice-in-Wonderland version of our labor laws;[24] few would doubt, however,

---

24. Note that this idea is not entirely outlandish in every possible context, as evidenced by this example. Suppose that a company like General Motors, all plants of which are now represented by the United Auto Workers, opens a new plant in a different geographic location. Under current labor law, the new GM plant could not be "accreted" to the UAW's existing bargaining unit and covered by the parties' collective agreement unless the union persuaded a majority of the new work force in the plant to sign cards authorizing such a step. In fact, if General Motors insisted, the UAW would have to win a secret ballot election conducted by the NLRB at the new plant. The aim of this body of accretion law (which is briefly reviewed in Charles J. Morris, ed., 1 *The Developing Labor Law: The Board, the Courts, and the National Labor Relations Act* 2nd ed., pp. 369–371 (Washington, D.C.: Bureau of National Affairs, 1983)) is to protect employees from being swept into a bargaining unit against their wishes. Indeed, if General Motors were to sell

that in such a setting union density trends and figures would look profoundly different from those we observed in the last quarter-century. Simple inertia would preserve the unionized starting point in most employment settings: recall the survey data indicating that employees are generally satisfied with their incumbent unions as well as with their incumbent employers. Even in locations where there was some employee discontent with the union representatives, the proponents of the nonunion option would face an arduous uphill struggle to persuade a majority of their colleagues to enter that unknown world, especially since everyone would be aware that such a move would be considered a real slap in the face to the union officials who would continue to exercise managerial authority over the employees' jobs and careers. I re-emphasize that from a purely formal point of view, the employees' freedom of choice with respect to this alternative regime would be precisely the same as it is now under the NLRA: only the legal starting line and the party holding managerial power have been changed. But because the initial inclinations of many employees about a union versus nonunion shop are generally rather tentative and ambivalent, the obstacles posed by these legal arrangements and institutional incentives would exert a substantial dampening effect on the likelihood that the latent demand for a nonunion workplace would eventually bear fruit.

I do not for a moment suggest that all new plants and offices should start out unionized unless otherwise voted in order to expand the scope of union representation in this country. Rather, I proposed this thought experiment in order to bring into relief the powerful, albeit

---

an existing plant to a successor employer, the successor would not be bound by the existing UAW contract (see NLRB v. Burns International Security Services, Inc., 406 U.S. 272 (1972)), and would be bound by the union's bargaining authority only if there were sufficient continuity in the work force. So if the successor chose to use its freedom from the collective agreement to hire a substantially different work force for this plant, there would be no union representation in the plant until the union positively established a majority position there (see Howard Johnson Co., Inc. v. Detroit Local Joint Board, Hotel and Restaurant Employees, 417 U.S. 249 (1974)). Again, the manifest aim of this doctrine is to protect employee free choice under the Act. But despite the fact that union representation may have a long history in an enterprise and even in a particular plant, any material change of the types described above will immediately produce a reversion to the supposedly natural nonunion status, at least until the union can overcome employee inertia and employer resistance enough to re-establish collective bargaining. In my opinion there would be no logical incompatibility—and in fact there would be a positive affinity—with employee free choice if the law were changed to provide that plants which change owners shall remain union unless the employees freely choose to dispense with collective bargaining.

largely invisible, influence exerted by the ground rules of the representation contest, which we tend to take for granted.

A typical group of employees who are potential candidates for a union organizing drive start out with somewhat amorphous feelings of discontent about their current job and a vague inclination toward collective bargaining as a means of improving working conditions. But these employees also know that to translate such incipient feelings into an enduring union presence will require a grueling effort. Even in units where the employees were initially organized for a certification petition to the NLRB, more often than not the union effort fails, and a great deal of damage is inflicted on many of the participants. So the prospect of such a traumatic venture[25] is a major inhibitor to employees' getting interested in and involved with an organizing effort in the first place (and consequently becoming part of the NLRB caseload and statistics, which in turn are grist for the mill of empirical researchers). As it becomes apparent that the real odds of securing a union contract are very low, most employees are apt to persuade themselves that their working conditions are reasonably satisfactory, so that they do not really need union representation to improve them.[26] Other employees who feel more discontented will leave for better jobs, to the extent they are available. Finally, as I noted in the last chapter, growing numbers of American workers who have less-than-happy prospects in the outside labor market are turning to lawyers to represent them in lawsuits over their grievances.

The judgment I arrived at in Chapter 2 is that such legal representation and employee litigation is not as constructive a response to this workplace problem as would be an employee organization and voice

25. I refer at p. 114 to a 1984 Lou Harris Poll of a national sample of nonunion, nonmanagerial employees, in which 59 percent of the respondents said that they expected there would be trouble and tension during a representation campaign in their workplace, and 43 percent believed that their employer would fire, demote, or take other retaliatory measures against employees who visibly supported the union. In a 1988 Gallup Poll, 69 percent of the respondents agreed (and only 21 percent disagreed) with the proposition that corporations sometimes harass, intimidate, or fire employees who openly speak out in favor of a union.

26. Among psychologists this response is known as cognitive dissonance or adaptive preferences. These terms mean that if people know that a particular option is not realistically available to them, they will gradually adapt their preferences to the situation and exhibit little interest in pursuing the unavailable option. See Cass R. Sunstein, "Legal Interference with Private Preferences," 53 *University of Chicago Law Review* 1129, 1146–50 (1986), for a lawyer's discussion of this phenomenon with references to the scientific literature.

inside the firm. The policy implication from my argument in this section, then, is that those who are interested in improving the conditions of workers within the loose confines of the labor market would be better advised to invest their scarce political and legal resources in altering our labor laws rather than our employment laws. In other words, employees should be afforded a better chance to secure through their own group efforts such benefits as protection against unjust dismissal, rather than having to wait for legislators or judges to establish and enforce regulatory laws for each issue as and when it comes to the fore.

The Intellectual Challenge to Unionism

The foregoing section explains how the failure of American labor law to contain employer resistance to union representation bears a substantial share of the responsibility for the general decline of unionization, which in turn has added measurably to the impetus for more and more government regulation of wrongful dismissal and other employment matters. But even though establishing such a factual connection is a necessary part of the case for labor law reform, it is by no means sufficient. One must also make a persuasive case that the gradual demise of private sector collective bargaining is an unhappy result for the American worker and the political economy. Although this value judgment is a central premise of the NLRA, the fact that the policy was accepted by Congress in 1935 is no better an argument for its contemporary virtues than was the common law adoption of the at-will doctrine a half-century earlier.

At the heart of the Wagner Act were three judgments: collective bargaining is a valuable institution for the reduction of inequality of bargaining power in the workplace and therefore deserves encouragement from the law (Preamble); workers should enjoy a positive statutory right to use this instrument to improve their conditions of employment if the majority of the employees want it (Sections 7 and 9(a)); and this right should be protected from employer coercion by outlawing a variety of unfair labor practices (Section 8). It is not surprising, then, that as employer suppression of union representation became so widespread in the eighties, so respectable in American business circles, there should also emerge scholarly justification for that employer behavior. The revisionist theory rejects the fundamental premise that collective bargaining is a desirable institution that employees are entitled to have if they want it, and defends the employer's use of its powers of hiring and firing to maintain a union-free environment in its plants.[27] This view of the Wagner Act is in much the same intellectual vein as the defense of employment at will that I sketched earlier. Such an affinity is to be expected, since collective bargaining is an institution designed to regulate the prerogatives management enjoys in an unfettered labor market, not simply with respect to dismissal, but over every facet of the employment relationship.

One possible rendering of the current labor law is that it does no more than offer workers freedom of choice about collective bargaining without implying any particular endorsement of that institution. That intepretation is much more plausible after the reform of the NLRA by the Taft-Hartley Act in 1947, which made clear that workers had a right *not* to have collective bargaining if that was their majority verdict, and protected their freedom against a variety of *union* tactics that might coerce them in that choice.[28] Since the law has deployed a variety of highly effective remedies against coercive top-down organizing tactics by unions (particularly the use by unions of their traditional weapon, the secondary organizational boycott), simple substantive neutrality could justify reforming the NLRA to provide effective protection against widespread employer intimidation of workers' decisions about collective bargaining.

The problem with this standard liberal refrain for labor law reform is that it adheres unquestioningly to the assumption of the original Act, that it is the freedom of choice of *employees* that should count; that the law should guarantee to workers the right of self-determination about

27. The most explicit statement of this position appears in Richard A. Epstein's highly provocative article, "A Common Law for Labor Relations: A Critique of the New Deal Labor Legislation," 92 *Yale Law Journal* 1357, 1370–75, 1382–85, 1392–94 (1983); see also Julius G. Getman and Thomas C. Kohler, "The Common Law, Labor Law, and Reality: A Response to Professor Epstein," 92 *Yale Law Journal* 1415 (1983); and Richard A. Epstein, "Common Law, Labor Law, and Reality: A Rejoinder to Professors Getman and Kohler," 92 *Yale Law Journal* 1435 (1983). Dan C. Heldman, James T. Bennett, and Manuel H. Johnson, in *Deregulating Labor Relations* (Dallas: The Fisher Institute, 1981) also systematically criticize the NLRA for its positive protection of union representation and collective bargaining (pp. 49–76) and propose the repeal of the entire Act (pp. 141–154).

28. For close reviews of the complex relationship between the purposes and policies expressed by the Congress in the Wagner Act and Taft-Hartley Act, see James A. Gross, "Conflicting Statutory Purposes: Another Look at 50 Years of NLRB Law-Making," 39 *Industrial and Labor Relations Review* 7 (1985); and Charles J. Morris, "The NLRB in the Dog House: Can an Old Dog Learn New Tricks?" 24 *San Diego Law Review* 9, 11–17 (1987). I agree with Morris that even after Taft-Hartley encouraging collective bargaining remains an explicit policy objective of the NLRA.

whether to shift the representation with their employer from an individual to a collective basis. The fact is that there are two parties to this relationship—the employees, who supply their labor, and the employer, which supplies its capital. Each is vitally affected by the presence or absence of collective bargaining. The law does ban the so-called "discriminatory" discharge and the "yellow dog" contract, actions that are said to "intimidate" employees in their choice. But emotional overtones to our characterization of such employee actions are apt only if we assume that the workers start with an inalienable statutory right to choose union representation. Without the tacit assumption that only the workers "own" a voice in the decision, one could fairly characterize such employer action as no more than the exercise of its own choice about whom to hire or fire by conditioning offers of employment on the workers' accepting that the plant remain nonunion.[29] If we ask why the employer should be free to insist on such an agreement, the simple answer is that the employees enjoy the reciprocal freedom to reject or to quit a job unless the employer agrees to deal with them through a union.

One answer to this mutuality objection—the one that historically underlies our labor laws—is that collective bargaining is a substantively valuable institution (at least if freely chosen by workers), and that lodging the power of decision with the employees is more conducive to the development of union representation than would be leaving it to bilateral dealings between the firm and its individual workers. It is precisely this assumption which now seems questionable in the popular mind,[30] for reasons that have long been argued by prominent economists,[31] and that are now seeping into legal scholarship, especially of the law and economics genre.[32]

29. See Epstein, "A Common Law for Labor Relations."

30. A particularly good account of popular misgivings about contemporary American unionism is an article by Robert M. Kaus, "The Trouble With Unions," *Harper's* 23–35 (June 1983). To much the same effect but in a somewhat more scholarly vein is Daniel K. Benjamin, "Combinations of Workmen: Trade Unions in the American Economy," in Lipset, ed., *Unions in Transition*, p. 201.

31. See, e.g., Henry C. Simons, "Some Reflections on Syndicalism," 52 *Journal of Political Economy* (1944); Charles Lindblom, *Unions and Capitalism* (New Haven: Yale University Press, 1949); H. Gregg Lewis, "The Labor Monopoly Problem: A Positive Program," 59 *Journal of Political Economy* 277 (1951); and Milton Friedman, "Some Comments on the Significance of Labor Unions for Economic Policy," in David M. Wright, ed., *The Impact of the Union*, pp. 204–234 (New York: Harcourt Brace, 1951).

32. A number of distinct though related strands can be identified in the recent incursion of the law and economics fraternity into the world of labor law. One such strand is professedly positive: it claims only to demonstrate how the NLRA and its jurisprudence implements the statutory policy fostering and protecting (within limits)

From the point of view of Senator Wagner and the other authors of the NLRA, the aim of the labor unions and the labor laws was to give employees the bargaining power they needed to win better wages from their employers, not only for the benefit of workers and their families, but also to expand the level of purchasing power in the broader economy.[33] But from the neoclassical economic point of view, labor is a commodity, a factor of production for which the terms of exchange are ideally determined in competitive markets. Unionization of workers introduces a cartel into this market, an organization that attempts to monopolize the supply of labor to the firm in order to extract a premium wage that is higher than the wage that would be set in a competitive labor market. Further, to defend any economic "rent" it may win, the union must also deploy elaborate devices to regulate management's use of labor in its operations. Viewed from this vantage point, the effort by labor law to foster the development of private labor cartels and then to shield them from normal antitrust scrutiny of their

---

the cartelization by unions of what would otherwise be a freely competitive and efficiently operating labor market. Prominent examples of this genre of commentary are Richard A. Posner, "Some Economics of Labor Law," 51 *University of Chicago Law Review* 988 (1984); and Thomas J. Campbell, "Labor Law and Economics," 38 *Stanford Law Review* 991 (1986).

A second strand is frankly normative. Accepting the foregoing law and economics analysis of the function of our labor law, scholars of this persuasion argue that such statutory policy is undesirable on allocative, distributional, and libertarian grounds. I referred earlier to proposals by Epstein and by Heldman, Bennett, and Johnson (note 28) to dismantle entirely the legal apparatus erected under the NLRA that now gives affirmative encouragement and protection to unions. In another piece in this vein, Robert H. Lande and Richard O. Zerbe, Jr., "Reducing Unions' Monopoly Power: Costs and Benefits," 28 *Journal of Law and Economics* 297 (1985), argue that the restraints of antitrust law should be reimposed on unions whenever they attempt to represent employees of several firms which are in a vertical or horizontal relationship in the same markets, because we should try to enhance competition by and for labor, rather than let it be obstructed. My argument in the next section will be that our current labor laws do almost nothing to maintain a union cartel in the labor market, and that unions themselves, moreover, can do remarkably little to sustain a cartel and extract a monopoly rent from what would otherwise be a competitive marketplace. In Chapter 4 I shall develop as an alternative to the price-auction theory a different conception of the employment relationship and real-world markets, a position similar to the one adopted by Douglas L. Leslie, "Labor Bargaining Units," 70 *Virginia Law Review* 353 (1984), and by Michael L. Wachter and George M. Cohen, "The Law and Economics of Collective Bargaining: An Introduction and Application to the Problems of Subcontracting, Partial Closure and Relocation," 136 *University of Pennsylvania Law Review* 1349 (1988), in their respective analyses of these specific issues in contemporary labor law.

33. For an astute economist's critique of the objective of expanding purchasing power, see Daniel J. B. Mitchell, "Inflation, Unemployment and the Wagner Act: A Critical Reappraisal," 38 *Stanford Law Review* 1065, 1066–82 (1986).

anticompetitive tactics is socially undesirable in terms of both allocative efficiency and distributional equity.

This critique of collective bargaining measures its performance against an ideally functioning, free and competitive labor market. In such a market workers compete with each other to sell their labor to firms bidding for their services at a price that tends to reflect the value of an employee's contribution to the production of goods and services that consumers want to buy. Workers of different qualifications will be offered and will fill jobs for which their talents are best suited, because this is how they can be rewarded for their greatest contribution to the output of the firm that employs them. The prospect of such a reward is what gives employees the incentive to work as well as they can for their immediate employer, and also to enhance their personal qualifications (their "human capital"), which will enable them to get a better job in the future. What protects workers from exploitation by their more powerful-seeming employers, which might be tempted to deny employees appropriate payment for their true contribution to the firm's output, is the presence of a great many other employers in the market who are always looking for more and better workers, and who have an incentive to bid for the services of any worker who is being paid less than he is worth.[34]

To the extent that a labor market functions close to this ideal, unionization of workers will distort its operation. The purpose of a union is to organize workers into a cartel in order to eliminate any competition between its members in the sale of their services. As in any cartel, the ultimate aim is to raise the workers' price (the level of wages and benefits) above what the market determines to be their actual productivity in the economy. This union-created premium above the free market wage accrues to the benefit only of members of the favored group. However, to preserve their rent from erosion through the ever present forces of competition in the market, the unionized workers also have to deploy their enhanced bargaining power to establish a variety of constraints within the firm. The overall compensation package must be broken down into a large number of wage rates; each of these rates must be attached to specific job classifications with their own detailed descriptions; and these jobs have to be allocated in accordance with an elaborate set of rules and procedures regulating who will get the assignment, the promotion, the layoff, or the dismissal.

34. This is the argument in Milton Friedman and Rose Friedman, *Free To Choose: A Personal Statement* (New York: Harcourt Brace Jovanovich, 1979), in particular Chapter 7, "Who Protects the Worker?" pp. 218, 235–236.

The entire costly package must also be protected from the substitution of nonunion labor (through restraints on subcontracting or "out-sourcing") or capital (through limits on automation and technological change) when those alternatives appear cheaper by comparison.

As this process plays itself out, it generates a number of harmful consequences for the economy. The efficiency of the unionized firm is reduced, not only because of contract restraints on the flexibility of management, but also because the higher cost of unionized workers eventually leads to a greater than optimal use of technology in place of human labor. This release of a number of workers from the unionized sector leads to crowding of the nonunion labor market, reduction in the wages paid to nonunion workers, and greater substitution of cheaper labor for capital than is ideal for the economy as a whole. The cumulative result of these various forms of misallocation of resources engendered by the union wage premium is a reduction in the efficiency of the economy and a deadweight loss to all who share in its product.

Nor can one take consolation in the thought that such allocative effects are the price of a collective bargaining process that redistributes income from capitalists to workers. Assuming reasonably competitive financial markets, in the longer run the gains for unionized workers must come largely out of the pockets of nonunion workers: either from directly reducing their pay (through the above-mentioned "crowding" effect), or indirectly from the increased prices all workers must pay for higher-cost, union-produced goods and services. When we recall that the source of the price-generated redistribution is a process that had already raised the wages of union members relative to wages of comparable nonunion workers, the consequent increase in consumer prices seems to add distributional insult to allocative injury.

Undeniably, specific groups of workers find collective bargaining to be to their private advantage. But the implication of the foregoing analysis is that it was a fundamental mistake for public policy to encourage the spread of the institution by giving workers a unilateral, legally protected right to have union representation simply because workers believe the benefits to them will outweigh the detriments that are largely borne by others.

Indeed, collective bargaining seems to be an even more damaging intrusion on the labor market than is legal regulation. The logic of this critique of unionization does not imply that one must be entirely wedded to anything that results from the free market. For example, one might well believe that the harms inflicted by hazardous workplaces or arbitrary dismissal procedures are simply too great to warrant relying on the marketplace to contain them: in those cases one would favor the enactment of laws to protect these crucial interests of workers as human beings.[35] The virtue of using the law for this purpose is that it focuses only on the specific problems of concern, and it provides its benefits to every worker who needs them, whether organized or not. Relying on collective bargaining to produce a specific form of protection for workers on the job—protection against unjust dismissal, physical injury, or whatever—ignores the fact that bargaining would not be confined to that aim. Inevitably, union representation will be used (indeed, it probably will be used mainly) to enhance the earnings of specific groups of workers who are favored by such a reconstructed market.

In fact, the apparent source of the growing business resistance to unionization is located in precisely the same unfortunate results of collective bargaining. The sixties through the seventies saw a near doubling of the wage premium enjoyed by unionized employees over similarly qualified but unorganized workers in the same industries and occupations. The existence and prospect of such a wage premium spurred the efforts of nonunion employers to avoid unions by fair means or foul, and of already unionized firms to plan their future investment and expansion so as to reduce their exposure to collective bargaining. From the point of view of the neoclassical critique I just sketched, such vigorous resistance to unionization by American employers in pursuit of their own private interest in lower labor costs should actually be applauded for having served (through Adam Smith's invisible hand, as it were) the public interest of a more competitive labor market. And the inevitable policy implication of this diagnosis is that, far from tightening up NLRB restraints on such employer opposition, we should aim to dismantle our labor laws entirely, and to replace them with the standard antitrust scrutiny now directed at anticompetitive action by firms.

The Permeable Cartel

As I intimated earlier with respect to the defense of employment at will, I consider this view of collective bargaining to be a serious challenge to the conventional wisdom of liberal labor lawyers—those who believe that the only question is how to make our labor laws more

35. Charles Fried espouses this position in "Individual and Collective Rights in Work Relations: Reflections on the Current State of Labor Law and Its Prospects," 51 *University of Chicago Law Review* 1012 (1984). Fried goes on to argue that labor unions and labor law are no longer the social instruments best suited for providing such protection to workers.

effective in practice rather than how to justify their existence in principle. However, I believe that this assessment is flawed in two key respects. First, even within its own market-oriented frame of reference, it draws too stark a contrast between the operation of a labor market founded on employer contracts with individual workers and one based on employer contracts with groups of workers. Second, the market frame of reference is too narrow, because it ignores the crucial independent dimension of how best to structure the governance of a workplace to resolve a variety of problems in the life of workers that are not reducible to the efficient delivery of goods and services to consumers.

I grant the premise that a major role of the union is to pool the bargaining power of an entire unit of employees so as to increase the compensation that the employer would otherwise pay them in an unorganized nonunion setting. But the emergence of collective bargaining by no means transforms the labor market from an idealized state of pure competition into one dominated by powerful union cartels. Neither of these polar conceptions accurately reflects the actual process of wage determination in the union or the nonunion context.

The nonunion labor market itself does not conform to the textbook price/auction model, in which a multitude of employers bid against each other for the services of workers, with market prices being continually adjusted so as to equate supply with demand, and the overall process serving to allocate workers to positions of highest marginal productivity, where they can receive wages commensurate with their economic contribution. The reality experienced by most workers is quite different. Initially they apply for a job in a queue with many other applicants. The potential employer is a corporate firm that has pooled the capital of a large number of investors and installed a management team to run the organization. The management includes a personnel department that establishes the structure of wages, benefits, and conditions to be offered to all the applicants for the jobs. The individual worker has no effective power to negotiate a different compensation package for himself alone. Each individual must either take the job as is or leave it to another applicant in the queue. It is also rare that a firm regularly adjust its wage levels (up or down) to changing flows of applicants for its jobs.

Of course, if the worker "leaves" this job, he can and will look for a position with another employer—probably with a firm organized and run in much the same bureaucratic fashion. The viability of this option will depend on a variety of factors: the nature of the occupation and the number of firms that make use of it; the worker's mobility in the region or beyond it; the amount of information he has about wages, benefits, and other significant features of various jobs and firms; and the tightness or slackness of the general labor market. Employees who search seriously for alternative jobs (as do scholars who investigate this problem) usually find remarkable diversity in the pay and working conditions offered by different firms in the same local market for what appear to be homogeneous levels of worker skill.[36] And it is the personnel department that takes the initiative in setting the wages and establishing the conditions for each individual employer.

I do not mean to overstate this point. Rarely does a firm enjoy a monopsonistic position vis-à-vis workers; in fact, there are only a few specialized skill groups, such as air traffic controllers, for whose services there is only one significant purchaser. The presence of other employers prepared to hire away its current and potential employees places definite market limits on the ability of any one management team to impose comparatively unattractive wages and working conditions on its present work force. But the variety of imperfections in real labor markets place fairly loose constraints on the level and type of compensation that any one firm need offer; and the judgment about where to locate the firm within that market range is actually made by the "visible hand" of corporate management.[37]

In fact, many believe it was the organization of more and more employers into large bureaucratic firms that first led workers to organize themselves into unions that could bargain collectively with such employers.[38] And the image of the union as a monopolistic cartel fits as awkwardly with the reality of what unions do in "selling" labor as does

36. For recent documentation of this phenomenon see William T. Dickens and Lawrence S. Katz, "Inter-Industry Wage Differences and Industry Characteristics," in *Unemployment and the Structure of Labor Markets*, p. 49, Kevin Lang and Jonathan S. Leonard, eds., (New York: B. Blackwell, 1987); and Alan B. Krueger and Lawrence H. Summers, "Efficiency Wages and the Inter-Industry Wage Structure," 56 *Econometrica* 259 (1988). For a review of the patterns and the significance of such pay diversity, which has persisted over time and across national boundaries, see Alan B. Krueger and Lawrence H. Summers, "Reflections on the Inter-Industry Wage Structure," in Lang and Leonard, eds., *Unemployment and the Structure of Labor Markets*, p. 17.

37. Not coincidentally, the classic account of the rise of corporate enterprise in America is titled *The Visible Hand: The Managerial Revolution in American Business*, by Alfred D. Chandler, Jr. (Cambridge, Mass.: Belknap Press, 1977). The book omits almost entirely the evolution of the management of labor, a gap that has been ably filled by Sanford M. Jacoby, *Employing Bureaucracy: Managers, Unions and the Transformation of Work in American Industry, 1900–1945* (New York: Columbia University Press, 1985).

38. See Christopher L. Tomlins, *The State and the Unions: Labor Relations, Law, and the Organized Labor Movement in America, 1880–1960*, pp. 10–20 (New York: Cambridge University Press, 1985)

the image of an impersonal market fit with the reality of what corporations do in purchasing labor.

Labor unions do not function as cohesive organizations which unilaterally set prices that a multiplicity of small unorganized consumers must accept, or else do without their services.[39] Instead, a trade union engages in collective bargaining about wages and working conditions with a corporate employer on the other side of the table, with a management organization that may be larger and is almost certainly more cohesive than the union. An effective union wields the power to deny the employer the services of all its members unless and until management makes an acceptable offer at the bargaining table. The NLRA provides some (rather modest) assistance to the union in this effort by giving the representatives selected by the majority of employees the exclusive authority to negotiate on behalf of the entire unit. This prohibits the employer from dealing directly with individual employees to see whether they would be willing to accept less than the union is insisting on.[40] But in that respect labor law and labor relations basically mirror the operation of corporate law and organization, under which a designated part of the management team develops the compensation policy and bargaining position of the firm. The union is unable to deal directly with individual managers or investors to see whether they would propose more money than has yet been offered at the bargaining table. Under both the common law and the labor statute, the management team is able to deny union members access to all the jobs in its plants unless the union accedes to the firm's position on what it will pay for their services. Looking simply at the relationship between these two parties, then, the reason why one side does not enjoy monopoly power in this situation is because the other side is ready and willing to act as a countervailing force to the exercise of any such power.

If one looks beyond the immediate relationship, it is true that the firm cannot deny its employees access to *any* jobs, but only to its own

39. Some unions, such as the American Federation of Musicians, function in somewhat that way (see David E. Feller, "A General Theory of the Collective Bargaining Agreement," 61 *California Law Review* 663, 724–736 (1973); and Robert A. Gorman, "The Recording Musician and Union Power: A Case Study of the American Federation of Musicians," 37 *Southwestern Law Journal* 697 (1983)); but such unions are very much the exception in contemporary industrial relations.

40. See J. I. Case Co. v. NLRB, 321 U.S. 332 (1944); and Railroad Telegraphers v. Railway Express Agency Ltd., 321 U.S. 342 (1944). In Chapter 6 I shall address further the nature and significance of the authority that the majority's union receives under Section 9(a) of the NLRA.

jobs. If their employer has not made them a generous enough offer, union members are free to look elsewhere for jobs that will better satisfy their expectations. But the employer enjoys an analogous freedom. Although the law requires employers to bargain in good faith with unions to try to arrive at collective agreements, freedom of contract is the legal principle that governs these negotiations.[41] This principle means that the employer is not required to make a wage offer of any particular level of "reasonable" generosity, nor need the employer confine itself to the labor of the union members at their asking price if it wants to operate its plants. If the union does not accept the offer made by the employer, once bargaining reaches an impasse the employer is entitled to implement its position unilaterally. If they do not like the employer's terms (too small a wage increase, say, or even a wage cut), the employees can collectively refuse to work under them (in other words, go on strike); but the employer is then legally entitled to hire other workers to fill the jobs at the pay that the firm was prepared to offer the strikers.[42]

In practice, the legal freedom of the employer to continue operating with strike replacements is severely limited (just as is the union member's legal freedom to find a job elsewhere at better wages than this employer is paying). Indeed, unions have always tried to achieve their goal of insulating wages from the forces of market competition by extending their organization of the work force far beyond the confines of a single plant of one employer. Such a broad reach is important for forcing the employer to agree with the union rather than operate with nonunion labor. But the capacity of even the largest, most powerful national unions to act as a cartel can be highly permeable in practice with respect to a strike in any one unit. Some of the unit members may choose to stay at or go back to work; the firm may utilize people from other parts of its work force (supervisors or transferees from other locations); replacements may be recruited from off the street; the work may be done and the product supplied from other plants in the enterprise. Though the practical feasibility of each of these tactics depends very much on the time and place, all have proved

---

41. See generally Weiler, "Striking a New Balance."

42. Ever since the Supreme Court's decision very early in the life of the NLRA in NLRB v. Mackay Radio and Telegraph Co., 304 U.S. 333 (1938), the employer has been legally entitled to hire even *permanent* replacements for striking employees. It was held recently that even if the *employer* initiates the work stoppage through a lockout, hiring at least *temporary* replacements is legal. See Operating Engineers v. NLRB (Harter Equipment), 829 F.2d 458 (3d Cir. 1987).

viable indeed in the economic and industrial relations environment of the eighties.[43]

Nevertheless, employer operation during a strike is still an occasional rather than a common occurrence in established bargaining units. To that extent, then, unions are usually able to monopolize the supply of labor to the firm and, by the withdrawal of such labor, to inflict economic costs on the firm, from which management can get relief only by improving its wage offer. But by the same token such union action is a two-edged sword. A strike inflicts reciprocal economic costs on the union members, which they can avoid only by having the union representatives moderate their wage demands at the bargaining table. Although individual employees are always free to look for jobs in other firms, it is rare that any significant proportion of a sizable bargaining unit will be able to find temporary jobs elsewhere during a strike of their regular employer. Which side will have to compromise its negotiating position the most will depend on the overall financial resources of each for cushioning the impact of the work stoppage and on the economic soundness of their respective bargaining positions. Typically, though, the bipolar union-management relationship involves a balance of power between the two sides, in which the employer has the incentive and the resources to restrain the effort by the union to extract a significant premium from its control over the supply of labor to the enterprise.

One can think of cases in which a large national union dealing with a small firm has far greater resources in the conflict. The firm's employees go on strike, the firm has no other supply of labor and thus must shut down its operations, the reduction in revenue is not matched by a reduction in fixed costs, and the firm is placed under severe financial pressure to settle the strike. Meanwhile the union is able to pay generous strike benefits to a relatively small unit of strikers, and, indeed, may be able to place many of its members in jobs elsewhere, through its hiring hall or other contacts. These would seem to be circumstances in which the union's monopoly power could secure it a very favorable contract settlement.

43. See Charles R. Perry, Andrew M. Kramer, and Thomas J. Schneider, *Operating During Strikes: Company Experience, NLRB Policies, and Governmental Regulations* (Philadelphia: Industrial Research Unit, Wharton School, University of Pennsylvania, 1982). Unquestionably, a union's leadership wields far *less* control over current or prospective employees deciding whether or not to work in a struck plant than does management over the shareholders in the firm's decision on whether to accede to the union's demands or to face up to a strike (as well as whether or not to operate during the strike).

Interestingly, even this apparently impressive degree of union leverage will be contained by external economic forces. The employer's demand for labor and its effective ability to pay for labor is derived from the consumer demand for the goods and services that the labor will produce. Even if a particular employer seems unable to match directly the economic resources of the union, the union's ability to translate the employer's disadvantage into a premium wage is indirectly constrained by the freedom of consumers to decline to pay for the firm's products a price inflated by excessive contract settlements. Consumers have this freedom because they can buy from nonunion firms, from firms represented by the same union but that have greater resources with which to resist the union's wage demands, or from firms represented by other unions (perhaps in other countries producing the same product or in other industries producing substitute products). The consequence is that even though the union in our example may be able to use its bargaining power to achieve very high wage rates for all the work done by its members for the firm, it will soon find that very little work is actually being done at the premium rates.

A final argument is that although a union might not be able directly to control consumers in their product choices, it can do so indirectly by organizing all the firms that can satisfy a particular consumer demand. To my mind, this is the only serious cartel problem presented by collective bargaining.[44] Organization of the entire product market is especially serious because it can sharply reduce the incentive to resist rich wage demands, even for large employers that have the economic resources to do so. If all the employers in a product market have confidence that a union which represents both them and their competitors will secure a common wage settlement—through either coalition bargaining with an employers' association (like the Teamsters with the trucking firms) or pattern bargaining (like the UAW with the auto manufacturers)—there is no reason for any one of these firms to absorb the immediate financial costs of taking a strike in pursuit of reasonable long-term settlements. Its higher wages can simply be passed on to consumers as a uniform ingredient of the product price—and this economic rent in the wage rate will, in turn, produce the undesirable allocative and distributional consequences sketched earlier.

Although such a scenario is a real possibility, one should not overestimate either its probability or its magnitude, especially as an endur-

44. See the analyses by Lewis, "The Labor Monopoly Problem," by Lande and Zerbe, "Reducing Unions' Monopoly Power," and by Campbell, "Labor Law and Economics."

ing phenomenon. New market entrants regularly appear on the scene to supply consumers with a particular product or an acceptable substitute at a price they are prepared to pay. As noted earlier, such new firms start out nonunion, and it usually takes considerable time and effort for a union to organize the employees and secure a collective agreement from the firm so as to bring the wages up to the industrial scale. If the firm is located outside the region, the industry, or even the country, or if it is prepared to fight to remain union-free, such organization may never take place.[45] If a high union premium has been built into the wage scale and the product price, there is a much stronger incentive for entrepreneurs to enter this market, to undercut the incumbents who are locked into union contracts, and to pocket for themselves the rents that the union secured for its own members in the industry wage scale. The experience of this unstable quality of the supposed monopoly union wage provides a substantial incentive for astute unionized firms to expend some of their resources in resisting rich union contracts that might come back to haunt them later on. All in all, this variety of competitive market restraints on the collective bargaining process accounts for the comparatively modest wage premium that unions have been able to secure for their members.[46]

Having discounted the more inflated generalizations about unions' supposed monopoly power, it would be naive to downplay the high level of market power that a few unions have been able to deploy at various times and places. As good an example as any is the airline pilots' union in the seventies. This was a relatively small occupational group in the industry; the employees in question were highly skilled, indispensable for the operation of the airline, and not easily replaceable in a strike; they were members of a union that had organized almost the entire industry; and the union negotiated with employers that were not easily

45. Thus the construction industry, which rightly or wrongly is considered by many to be a stronghold for monopolistic and inefficient unionism, has witnessed a sharp increase in nonunion open-shop construction over the last two decades (see Clinton C. Bourdon and Raymond E. Levitt, *Union and Open-Shop Construction: Compensation, Work Practices, and Labor Markets* (Lexington, Mass.: Lexington Books, 1980)). The building trade unions have been able to do very little about this development, given the particularly unfavorable way that the NLRA representation model deals with attempts to organize workers in this distinctive industry with its unusual employment structure. See Jan Stiglitz, "Union Representation in Construction: Who Makes the Choice?" 18 *San Diego Law Review* 583 (1981).

46. A recent careful survey of the empirical literature, which took account of the multitude of other factors that influence pay determination, concluded that the average compensation differential specifically attributable to unionism was somewhere in the range of 10 to 15 percent; see Barry T. Hirsch and John T. Addison, *The Economic Analysis of Unions: New Approaches and Evidence* 116–154 (Boston: Allen and Unwin, 1986).

able to cushion themselves against the financial losses in a strike (one cannot, after all, stockpile seats on an airline flight). In that setting the pilots were able to achieve a very high union wage effect, a premium of 50 percent or more above the wage that would have been needed to attract that quality of labor into the industry.

But the true lesson of the pilots' case is much more complicated than the effects of a simple union cartel in the labor market. The airline/pilot industrial relations system was actually dependent on an airline cartel in the product market.[47] This cartel was created by a system of government regulation that allocated routes and fixed fares so as to deny consumers the ability to choose alternative carriers on the basis of price. That meant that union and management negotiators of airline collective agreements were largely insulated from the constraints of consumer reaction to their settlements. When deregulation of the airline industry came into effect at the beginning of the eighties, permitting nonunion carriers (such as People Express) to compete on the basis of their lower pilot compensation and lower fares, this entire *modus vivendi* of airline collective bargaining collapsed like a house of cards. Concession bargaining, two-tier wage schemes, Chapter 11 rejection of collective agreements, and a variety of other reactions to the new marketplace soon dissipated most of the rent built into the wage rates and other benefits in the pilot contracts.[48] Somewhat the same scenario has played itself out in the auto industry in the eighties, as the hitherto geographically insulated domestic auto market has been penetrated by non-UAW (*not* nonunion) manufacturers in Japan, Germany, and elsewhere.[49]

The lesson of the pilots' case is that a union is not and cannot be a cartel that exercises true monopoly power in an otherwise competitive market. Econometric analysis of union wage effects shows that the really sizable wage premiums are located in industries in which there are already significant restraints (legal, geographic, capital, or other) on competition in the product market.[50] In such industries unions

47. See C. Vincent Olson and John M. Trapani III, "Who Has Benefited from Regulation in the Airline Industry?" 24 *Journal of Law and Economics* 75 (1981).

48. For a comprehensive review, see Peter Cappelli, "Airlines," in David B. Lipsky and Clifford B. Donn, eds., *Collective Bargaining in American Industry: Contemporary Perspectives and Future Directions*, p. 135 (Lexington, Mass.: Lexington Books, 1987).

49. See Harry C. Katz, *Shifting Gears: Changing Labor Relations in the U.S. Automobile Industry* (Cambridge, Mass.: MIT Press, 1985); and Harry C. Katz, "Automobiles," in Lipsky and Donn, eds., *Collective Bargaining*, p. 13.

50. See the empirical studies by Thomas Karier, "Unions and Monopoly Profits," 67 *Review of Economics and Statistics* 34 (1985); Michael A. Salinger, "Tobin's *q* Unionization

wrest for their worker members a portion of the rents that the firms are already extracting from consumers for the benefit of their shareholders. In the labor market itself, the effect of collective bargaining is to reduce the dispersion of earnings in the immediate bargaining orbit, as well as to bring the wages and benefits paid to the less educated, blue-collar union worker up closer to those paid the better educated, white-collar nonunion worker.[51] As I noted in the opening chapter, one of the striking features of recent economic trends in our increasingly union-free environment has been a sharp increase in the inequality of earnings and assets in this country.[52] Of course, whether or not one believes that it is good to have thus weakened the power of workers who have traditionally been (or wanted to be) union members in order to maintain or improve their share of the economic pie vis-à-vis the owners of greater financial and human capital depends on one's underlying views about the virtues and vices of distributional equality.

But one must also recognize that the distributional effects of union representation, though substantial, are not dramatic. The broader market economy, national and international, places real limits on the leverage that workers can gain from unionization, whether or not their initial organization is protected and encouraged by effective labor laws. I have always believed that in analyzing policy problems one should be wary of sweeping analytical generalizations, whether they are drawn from economic or philosophical theory. But with respect to the intellectual position concerning the premises and goals of our national labor law policy, namely that the NLRA fosters strong union cartels that extract substantial economic rents at the price of a malfunctioning economy, the generalization that is closest to the truth is that a law which permits unions will not produce these consequences in an otherwise competitive industry, and a law which prohibits unions will not prevent those consequences in an otherwise oligopolistic industry.

---

and the Concentration-Profits Relationship," 15 *Rand Journal of Economics* 159 (1984); and Richard B. Freeman, "Unionism, Price-Cost Margins and the Return to Capital" (NBER Working Paper, 1983). For different views about the policy implications of this tendency, compare Freeman and Medoff, *What Do Unions Do?* pp. 184–190, and Hirsch and Addison, *The Economic Analysis of Unions*, pp. 208–215.

51. See Freeman and Medoff, *What Do Unions Do?*—in particular Chapter 5, "Labor's Elite: The Effect of Unionism on Wage Inequality," pp. 78 and 90–93.

52. See Frank Levy, *Dollars and Dreams: The Changing American Income Distribution* 75–78 (New York: Russell Sage Foundation, 1987); and Harrison and Bluestone, *The Great U-Turn*, pp. 117–128.

4 · The Sources and Instruments of Workplace Governance

Why Labor and Its Market Are Singular

People and Machines

The previous chapter's discussion of collective bargaining assumed the basic validity of the market paradigm, but argued that unionization does not involve a particularly harmful form of cartel. The reason is that the actual level of competition in real world markets is already reduced by the presence of large corporations that pool the capital of a large number of shareholders and wield substantial, though by no means unlimited, power in the market, both as employers purchasing labor from workers and as producers selling goods to consumers. Thus to give workers an analogous legal facility with which to pool and sell their services does not (or so I have argued) add significantly more imperfection to the overall workings of our economy.

The foregoing argument, however, is open to an immediate rejoinder. There is good reason to believe that the accumulation of capital and other resources in corporate firms enhances long-term technological and organizational productivity, and that these gains from the corporation outweigh whatever short-term inefficiencies stem from greater concentration and lessened competition in a corporate economy.[1] But if one assumes (as I do) that unionization hampers the

---

1. See Alfred D. Chandler, Jr., *The Visible Hand: The Managerial Revolution in American Business* (Cambridge, Mass.: Harvard University Press, 1977); and Oliver E. Williamson, *The Economic Institutions of Capitalism: Firms, Markets, Relational Contacting* (New York: Free Press, 1985) for historical and analytical accounts of how the integration of economic functions in modern corporate organizations enhances productivity and reduces transaction costs, thus dominating any losses in allocative efficiency from the displacement of market transactions for these activities.

efficient operation of the labor market, at least to some extent and in some settings, the institution must contribute something of significance in order to justify the encouragement that the law now gives to union organization (and, even more, to justify the greater protection that a reformed labor law might provide against increasing employer resistance).

As a prelude to the positive case I will make for collective bargaining, I shall restate the basic argument against it, but in a more concrete and vivid fashion. The argument, we recall, is that labor should be treated like any other commodity, freely exchanged in competitive markets and regulated as little as possible by either the law or collective bargaining.[2] Labor has traditionally been supplied by human beings. More recently, though, we have developed the technical capacity to supply a substitute form of labor—robots. Robots are often preferred over humans because they are less prone to error, they are not endangered by exposure to toxic substances, and they are simply cheaper. Suppose, then that all the producers and owners of robots banded together into an organization to monopolize the supply of robotic services. The aim of this robot cartel would be to raise the price that the members could charge auto manufacturers and other industrial users for the rental or outright sale of their robots. Such an organization and its action would constitute a clear-cut violation of antitrust law, a restraint on the competitive robot market. Such a restraint on trade could not be justified because General Motors, for example, is itself a huge corporation with major resources and advantages in dealing with its suppliers and dealers. Why, then, does the law permit the UAW to monopolize the sale of the services of its members to GM? What benefits are derived from the organization of workers which could justify whatever imperfections unionization introduces into the labor market?

It is not enough to say that a robot is a machine whereas a worker is a human being. At issue here is precisely the difference, if any, this should make (and of course the owners of robots are also human beings, e.g., as shareholders of the firms that make and sell them). One can point to certain obvious differences between a machine and a human which might seem to justify some difference in their legal treatment. For example, if a robot is severely damaged it can be discarded

2. See the pieces cited in notes 30–32 in Chapter 3. See also Daniel R. Fischel, "Labor Markets and Labor Law Compared with Capital Markets and Corporate Law," 51 *University of Chicago Law Review* 1061 (1984), for some interesting parallels between labor and capital as factors of production in a market economy.

with concern only for the financial loss, which is surely not the case when a worker is injured on the job. But while the proponent of the market as a general matter could concede that legislation might be justified to deal with such distinctively human and especially pressing concerns,[3] the basic claim is that a free contract arrived at in a competitive market is presumptively the best way to structure the sale of a worker's services to his employer. After all, that is how we expect human beings in their capacity as consumers to deal with General Motors, relying on the presence of competitors such as Ford or Toyota to ensure that the lone individual is not exploited by the large GM organization.[4] So also, then, should human beings deal with GM in their capacity as workers, relying on the same freedom to choose among competitor employers to protect workers from unfair treatment and undesirable conditions.[5]

A major premise of this book is that there are fundamental differences between the market for the labor of a human being and markets for other commodities, including the labor of a robot; these differences are (and should be) manifested throughout the entire employment relationship, not only with respect to exceptional concerns such as workplace safety. As good a way as any to appreciate the nature and significance of such differences is to reflect briefly on some peculiar features of contemporary employment, features that are widespread in the real world but anomalous in neoclassical economic theory.[6]

3. See Charles Fried, "Individual and Collective Rights in Work Relations: Reflections on the Current State of Labor Law and Its Prospects," 51 *University of Chicago Law Review* 1012 (1984).

4. See Alan Schwartz and Louis L. Wilde, "Imperfect Information in Markets for Contract Terms: The Examples of Warranties and Security Interests," 69 *Virginia Law Review* 1387, 1402–20 (1983), explaining how comparison shopping by only a limited number of consumers drives a market with numerous sellers toward lower prices and higher quality for the majority of the customers.

5. The classic piece by Armen A. Alchian and Harold Demsetz, "Production, Information Costs, and Economic Organization," 62 *American Economic Review* 777 (1972), begins by emphasizing how fundamentally parallel are the contractual, nonauthoritarian relationships between the grocer and his customers on the one hand, and the grocer and his employees on the other; both the customer and the employee are equally free to leave for another shop if they do not like how they are being treated here.

6. These features of the world of work were documented initially through detailed field research by the original specialists in labor economics in the United States, such as John Dunlop of Harvard and Clark Kerr of Berkeley. These scholars set out in the forties and fifties to test how realistic were the standard assumptions and implications of economic analysis as applied to the labor market by such general theorists as Sir John Hicks (in his *The Theory of Wages* (London: MacMillan, 1932)). Through meticulous observation, Dunlop and his confrères demonstrated that the world of work was quite different from

Rigidity of Wages. Perhaps the most widely noted such phenomenon is that when the general demand for labor drops in the economy, the wages and benefits paid to workers usually do not drop; indeed, nominal compensation typically continues to rise. It is true that when severe drops occur in the demand and consequently in the price for particular product lines, special (and usually traumatic) wage concessions may be negotiated in the affected industries (say, in steel or airlines), so that the firms' costs of production can be brought into line with their shrunken revenues. But a general decline in economic activity coupled with a substantial increase in unemployment in the overall labor market is rarely used by employers as a reason to reduce wages to a level which would be sufficient to attract and keep workers who are in surplus supply. Instead, the standard way in which firms adjust to a reduction in consumer demand is to lay off workers and reduce production rather than cut employee wages in order to reduce consumer prices and thereby maintain sales and production. This downward "stickiness" of wages has emerged as the central problem for contemporary macroeconomic policy, since it is the source of persistent stagflation—a combination of rising prices and substantial unemployment which was especially virulent throughout the seventies.[7] It is this combination which leads policymakers deliberately to induce severe recessions, as they did in the early eighties, to try to wring wage and thence price inflation out of the economy; even such drastic measures have met with only partial suc-

---

other market settings, that the differences occurred as frequently in nonunion as in union environments, and that collective bargaining was as likely to worsen the efficiency of real-world labor markets. But in the sixties and seventies the center of gravity in labor economics scholarship shifted toward the University of Chicago, with its economists' preference for a pure competitive model of any market setting and their historic distrust of supposed labor union monopolies. It was natural, then, that the Chicago intellectual persuasion would heavily influence the first attempts by legal scholars in the early eighties to interpret and evaluate labor and employment law from an economic point of view. Ironically, in the same decade as this economic approach to the law at work was getting seriously underway, a group of younger, empirically oriented labor economists applied the new tools of econometric analysis to population-wide survey data sets to corroborate most of the judgments made by Dunlop and their other intellectual forbears. Bruce E. Kaufman, ed., *How Labor Markets Work: Reflections on Theory and Practice* (Lexington, Mass.: Lexington Books, 1988), presents a revealing account of these swings of the pendulum in labor economics, as well as a detailed review of the correspondence between the research findings of the 1940s and the 1980s. In the text I shall refer to just a few of the highlights of this research and its implications for how we interpret the realities of the world of work with which labor and employment law must operate.

7. See generally Arthur M. Okun, *Price and Quantities: A Macroeconomic Analysis* (Washington, D.C.: Brookings Institution, 1981); compare with John T. Dunlop, "The Task of Contemporary Wage Theory," in George W. Taylor and Frank C. Pierson, eds., *New Concepts in Wage Determination*, p. 117 (New York: McGraw Hill, 1957).

cess. Whatever may be the source or the cure of such inflexibility in wage levels,[8] what is significant here is the sharp contrast between the labor market and the market for nonhuman commodities. A slump that hits the economy will have a downward impact on the price paid by firms such as General Motors to almost all its suppliers (including vendors of robots), who will themselves have a surplus of product to sell, and to whom GM will feel no obligation to continue paying pre-slump prices or maintain the suppliers' income. Although it is not unique, the labor market is very much a special case in this respect.

Distribution of Wages. Not only are rates of pay not particularly influenced by changes in short-term demand for labor, but they are not strongly correlated with the long-term productivity of the individual worker. Within the firm, the distribution of wages among employees is far more compressed than is the range of differences in their relative productivity, even where such differences can be individually metered.[9] The larger, more sophisticated firms use job evaluation programs that establish rates of pay for the job, not for the individual; and as we saw earlier, progress along that salary scale is based more on length of service than on apparent "merit."[10] Though the outside market becomes relevant when the firm must decide where to peg its internal wage structure in the community pay spectrum, surveys conducted of local wage patterns find that there is still a wide disparity in wages paid by different firms for the same type and quality of work. Even more curious, there is a systematic tilt in this pay range under which the larger, more capital-intensive, more profitable firms pay considerably higher wages (and benefits) for the same workers than do their smaller counterparts.[11] The

8. Charles L. Schultze, "Microeconomic Efficiency and Nominal Wage Stickiness," 75 *American Economic Review* 1 (1985), provides a useful review and analysis of several explanations for this phenomenon. An intriguing prescription for the problem is offered in Martin L. Weitzman, *The Share Economy: Conquering Stagflation* (Cambridge, Mass.: Harvard University Press, 1984), proposing the extensive use by firms of revenue or profit sharing with their employees in place of a substantial portion of the present fixed wage scale.

9. For reports of detailed research documenting this phenomenon in different contexts, see George A. Akerlof, "Labor Contracts as Partial Gift Exchange," 97 *Quarterly Journal of Economics* 543 (1982); and Robert H. Frank, "Are Workers Paid Their Marginal Products?" 74 *American Economic Review* 549 (1984); see also Robert H. Frank, *Choosing the Right Pond: Human Behavior and the Quest for Status*, pp. 58–98 (New York: Oxford University Press, 1985).

10. See James L. Medoff and Katharine G. Abraham, "Are Those Paid More Really More Productive? The Case of Experience," 16 *Journal of Human Resources* 186 (1981).

11. See Richard A. Lester, "Wage Diversity and Its Theoretical Implications," 28 *Review of Economics and Statistics* 152 (1946); compare with Alan B. Krueger and Lawrence H. Summers, "Reflections on the Inter-Industry Wage Structure," in Kevin Lang and

implication, then, is that employees as a group are allowed to share in the overall economic success of their employers even if their individual performance is no better than that of workers in less successful firms; and these wages are distributed in a relatively egalitarian manner within this group of employees, rather than related strongly to individual productive merit. The other side of the coin is that large powerful firms like General Motors and IBM, which can command a discount on almost everything else they buy (money and raw materials as well as robots), pay a premium when they buy labor from human beings.[12]

Internal Labor Market. The allocation of attractive jobs in the more successful firms is done in accordance with what has been called an internal labor market.[13] The selection of workers to be promoted, for

---

Jonathan S. Leonard, eds., *Unemployment and the Structure of Labor Markets*, p. 17 (New York: B. Blackwell, 1987). Inter-firm and inter-industry wage distribution is also important in quite a different context. It turns out that men are much more likely to be employed by higher-paying employers than are women; see Francine D. Blau, *Equal Pay in the Office* (Lexington, Mass.: Lexington Books, 1977). This tendency explains a larger percentage of the current gender gap in pay than does the fact that women are more likely than men to occupy lower-paying jobs in the same firm (see George H. Johnson and Gary Solon, "Estimates of the Direct Effects of Comparable Worth Policy," 76 *American Economic Review* 1117 (1986)), and in turn imposes severe limits on the obtainable benefits even if it were possible successfully to implement a program of comparable worth revaluation of sex-segregated occupations. See Paul C. Weiler, "The Wages of Sex: The Uses and Limits of Comparable Worth," 97 *Harvard Law Review* 1728, 1789–93 (1986).

12. I emphasize the point that these firms pay higher wages even for workers of the same individual ability. The reaction to an earlier draft of this book from several readers of the law and economics persuasion was that this claim is not and cannot really be true. Since a company such as IBM actually hires workers of higher quality, argue these readers, it is the quality advantage that justifies paying the additional wage premium; after all, isn't that exactly what one would expect from employers in an economy in which the aggregate compensation for labor is roughly four times that for capital (so that a wage premium of only 10 percent would cut into potential profits by at least 40 percent)? But whatever the explanation for why larger, more profitable companies find it efficient to pay higher wages for the same worker quality (a subject on which I will comment later), I insist on the accuracy of the empirical claim in the text. Although a considerable portion of the significantly higher wages and benefits paid by firms like IBM and GM does purchase for them a better qualified and more productive employee, econometric analysis of the relative magnitudes of the wage and labor quality gaps shows that a substantial part of the wage premium is not explained by higher quality. This has been demonstrated not simply by cross-sectional comparisons of the measured human capital embodied in workers from different firms, but also by longitudinal analyses which track the wage increases and decreases experienced by individual workers as they enter and leave the higher-wage firms. Thus a company like IBM systematically offers workers a significantly higher compensation package than the same workers were able to obtain either before *or after* their employment at that firm.

13. For an extended treatment of this concept and its operation, see Peter B. Doeringer and Michael J. Piore, *International Labor Markets and Manpower Analysis*, 2nd ed. (Armonk, N.Y.: M. E. Sharpe, 1985). A key early piece in the development of this notion was Clark

example, is made by posting the job vacancy to solicit applications from current employees, then picking one of the internal contenders to fill the position. Only if no suitable candidate can be found inside the firm will the search be broadened to look at outside applicants. To the extent promotion is based on relative ability, it can serve as a substitute for merit pay in that it motivates workers to do better in their present job in order to improve their chances in the competition for better positions. Most firms rely not simply on incumbency, but also to a considerable extent on seniority as a criterion for promotion decisions (seniority counts very heavily for layoffs), thus reducing the level of competition even among workers in the firm.[14] Whatever may be the range and mix of administration and market inside the work force, incumbent employees in these firms are almost entirely insulated from the outside market in the allocation of jobs: they need not worry greatly about an outsider's persuading the company that he will do better in filling a vacancy, and they need worry hardly at all about an outsider's offering to do the work more cheaply in the case of a surplus of employees in a recession. Again, this pattern is almost totally limited to the purchase and sale of human labor, by contrast with the market for almost any other commodity.

Career Employment. These standard features of contemporary employment are closely connected to the phenomenon I described earlier: the long-term career relationship of the worker to the firm. Indeed that kind of relationship is likely to be induced and reinforced by this pattern of administration of job opportunities, wages, and benefits. The implication I drew from the earlier discussion was than an individual's present job becomes more and more valuable to him as he commits more and more of his working life to it while working his way up the internal labor ladder; and that this presents a compelling case for some

---

Kerr's "The Balkanization of Labor Markets," in *Labor Mobility and Economic Opportunity,* p. 92 (New York: Technology Press of M.I.T. and John Wiley and Sons, 1954). Paul Osterman, *Employment Futures: Reorganization, Dislocation and Public Policy* (New York: Oxford University Press, 1988), in particular Chapter 4 on "The Reorganization of Work Within Firms" (pp. 60–91), analyzes more recent trends in the industrial and the salaried models of the internal labor market, to which I alluded in Chapter 2 and to which I shall return in Chapter 5.

14. See Fred F. Foulkes, *Personnel Policies in Large Nonunion Companies* (Englewood Cliffs, N.J.: Prentice-Hall, 1980), in particular Chapter 7, "Promotion Systems," pp. 123–145; and James L. Medoff and Katharine G. Abraham, "Length of Service and Layoffs Within Union and Nonunion Work Groups," 37 *Industrial and Labor Relations Review* 87 (1984). Compare Richard A. Lester, *Hiring Practices and Labor Competition* (Princeton, N.J.: Princeton University Press, 1954).

kind of protection against arbitrary dismissal from the firm and expulsion into the outside market. The crucial point is that the pattern of workers committing themselves to jobs and becoming locked into relationships that can last for decades reduces and inhibits the play of market forces that function most effectively in settings where there is flexibility and mobility in the competition for services.

A number of general comments can be made about these features of the world of work. First, I do not suggest that they are inevitable and universal. Indeed, as we shall see, this employment pattern is of relatively recent vintage.[15] There are many contemporary examples of occupations marked by more casual relationships and more influenced by standard market forces; jobs that range in quality from the migrant farm laborer to the entertainment personality in theater, television, sports, and so on. But the majority of jobs filled by people who are committed to stay in the labor force take the form of this structured career arrangement: in such jobs internal administrative regulation has much more influence than does conventional supply and demand from the external market.[16]

Nor can we bracket these observations from our analysis by assuming these practices to be the hallmark primarily of unionized or union-like public employers—organizations that are supposedly less productive than they might be because they are not required by the market to be efficient in their use of labor. It is fair to say that the origins and impetus of this kind of employment structure are to be found in collective bargaining,[17] and that they continue to remain more pronounced in the union sector.[18] However, administration of employment along the lines I have sketched is also a visible and regular characteristic of nonunion firms; and, even more significantly, of the more

15. See Sanford M. Jacoby, *Employing Bureaucracy: Managers, Unions, and the Transformation of Work in American Industry, 1900–1945* (New York: Columbia University Press, 1985), for an account of the struggle in the first half of this century between the market and the bureaucratic models for treating employment inside the firm.

16. I should reiterate the point made in Chapter 2 that research has documented a variety of specific shapes that administered career employment may take, some systems being more prevalent in blue-collar than white-collar employment or in manufacturing rather than service industries. See Osterman, *Employment Futures*. Again, this phenomenon was a commonplace to the progenitors of American labor economics.

17. See Jacoby, *Employing Bureaucracy*; and Sumner H. Slichter, James J. Healy, and E. Robert Livernash, *The Impact of Collective Bargaining on Management* (Washington, D.C.: Brookings Institution, 1960).

18. See generally Richard B. Freeman and James L. Medoff, *What Do Unions Do?* (New York: Basic Books, 1984); and Slichter et al., *The Impact of Collective Bargaining*.

successful, more profitable nonunion firms that other employers try to learn from and to emulate.[19] In other words, employers like IBM, General Motors, and the federal government behave very differently in their purchase of labor than in their purchases of other commodities in the marketplace.

Why Treat Human Labor Differently?

The next question is, what is the explanation for the remarkable differences in the market treatment of humans and of robots? In that explanation may be found inspiration and justification for public policies that would alter even more dramatically the market for labor, whether such policies take the form of reconstruction of the labor market through collective bargaining or replacing the market with legal regulation.

It is not difficult to understand why an internal labor market (actually internal labor *administration*) is attractive to the worker who is party to an employment contract. Workers naturally prefer to live in an environment where they have reasonable assurances about what their competition will be, an expectation of advancement in the firm in times of prosperity, and confidence that they will retain their job (or at least be recalled to it) in times of adversity. Employees will find these kinds of assurances and expectations to be far more reliable if judgments about work and pay are insulated from the forces of direct competition with other workers and the sudden shocks to which market competition is prone.

There are two additional reasons most workers prefer such administrative regulation. First, in the modern world a job is the major foundation for the economic welfare of individuals and families; not merely the source of immediate take-home pay, but also of much of the network of insurance protection against illness, disability, aging, and so on. But unlike the owners of almost any other income-producing assets (owners of robots, for example), the worker cannot separate himself from his labor: he cannot diversify his risk by doing business with a variety of customers, some of whom may treat him poorly but most of whom will not. Since at any given time a worker must place all his eggs in one basket, as it were, having a sense of security about what will

19. See generally Foulkes, *Personnel Policies*; and Michael Beer, Bert Spector, Paul R. Lawrence, D. Quinn Mills, and Richard E. Walton, *Managing Human Assets* (New York: Free Press, 1984); and Thomas A. Kochan, Harry C. Katz, and Robert B. McKersie, *The Transformation of American Industrial Relations* (New York: Basic Books, 1986).

happen in his current job is far more important than in virtually any other market setting. And for the reasons I gave earlier, it is terribly difficult for workers to spread the risk over time by moving to a comparable new job from one that has proved unstable or unpleasant.

Abstracting from the serious financial costs created by the loss of a job and its perquisites, there are important personal values implicated in the treatment of people at work. Work is not merely an economic function whereby people produce goods and services that are useful to and will be bought by others (although certainly this market exchange dimension is very important). For the employee work is also a major source of personal identity and satisfaction, of his sense of self-esteem and accomplishment, and of many of his closest and most enduring relationships. But at the heart of the employment contract is an undertaking by the worker to subject his person to the authority and direction of the employer (again, in marked contrast to the undertaking made by the owner of the robot). The exercise of such managerial authority is closer, more regular, and often more salient to the worker than is the exercise of government authority. For many of the same reasons we as citizens feel entitled to fair treatment at the hands of government officials, we also feel entitled to comparable consideration from management officials.[20] And as their initial quest for decent compensation and protection on the job is gradually satisfied, workers feel and assert a further claim to meaningful involvement in and influence over the process by which is fashioned the web of workplace rules, with their often fateful human consequences for the employees' lives, both on and off the job.

This is not to imply that even the fairest of treatment by the most responsive of employers guarantees the protection of employees against all adverse happenings at work. Just as governments cannot avert many natural or socioeconomic disasters, so also firms encounter shifts in their external product and capital markets that make them unable to satisfy their workers' expectations of stable employment and rising wages. Few employers guarantee and few employees expect lifetime employment, come what may.[21] But when one considers, instead, the employer's decision to dismiss a particular individual for

20. Thus as new substantive and procedural standards are established for the government's treatment of citizens, standards for such activities as the use of lie detectors or drugs tests, the same claims will naturally be asserted against private employers.

21. Even firms which have traditionally held out this expectation to their salaried employees are finding that living up to such a commitment has become very difficult on account of recent changes in product, capital, and labor markets. See Osterman, *Employment Futures*, pp. 77–81.

disciplinary reasons—with the stigma being fired inflicts and the sense of resentment if there was no cause—or, conversely, the decision to favor someone in the award of a raise or a promotion, it is not hard to fathom why workers want their employers to respect, in some fashion or other, the values of personal integrity, equality, and due process that are imposed on government.

This brief sketch of the reasons employees normally prefer administrative regulation to market competition simply repeats what should be evident from our own personal experience. Less obvious, though, is why that facet of the employment relationship should be acceptable to so many employers. Why is self-regulation of management's authority over the work force adopted voluntarily by so many firms, without any significant present-day pressure from either the law or union organization?

Employers did not always perceive that this policy would be to their advantage. Acceptance of the career-type employment relationship dates back no earlier than World War II, and more than half a century of struggle was required to bring it about. The initial organization of factory work in the late nineteenth century was very much in accordance with the market paradigm—the "drive system" as it was called.[22] In this system, the foreman in charge of a division of the firm's operation recruited the employees he needed from a nomadic population of available workers. The overall wage level went up or down according to conditions in the labor market, and individual workers were paid in accordance with their productivity, measured on a piecework basis or simply assessed by the foreman. If the work load in the factory slackened, the redundant employees were let go with no expectation of a future preference in rehiring based on their previous service; neither was there any regular practice of preferring incumbent workers for promotion into whatever more skilled and attractive jobs happened to open up. In that setting, there was no basis for the employer's devising benefit packages to protect employees against misfortunes that might occur at some time in the future. Indeed, if workers became less productive because of disability or age, they would simply be replaced by younger, more able-bodied workers, who were better able to meet the

---

22. There is a wonderful description in Jacoby, *Employing Bureaucracy*, 16–23, of the drive system which predominated for factory labor before 1915 in the heyday of pure at-will employment, a system which eerily foreshadows the conception of employment celebrated by Richard A. Epstein in his "In Defense of the Contract at Will," 51 *University of Chicago Law Review* 947 (1984).

rigors of factory life. From a socioeconomic perspective, the employment relationship (particularly in manual work, which comprised the majority of jobs at the time) was truly casual and episodic; thus the law's adoption of a strong presumption of an at-will contract was very much in accordance with workplace life.[23]

The interesting question, then, is why has this model almost entirely disappeared from the life, if not the law, of the factory and office, to be replaced by the system of internal administration I just described? One possibility is that employers wanted the benefit of bureaucratic rule, through which senior management could control the exercise of power by people lower down in the hierarchy, and thereby reduce the risk of arbitrariness, favoritism, and simple erratic behavior by their foremen.[24]

While this preference for rules over discretion likely has something to do with the transformation of work, it will not nearly serve as a full explanation. First, supervisory discretion was the price of the firm's having the flexibility to respond to changing market cues: sacrificing it could cost the employer more than regulation would gain. In other words, while one can readily see that the drive system exposed individual employees to considerable risk of arbitrary and discriminatory action, that will not explain why employers would dispense with an arrangement in which they could and did hold the foreman to account for the bottom-line labor productivity and costs produced by whatever style he used in managing his work force.

Second, even a system of bureaucratic rules that proved to have net advantages over market discretion would not explain the *content* of the rules I described, such as the egalitarian tilt to the wage structure or the tendency to reward service more than performance in bestowing jobs and benefits. It is easy to understand why the average employee would be interested in equality and seniority; but what about the employer who, one presumes, is primarily interested in productivity and profitability? What are the special features and challenges of the labor of a human being as far as the employer is concerned? Why might the more rigid administration of a career employment relationship be ultimately more productive than the more flexible, market-oriented, casual relationship with which modern industrial life began?

Recruitment. One unique feature of human labor is that the worker is

23. See Matthew W. Finkin, "The Bureaucratization of Work: Employment Policies and Contract Law," 1986 *Wisconsin Law Review* 733.

24. David E. Feller makes this argument in "A General Theory of Collective Agreement," 61 *California Law Review* 663, 760–771 (1973).

a peculiarly *free* factor of production in the sense that he can leave his job at will. An employer cannot buy and own a worker as it can a robot; indeed, the employer cannot even negotiate a specifically enforceable contract of employment with him.[25] But when workers leave their jobs, others must be recruited to fill their places. The recruiting process itself imposes significant costs on the firm; not merely on the personnel department, which must do the initial advertising and screening, but also on the operating divisions, which must interview and judge the suitability of candidates. The magnitude of these costs can vary widely, depending on the nature of the job, the skills required, the number of applicants, and so on, but on occasion they can be substantial indeed.[26] It is now not uncommon for employers to contract out the search process to consulting firms that specialize in recruiting and charge a sizable fee for their service. So the firm has an immediate tangible interest in keeping recruitment costs down by reducing the turnover in its present work force and consequently the number of vacant positions it will have to fill. Since it cannot use the law to force a worker to stay on the job, the employer has to design its employment relationship in a way that gives its workers strong incentives to stay. This is an initial explanation, then, for the variety of features of contemporary employment that mark its transition from the casual to the career form, even though the career form might seem to interfere with the operation of simple, short-term market forces.

Training. Only the smaller share of the financial costs of worker turn-

25. I recognize that an employer can draw upon a powerful legal device in its efforts to inhibit workers from deciding to quit their job: judicial enforcement of employee covenants not to engage in post-employment competition with the firm. However, the narrow limits which most courts have placed on the enforceability of such clauses—requiring that the covenant be reasonably limited in geography, duration, and content to the tangible interests of the firm in its customers lists, trade secrets, and the like—make noncompetition covenants effective only with respect to exceptional categories of employees. For interesting recent analyses of this topic see Paul H. Rubin and Peter Shedd, "Human Capital and Covenants Not to Compete," 10 *Journal of Legal Studies* 93 (1981); and Jordan Leibman and Richard Nathan, "The Enforceability of Post-Employment Noncompetition Agreements Formed After At-Will Employment Has Commenced: The 'Afterthought' Agreement," 60 *Southern California Law Review* 1465 (1987).

26. Consider, for example, the expenditures of time and money required to recruit a tenured professor for a university faculty. More generally, Daniel J. B. Mitchell and Larry J. Kimbell, "Labor Market Contracts and Inflation," in Martin Neil Baily, ed., *Workers, Jobs, and Inflation*, p. 216 n. 39 (Washington, D.C.: Brookings Institution, 1982), report that a 1979 survey of Los Angeles employers found that recruitment and initial training costs of replacing employees ranged from over $2,000 for each office worker, to over $3,500 for production workers, to over $10,000 for salary-exempt workers.

over is attributable to the recruiting process. By far the most significant expenditures are those required for training the newly hired worker to perform in the vacant position. Very few jobs have demands which are so rudimentary or necessary skills which are so adequately taught elsewhere that a newcomer can step in and do a satisfactory job immediately. At a minimum, the new employee will have to learn the location and idiosyncrasies of the physical equipment and the routines and expectations of fellow workers. Typically, much of the necessary basic knowledge and skills for the position will have to be learned on the job rather than at school; either because learning by doing is the soundest pedagogical technique for teaching certain skills, or because the relevant aptitudes are peculiar to a particular firm's operations, so that only that firm has the means and the economic incentive to provide such training. In either case, the firm must expend its own money in paying both the new employee to learn the job and fellow employees to teach him. The employer considers it reasonable to make this investment in the enhanced capacities of its workers because it expects to get a return on the investment in better performance and productivity over the years.[27] But the resulting human capital is in fact embodied in and owned by the worker, who, as I noted above, is legally free to move elsewhere whenever he wants, and in doing so to liquidate instantly the capital investment made in him by the firm. This provides an even stronger incentive for the employer to make another investment in designing attractive employment terms that will reduce turnover in its work force.

Motivation. To secure its side of the employment bargain, the firm must do more than simply retain its employees in their jobs: it must also elicit the optimum level of performance while they are there. This objective confronts another specifically human characteristic. Unlike robots, one cannot program workers to produce a desired response on command, day in and day out. Even with a given level of teaching and training, human beings display a remarkable range in potential performance, the full gamut from perfunctory to consummate.[28] Although the labor market gives employers considerable leeway in specifying the level of compensation, working conditions, and other treatment of

27. Pathbreaking analyses of this phenomenon can be found in Gary S. Becker, "Investment in Human Capital: Effects on Earnings," 70 *Journal of Political Economy* 9 (1962); and Walter Y. Oi, "Labor as a Quasi-Fixed Factor," 70 *Journal of Political Economy* 538 (1962).

28. These terms are used in Oliver E. Williamson, *Markets and Hierarchies, Analysis and Antitrust Implications: A Study in the Economics of Internal Organization*, p. 69 (New York: Free Press, 1975).

their employees, the employees retain comparable control over the intensity and quantity of personal effort that they will put forth in exchange for what their employer is offering them. The significance of this dimension is testified to by recent polls, which show that although the vast majority of American workers would like to work up to their potential, only about a quarter of them feel that they are now doing so.[29] Employers, of course, can adjust the benefits they pay to the level of productivity that they expect to receive from their employees (and vice versa). But if our goal is not simply profitable businesses, but also a productive economy that supplies its citizens with more and more "good jobs at good wages," then it is essential to motivate employees to make a strong, willing commitment to the success of the enterprise, rather than simply to do the bare minimum necessary to keep their job.[30] That kind of esprit de corps can be undermined in a number of ways. The work force may get the feeling that individual employees are being treated arbitrarily and unfairly (treatment that is perceived as damaging even if administered to one's fellow workers and friends, not only to oneself).[31] Alternatively, the employees may feel that the business is being run primarily for the short-term goal of raising the rate of return on the shareholders' investment, without a reciprocal management commitment to improve workers' pay and preserve their jobs. Indeed, polls have found that fewer than 10 percent of American workers now believe that if they were to put forth extra effort and thereby enhance the productivity of their operations, it would redound

29. Daniel E. Yankelovich and John Immerwahr, *Putting the Work Ethic to Work* (New York: Public Agenda Foundation, 1983).

30. See Beer et al., *Managing Human Assets.* The phenomenon of reciprocal discretion retained by both parties to the employment relationship is at the heart of the work of Harvey Leibenstein, who has depicted and analyzed the broad variation in what he calls the X-efficiency of firms and economies; see his *Beyond Economic Man: A New Foundation for Microeconomics* (Cambridge, Mass.: Harvard University Press, 1976); and *Inside the Firm: The Inefficiencies of Hierarchy* (Cambridge, Mass.: Harvard University Press, 1987). Leibenstein argues that while the emergence of well-paying jobs for highly motivated employees is certainly a viable possibility, it is by no means inevitable; in fact, this ideal is constantly in danger of being undermined by employer exploitation and employee distrust, especially as work becomes more specialized and organizations become larger and more hierarchical. The unfortunate fact, then is that low-paying jobs for poorly performing employees are an equally viable equilibrium solution to this labor market dilemma. Leibenstein shows that the particular point occupied on the X-efficiency spectrum by a firm, an industry, or a national economy is determined to a considerable extent by the institutional and cultural devices that the firm, industry, or economy has fashioned to respond to this "prisoner's dilemma" lying at the heart of modern employment.

31. This principle is illustrated by the case described in Akerlof, "Labor Contracts."

much to their personal benefit rather than just to their employer's.[32] In such an environment, no wonder so many employees feel no particular reason to make sacrifices and try harder in pursuit of a corporate goal, the achievement of which they may not be around to see, let alone to benefit from. Thus the essence of good personnel practice consists in the communication of a very different message to one's work force in order to enhance its morale and its productivity.[33]

Cooperation. Modern production is much more a social than an individual process. It is hard to imagine many goods and services that are produced and supplied by a single worker.[34] The most efficient enterprise then, is not necessarily the one with the most stable, well-trained, and highly motivated individual workers; it is the one with the most cohesive and cooperative *team* of workers.[35] What a productive team requires are people who complement each other in filling the wide variety of roles in any complex enterprise, with some positions being more attention-getting and rewarding, but with even the journeymen performers being indispensable to the functioning of the whole. Teamwork also requires a willingness on the part of everyone to cooperate with fellow employees in the constantly recurring situations where they interact. A vital example of this is the willingness of veteran employees to transmit the lore of the shop, the equipment, and the position to the newcomer who is being trained on the job.

Again, this sense of cooperation can be threatened by such market-oriented employment practices as attempting to match each worker's

32. Yankelovich and Immerwahr, *Putting the Work Ethic to Work.*

33. This theme receives markedly greater emphasis from Japanese management, which has long adhered to the practice of lifetime employment for a substantial core of the work force, and which distributes wages and benefits in a significantly more egalitarian fashion as between workers and executives (or shareholders). Thus when Japanese workers were asked the same question about the results of extra effort that was posed to American workers, more than 90% of the Japanese responded that they would receive some of the benefits of their extra effort and productivity. Striking evidence of the difference the Japanese style of management can make is to be found in Ramchandran Jaikumar, "Post-Industrial Manufacturing," 64 *Harvard Business Review* 69 (Nov.–Dec. 1986). For recent broader speculations on the long-range dynamic efficiency of the cultural constraints imposed on the operation of the Japanese labor market, see Leibenstein, *Inside the Firm;* Ronald P. Dore, *Taking Japan Seriously: A Confucian Perspective on Leading Economic Issues* (Stanford: Stanford University Press, 1987); and Robert B. Reich, *Tales of a New America* (New York: Times Books, 1987).

34. To take one example, even a newspaper columnist who writes his own unedited column, typing it directly into the computerized typesetting system, is dependent on an elaborate network of people to get the paper printed, delivered, and sold.

35. See generally Thurow, *The Zero-Sum Solution,* in particular Chapter 6, "Constructing an Efficient Team" pp. 135–182.

pay and benefits precisely to his marginal productivity, where the actual contribution of any individual to the group product is very difficult to measure, at least in a way that will be evident to fellow workers;[36] or setting up a competition for scarce jobs, so that the veteran employee knows that if he trains the newcomer too well, the latter will be able to beat him out for promotions or even bump into the veteran's own job in a layoff. The aim of creating a cooperative, complementary team of employees helps explain, then, not simply the development of *rules* which limit supervisory arbitrariness to preserve morale, but also the *content* of such widespread standards as seniority in the allocation of positions, and pay systems that evaluate the job, not the person. While such administrative restraints on the operation of market incentives might seem to sacrifice certain immediate spurs for individual productivity, their broader value consists in the reinforcement they give to the cooperative attitudes needed for a productive work team.[37]

How can we sum up these reflections on employment practices in modern industry, especially in the more successful firms? The secret of a productive operation is not necessarily to be found in direct reliance on market forces—that is, on flexible adjustment to the changing supply and demand for labor, monetary incentives paid to individuals with the greatest marginal productivity, and other implications of the neoclassical economic model (which were manifested in the late-nineteenth-century drive system). Workers present a very different kind of challenge to the firm and the market. Unlike robots, human beings are mobile, educable, motivatable, and collegial. Not only do workers have particular needs and expectations from the supply of their labor, but it is a commodity that their employers must treat in a special way as well.

36. Consequently, although American managers and workers alike endorse the general principle of basing an individual's pay on his performance, managers encounter great difficulty in devising sensible programs which will be acceptable to workers for putting the idea into practice. Part of the problem is that workers are prone to overestimate their own relative performance, typically placing themselves in the 80th percentile. See H. H. Meyer, "The Pay-for-Performance Dilemma," 1975 *Organizational Dynamics* 3, 39. Recent analysis of the problems and pitfalls of "pay for performance" has engendered considerable skepticism about its general value: see Beer et al, *Managing Human Assets*, pp. 139–151.

37. For an illuminating depiction of this philosophy at work at some of the country's most successful law firms, which divide up their partnership pie on the basis of strict seniority in the firm, see Ronald J. Gilson and Robert H. Mnookin, "Sharing Among the Human Capitalists: An Economic Inquiry into the Corporate Law Firm and How Partners Split Profits," 37 *Stanford Law Review* 313 (1985).

This is not to imply that internal labor administration is necessarily more productive and more advantageous to the firm than the old market-oriented drive system. While some evidence points in that direction, the case is still open, especially when one recalls the key feature of this system: that bigger, better firms feel they must pay significantly higher wages and benefits for the same workers.[38] Certainly it was *not* typically the case that management fashioned these features of the employment relationship to insulate workers from direct exposure to the market because management believed it would be more efficient for the firm. What actually happened was that workers originally developed these practices through their unions and eventually, by means of collective bargaining, forced their adoption throughout modern industry. Once that happened, the management of nonunion firms had a strong incentive to emulate voluntarily the pattern set by collective bargaining relationships in order to avoid being organized themselves.

As the threat of unionization recedes, the psychology of the firm is becoming somewhat subtler. A younger, more heterogeneous work force has emerged, one whose collective consciousness has been formed much more by the protest movements of the sixties than by the Great Depression of the thirties. Not only does the new worker find it natural to demand a more satisfying and interesting job, but also it is apparent that many employers treat their employees in a civilized and humane manner and still prosper. Thus any firm that deviates too far

---

38. Some positive evidence on this score can be found in a fascinating case study by Daniel M. G. Raff and Lawrence H. Summers, "Did Henry Ford Pay Efficiency Wages?" 5 *Journal of Labor Economics* S57 (1987). This paper analyzes in depth Henry Ford's famous decision in January 1914 to double the average wages in his auto plant to five dollars a day, a decision which, the authors show, increased worker productivity and consequently Ford's profits. Some of the productivity improvement resulted from a drastic reduction in employee turnover: the higher wages were paid only after six months of service, and turnover in the Ford plants dropped from 400 percent to 25 percent per year. However, most of the productivity gains were attributable to subtler morale factors, bolstered by Ford's explicit announcement that doubling wages was his way of sharing with the workers the large profits generated by his assembly-line operation (thus providing some empirical corroboration of Akerlof's theory, in "Labor Contracts," of the labor contract as a form of reciprocal gift giving, at least in part). The Ford study is only a single case, and one must be wary of deriving overbroad generalizations from it; however, there is further confirmation of its lesson in a broad systematic investigation of what later happened to plant productivity in the auto industry when workers became dissatisfied with their treatment on the job: see J. R. Norsworthy and Craig A. Zabala, "Worker Attitudes, Worker Behavior, and Productivity in the U.S. Automobile Industry, 1959–76," 38 *Industrial and Labor Relations Review* 544 (1985).

from this pattern, that chooses to deny its employees the kind of consideration all its counterparts provide, does so at its own peril. In sum, the employer may receive its side of the employment bargain—a stable, trained, motivated, and cooperative team—only if it treats its work force in accordance with norms of behavior that exhibit respect for the employees as human beings.[39] Whatever the explanation, this conclusion is now commonplace in the teaching of human resource management. It is gradually seeping into labor economics, but it has not yet surfaced in the recent efforts by the law and economics school to tackle labor and employment law.[40] To the extent that one wants the future evolution of labor law policy to be informed and influenced by economic analysis, it is critical that labor economics be founded on careful empirical investigation of how labor markets respond to the peculiar needs and concerns of this distinctively *human* commodity, rather than on an effort to force the employment relationship into the procrustean bed of an economic model that accounts quite well for what happens in only certain markets—in markets for money, natural resources, and other inanimate commodities.

Instruments for Workplace Governance

Government Regulation

My operating premise, then, is that standard market forces do not advance us very far in understanding and predicting the actual shape of the employment relationship. There are far too many issues that must be faced—workers' wages, benefits, guarantees, work assignments, and responsibilities—and the precise solutions will vary markedly from firm to firm, industry to industry, and nation to nation. Because the general trend is more and more toward the career-type employment relationship in which both worker and employer make considerable investments and from which each draws considerable value, the power of external labor market competition is considerably attenuated. Neither party can readily duplicate its current situation with an alternative bidder for the employer's job or the worker's services. The resulting gap between loose market constraints and a de-

---

39. Some revealing empirical evidence for this hypothesis can be found in Daniel Kahneman, Jack L. Knetsch, and Richard H. Thaler, "Fairness as a Constraint on Profit Seeking: Entitlements in the Market," 76 *American Economic Review* 728 (1986).

40. An important exception to this generalization appears in Douglas L. Leslie, "Labor Bargaining Units," 70 *Virginia Law Review* 353 (1984), especially at pp. 364–380.

terminate content to the relationship must be closed by some authoritative decisions made for the enterprise.

Four candidates emerge for the exercise of such discretionary authority. Selection from among them will ultimately turn on whether the authority is ideally lodged inside or outside the firm, and whether it should be exercised unilaterally or bilaterally. If one's preference is for external neutral authority, the natural candidate would be government regulation. If one wants decisions about employment conditions to be made inside the enterprise, the basic options are management or the workers themselves operating through some kind of organized mode of representation. Either of these parties could be empowered to make its judgments unilaterally; however, if one prefers bilateral agreement, the likely technique would be collective bargaining between management and a union representing the employees. In practice one probably would have a blend of some if not all of these devices, with varying degrees of control exercised over different issues. For analytical purposes I shall try to depict the comparative value of each candidate taken on its own.

Let us first consider government regulation, the instrument we explored in detail earlier in connection with unfair dismissal. With respect to that problem and a growing number of other employment concerns, this regulatory option has attracted considerable support across the intellectual spectrum.[41]

External legal control of the workplace has evident virtues. An agency of government—legislative, administrative, or judicial—tackles a particular problem that appears serious and urgent: plant closings and job losses, or the tension between work schedules and parental responsibilities. The public authority canvasses the merits of the problem as a somewhat neutral and detached arbiter which can weigh the interests and priorities of each side. The solution devised is then em-

41. A preference for legal regulation rather than collective bargaining as the instrument for protecting the key interests of the employee is expressed in such divergent writings as Fried, "Individual Collective Rights" (the perspective of classical liberalism); David M. Beatty, "Ideology, Politics and Unionism," in Kenneth P. Swan and Katherine E. Swinton, eds., *Studies in Labour Law*, p. 297 (Toronto: Butterworths, 1985) (the radical liberal view); and Katherine Van Wezel Stone, "The Post-War Paradigm in American Labor Law," 90 *Yale Law Journal* 1509, 1579–80 (1981) (the critical legal studies position). Other scholars from that movement, in particular Karl Klare, are less enamored of the virtues of substituting government regulation for more effective worker participation and influence in workplace decisions; Klare's sentiment is echoed in other writings of the three people cited in this note. In Chapter 5 I shall take up this alternative critique of union representation and collective bargaining.

bodied in a legal entitlement that the affected party can call on the state to implement, rather than having to face the vicissitudes of the marketplace. The expectation is that the disparate economic bargaining power wielded by the employer in the workplace will be corrected by the greater clout wielded by the worker as a voter in the political arena. Especially for those pressing human needs that we are unwilling to entrust to the pure market, the instrument of law—of enforceable individual rights—can be used instead to establish a basic social safety net for all workers.

However, even when the lawmaking process functions as sensibly as it is supposed to—which too often it does not—legal regulation has certain major weaknesses, some of which we glimpsed in our earlier look at the discharge problem.

First, government regulation is inherently limited in scope. Many pressing employee concerns are considered to be beyond the reach of sensible legal intervention, including the obvious issue of what wages and benefits should be paid for the host of different jobs in our vast and decentralized economy. Indeed, for the last decade we have been unable to find the political will even to maintain the real value of a *minimum* wage standard, which directly touches only a tiny handful of low-paying jobs. It is understandable, then, that judges and legislatures have so far shied away from the recent flirtation with a "comparable worth" policy as an attempt to rectify the historic undervaluation and underpayment of so-called women's work.[42] Even proponents of this extension of the antidiscrimination policy have suggested only that individual firms be legally required to establish a more equitable relation between the compensation they pay for such predominantly female jobs as secretary or nurse, as compared to such male-dominated jobs as electrician or accountant. They have not dreamed of tackling what turns out to be a much larger component of the gender earnings gap, the fact that women tend to work in lower-paying industries such as retail sales and financial services, while men make up a much larger share of the work force in such historically well-paying (and unionized) industries as construction or steel.[43]

---

42. See Weiler, "The Wages of Sex"; and Henry J. Aaron and Cameron M. Lougy, *The Comparable Worth Controversy* (Washington, D.C.: Brookings Institution, 1986). For a recent study that focuses on the revaluation of state and local government employees in Minnesota, see Sara M. Evans and Barbara J. Nelson, *Wage Justice: Comparable Worth and the Paradox of Technocratic Reform* (Chicago: University of Chicago Press, 1989).

43. See Weiler, "The Wages of Sex," pp. 1788–93; Aaron and Lougy, *Comparable Worth*, pp. 13–15; also George H. Johnson and Gary Solon, "Estimates of the Direct Effects of Comparable Worth Policy," 76 *American Economic Review* 1117 (1986).

There are, of course, many other workplace problems that the government is prepared to tackle. Lawmakers find, though, that the legal instruments with which they try to alter the flawed outcomes of the labor market are themselves of rather imperfect quality.

So, for example, if one wants to employ fairly precise, easily administered standards like those promulgated under OSHA, these rules can be formulated for only a few generalizable and recurring problems, such as the dangers of lacerations by machine tools or shocks from electrical equipment, not for the host of idiosyncratic contextual events that produce the burgeoning number of back injuries. That is why it is estimated that less than 20 percent of all workplace accidents are of the type governed by OSHA standards,[44] which means in turn that even full compliance by employers with all legal safety requirements set by the government would produce only a modest reduction in employee injuries.[45]

To take another example, the recently enacted and hotly contested Worker Adjustment and Retraining Notification Act (WARNA) requires firms to do no more than give their employees some advance notice before a plant closing or mass layoff. Admittedly employees reap some value from having time to ready themselves for the upcoming loss of their present job and to look for a replacement position if any are to be found. But by the same token, it is clear that a much more valuable protection for workers would be a guaranteed opportunity for retraining and reassignment to a new position, or for meaningful severance benefits as compensation for the loss of time and service invested with the firm. The fact is, however, that Congress finds it far easier to write a term like "60 days" into an across-the-board legal requirement of minimum notice than it does to tackle the complex question of what more tangible response to impending job losses would be both equitable and affordable across our heterogeneous and ever-changing economic landscape.

Of course, this particular regulatory difficulty can be avoided if the government adopts a general standard rather than prescribe specific rules. As we saw earlier in the wrongful dismissal area, it is simply not possible to spell out the metes and bounds of when it is legally permissible to discharge employees, whose positions range from factory worker to construction worker, from professional athlete to university

---

44. See John M. Mendeloff, *Regulating Safety: An Economic and Political Analysis of Occupational Safety and Health Policy* 94–98 (Cambridge, Mass.: MIT Press, 1979).

45. See Ann P. Bartel and Lacy Glenn Thomas, "Direct and Indirect Effect of Regulation: A New Look at OSHA's Impact," 28 *Journal of Law and Economics* 1 (1985).

professor. Instead, we use such vague phrases as "just cause" or "good reason," which enable us to postpone the judgment about the precise dictates of the law until we can appreciate the special needs and factors in particular contexts. So OSHA, for example, contains a "general duty" provision that requires each employer to "furnish . . . his employees employment which [is] free from recognized hazards that are . . . likely to cause death or serious physical harm."[46] Again, this provision gives the government agency the luxury of dealing with the broad spectrum of injuries that can occur, without having to pin itself down to an explicit legal formula that may have unfortunate implications for unanticipated cases.

Unfortunately, the general language that is an advantage for the regulator imposes corresponding burdens on the citizen, employee as well as employer. From the latter's point of view, the absence of clear legal guidelines for what constitutes a good reason for discharge, or for what is a recognized (and preventable) hazard of serious injury, means that the firm will not know for sure whether its action was legally proper until long after it has had to commit itself to a particular course of action. And as we saw in the case at the start of this book, the price of guessing wrong—in that instance, of enforcing a new drug testing program by dismissing employees who refused to cooperate—may well be a huge monetary damage award.

By and large, their appreciation of this employer concern influences the elected branches of government to restrict sharply the firm's risks from guessing wrong. For example, the penalties for initially violating OSHA's general duty clause are quite mild. But courts display little such inhibition. After all, for several decades now judges have successfully imposed more and more common law liability on manufacturers and other enterprises for creating a risk of physical injuries with their products and activities.[47] Present judicial sentiment seems to be that the same ambitious effort should now be made to protect employees from the economic and psychological trauma of an improper discharge.

46. See Richard S. Morey, "The General Duty Clause of the Occupational Safety and Health Act of 1970," 86 *Harvard Law Review* 988 (1973); and Mark A. Rothstein, *Occupational Safety and Health Law*, 2nd. ed., pp. 159–176 (St. Paul, Minn.: West Publishing, 1983), for brief reviews of the history and interpretation of the general duty clause.

47. For diametrically opposite reactions to this judicial trend see Paul Brodeur, *Outrageous Misconduct: The Asbestos Industry on Trial* (New York: Pantheon Books, 1985), and Peter W. Huber, *Liability: The Legal Revolution and Its Consequences* (New York: Basic Books, 1988).

I suspect that judges are right in surmising that the threat of an expensive damage award will prove to be a potent disincentive to firing employees for recognizably bad reasons. The problem is that it may also produce undue risk aversion among American employers, making them unwilling to take the chance of firing employees even for what are believed to be good reasons. In many cases dismissal would be useful in enforcing standards of employee performance that would enhance the productivity of the enterprise, but the personnel manager is dubious about whether the grounds for dismissal can be documented and sustained in a trial before a jury whose sympathies often are tilted toward the individual employee who is out of work and battling a large corporation.

The other side of the coin is that there is still no guarantee that even an ambitious program of government regulation can deliver what it promises to the employees on the credit side of the regulatory ledger. After all, management remains in charge of the firm, wielding direct control over the workplace. External legal rules will alter the firm's market inclination only to the extent that there are real teeth in the enforcement of the rules. The deterrent strength of the law is a function of the procedures by which violations are investigated and the severity of the sanctions meted out when violations are detected. The problem is that each of these dimensions itself rests to a considerable extent on the resources that can be deployed by and on behalf of the workers themselves, the intended beneficiaries of the protection that was supposed to be afforded by the government.

Some legal programs—OSHA is again an example—do have a government inspectorate to carry the enforcement load; however, OSHA has always suffered from the inability of a comparative handful of inspectors to monitor hundreds of thousands of work sites in this country in order to ensure even a modest level of ongoing compliance with legally mandated standards. Even violations detected in the course of an inspection typically generate only mild monetary penalties. It is not surprising, then, that the consensus of research from the first decade of OSHA is that this legislation has produced only a modest reduction in the overall level of workplace injuries.[48] And a key

---

48. The most recent and sophisticated demonstration of this point is presented in W. Kip Viscusi, "The Impact of Occupational Safety and Health Regulation, 1973–83," 17 *Rand Journal of Economics* 567 (1986). I have analyzed this and other appraisals of OSHA's impact in Paul C. Weiler, "Legal Policy for Workplace Injuries" 85–93 (ALI Working Paper, 1986).

variable that positively influences both the likelihood of OSHA inspections and the size of penalties is whether the employees have been organized into a union with the experience and clout to insist on more effective administration of the law for the benefit of its members.[49]

Many regulatory programs, though, put the onus on the worker to enforce these legal rights on his own. This is true not only of the recently developed common law remedy of wrongful dismissal, but also of such long-standing programs as workers' compensation for occupational injuries that OSHA was unable to prevent. So the primary responsibility for representing the employee and for securing his rights under these laws falls to the litigator.

In a number of contexts such legal help has not been very fruitful, particularly when the employee who wants to take his employer to court also wants to continue working in the employer's plant or office. We saw earlier that the prospects for successful reinstatement after an unjust dismissal are bleak in an unorganized workplace;[50] research has also shown that, in practice, workers' compensation benefits are claimed significantly less frequently by nonunion employees.[51] The explanation is quite simple. To translate abstract legal rights on the books into practical guarantees in the workplace, the employee needs to be informed what his rights are and must secure assistance in asserting claims against unwilling managers. A lawyer may be able to provide the necessary information but will be unable to offer much sense of security to the individual worker contemplating such a challenge. And if the aim of a law such as WARNA is to enable employees to erect on the floor of a minimum legal guarantee (notice of impending plant closing) more constructive solutions to the underlying problem, such as work sharing, job banks, retraining opportunities, early retire-

49. This conclusion is documented in detail by the research of David Weil on the distribution of inspections and fines under both OSHA and the Mine Safety and Health Administration (MSHA): see David Weil, "Government and Labor at the Workplace: The Role of Labor Unions in the Implementation of Federal Health and Safety Policy" (Ph.D. diss., Harvard University, 1987). Interestingly, the size of market incentives for safety through compensating waste differentials is also sharply increased by the presence of collective bargaining: see Craig A. Olson, "An Analysis of Wage Differentials Received by Workers on Dangerous Jobs," 16 *Journal of Human Resources* 167, 180–185 (1981). For a more general treatment of unions and safety, see Lawrence S. Bacow, *Bargaining for Job Safety and Health* (Cambridge, Mass.: MIT Press, 1980).

50. See Chapter 2, pp. 85–87.

51. See Richard J. Butler and John P. Worrall, "Workers' Compensation: Benefits and Injury Claims Rates in the Seventies," 65 *Review of Economics and Statistics* 580, 586–589 (1983).

ment on pension, or even an employee buyout of the endangered operation—then, *a fortiori*, there is little likelihood that unorganized and unrepresented workers can possibly achieve any such outcome.

These kinds of objections do not apply, of course, to the common law action for wrongful discharge. In that situation the employee was dismissed from the workplace and is unlikely to return, and so he seeks the assistance of a lawyer in obtaining monetary compensation for the losses that he has suffered. One thing that our legal system can do quite effectively is to force a guilty party to pay money to its victim for his injuries. But as we saw earlier, the flaw in that type of regulatory instrument is that such legal help is much more likely to be available to the managerial or professional employee. It is these people whose potential damage awards are likely to be valuable enough to warrant a lawyer's investing his scarce time and money in pressing a chancy claim against the employer; because it is these employees who lost the sizable salaries, benefits, and other perquisites that they had enjoyed in their position. The irony is that the very legal principle that judges fashioned to protect employees who appeared to be unable to protect themselves in the labor market ends up in practice to deliver the vast majority of its benefits to upper-level employees who have proved themselves capable of doing quite well in several other respects in the same labor market.

This recital of the various limits and flaws in government regulation is not meant to imply that it may not be *necessary* in a variety of contexts. As was indicated by my earlier detailed exploration of the wrongful dismissal issue, often there are even greater limits and flaws in the protection afforded by the unregulated labor market; and through careful design of a streamlined administrative program, the government may be able to provide a significantly better balance between the legitimate needs of employer and employee. My basic point is that external legal controls are unlikely to be *sufficient* to provide employees with the ideal level of protection in the absence of some organization and representation of those employees in their workplace.

Certainly some technique for effective representation of the employees as a group in the firm is indispensable if we are to achieve even a modicum of *participation* by the employees in the definition of their rights and guarantees—the second dimension along which one must appraise alternative governance mechanisms. In other words, even holding constant the adequacy and affordability of our network of protective standards, there is an important independent value in having the employees themselves play a meaningful role in devising, monitoring, and enforcing their workplace safety net.[52]

Of course, the employee as voter exerts some influence on the way legislators, if not courts, respond to worker needs. In practice, though, the effectiveness of participation by ordinary workers in the political arena is itself dependent on the extent to which they are organized into a body through which they can understand and voice their concerns, not simply about their immediate job, but about a variety of other issues as well.

From that perspective, one may be even less enchanted by the gradual replacement of union negotiation by government regulation as the major institutional response to the failings of the labor market. With respect to issues such as wrongful dismissal or workers' compensation, for example, the person whom the nonunion employee actually sees, and then only as an isolated individual, is the lawyer who files and litigates a claim on his behalf. Without the resources of a large and effective union movement, employees as a whole can only hope that these trial lawyers will represent the real interests of workers as well as of attorneys when the broader policy dimensions of such programs are being addressed in the political arena.

I recognize that with respect to antidiscrimination laws, a variety of organizations such as the National Association for the Advancement of Colored People (NAACP), the National Organization of Women (NOW), or the American Association of Retired People (AARP) have emerged as defenders of the legal protection enjoyed by their respective constituencies. It was vital that institutions such as these evolve, groups whose role was to speak for black workers, for example, when their interests conflicted with those of the white employee majority or with the interests of employers for which both blacks and whites worked.

But the latent consequence of the gradual development of this network of specialized representative bodies, each functioning in the orbit

52. See Cass R. Sunstein, "Rights, Minimal Terms and Solidarity: A Comment," 51 *University of Chicago Law Review* 1041 (1984), criticizing Fried, "Individual and Collective Rights," from this perspective. It is for reasons such as these that Karl Klare is dubious about the value of government regulation as the instrument to repair what he believes are major flaws in the traditional "contractualist" nature of collective bargaining under the NLRA. See Klare's "Judicial Deradicalization of the Wagner Act and the Origins of Modern Legal Consciousness, 1937–1941," 62 *Minnesota Law Review* 265, 308 n. 150 (1978); and his "Traditional Labor Law Scholarship and the Crisis of Collective Bargaining," 44 *Maryland Law Review* 731, 767–772 (1985).

of legislation dealing with the concerns of a particular category of employees, is that too often the focus of attention is on problems that divide one group of workers from another—problems like the conflict between affirmative action and seniority when the employer has chosen to permanently lay off a substantial number of employees; or the struggle for a more equitable pay structure for female-dominated job categories in an industry that ranks at the lower end of the pay spectrum for its entire work force. However valuable may be the efforts of specific rights-based organizations such as the NAACP and NOW, they do not satisfy the need for a broader kind of union of employees as employees, an institutional mechanism through which workers can reflect on and understand their common experiences on the job and seek solutions for the problems they all face together. While some of these common problems may well be addressed by the legislators and administrators responsible for broad-ranging statutory programs such as OSHA, ERISA, and WARNA, for the reasons I gave earlier most employee concerns must inevitably be addressed and solved within a particular enterprise and industry.

Management Control

The foregoing is intended not as a brief against any use of legal regulation, but as a caution against undue reliance on its value. The vast bulk of employment issues will be and should be handled inside the firm. Individuals in the enterprise are much better able to identify their special problems and the solutions that make most sense for them (if not for everyone else); no particular formalities need be followed in adopting new standards of behavior and seeing whether they have been complied with; and once a directive has been issued by someone in authority, the same individual can be relied on to see that the directive is carried out. When we look inside the enterprise, though, we find two basic constituencies: the shareholders, represented by a management team, and the work force, which may or may not have organized representation. An initial question, then, is whether either of these groups has a plausible claim to ultimate authority in the firm, including the power to make decisions about what the conditions of employment will be.

In the dominant American tradition the shareholders have always staked out the more powerful claim. They are the legal owners of the enterprise. Their representative, the board of directors, selects a management team to run the enterprise for the benefit of the shareholders. Within the considerable play left in the joints of the present-day labor market, management establishes the conditions of employment for the firm's jobs—conditions that workers can either take or reject, depending on their opportunities elsewhere. In making its decisions the management team is largely insulated from real control by the scattered population of shareholders. Senior managers, then, are in a position from which they can consider the claims not only of the shareholders but also of other key stakeholders, such as labor, and balance their respective claims in a way that keeps them all willing to contribute to the success of the enterprise.[53] One does not have to assume that the managers' exercise of authority will be ideal in every respect to conclude that it is certainly better than the alternative we just considered—the government.

Lodging essentially unilateral authority in management is *not* a recipe for exploitation of workers. In fact, this is the basic regime throughout much of American business, a world in which most employees are nonunion and most employment practices are largely unregulated by the government. We know that rather than systematically exploit their workers, a large number of American firms have developed a highly sophisticated capacity for human resource management, administered by people who fully recognize (even if some economists and lawyers do not) the fundamental differences between their employees' labor and other commodities purchased by the firm. Numerous nonunion employers now regularly pay wages well above the market minimum; they have designed sophisticated benefit and insurance packages; they have adopted formal criteria and procedures to insure that employees are treated fairly by their supervisors; and more and more firms are even creating programs to give workers a direct influence over how they do their work, how to raise productivity in their area, and how to improve the quality of their working life.[54] And the reason that management has been moved to such innovations is that it now realizes (even if it did not a half-century ago) that it is good business practice to devise terms and conditions of employment that will attract good workers, keep them motivated and cooperative while they are on the job, and retain them when competitors offer them inducements to leave. In other words, the ultimate source of protection for the em-

53. See generally, Alchian and Demsetz "Production, Information Costs," and Fischel, "Labor Markets."

54. See generally Foulkes, *Personnel Policies*, and Beer et al., *Managing Human Assets.*

ployee as against management need not be the government or a union, but simply the presence of other employers bidding for the services of workers like him.

Having acknowledged the real virtues of managerialism, one must not be blind to its characteristic weaknesses, the limits on even a benign employer's empathy and altruism.

Limited Empathy. To establish an employment package that will best satisfy the needs and interests of its employees within the scope of the available resources, management must know what these needs and interests are. But because human resource managers, especially at the executive decision-making level, are not ordinary workers in the office or on the shop floor, they cannot learn from their own personal experience what their employees would like. Of course, management can ask its employees informally, but the response is often only anecdotal, and it may be guarded because of employees' anxiety about complaining to or about someone who has power over them. Sophisticated personnel departments sometimes conduct systematic surveys of their employees to learn their views. However, there are severe constraints on the understanding one can obtain from a survey, especially concerning what priorities and tradeoffs workers would prefer in a complex, multidimensional employment package. Indeed, policy judgments must often be made about important issues that many employees have never even thought about, much less had a chance to study and evaluate in the course of meaningful discussions with their fellow employees.

The traditional assumption of economists is that the employer will get helpful signals from the labor market into which it regularly loses employees and from which it tries to replace them, perhaps through interviews conducted by the personnel department to find out what attracts workers to and bothers them about a certain firm. One needs only a modest sample of workers doing such comparison shopping between jobs to derive a fair indication of whether a particular employer's pay and conditions were satisfying its employees.[55] The problem with this signaling process in the labor market, though, is that it relies on a skewed sample—the younger, junior, *marginal* employees who are entering or exiting the firm and whose interests are likely to be quite different from those of the older, senior, *average* employees who are making their career in the firm. To the extent one places a priority

55. See Schwartz and Wilde, "Imperfect Information."

on satisfying the situation of the older group, even the better nonunion employers will tend to miss this mark somewhat.[56]

Limited Altruism. However, the question is not simply how best to allocate the available resources among the employees in accordance with their wishes. One must also decide how much of the firm's resources will be expended on the work force as a whole. This brings into play the basic conflict of interest between labor and either consumers or capital. While management must mediate among these interests to a substantial extent, it is not a neutral arbiter. At crucial points managers can be expected to tilt toward the shareholders who select them through the board of directors, and toward the consumers upon whose continued patronage the shareholders' rate of return ultimately depends. One point at which this conflict surfaces is in the division of the economic surplus generated from the continuing relationship of employee and firm—stemming from the fact that each is worth more to the other than to anyone else. In such distributive bargaining, management, acting at the behest of the shareholder, tends to fare much better than the individual employee, because any one employee is far more fungible to the firm than is the employer to a particular worker.[57]

A second illustration of the same orientation of managerial authority concerns management itself as an independent constituency. Even ignoring the issue of compensation of executives (which will be influenced somewhat by how well they do for the shareholders), managers have an interest in preserving their discretionary power.[58] The result is that even the good employer that provides very attractive benefits and

56. See Freeman and Medoff, *What Do Unions Do?* Earlier I commented on the significance of this point for the crucial issue of unfair dismissal. The large body of empirical research reported and analyzed by Freeman and Medoff makes it clear that this phenomenon—the divergent tilts in the individualist and the collectively organized labor markets—extends across the entire spectrum of employment conditions, both monetary and nonmonetary. The reasons why an enterprise should focus on the career employee in the design of its employment package (and why the better nonunion firms attempt to do so) are implicit in the entire line of argument in this book.

57. One can imagine examples of virtually irreplaceable employees, such as the star actor in a highly rated television series, but these cases are very much the exceptions which prove the rule.

58. An important illustration of this tendency appears in the recent and illuminating book by Shoshana Zuboff, *In the Age of the Smart Machine* (New York: Basic Books, 1988). Zuboff shows how, at critical forks in the road to a computerized workplace, management often makes key design choices which enlarge its own effective control over the work force, rather than build into the new technology features which would enhance employee understanding of, and concomitant autonomy and power over, the job and the enterprise itself.

conditions to its workers will rarely allow these benefits to be locked up in a legally enforceable contract. Even the open-door procedures we looked at in Chapter 2, which allow appeals of supervisory discipline or dismissal to senior management, do not permit further appeals of unfavorable decisions from that quarter to an outside arbitrator applying a just cause standard.[59] Finally, as we shall see in the next section, employee stock ownership plans (ESOPs) are usually carefully drafted to ensure that management retains control of the firm.[60] A particularly revealing illustration of that tendency is the rapidly growing incidence of unilateral employer termination of pension plans; the "surplus" funds originally accumulated to give the retirement income of workers some protection from inflation are returned to the coffers of the firm for its financial uses.[61]

Most pension plans are of the defined benefit rather than the defined contribution type; that is, rather than simply provide a guaranteed financial contribution to a pension account for each employee, the employer commits itself to pay the employee a specified benefit when he retires. Thus rather than the employee's having to take responsibility for making the investment decisions needed to insure that an appropriate income will be available on retirement (as he would under an IRA), workers can rely on their employers to perform that role for them. The size of the pension benefit will typically be based on the compensation being earned by the employee at or near the end of his tenure with the firm. Such a formula provides the employee with valuable protection against inflation during the span of a lengthy working

59. See Chapter 2, pp. 72 and 77.

60. See generally, Joseph R. Blasi, *Employee Ownership: Revolution or Ripoff* (Cambridge, Mass.: Ballinger, 1988).

61. This phenomenon has recently attracted a great deal of political attention as evidenced, for example, by congressional hearings on the matter. See *Overfunded Pension Plans*, Joint Hearing Before the House Select Committee on Aging and the Subcommittee on Labor-Management Relations of the Committee on Education and Labor, 99th Congress, lst Sess. (1985); and *Overfunding and Underfunding of Pension Plans*, Joint Hearings Before the Senate Committee on Labor and Human Resources and the House Committee on Education and Labor, 100th Congress, 1st Sess. (1987). The best scholarly treatments of this subject from a legal perspective are Norman P. Stein, "Raiders of the Corporate Pension Plan: The Reversion of Excess Plan Assets to the Employer," 5 *American Journal of Tax Policy*, 117 (1986); and Norman P. Stein, "Reversions from Pension Plans: History, Policies and Prospects," 44 *Tax Law Review* 259 (1989). The best study from an economist's perspective is Richard A. Ippolito, *Pensions, Economics and Public Policy* (Homewood, Ill.: Dow Jones-Irwin, 1986), in particular Chapter 13 on "Terminations for Reversion," pp. 253–257. My own brief review of this problem relies primarily on the evidence and arguments in the works cited in this note.

career. Indeed, employees find this kind of retirement protection to be so valuable that they willingly pay for the extra funding needed by foregoing additional wages while they are still employed.[62]

Assuming that the employer contributes the funding that is actuarially required to meet the future "final average earnings" obligation of the plan, the employer is itself protected against subsequent inflation, because the inflation premium in the investment earnings of the pension plan will naturally generate money necessary to protect the promised retirement benefits against loss of their real value.

However, this implicit understanding—in Arthur Okun's phrase, the "invisible handshake"—between employer and employee is not explicitly protected under the current law. ERISA requires that employers fully fund their pension obligations, and also states that the tax-sheltered assets accumulated must be used for the benefit of the plan participants, not the employer. However, ERISA also permits the employer to terminate its pension plan as long as the firm satisfies its current obligations to all participants; and then provides that any surplus generated as a result of "actuarial error" will revert to the employer. The rationale of the law seems to be that as long as the employees' rights have been protected, the employer which bears the risk of a deficit should also get the benefit of any surplus.

The problem is that ERISA, at least as it was interpreted by the Reagan administration, permits the employer to terminate a defined benefit plan by purchasing for each of its employees (as well as its retirees) an annuity that is based on their present salary rather than the final salary they would probably be earning ten or twenty years later upon retirement. So the inflation premium which has been accumulated in the fund to pay for the higher benefit promised on retirement is now treated as surplus to the much lower benefit payable on earlier termination of the plan. The so-called actuarial error is the product of this entirely artificial legal distinction which denies employees the benefit of a pension bargain for which, economic analysis demonstrates, the employees themselves have paid with earnings foregone in previous years.[63]

---

62. Ippolito, *Pensions*, pp. 36–62, provides an elegant empirical demonstration of the fact that employees pay more for such anticipated real pension protection than they do for plans under which the employer merely contributes nominal dollar amounts.

63. The pieces by Stein, "Raiders" and "Reversions," provide very careful analysis of the current status of this tangled legal problem. To my mind, Stein also makes a telling case against the legal entrée (the nature of which I will spell out in the text) that was extended to employers by the 1984 Joint Implementation Guidelines of the Department of the Treasury, the Department of Labor, and the Pension Benefit Guarantee Corporation. Unfortunately, so far the courts have been prepared to accept the government's interpretation

This legal loophole was not discovered and exploited until the early eighties. Before the present decade pension termination and reversion was a very rare event: only $2 million of pension assets reverted to employers in 1979 and in 1980. In the more difficult economic climate of the early eighties, a number of employers discovered that they could, in effect, borrow these funds from their pension programs to tide them over their financial straits. But once that possibility became visible on the balance sheets of public corporations, it proved irresistible in the new capital markets of the mid-eighties. Hostile takeovers by outside raiders as well as leveraged buyouts by inside managers could readily be financed with these apparently idle assets. Indeed, even managers who might have felt some personal compunction about initiating a pension plan termination often feel compelled to do so as part of a takeover defense strategy, in order to remove that surplus from their accounts. These employers often restart the pension plan for their active employees, but only on a seriously underfunded basis when measured against the real pension promised upon retirement. The stark result is that during the eighties nearly $20 *billion* of "surplus" assets were stripped from American pension funds—nearly 50 percent of the total assets in the plans that were terminated—to be used for the benefit of employers.

Clearly this trend makes little sense as matter of public policy. From the perspective of tax policy, for example, the federal treasury was in effect allowing firms to invest money in a tax-free account until they wanted to draw on it and use it years later. In the Tax Reform Act of 1986, Congress responded to this facet of the problem by imposing a flat 10 percent excise tax on all such reversions.[64]

This step, however, did not respond to the strains posed on pension policies by the nonindexed feature of private pensions. In the seventies most firms used the high inflation dividend they earned on their pension assets to award ad hoc benefit increases to retirees, in order to make good on an implicit contract of protection against undue erosion in the real value of the pensions initially promised to the work force. But in the eighties, with more and more pension plans being stripped of the funds that might have been used for this purpose, far fewer ad hoc increases

---

(see, e.g., Blessitt v. Retirement Plan for Employees of Dixie Engine Co., 848 F.2d 1164 (11th Cir. 1988)), with distressing consequences that will be described in the text.

64. Note, however, that the new tax on reversions was itself part of a broader tax package that reduced the corporate tax rate by roughly 10 percent. In addition, propelled by its fascination with the idea of employee stock ownership (which will be considered in the next section), Congress exempted from the new excise tax any pension reversion funds that the employer chose to use in financing an ESOP.

were being made in fixed pension benefits that continued to be steadily eroded (albeit at a slower pace) by the inflation of that decade.

My primary concern, though, is the lesson this tale offers for the labor market and labor policy about the limits of managerial empathy and altruism toward workers. I concede that the labor market often generates considerable protection of employee interests. In fact, the very development of the defined benefit/final average earnings pension formula shows that good human resource managers will make a sincere effort to understand the needs and priorities of their career employees and offer them somewhat greater rewards than the firm absolutely must provide to function in a competitive labor market. And firms that think about the longer term will be concerned about their loss of reputation and morale if the employer later reneges on an undertaking that its employees feel is morally, if not legally, binding.[65]

But just as we saw earlier with respect to wrongful dismissal, even the inhibiting reputation factor leaves considerable room for opportunistic behavior by individual managers before the employees realize what is going on and begin to react against it. And the pension problem is much worse than wrongful dismissal in that regard. First, the details of pensions are extremely arcane and difficult to understand for almost all employees. Second, the new brand of capitalism generates nearly irresistible temptations to groups of financial players to exploit the huge short-term opportunity presented by the pension surplus situation and to let the future relationship between the enterprise and its work force take care of itself. The accumulation of numerous instances of this kind of overreaching by managers, with the resulting harms inflicted on employees, in turn often impels the government, through either the legislative or the judicial branch, to step in and provide some guarantee of fair treatment that the market cannot visibly insure. We have yet to see, though, that Congress is up to this challenge with respect to the pension reversion problem.

Worker Control

Among those who recognize how difficult it is for government to devise and implement meaningful external restraints on management's

---

65. For a formal analysis of the scope and limits of such reputational factors in securing performance of the "implicit" labor contract, see H. Lorne Carmichael, "Reputations in the Labor Market," 74 *American Economic Review* 713 (1984); compare, with respect to the product market, Benjamin Klein and Keith B. Leffler, "The Role of Market Forces in Assuring Contractual Performance," 89 *Journal of Political Economy* 615 (1981).

conduct of the enterprise, some will be attracted to quite a different option—control of the enterprise by its workers.[66] This means not merely employee involvement in the day-to-day operation of the plant, a process designed to enhance worker morale, productivity, and quality,[67] but conferring upon workers the ultimate authority over enterprise decisions, whether through full ownership (in the sense of the right to the residual profits of the firm) or otherwise. Under such a regime, the suppliers of labor rather than of capital would be entitled to make the key decisions about the firm's product lines and technology, the reinvestment or the payout of its revenues, and all other matters crucial to the firm's future, including, naturally, the terms and conditions of its employment package. In that setting one could feel confident that the employees would secure the blend of protection and participation that they really want.

In fact, the federal government currently pursues at least one version of that objective with an extensive system of tax incentives provided to ESOPs. Since the idea first appeared in a piece of 1973 legislation,[68] the federal treasury has provided roughly $15 billion in tax benefits to companies that allocate to their employees some equity stake in the firm. By the end of 1987, it was estimated that nearly 9,000 companies had adopted ESOP plans which together held $19 billion of stock in trust for almost eight million participating employees.[69] Those figures seem to indicate that remarkable progress has been made toward giving American employees an equity stake in the (ideally growing) capital assets of

66. Thus Reich, in his *Tales of a New America*, after having depicted (pp. 130–151) the dilemma of eroding worker trust and team productivity produced by the pursuit of financial profits (of which pension reversion is just one instance) in our new capital markets, suggests worker ownership as a solution (pp. 245–248). In the context of workplace injuries, see the recent book by Charles Noble, *Liberalism at Work: The Rise and Fall of OSHA* (Philadelphia: Temple University Press, 1986), which offers a vigorous critique of the "liberal" attempt to regulate the safety decisions of a management team whose authority rests on private ownership in a capitalist economy, then suggests that a fully adequate response to this particular problem will come only from active worker participation in and control over these decisions.

67. I will take up this option in the next chapter; here I refer the reader to John F. Witte, *Democracy, Authority, and Alienation in Work: Workers' Participation in an American Corporation* (Chicago: University of Chicago Press, 1980). This is the best empirical study I have seen of the experience of a group of nonunion workers with the involvement model. The findings of Witte's research on worker attitudes toward enhanced participation in the affairs of the workplace are relevant to several of the points discussed in this chapter.

68. The Regional Rail Reorganization Act of 1973. The more general use of the ESOP was first established in Section 407(d)(6) of the Employee Retirement Income Security Act of 1974 (ERISA).

69. See *The Employee Ownership Report* (Oakland, California: National Center for Employee Ownership, Sept–Oct. 1988), p. 1, col. 3.

their employers, providing the employees with a personal incentive to work harder for the success of the enterprise, and serving as a vehicle through which the employees can influence and control the direction of the firm on which so much of their future lives depend.[70]

However, this sunny picture is quite misleading. The vast majority of ESOP plans (comprising 90 percent of the participants and 80 percent of the assets)[71] took the form of tax credit ESOPs (TRASOPs), under which the federal government in effect gave American companies roughly one dollar in tax savings in order to create $1.25 of stock ownership for employees.[72] When Congress finally appreciated the nature and dimensions of this particular tax break, the TRASOP program was repealed as part of the broader Tax Reform Act of 1986. That leaves as the major instrument for promoting employee ownership the classic ESOPs (leveraged or not), which for about $1.5 billion in tax expenditures have secured about $4 billion in stock ownership (only about 0.2 percent of total corporate equity) for the benefit of about one million workers (or less than 1 percent of the work force).[73]

Even this apparently more economical tax inducement features a number of characteristic ills of managerialism sketched in the previous section. Recall that the crucial decision about whether to create or terminate an ESOP is made by the employer—that is, by its senior management and corporate board—not by the employees or the broader community. So the government has considered it necessary to erect an elaborate array of tax incentives to make such a step financially appealing to the employer.[74] But in that setting such incentives pro-

70. For a recent strong endorsement of the ESOP idea, see the Cuomo Commission Report, *A New American Formula for a Strong Economy* 176–180 (1988). For a more skeptical view, with which I am basically in accord, see Raymond Russell, "Using Ownership to Control: Making Workers Owners in the Contemporary United States," 13 *Politics and Society* 253 (1984).

71. See U.S. General Accounting Office, *Employee Stock Ownership Plans: Benefits and Costs of ESOP Tax Incentives for Broadening Stock Ownership* 19 (Washington D.C.: U.S. General Accounting Office, December 1986), hereinafter cited as "GAO Study."

72. GAO Study, p. 31.

73. Blasi, *Employee Ownership*, p. 117.

74. Among the key tax incentives provided to employers to set up ESOP programs are the following provisions. First, all dividends paid to ESOPs are tax deductible (as contrasted with dividends paid on shares owned by non-ESOP investors), whether the dividends are distributed in cash to employees or are used to pay the principal (up to 25 percent of the total annual payroll) and interest on the loan secured by the leveraged ESOP to purchase the shares. In addition, banks may exclude from taxable income half of their interest earnings on loans to ESOPs, and some portion of the bank's tax savings presumably accrues to the benefit of the borrowing corporation. A shareholder who sells

duce certain patterns of behavior that work to the advantage of the people charged with the decision of whether or not there will be any employee ownership of a firm, as follows:

1. Among the major reasons for creating ESOPs is the desire to find a favorable market for the sale of the owner's personal shareholdings in the firm, or to help incumbent management fight hostile takeover bids, either by placing the stock in friendly hands or by removing the company from play by taking it into private ownership.[75]

2. Participation in the plan (in terms of eligibility and especially of quantity of accumulated stock) is sharply tilted toward upper-level managerial and salaried employees and away from ordinary production workers (particularly if they are unionized).[76]

3. Stock voting rights are either not passed through to the employee at all or apply only to certain decisions and after the employee owns the stock for a long time.[77] In the meantime a trustee selected by and effectively accountable to management votes the stock and makes other key decisions about the program. One such decision is the valuation of the stock that the employees receive under the ESOP, as compared with the value of the shares retained by the founding owner, the senior executives, et al.[78]

4. Employees who are covered by such ESOPs often experience little

---

at least 30 percent of the outstanding shares of the company to an ESOP may roll over his capital gain on the sale by purchasing qualified replacement property (other corporate securities, for example) within one year of the sale. If the estate of the shareholder sells the decedent's shares in the employer corporation to an ESOP, the estate may shelter 50 percent of the proceeds of the sale from the liability for estate taxes. Finally, if the employer transfers to an ESOP the surplus assets from termination of a pension plan, the reversion will be exempt from the 10 percent excise tax established in 1986 for such reversions. See, generally, Blasi, *Employee Ownership*.

75. See GAO Study, p. 20.

76. See Blasi, *Employee Ownership*, p. 44. The NLRB recently gave its blessing to the exclusion of union members as such from eligibility for participation in the firm's ESOP: see *Handleman Co.*, 283 NLRB No. 65 (1987).

77. In the case of publicly held employer corporations, the employees may vote their ESOP shares on all corporate matters only after the shares have been allocated to their accounts. For leveraged ESOPs, the shares are actually allocated to the employee accounts only as the loan for the ESOP is paid off, thereby figuratively releasing the shares from the security for the loan. In companies for which the stock is not publicly traded, employees are still entitled to vote only allocated shares and then only with respect to the approval or disapproval of certain corporate decisions such as mergers, liquidations, or sales of substantially all the assets of the trade or business. See Blasi, *Employee Ownership*.

78. See Freeman, "ESOP Valuation Issues," in Leon E. Irish, Ronald L. Ludwig, and Ronald S. Rizzo, eds., *The New Attractions of Employee Stock Ownership Plans*, p. 383 (Englewood Cliffs, N.J.: Prentice-Hall, 1988).

change in their daily life on the job, in their relations with their supervisors, and in their influence over the plans of the firm.[79]

Notwithstanding the foregoing tendencies, there are many cases in which the ESOP has functioned in accordance with the aspirations of its proponents. These plans were adopted to give employees a real stake in the enterprise; stock is distributed broadly and equitably across the entire work force; voting rights are passed through quickly and are exercised extensively by the employees; and the atmosphere and culture of the firm and its workplace have been transformed as a result. But where, as here, securing these policy objectives depends on an enlightened management response to a variety of tax incentives, the evidence is clear that in a disturbingly large number of situations the ESOP program has been prone to all the failings listed above.

In the debate about the ESOP program, a standard response to the criticism sketched here is that employees have no real grounds for objecting to what is, in effect, a gift of stock from the employer, given to induce greater productivity from its work force. Even discounting the fact that the federal treasury has made a very sizable contribution to that gift, the remaining part is by no means a free benefit for the employees. To the extent that the firm incurs any real cost (net of productivity gains) in such stock transfer to its employees, the added labor cost will limit the amount that the employer will expend on salaries and other benefits for the employees.[80] It is by no means evident that most employees would agree that accumulating the stock of their employer is a preferred mode of compensation if the stock comes with no effective voice in the affairs

79. See Blasi, *Employee Ownership*, pp. 201–219; and GAO Study, pp. 41–43.

80. Thus, for example, Roger C. Siske and Leslie A. Klein, "Employee Stock Ownership Plans," in Irish, Ludwig, and Rizzo, eds., *Employee Stock Ownership Plans*, p. 21 state that "[T]he employer contributions to the ESOP . . . represent business expenses of the corporation. . . . The use of an ESOP therefore makes sense only if total compensation to employees, including ESOP contributions, represents a reasonable aggregate payroll package." Striking corroboration of this economic tendency is to be found in the ongoing dispute at the Polaroid Corporation. There senior management instituted an ESOP for the workforce hoping, *inter alia*, to fend off a hostile takeover. At the same time, the employees were required to absorb a 5 percent across-the-board salary cut to pay for the stock which was being placed in their names in order to avoid any dilution of the equity of existing shareholders. Ironically, it was the outside bidder for the firm that went into the Delaware courts to challenge (unsuccessfully) the validity of the ESOP program under corporate takeover law. The employees had absolutely no voice in the initiation of the program, and no legal foothold from which to defend their own interests. See Shamrock Holdings, Inc. v. Polaroid Corporation, 559 A.2d 257 (Del. Ch. 1989) and 559 A.2d 278 (Del. Ch. 1989); see also "Polaroid's Success in Avoiding Takeover May Rest on Its Use of ESOP as a Defense," *Wall Street Journal*, July 22, 1988, p. 22, col. 3; and "Worker Ire May Hurt Polaroid's Defense," *Boston Globe*, July 23, 1988, p. 12, col. 2.

of the firm. After all, by contrast with the standard pension plan, for example, which is required prudently to diversify its portfolio among a variety of financial assets, the employee under an ESOP may be entrusting a sizable share of his future retirement estate to the fortunes of a single firm, which could as easily fail as flourish.

This brief recitation of the problems of ESOPs will be familiar to those who have studied and debated the program. Indeed, looking back at the evolution of ESOPs, it is both striking and ironic how closely the government has had to regulate the design and administration of ESOPs to protect employees from a variety of potential abuses in a program that might have been applauded as an indigenous participatory alternative to external legal control of the workplace.

In any event, one clear lesson from this account is that there is a fundamental difference between mere employee *ownership* of equity stock and actual exercise of *control* over decision-making in the firm. Indeed, to the extent that the main objective is to have employers give their workers a greater financial stake in the enterprise (so as to enhance employee commitment and productivity), the aim should be pursued through profit-sharing plans, which permit the employee to invest the proceeds in assets from which the return will be most attractive and secure.[81] But if we are primarily interested in giving employees the major role in the governance of the firm, we must consider measures that are much farther reaching than the ESOP—for example, a law that would confer on the work force the right to select and dismiss the directors and managers who will represent their interests in the operation of the firm, accompanied by a direct employee vote on the key strategic decisions the enterprise must make from time to time.

For American workers right now, such a governing role in the firm is not a viable possibility in a political economy based on fundamental premises (legal and otherwise) antithetical to the idea of worker control. This is not to ignore the occasional examples of true worker control in this country. Interestingly, perhaps the most common illustration will

81. Thus Stephen Bloom, "Employee Ownership and Firm Performance 248–254 (Ph.D. diss. Harvard University, 1985), found no net performance advantage of ESOP over non-ESOP firms once he controlled for other relevant characteristics. However, Douglas Lynn Kruse, "Essays in Profit-Sharing and Unemployment" 64–69, 88–89 (Ph.D. diss. Harvard University, 1988), while confirming Bloom's findings regarding the lack of impact of ESOPs as such, did observe a positive correlation between firm productivity and real profit sharing with the employees. These research findings corroborate the point made in the text, that ESOP programs generally deliver too little tangible advantage to workers to motivate them to improve their performance and productivity (though ESOPs probably do generate substantial tax-supported advantages for previous owners of the firm or for senior management).

be quite familiar to the legal mind: almost all law firms are governed by all the partners who work in them, rather than by those who may have invested capital in the firm.[82] Needless to say, in this context the scope of the "worker" constituency is highly restricted; it almost invariably excludes the associate lawyers and nonlegal staff, who outnumber the partners in most major law firms. However, some enterprises are run using a process of participatory self-management by the entire work force, professional and nonprofessional, skilled and unskilled. These tend to be small social service organizations established by activists committed not only to the welfare of their clientele, but also to the principle of equal participation as the ideal mode of governing the affairs of a workplace community.[83]

There is one really instructive example of a sizable enterprise manufacturing a product through technology requiring significant capital investment, but which is actually controlled by the ordinary blue-collar work force. This is the case of the cooperatives which have been a significant feature of the plywood industry in the Pacific northwest for the last fifty years.[84] Despite the paucity of examples,[85] there is a vast literature and increasing advocacy promoting worker control. This is a broad and complex subject that I cannot adequately address within the confines of this book. However, I shall make a few observations about the issues and the arguments to serve as a bridge between my discussions of managerialism and collective bargaining.

The case for worker authority is a simple and appealing one, especially from the point of view of the political theorists, who tend to be its

82. See Raymond Russell, "Employee Ownership and Internal Governance," 6 *Journal of Economic Behavior and Organization* 217 (1985) for extended discussion of the professional firm and other examples (such as certain taxi companies) of worker control in the service sector.

83. The best known and most systematically researched example of such an organization is the Helpline Project, described in Jane J. Mansbridge, *Beyond Adversary Democracy* (New York: Basic Books, 1980).

84. The experience of the plywood cooperatives is the subject of a first-rate empirical study by Edward S. Greenberg, *Workplace Democracy: The Political Effects of Participation* (Ithaca: Cornell University Press, 1986).

85. It is no accident that the authors of the three important pieces of empirical research to which I refer in this section—Witte, Mansbridge, and Greenberg—are all political scientists. Likewise Robert A. Dahl, perhaps the preeminent political theorist/scientist of this generation, has in recent years became an ardent devotee of worker control as the centerpiece of an economic democracy; see, e.g., his *A Preface to Economic Democracy* (Berkeley: University of California Press, 1985). In my view, a necessary precondition to such a political position is the evidence and analysis from contemporary labor economics on the nature and significance of the career employment relationship, which clearly establishes the need for some mode of governance within the rather loose confines of a market economy.

major scholarly advocates. The premise of our political democracy is that people should have a voice in and meaningful influence on decisions that affect primarily their interests. This principle seems just as applicable to decisions affecting people in their capacity as workers as it is to decisions affecting people as consumers and financers of government services. How much pay will be earned for different kinds of work? What insurance or retirement benefits will be available as protection against the vicissitudes of life? Who will get promoted or dismissed? All these issues are of immediate and vital concern to employees and their families. The stake of each individual worker in an enterprise—all of whose eggs are in this one basket—is much greater than that of the typical shareholder, who is likely to have a rather small and easily liquidated investment in any one firm and thus (or so it is argued) little incentive to exercise even the authority that he currently has under the law.[86]

Granted, as the firm gets larger and its problems more complex, it will probably need professional management, people who specialize in this role and who can focus all their time and energy on the various facets of running an ongoing enterprise—finance, human resources, and the like. But although self-management and coordination by the workers as a group—pure participatory democracy—may be viable for only the smallest of firms, management by specialists selected by and accountable to the employees—representative democracy—is considered to be a preferred mode of governing the firm, because it is far more responsive to the felt needs and concerns of the workers than would be a management team selected by and accountable to shareholders.[87] Not only does such an arrangement seem more in accord with the fundamental principles of our democracy, but it is anticipated that it will also produce positive results for our political economy. Empowering workers to par-

86. See Edward S. Herman, *Corporate Control, Corporate Power* (New York: Cambridge University Press, 1981), for an extended treatment of this point from the perspective of the issues of shareholder ownership and control. I am aware, of course, of the current belief among the law and economics fraternity that the market for corporate control through potential unfriendly takeover bids gives even a large, scattered pool of small investors an adequate means of insuring that senior management will respond to their interests; see, for example, the debate in the recent "Symposium: The Risks and Rewards of Regulating Corporate Takeovers," 1988 *Wisconsin Law Review* 353. Even granting the empirical validity of this claim (about which I am agnostic), the major argument for worker control is that it is the *workers'* interests which should really count in this matter.

87. See Russell, "Employee Ownership," on the importance of clearly distinguishing, in the debate over worker control, between direct, nonhierarchical peer group coordination and the exercise of hierarchical authority by a management team which is ultimately responsible to the work force.

ticipate in decisions that affect them in their immediate daily lives on the job will educate and induce the same workers to perform that role in the more remote outside polity.[88] And worker control is also considered to be an ideal instrument for eliciting from American workers the voluntary cooperation, commitment, and occasional financial sacrifices which may be necessary for a productive enterprise in an increasingly competitive international economy.[89]

That is, I believe, a fair distillation of what is primarily a political theorist's argument for worker control. The economists whose work on this subject I have read tend to be more skeptical.[90] Naturally enough their starting point is the fact that in our economy worker control is thoroughly atypical. Because no law prohibits the creation of employee-owned firms, the economist presumes that if such firms did in fact enhance worker satisfaction and performance, they would have flourished and would be widely emulated. But worker control has not become a prominent feature of the economic landscape; consequently the economist looks for the explanation in deficiencies of this organizational form in the labor, consumer, or capital markets.

An initial difficulty that arises in the labor market is that there is a cost as well as a benefit to participation—the expenditure of worker (and management) time. The more involvement the employees have in the affairs of their employer, the more that will be required from them for its exercise.[91] It is true that worker participation might increase the

88. A frequently cited statement of this argument can be found in Carole Pateman, *Participation and Democratic Theory* (Cambridge, Eng.: Cambridge University Press, 1970).

89. See the recent arguments to this effect in Reich, *Tales of a New America*, and the Cuomo Commission Report, *A New American Formula*.

90. A short and gracefully written statement of the economists' point of view is Herbert Simon's "What Is Industrial Democracy?" *Challenge* 30 (Jan.–Feb. 1983). More extended and analytical treatments are to be found in Williamson, *Economic Institutions*, in particular Chapter 12, "Corporate Governance," pp. 298–325; and Michael Jensen and William Meckling, "Rights and Production Functions: An Application to Labor-Managed Firms and Codetermination, 52 *Journal of Business* 469 (1979). For a useful recent review from this perspective, see Henry B. Hansmann, "Ownership of the Firm," 4 *Journal of Law, Economics, and Organization* 267 (1988).

91. In the Helpline Project studied by Mansbridge, *Beyond Adversary Democracy*, workers spent an average of seven hours a week in meetings and discussions about management of their enterprise. As I noted earlier, however, Helpline featured nearly pure self-management by all the workers, which maximized the time required for discussing the coordination of their activities. In the plywood cooperatives studied by Greenberg, *Workplace Democracy*, the ordinary worker spent significantly less time on such activity, attending only a few shareholder meetings every year. However, far greater demands were placed on the worker directors elected to the boards of the cooperatives, since it was they who actually supervised the management team throughout the year. This heavy burden

level of firm productivity enough to fully offset these extra time costs, but I know of no empirical demonstration that this offset does (or does not) occur. If it does not, then the additional cost of worker involvement must be paid for either by increasing the hours or reducing the pay of the affected workers.[92] I have argued that employee participation is an important value, which should be respected in the governance of the workplace. But that does not imply that American workers should be forced to accept this arrangement if it requires a significant sacrifice in such tangible outcomes as a well-paying job or decent working conditions, which workers generally rank higher than participation.[93] Thus if the price of the time spent in worker control is a considerable reduction

greatly reduced the appeal of serving on the boards and increased turnover in board membership, with consequent negative effects on the quality of worker control over decisions of the professional managers.

92. This is what law firms must do, at least implicitly, when they account for the time spent by partners in the governance of the firm. Participation in the firm is confined to the narrow constituency of the partnership, a group much more homogeneous in its interests than it would be if, say, secretaries and paralegals were included. This homogeneity has the virtue (at least from the partners' point of view) of reducing the amount of time spent on resolving differences of views. The benefit of homogeneity may help account for the fact that the plywood cooperatives typically exclude from the ownership constituency such diverse groups as the management team, the office staff, and certain employees with specialized skills and/or roles within the operations. See Greenberg, *Workplace Democracy*, pp. 60–61.

93. See Robert P. Quinn and Graham L. Staines, *The 1977 Quality of Employment Survey* p. 57 (Ann Arbor: University of Michigan, 1979), reporting on a population-wide survey of American workers; their results on this issue are corroborated by surveys of the specific employee groups studied by Witte, *Democracy, Authority, and Alienation*, pp. 41–47, and Greenberg, *Workplace Democracy*, pp. 34–36. Some might discount these survey findings on the ground that they show only that workers who have little or no experience with participation tend to downplay its value relative to more tangible rewards from the job. A major flaw in this apparently obvious response is that the longitudinal surveys by Witte and Greenberg found little or no increase in appreciation for the participatory process among workers who had in fact had several years' experience with it. Thus when Greenberg asked his worker-shareholders whether they would choose to work in another cooperative if they were to leave their present company, 27 percent said they definitely would *not* (versus 17 percent who said they definitely would), and 30 percent said it would not be a positive factor (versus 17 percent who said it would be); *id.* at 91. Essentially the same point is made by Witte, *Democracy, Authority, and Alienation*, pp. 148–150.

Many employees do, of course, place a high value on being involved in decisions which affect their working life: there are quite a number of such individuals on the Harvard Law School faculty. If one assumes that a regime of worker control will have a relatively limited scope, one could solve the problem described in the text by the simple process of self-selection and sorting (as occurred in the Helpline Project, see Mansbridge, *Beyond Adversary Democracy*). However, the issue I am considering is whether it would be good public policy to make worker control the normal mode of workplace governance; if so, one has to deal with the attitudes and the aspirations of the typical American worker as disclosed in these surveys.

in the worker's pay or leisure, enterprises organized in this fashion may risk being unable to attract and retain employees of the quality they want.

Suppose the firm were to respond to this labor market problem by adding the extra costs of employee involvement to its consumer prices. That possibility raises the more general issue of the inescapable conflict of interest between worker and consumer. Workers tend to be interested in higher wages, while consumers want lower prices; workers would prefer a somewhat more leisurely pace on the job, while consumers want faster service. When one reflects on this complication from the point of view of abstract political principle—who should be entitled to a voice in the affairs of the enterprise?—it is no longer so clear that only the employees can stake out a strong claim, because the firm's clientele also has a vital interest in its goods and services. In practice, we do not usually worry about giving consumers a political voice, because we assume that their ability to choose between competing suppliers gives them sufficient influence over the firm's decisions about the prices of its products and the quality of its service.[94] But if a major reason workers want more control over their employer is to make the employer more responsive to employee interests—such as increases in pay or reductions in job hazards—the economist might worry that a firm tilted too much in that direction would be prone to failure in a competitive market.

Again, this is a largely speculative concern: there is no documented evidence that worker control is incompatible with business success.[95]

94. This solution is not sufficient, however, for consumers with little ability to choose among different suppliers, especially consumers who are already committed to and reliant upon a particular supplier. Consider, for example, the student in a university, the patient in an extended care facility, and the individual whose life is insured by a particular insurer. Interestingly, as pointed out by Hansmann, "Ownership of the Firm," it is the consumer-owned firms (including mutual life insurance companies which are "owned" by their policyholders) that constitute the most significant present-day alternative to investor ownership, not worker control.

95. There have been some recent highly publicized employee buyouts of firms which subsequent failed: examples are the Rath Packing Company (see Tove H. Hammer and Robert N. Stern, "A Yo-Yo Model of Cooperation: Union Participation in Management at the Rath Packing Company," 39 *Industrial and Labor Relations Review* 337 (1986)); and Hyatt-Clark Industries (see "A Noble Experiment Goes Bankrupt," *New York Times*, Sunday, May 3, 1987, sec. III, p. 1, col. 5). However, it is by no means clear that failure could have been avoided in either instance by a conventionally controlled firm, which would have had to deal with the major product market strains facing the meat packing industry in the first case, and the auto parts industry in the second. The experience of the northwest plywood cooperatives, which were not founded in such a crisis atmosphere and which have flourished for decades, may well be a better index of the economic viability of worker ownership. See generally Frank H. Stephen, ed., *The Performance of Labor-Managed Firms* (New York: St. Martin's Press, 1982).

However, one suspects that such uneasiness is likely to be especially felt by the suppliers of capital, the other major constituency of the firm.

The infusion of capital needed by any substantial business can be obtained through loans with fixed interest rates, repayment schedules, and security against default. Alternatively, the necessary capital can be raised through equity shares that promise the investors only the residual profits of the enterprise, however large or small they may be. In the loan market, the difficulty encountered by worker-controlled firms is that the employees may not have the wherewithal to meet substantial payments for principal and interest, nor will they have the assets to provide adequate security in case of default (recall that the employees' human capital is not a legally deployable asset for this purpose). If the firm looks for equity capital on terms that imply not only the promise of future profits but also the risk of future losses, the capital will not easily be forthcoming without the firm's ceding ultimate control to the investors who are asked to bear the residual risk. It is true that the employees, too, will suffer significant losses from a decline in the employer's business, to the extent that their current jobs, in which they have invested much of their working lives, are worth more than any alternative jobs they are likely to find. But the equity shareholders, taken as a single constituency in the firm (rather than as individuals who have probably diversified their investment portfolio), stand to lose their entire investment if the firm fails, because their capital goes to pay off all prior creditors (including the workers' claim to back pay and benefits). Given this distribution of the risks, it is argued[96] that the natural market solution to the problem of raising venture capital is to locate ownership and control in the shareholders, so that they can better protect themselves and thereby reduce the price at which they can be induced to provide their capital.

Like the earlier political case for worker control, the various economic qualms on the subject are almost entirely *a priori* and conceptual in nature. Only recently have systematic empirical analyses of the relatively few extant cases begun to appear.[97] My own reading of this research suggests two tentative but counterintuitive judgments. First, contrary to the expectations of the economists, worker control does seem to be a viable mode of organization in the marketplace. The plywood cooperatives, for example, give ordinary workers in their plants meaningful control over the professional management that they

96. Most prominently by Williamson, *Economic Institutions* pp. 298–325.
97. The best of these studies are Witte, *Democracy, Authority, and Alienation*, Mansbridge, *Beyond Adversary Democracy*, and Greenberg, *Workplace Democracy*.

hire to run sizable and complex organizations successfully in a competitive product market. However, contrary to the hopes of the political theorists, this experience does not appear to alter sharply the nature of the job and the workplace environment, nor the attitudes and aspirations of its worker owners (on or off the job).[98]

If these judgments are valid, they suggest how complicated this topic really is. Whether or not one would conclude after broader and deeper analysis of the issue that worker control of American industry is so worthwhile that it should be seriously fostered by an affirmative public policy is a question I will not purport to answer here. But I do not have to arrive at a final verdict one way or the other, because there is simply no prospect on the horizon for any policy of true worker control (as contrasted with greater or lesser degrees of employee stock ownership).

Still, it is important to have rehearsed and understood the debate about this institution. The lesson that emerges from working through the arguments is that employee control is prone to the same characteristic tilt as shareholder control. Whenever the exercise of authority in the firm is directly accountable to only one of its constituencies, whichever it might be, there is a risk that the dominant group's decisions will downplay the needs and concerns of the other groups with a comparable stake in the enterprise. On the other hand, important political and economic reasons remain for giving career employees a meaningful voice in the affairs of the firm to which they have committed much of their working lives. If the American polity is not prepared to go all the way with this strong version of worker voice, then decent respect for the interests of employees will require that they be provided with something else. In the American tradition, that something else has long been union representation for purposes of collective bargaining.

98. These are the consistent conclusions of Greenberg, *Workplace Democracy*, studying the effects of worker ownership, and of Witte, *Democracy, Authority, and Alienation,* studying the effects of substantial employee involvement in a firm owned by its shareholders. The record of the plywood cooperatives with respect to job safety is an enlightening but depressing testimonial to the limited effects of changing the locus of control within the enterprise. Apparently, the worst accident records of the northwest plywood industry are held by the cooperatives, which tend to be much less attentive to OSHA than are the conventionally owned plywood firms. See Greenberg, *Workplace Democracy*, pp. 85–87. This uncomfortable fact has not yet sunk home among the radical analysts of the workplace safety problem (e.g., Noble, *Liberalism at Work*), who are prone to pin the blame for workplace accidents on capitalist owners' ignoring the interests of their workers.

Union Representation

Within the analytical framework of this section, the place of union representation and collective bargaining should now be readily apparent. Rather than the unilateral exercise of authority by managers who are directly accountable only to shareholders or to workers, some measure of bilateral sharing of authority between the two constituencies should be established. The shareholders of the firm will still have a management team to advance and protect their interests, but this management would have to deal with a comparably cohesive and sophisticated team to represent the employees. In that setting the function of collective bargaining is to supply a remedy for each of the characteristic flaws in managerialism that I pointed out earlier.

Voice. Unionization allows the employees to come together as a group, discuss and learn how they might want their working conditions improved, figure out their priorities in distributing whatever added resources will be offered by their employer, and voice these concerns and proposals without fear of reprisal against any individual worker who challenges the customary way management has operated. In particular, union representation is the vehicle through which the average career employee asserts his needs in contrast with either the casual employee who can pick up and go elsewhere, or the exceptional employee whom the employer will make a special effort to satisfy on its own. This is not just a speculative point: recent research has amply documented the hypothesis that a more egalitarian distribution of wages, rewards for long service in the design of fringe benefits and the allocation of desirable jobs, protection against unfair treatment and dismissal, and the other priorities of the average career employee are emphasized much more in union than in comparable nonunion firms.[99]

Nor is this simply a matter of satisfying the preferences of one interest group or another, with no broader social value. For all the reasons I have given, the average career employee is in the segment of the work force that is least able to rely on a competitive market to advance its concerns, and that has the greatest need to establish an employment relationship which will enhance its commitment and productivity. Unsurprisingly, then, the same research that demonstrated the above-noted differences in actual employment terms between union and nonunion firms also showed that unit labor productivity in the unionized private sector firm is often significantly greater than in its non-

99. See generally Freeman and Medoff, *What Do Unions Do?*

union counterpart.[100] Although the finding that unionization has a positive overall impact on productivity remains controversial,[101] there is strong corroboration of the more limited claim that the voice mechanisms of collective bargaining better communicate the true interests of employees. The fact is that the better nonunion firms have regularly learned from and adopted the important innovations in conditions of

100. See the research reviewed in Freeman and Medoff, *What Do Unions Do?* in particular Chapter 11, "Unions: Good or Bad for Productivity?" pp. 162–180. The most detailed and unshakeable of these research results come from the longitudinal study of the cement industry by Kim B. Clark, "The Impact of Unionization on Productivity: A Case Study," 33 *Industrial and Labor Relations Review* 451 (1980); and from a series of studies by Stephen G. Allen on different segments of the construction industry: "Unionized Construction Workers Are More Productive," 99 *Quarterly Journal of Economics* 251 (1984); "Unionization and Productivity in Office Building and School Construction," 39 *Industrial and Labor Relations Review*187 (1986); and "Can Union Labor Ever Cost Less?" 102 *Quarterly Journal of Economics* 347 (1987). A recent study of the impact of collective bargaining in a partially unionized multiplant firm also found that collective bargaining had a substantial positive effect on productivity: see Robert N. Mefford, "The Effects of Unions on Productivity in a Multinational Manufacturing Firm," 40 *Industrial and Labor Relations Review* 105 (1986). By contrast, on the basis of the research reported so far, the effect of unionization on productivity in the public sector appears to be neutral: see Ronald G. Ehrenberg, Daniel R. Sherman, and Joshua L. Schwarz, "Unions and Productivity in the Public Sector: A Study of Municipal Libraries," 36 *Industrial and Labor Relations Review* 199 (1982) ; Stephen G. Allen, "The Effect of Unionism on Productivity in Privately and Publicly Owned Hospitals and Nursing Homes," 7 *Journal of Labor Research* 59 (1986) ; and Eli M. Noam, "The Effect of Unionization and Civil Service on the Salaries and Productivity of Regulators," in Joseph D. Reid, Jr., ed., in *New Approaches to Labor Unions*, pp. 157–170 (Greenwich, Conn.: JAI Press, 1983).

101. For an extended critique of the research and literature on this subject, see Barry T. Hirsch and John T. Addison, *The Economic Analysis of Unions: New Approaches and Evidence* (Boston: Allen and Unwin, 1986), in particular Chapter 7, "Unions and Economic Performance," pp. 180–217. Hirsch and Addison are dubious about the union productivity effects described by the research of Freeman and Medoff and their associates in *What Do Unions Do?* in part because of the difficulty of pinning down the precise sources and mechanisms of these productivity gains. Some gains can be specifically attributed to the increase in employee tenure and reduction in turnover produced by an institution such as unionism, which is responsive to the interests and concerns of career employees. When measured, however, this factor appears to account for less than half of the improvement in productivity. It is speculated that a considerable portion of this improvement is the result of the union "shock effect" on the firm's management, which must strive to run a considerably more efficient operation in order to pay for the additional wages and benefits that employees tend to win through collective bargaining. This explanation fits nicely with the observed pattern of research results: the productivity improvements associated with unionism are confined to the private rather than the public sector, and the strongest improvements are observable in industries (such as construction) in which the union wage premium is the highest, and the need is thus greatest for more efficient use of the firm's labor and other resources to accommodate the additional costs.

As Addison and Hirsch admit (pp. 214–215), whether or not one believes that enhanced efficiency is likely to be the byproduct of the collective organization of employees depends to a considerable extent on one's prior assumption about whether there tends to be a con-

employment that have been developed through collective bargaining in unionized firms.[102]

Leverage. Even if the interests of the average nonunion employees are effectively communicated to management, they may not be adequately satisfied. That outcome requires enough employee leverage to extract a larger share of the firm's resources, a share that management is not inclined to give them voluntarily. Within the upper and lower bounds set by the labor, consumer, and capital markets, the balance of power in dealings between individual long-service employees and their employers will tend to favor the latter. The firm can lose and replace any one employee much more easily than the employee can lose and replace his job with the firm. What unionization does is coordinate the actions of the entire group of workers so that in the absence of a favorable contract offer from the employer, all the employees can withdraw their labor together. It is this collective loss of labor that the firm cannot so easily redress.

That does not mean that the employees' bargaining power can be instantly overwhelming. Any strike also costs the employees their paychecks and risks their jobs to permanent replacements, thus giving them a strong incentive to moderate their contract demands. However, the difference in relative bargaining power as between union and nonunion employees is amply demonstrated by the results. In financial terms, collective bargaining produces gains in total compensation that now average 10 percent to 15 percent.[103] For reasons I suggested earlier,[104] the bulk of these gains will come out of what the employer would otherwise take as its vastly greater share of the surplus from their mutually beneficial employment relationship, or from the rents available in an im-

---

siderable degree of X-inefficiency in American industry (see Leibenstein, *Beyond Economic Man*), a factor with which management must finally come to grips when faced with economic gains won by employees through collective bargaining. At a minimum, this argument is at least as plausible as the assumption subscribed to by a large portion of the law and economics fraternity (including many of its members who are highly dubious about unionism) that there is a significant amount of slack in corporate management that can be reduced, with a corresponding increase in productivity, by hostile takeovers and corporate restructuring. In my opinion it is distributionally more appealing to have the shock effect on management produced by a premium paid to the employees, rather than by a windfall to the shareholders. But however the debate may evolve about the scope and size of union productivity *gains*, what is most striking about the serious empirical research on this subject carried out over the last decade is that it has thoroughly exploded the stereotype of the union as cartel, which assumes, *a priori*, that collective bargaining by workers is inherently antithetical to a productive and competitive economy.

102. See Jacoby, *Employing Bureaucracy*; and Foulkes, *Personnel Policies*.
103. See Hirsch and Addison, *The Economic Analysis of Unions*, pp. 116–154.
104. See Chapter 3, pp. 132–133.

perfectly competitive product market. Thus the actual size of the union wage effect will depend a great deal on the circumstances which influence that surplus or those rents. But on the noneconomic side, the almost uniform difference between union and nonunion employment is that the terms and conditions enjoyed under a collective agreement—epitomized by the protection against unjust dismissal—are guaranteed as a matter of contractual right and enforced in an accessible grievance procedure ending in neutral and binding arbitration.[105] This is perhaps the best testimonial to the difference made by collective employee leverage, as compared to mere collective voice.

This review of the available options for workplace governance satisfies me that collective bargaining, as compared with managerialism, is significantly more likely to insure that the important concerns of workers will be reflected in the decisions of the enterprise in the broad leeway left by the market. The premise of collective bargaining is that the skilled and cohesive management team that represents the interests of the shareholders will be matched on the other side of the table by union leaders with comparable resources and incentives to advance the employees' interests. And though there is an admittedly arm's-length adversarial flavor to the process, the contract the parties eventually sign is much more likely than a legal edict from an outside government agency to be tailored to the special characteristics and needs of the common enterprise on which both the workers and the shareholders depend.[106]

105. To return briefly to the issue of pension reversions, the econometric analysis reported in Ippolito, *Pensions*, p. 240, found that the single largest inhibitor to an employer contemplating such action is the presence of a union representing the employees.

106. It is sometimes argued (e.g., by Richard A. Posner, "Some Economics of Labor Law," 51 *University of Chicago Law Review* 988, 1000–01 (1984)) that if collective bargaining were really better attuned to the interests of workers, and thereby likely to increase their satisfaction and productivity in their jobs, one would expect employers to embrace rather than fight this process, which could make them more competitive. But in fact the price of a firm's stock tends to fall rather than rise when the employer is presented with an NLRB certification petition; see Richard S. Ruback and Martin M. Zimmerman, "Unionization and Profitability: Evidence from the Capital Market," 92 *Journal of Political Economy* 1134 (1984). This pattern implies that the determined resistance by American management to union representation corroborates the earlier theoretical argument about the economic vices of unionization.

The fallacy in the preceding argument is its assumption that what is bad (or good) for the employer is necessarily bad (or good) for the political economy as a whole. There is no doubt that employees' organizing themselves into a body which can wield power on their behalf inflicts costs on the special interests of the employer. Unions reduce the proportion of profits flowing to the shareholders by securing for the employees a sizable share of the rents generated in product markets that are geographically or technologically

In addition to the instrumental advantages of unionism in better protecting the interests of workers in the firm, union membership has intrinsic value as a process in which employees take the responsibility for defining, asserting, and, if necessary, compromising their concerns. At least when the system operates as it is supposed to,[107] employees in the factory or office select union leaders (from president to job steward) to represent them in dealings with the employer, and the employees themselves make a variety of group decisions, such as what position their union will take in contract negotiations, or whether to challenge the employer's treatment of individual claims under the contract. As I contended earlier in discussing the far-reaching program of full-fledged employee ownership and control, union representation is a vehicle through which workers can, at least to some extent, participate in and influence some of the most salient issues in their daily lives, and thereby equip themselves to play a more active role in the outside polity.

I do not purport to deduce from some abstract principle the conclusion that collective bargaining is inherently the ideal mode of governance for the workplace. There is no such abstract principle, and there is no single best way to govern all workplaces. But once we understand the nature and limitations of the available alternatives, it is plausible for us to suppose that in a multitude of settings union representation is as attractive a form of governance we have yet been able to devise. If this supposition is true, the policy conclusion which follows is that we should use our legal imagination and political resources to try to fashion a labor law regime that could avert the impending demise of unionization in the American political economy.

---

protected. Unions also place significant restraints on what was once legally unconstrained managerial power over the work force—subjecting company dismissal policies and their administration, for example, to the authority of a neutral arbitrator under a "just cause" contract term. American management has always been extremely unreceptive to the institution that undermines its authority in this way, and management is prepared to invest more and more firm resources in fending off union representation for employees. But management's aversion tells us no more about the social value of unionization than we can infer about the value of corporate takeovers from the similar antipathy exhibited by American management to the unfriendly takeover bid. The hostile takeover attempt, like unionization, inflicts significant costs on incumbent management, but may have redeeming social benefits which are not factored into management's decision whether to use the firm's resources to fend of an unwelcome intruder (see John C. Coffee, "Shareholders Versus Managers: The Strain in the Corporate Web," 85 *Michigan Law Review* 1 (1986)).

107. This it does *not* always do, as the next chapter will demonstrate.

5 · Alternative Futures for Worker Participation

Rigidity in Contemporary Collective Bargaining

I claim no particular novelty for my pluralist account of union representation and collective bargaining. My aim has been to defend this now traditional institution against a contemporary attack mounted largely (though not entirely) from the law and economics platform, and to base this defense on a more realistic and up-to-date picture of how work is actually organized in the contemporary labor market. However, in discussing labor law reform with business executives and their lawyers, I have found that to many of them my rather academic and analytical argument simply misses the mark. Indeed, most are prepared to concede the abstract principle. "Of course," they say, "we agree that American workers should have a right to collective bargaining if that is what they want. Isn't that what we have been vigorously advocating for Polish workers?" But then they shy away from any proposals for serious labor law reform, because the whole case seems remote from the American reality they now experience.

In other words, it is one thing to acknowledge that collective bargaining as an ideal type may be the preferred procedure for resolving workplace issues. However, the concept of union representation has been realized in a remarkable variety of shapes, at different times and in different nations, each version with its own social, economic, and political implications. Its critics lament that the distinctive style of unionism that has evolved in the United States is of a peculiarly unattractive stripe.[1] That is why so many business executives, who would

1. For example, in *The Rise and Decline of Nations: Economic Growth, Stagflation and Social Rigidities* (New Haven: Yale University Press, 1982), Mancur Olson paints quite an unflattering picture of the nature and functioning of American unionism, by comparison

agree as citizens that a trade union movement has been and should continue to be an important ingredient in a market economy and democratic polity, will fight hard as managers to keep unionization out of their own plants and offices in order to avoid the tangible difficulties it may cause to their particular enterprises. Of course, if the NLRA is reformed to give American workers a better chance to have union representation if they want it, whatever their employers might feel, the country will simply get more of the style of collective bargaining currently practiced by American unions. Thus it is the future prospect of what many in the business community have experienced in the past as an especially rigid and confrontational mode of union representation that makes management and its political representatives especially resistant to labor law reform.

A good index of the malaise that has allegedly enveloped U.S. collective bargaining is the evolution of the collective agreement itself. For example, whereas the first contract negotiated between the United Auto Workers and General Motors (in the late thirties) was only one page long, the agreement now covering each of GM's plants totals 500 pages.[2] Merely to specify how wages are to be paid, the contract contains a voluminous list of job classifications and pay rates, complex descriptions of what each job involves at a particular rate, and elaborate procedures and criteria for deciding who gets to do the work at which rate.[3] Similarly detailed regulations define the rights and obligations of the parties with respect to each of the fringe benefits, layoffs and promotions, and a multitude of other conditions of employment.

And all this is simply the basic collective agreement, the legislative framework for life in the plant. The contract language is then in-

---

with what he judges to be much more sensible versions of the institution in countries such as Sweden, West Germany, and Japan.

2. D. Quinn Mills, *The New Competitors: A Report on American Managers*, p. 245 (New York: Wiley, 1985). This is the combined length of the master GM-UAW agreement and the typical local agreement covering a particular GM plant. In the steel industry, the combination of the basic US Steel-Steelworkers contract and the several specialty agreements for pensions, health and welfare insurance, supplementary unemployment benefits, and vacations now totals 550 pages; see John P. Hoerr, *And the Wolf Finally Came: The Decline of the American Steel Industry*, p. 75 (Pittsburgh: University of Pittsburgh Press, 1988).

3. Harry C. Katz, in his book *Shifting Gears: Changing Labor Relations in the U.S. Automobile Industry* p. 39 (Cambridge, Mass.: MIT Press, 1985), reprints a figure from the GM-UAW contract which lays out part of the job and wage classification system and seniority ladder. Among the eleven carefully segregated jobs in only one area of the assembly operation are such positions as Installer Door Trim Panels, Installer Garnish Moldings, Lower Rear Assembly, and Arm Rest Assembly; just up the ladder are Installer Front Seats and Installer Rear Backs.

terpreted and elaborated by a vast array of grievance settlements, arbitration awards, and letters of understanding, all designed to put flesh on the 500-page skeleton. This complex exegesis is evidence of a frequently noted feature of American-style unionism: how deeply and how closely it regulates life in the plant.[4] The consequence is that management often feels hamstrung in its capacity to respond to changes in its environment—either in its product market, its technology, or its work force and their sentiments. Nor is such constraint due simply to the detail of such contractual regulation. Often a contract provision or arbitration precedent starts out as a sensible response to a tangible workplace problem. But once such a perquisite has been won and enjoyed by a particular group of workers it is perceived as a worker "right", and the political process inside the union makes it difficult for elected leaders to override their members' intense opposition to any concession in their "rights," even if a union leader would privately concede to his management counterpart that the contract term had become outmoded.

Even worse from management's perspective, the contract that will regulate affairs inside the plant is often the product of negotiations with a large national union. For example, the UAW has evolved into a national body which represents not only the employees of General Motors, but also the employees of other auto manufacturers and of the many auto parts firms, and, indeed, of businesses in a variety of unrelated industries. The UAW felt compelled to grow into a large organization so that it could draw upon resources sufficient for facing off with a giant corporation like General Motors. But having attained that advantageous position, the union leadership still considers it strategically necessary for both economic and political reasons, to impose on other smaller companies the same pattern of wage rates and fringe benefits that it has won for its members in the bellwether settlement with the bigger, more profitable firms. From the worker perspective, this practice is one of the historic virtues of trade unionism because it reduces the arbitrary disparity in wages paid by different firms and industries to employees of similar abilities, and thereby significantly lessens the degree of earnings inequality in the economy as a whole.[5]

4. For an analysis of this regulation and its implications, see Derek C. Bok, "Reflections on the Distinctive Character of American Labor Laws," 84 *Harvard Law Review* 1394, 1404–18 (1971).

5. Richard B. Freeman and James C. Medoff, in *What Do Unions Do?* pp. 78–93 (New York: Basic Books, 1984), present decisive empirical evidence of the significant net reduction in earnings inequality which has been produced by collective bargaining. One important component of the overall reduction is a decrease in the disparity in the earnings of workers with the same human capital who happen to be employed by different firms

However, the flip side of this benefit is that collective bargaining imposes considerable financial rigidity on the economy, since the market situation of the other firms and industries may be entirely unsuitable for a contract term that was arguably justifiable in the particular context in which it was first negotiated. According to this line of argument, then, the more important objection to present-day unionism is not that the union operates as a private cartel inside the firm, extracting exorbitant rents for its members, but rather that the union functions as an outside regulator, imposing on individual firms restraints that are much more profound than, and often as rigid and insensitive as, restraints placed on firms by the federal government.

The inefficiency of imposing such inflexible employment protections on management cannot be justified by asserting that it is a necessary byproduct of a process which gives employees an opportunity for meaningful participation in the firm and influence on their life at work. The "iron law of oligarchy" governs unions as much as it does businesses. Large unions are run by bureaucracies which often bear an uncanny resemblance to the corporate management with which they regularly do battle.[6] From the point of view of the worker, then, his union often appears to be simply another alien organization, one in which he also has relatively little voice, and against which he may occasionally want legal rights and protections. This is not to deny that in the triennial negotiation of the new contract, union leadership makes a considerable effort to learn what new benefits their members would like and what rights they most want to have preserved against management erosion.[7] The fact that collective bargaining is indeed respon-

---

and in different industries. Michael J. Piore and Charles F. Sabel, in *The Second Industrial Divide: Possibilities for Prosperity*, pp. 79–85 (New York: Basic Books, 1984), describe the system of post-World-War-II wage determination, which evolved after the enactment of the NLRA and the unionization of the major industrial sectors of the economy, and which made the egalitarian trend in earnings possible. On the basis of as yet unpublished calculations, Richard Freeman has concluded that the decline of union representation and the unraveling of the collective bargaining system over the last fifteen years is responsible for a considerable share of the growing earnings inequality which emerged during the same period, and which is depicted in Frank Levy, *Dollars and Dreams: The Changing American Income Distribution*, pp. 75–78 (New York: Russell Sage Foundation, 1987); and in Bennett Harrison and Barry Bluestone, *The Great U-Turn: Corporate Restructuring and Polarizing of America*, pp. 117–128 (New York: Basic Books, 1988).

6. For some illuminating reflections on this theme by the leading legal scholar on the subject of union democracy, see Clyde W. Summers, "Democracy in a One-Party State: Perspectives from Landrum-Griffin," 43 *Maryland Law Review* 93 (1984).

7. There is data corroborating this tendency in the research by Edward S. Greenberg on the plywood cooperatives in *Workplace Democracy: The Political Effects of Participation* (Ithaca, N.Y.: Cornell University Press, 1986). The control group for Greenberg's study were the

sive to the actual wishes and priorities of the average employee is graphically displayed in the pronounced difference between union and nonunion employment conditions. But if the initial moral aspiration of union representation was to democratize the workplace,[8] to give employees the ongoing experience of shaping their work environment, the current reality of American collective bargaining—in which professional union managers (many of them lawyers) negotiate and administer formal contract language in an artificial setting detached from day-to-day life in the plant—seems worlds removed from that ideal.[9]

---

employees of the conventionally owned plywood mills, which were typically unionized. When union members were asked about their involvement in union affairs, only a small fraction (16 percent in 1978 and 6 percent in 1983) said that they almost always attended union meetings; 75 percent said that they attended occasionally (p. 233). The occasion would almost certainly be at or around the time of contract negotiations, when nearly 80 percent reported that they actively discussed the issues in these negotiations (p. 52).

8. In explaining the philosophy which underlay the original NLRA, Senator Wagner stated: "The principles of my proposal were surprisingly simple. They were founded upon the accepted fact that one must have democracy in industry as well as in government; that democracy in industry means fair participation by those who work in the decisions vitally affecting their lives and livelihood; and the workers in our great mass-production industries can enjoy this participation only if allowed to organize and bargain collectively through representatives of their own choosing." The passage is quoted in Clyde W. Summers, "Industrial Democracy: America's Unfulfilled Promise," 28 *Cleveland State Law Review* 29, 34 (1979).

The major manifesto of the union movement as an instrument of democratic participation by employees in the workplace is the book by Clinton S. Golden and Harold J. Ruttenberg, *The Dynamics of Industrial Democracy* (New York: Harper and Brothers, 1942), written by two of the major intellectuals in the Steel Workers Union. A prominent theme in *And the Wolf Finally Came*, John Hoerr's book on the evolution of collective bargaining in the steel industry, is how far the industry's industrial relations system veered from that goal over the next forty years before finally and haltingly beginning to retrace its steps in this decade.

9. The problems of the elitism of union officialdom and the abstract legalism of "contractualist" collective bargaining receive special emphasis in the left's critique of American-style union representation. See, for example, Stanley Aronowitz, *False Promises: The Shaping of American Working Class Consciousness* (New York: McGraw-Hill, 1973), in particular Chapter 4, "Trade Unions: Illusion and Reality," pp. 214–263; Katherine Van Wezel Stone, "The Post-War Paradigm in American Labor Law," 90 *Yale Law Journal* 1509 (1981); and Karl E. Klare, "Critical Theory and Labor Relations Law," in David Kairys, ed., *The Politics of Law: A Progressive Critique*, p. 66 (New York: Pantheon, 1982). However, as both Stone and Klare make clear in their later writings—e.g., Karl E. Klare, "Workplace Democracy and Market Reconstruction: An Agenda for Labor Reform," 38 *Catholic University Law Review* 1 (1988); and Katherine Van Wezel Stone, "Labor and the Corporate Structure: Changing Conceptions and Emerging Possibilities," 55 *University of Chicago Law Review* 73 (1988)—their earliest critiques of the limitations of our collective bargaining system as it happened to evolve have not altered their views about the fundamental value of collective bargaining for American workers and the need to save the union movement in order to improve it.

However cramped might be the manner in which collective bargaining now satisfies the felt demand for greater worker participation in the affairs of the employer, the major overt opposition to the institution comes from American management. Employers find that too many unions seek to impose overly intrusive and inflexible restraints on the sensible conduct of their businesses. The resulting waste of energy and resources might have been tolerable, if not desirable, in the halcyon days of the fifties, when American enterprise dominated both its large insulated domestic economy and most foreign markets. However, dramatic changes in international competition have exposed the true weakness of American collective bargaining, its inability to adjust to new economic realities without employers' having to wage bruising battles to win concessions in outmoded contract terms. From this perspective, it would appear to be a serious mistake for the federal government to undertake major surgery on its labor legislation to save from extinction an institution which, whatever its analytical potential to the scholarly mind, functions so poorly in the real world of the eighties.

At the same time, it is also true that American employers have not been fighting the unionization of their employees simply to preserve unchallenged their traditional managerial prerogatives. For the last decade an ever-increasing number of businesses have been devising innovative programs of direct worker participation. The aim of such programs is to give employees a substantial measure of involvement in the affairs of the enterprise, but in a format that is sensitive to the immediate circumstances of each plant and firm, and that will be flexible in altering course as these circumstances change.

Such employee involvement plans (EIPs) take a variety of forms.[10] At the most rudimentary level, the organization of work is revised to give employees more leeway in their duties and the opportunity to rotate from one job function to another. Employees in different areas of the operation meet regularly in "quality circles" to discuss problems in the

10. There is a brief but useful catalogue of the different modes of EIP in Thomas C. Kohler, "Models of Worker Participation: The Uncertain Significance of Section 8(a)(2)," 27 *Boston College Law Review* 499, 500–513 (1986). Note that all of the various forms of direct employee participation in workplace decisions can be and have been adopted within the framework of a collective bargaining relationship. For descriptions of several such labor-management programs, see Thomas A. Kochan, Harry C. Katz, and Nancy R. Mower, *Worker Participation and American Unions: Threat or Opportunity?* (Kalamazoo, Mich.: W. E. Upjohn Institute, 1984). For more anecdotal reports of a variety of cases, mostly in unionized settings, see John Simmons and William Mares, *Working Together: Employee Participation in Action* (New York: New York University Press, 1985).

productivity and quality of output in their work area and to devise procedures for enhancing the efficiency of the firm's operations. In some instances joint QWL committees are formed with representatives of both employees and management. Their role is to take up a variety of worker concerns about the quality of their working life—an unpleasant physical environment, job hazards, work schedules, personality and disciplinary problems, and so on. A few firms have moved to a full-fledged team system of production in which employee groups are given substantial responsibility and autonomy in their area of the operation, in connection with issues such as how and when work is to be done, who will become members of the team through hiring or transfer, when and from whom parts and materials will be obtained, and which team members have performed well enough to merit bonuses or selection for team leader roles (or, on the contrary, which members have done poorly enough that they require discipline or even removal from the team).

Taken together, these recent developments imply that the emphasis of labor policy should shift from merely protecting employees from the harmful things that employers may do to them (and vice versa) in an assumedly adversarial relationship, to encouraging active participation by both sides in an effort to produce greater mutual benefits for each in an ideally cooperative relationship. Our priority ought to be to devise arrangements which will enable the firm to tap the insights and ingenuity of the work force in improving the efficiency of its operations and the quality of its product in a fast-changing and highly competitive marketplace; and which will at the same time allow employees to experience a sense of accomplishment and satisfaction from making an active and valuable contribution to the success of an enterprise in which they invest much of their working life.

What are the policy and legal implications of this alternative model for worker participation in America? Management would retain its basic position as the monitor and mediator of all the competing constituencies of the firm. It would have the ultimate authority and responsibility for designing an employment package which it considered sensible for and attractive to its employees. But a major feature of the package would be EIPs, serving as a regular institutional conduit through which the special needs and contributions of the employees would be channeled.

There are certain obvious obstacles to this promising development,[11]

11. These legal issues have provoked extensive legal commentary. Among the relevant pieces that I have found most helpful are Kohler, "Models of Worker Participation," and Charles C. Jackson, "An Alternative to Unionization and the Wholly Unorganized Shop: A Legal Basis for Sanctioning Joint Employer-Employee Committees and Increasing

and to help overcome them the focus of *labor* law reform should be to loosen up the anachronistic hold placed on so-called company unions by the NLRA. However, the program I just sketched is not rigidly wedded to the ideal of the free market—in particular, to the view that labor is just another commodity to be exchanged in a competitive marketplace. The option of external legal regulation would be held in reserve to deal with those especially serious human problems faced by workers and not adequately addressed by in-house procedures. (The legal doctrine of employment at will might well be the prime current candidate for such *employment* law reform.) This complementary array of instruments for workplace governance appears much more likely than actual (as opposed to idealized) collective bargaining to provide the ideal blend of flexibility and regulation in meeting the needs of both parties to the employment relationship.

Three Stages of American Unionism

The foregoing discussion is the strongest possible rejoinder to the more analytical argument I developed earlier for labor law reform. To deal with this counterattack, I shall break it down into its key components and take them up one by one.

To begin, I agree that there is much to criticize in the standard product of present-day collective bargaining. However, it is not clear precisely what significance should be attached to this point. After all, there is as much if not more to criticize about the standard operating procedures followed by American managers over the last two decades, including the policies of personnel management in nonunion firms.[12] However, no one would suggest that because of these visible failings shareholders should no longer have the right to have a management team represent their interests inside the enterprise, a team whose particular composition and practices can and should be changed when

Employee Free Choice," 28 *Syracuse Law Review* 809 (1977), two articles written from starkly contrasting value premises. Recently the U.S. Department of Labor produced its own analysis of the legal problems, published in a departmental report on *U.S. Labor Law and the Future of Labor-Management Cooperation*, pp. 36–65 (Washington, D.C.: U.S. Department of Labor, October 1987).

12. For a vigorous and frequently cited general critique of American managerial practices, see Robert H. Hayes and William J. Abernathy, "Managing Our Way to Economic Decline," 58 *Harvard Business Review* 67 (July–Aug. 1980). The accounts by Hoerr, *And the Wolf Came*, and Katz, *Shifting Gears*, of the failings of the industrial relations systems in the steel and auto industries show that the problems are attributable at least as much to the limited vision of their business executives as of their union leaders.

they have failed. Likewise, one must distinguish the question of whether workers should have a right to collective bargaining from the very different question of whether what they are doing with that right—that is, the contents of their collective agreements—is sensible, for themselves or for others. Granted that a good deal of the standard product of collective bargaining is somewhat out of touch with the realities of the contemporary workplace and marketplace; the point is that either side can press for changes in the traditional way of doing things. My argument about the principles that should be reflected in labor law reform is directed only at the fundamental issues of whether workers should have a meaningful collective voice in deciding the terms of any transformation of the employment relationship. The argument implies no blanket approval of the shape and content of the typical labor contract in American industry, content which neither present nor future labor law should dictate.

I recognize that to many people this may seem to draw too easy a distinction. If union representation has in fact produced an unhappy tilt in the employment relationship, that is surely a powerful argument against vigorous legal reforms that would help expand the reach of unionism as we know it to be, with all the inertial force that inhibits possible changes in the unions' standard *modus operandi*.

The flaw in the last contention is that it mistakenly assumes only a single essential version of American-style collective bargaining. In fact, collective bargaining has taken at least two fundamentally different forms in its one-hundred-year life in this country—the American Federation of Labor (AFL) "trade" model and the Congress of Industrial Organizations (CIO) "industrial" model.[13] Given that such a profound transformation has already taken place in American collective bargaining, it follows that there is no intrinsic, immutable character to the process. Thus to argue that as a matter of principle workers should enjoy an effective right to union representation does not imply an endorsement of the way currently unionized workers are using that right, nor any advice to newly organized workers to tread the same path.

I shall try to encapsulate a century of bargaining history in a few paragraphs.[14] First came the AFL trade model, which was dominant

13. A third, albeit short-lived, model of American unionism, the Knights of Labor movement, sought in the late nineteenth century to organize workers primarily for collective political action vis-à-vis the government, rather than for collective bargaining with their immediate employers. See Leon Fink, *Workingmen's Democracy: The Knights of Labor and American Politics* (Urbana: University of Illinois Press, 1983).

14. There is a vast literature on the contrasting AFL and CIO conceptions of union representation and collective bargaining. David E. Feller, "A General Theory of the

from about 1885 to 1935. The workers who enjoyed this kind of union representation were the skilled tradesmen in industries such as construction, shipping, railroading, printing, and music. These workers became skilled in their craft through a rather lengthy apprenticeship as a prelude to obtaining journeyman status. In many of these industries (epitomized by construction) the tradesmen would move from employer to employer, because the firms were quite small and needed workers with such skills for only specific periods of time. In those sectors the primary relationship and allegiance of the tradesmen would be to their union, which defended their craft and jurisdiction not only against the employer, but also against other trades and *their* unions. But in whatever industry they were employed, the skilled journeymen exercised a good deal of autonomy in their work. Usually there were no preset routines for the production operation, epitomized by the construction of large buildings custom-designed for particular clients and sites. That meant that the worker had to display his acquired skills and experience in dealing with the challenges he regularly encountered, rather than have a supervisor constantly tell him exactly what to do. Indeed, the foremen themselves were drawn from the craftworkers and remained members of the union as they occasionally moved from the status of supervisor on one job to journeyman on another.

In this occupational setting, the typical contract negotiated between a union and an employer was quite short, with standard contents tailored to the specific project conditions. The collective agreement would define the craft and work jurisdiction over which it applied; establish the appropriate ratio of employees (the number of supervisors and number of apprentices per journeyman) to be used on the job; specify the wage rates to be paid to the tradesmen and the employer's contribution to the benefit programs run by the union for its members; outline the general criteria for allocating work assignments in cases of promotion, layoffs or work sharing, and dismissal; and contain a "closed shop" provision requiring that all work of the craft type be performed by members of the union (who were often referred to the employer by the union's hiring hall). The mode of enforcing the agreement tended to be not outside neutral arbitration, but rather procedures internal to the union. For example, a conflict between a

---

Collective Bargaining Agreement," 61 *California Law Review* 663, 724–736 (1973), synopsizes this literature and provides an instructive analysis of how the respective trade and industrial models fit within the legal framework of the NLRA. Piore and Sabel, *The Second Industrial Divide*, pp. 115–124 and 205–220, contrast the craft and industrial models of workplace organization in the past and present economies.

supervisor and a journeyman about a disciplinary discharge would be heard and settled at a hearing held by a committee of the union, of which the parties to the dispute would both be members. The union's decision was enforceable through its control of the employer's labor supply under the closed shop provision, or simply through a strike of those currently working on the job. In turn, the union provided a significant degree of economic security to its members by limiting the number of new entrants into its apprenticeship programs and thence into the craft community, in order to assure the incumbents that a reasonable amount of work would be available to them at the wage levels and on the other terms established through collective bargaining. In sum, rather than put a premium on close, legalistic regulation of management to protect the employees, this model of union representation and the labor contract assumed and fostered a considerable degree of flexibility and autonomy on the part of the work crew on the job site; in part because many of the potential conflicts between employer and journeyman would be settled by the union and its leadership rather than by the firm and its management.

However attractive it may have been in its particular setting, this trade model was simply not responsive to the situation and the needs of the unskilled and semiskilled workers employed in vast numbers by such giant corporations as General Motors, U.S. Steel, and General Electric. These employees worked in a mass-production, assembly-line operation, originally in the insecure atmosphere of the drive system, where they were subject to the whims of omnipotent foremen. Then, as management of the workplace became more sophisticated and professional, it followed the lead of Frederick Taylor's "scientific management."[15] Under that system, engineers and other technical people would break the entire production process down into a large number of small steps, each allocated to an individual worker to perform as a single cog in a vast technological machine, closely monitored and controlled by supervisors. Under either the old drive system or the newer scientific management, there was a sharp divide between the small elite management team that decided what and how the work was to be done, and the large mass of labor that simply did what it was told. The new model of industrial unionism had to be developed for precisely these workers, who were to be organized into a single union of all the employees in the plant, the firm, and ideally the industry. The aim of this model of unionism was to humanize the employment relationship by winning more

15. See generally Daniel Nelson, *Frederick W. Taylor and the Rise of Scientific Management* (Madison: University of Wisconsin Press, 1980).

generous and more rational pay and benefit schedules, defining equitable criteria for allocating preferred jobs, protecting workers from arbitrary treatment or excessive pressures by supervisors, and generally by establishing a more secure and stable employment relationship between worker and firm. It was always one of the aspirations of industrial unionism to give employees a voice on the job, to provide ordinary workers a modicum of democratic participation in the life of the factory, both for the intrinsic benefits of workplace involvement and to train these workers to participate in the democratic life of the polity.[16]

Still, the natural assumption on both sides was that management would continue to run the enterprise and would have the prerogative of initiating changes in the firm's operation and work organization. The role of the union was to react to these decisions, to challenge them in grievance arbitration, and eventually to regulate by contract the exercise of management authority where it significantly affected employees. In order to protect their members from harmful treatment as well as to secure for them a growing share of the fruits of the enterprise, the unions themselves became sophisticated enough to deal effectively with corporate management. That meant that a union would be run by a bureaucratic leadership of full-time officials and skilled professionals, who negotiated pattern-setting agreements for the entire industry, of which any single unit of employees was just a small part.

Viewed in its historical context, the industrial model of collective bargaining was a rather remarkable achievement. It succeeded in transforming our sense of how work should be organized and how employees should be treated, not only in union but in nonunion companies as well.[17] There were, of course, significant limits on the scope of this process. Unions focused on the immediate interests of workers in securing tangible guarantees against economic exploitation and arbitrary supervisory action on the job, while management was left in charge of the broader direction of the enterprise. Thus, for example, auto industry negotiations established the compensation paid to the employees and the quality of the working conditions under which they labored, but did not address either the price or the quality of the cars sold to consumers.[18] The historical trajectory reflected an always expanding

16. See the references cited in note 8.

17. The effects of the industrial model are described in detail in the work of Sumner H. Slichter, James J. Healy, and E. Robert Livernash, *The Impact of Collective Bargaining on Management* (Washington, D.C.: Brookings Institution, 1960).

18. This particular die was cast with the outcome of the famous bargaining dispute between the UAW and General Motors in 1946. In that year the union sought large compensation increases after the years of wartime restraint, yet insisted that the com-

reach of the union contract into employer decisionmaking whenever such action seemed to threaten employee interests, regardless of the predilections of management or even the edicts of the Supreme Court.[19] However, there was a clear sense on the part of union leaders as well as business executives that collective bargaining should not venture beyond certain limits.

The fundamental challenge of the eighties arose from the fact that the ground had shifted dramatically under the massive apparatus of industrial-style bargaining, with its limited regulatory approach to the workplace. That shift was the result of a number of important trends.[20]

The first trend has altered the economic environment that made Henry Ford's assembly line so efficient and profitable for American employers, and consequently produced unions that could negotiate contracts to both establish rules for fair treatment on the job and secure for workers a lucrative share of the proceeds from such industrial organization. But to be economically viable mass production re-

---

pany agree to maintain its existing car prices. The result was that General Motors granted generous improvements in wages and benefits, but successfully held fast to its position that the nature of the company's relationship with its customers was not the business of the union. For a historical analysis of this key event in the evolution of U.S. labor-management relations, see David Brody, *Workers in Industrial America: Essays on the Twentieth Century Struggle*, pp. 172–214 (New York: Oxford University Press, 1980); and Horwell J. Harris, *The Right to Manage: Industrial Relations Policies of American Business in the 1940's*, pp. 129–154 (Madison: University of Wisconsin Press, 1982).

19. Thus unions regularly bargain over plant closing or relocation, automation, and other forms of industrial change, notwithstanding the decision of the Supreme Court in First National Maintenance v. NLRB, 452 U.S. 666 (1981), that such changes typically are not "terms and conditions of employment" within the meaning of Section 8(d) of the NLRA. Similarly, unions regularly bargain for inflation adjustments in the pensions paid to retired workers, notwithstanding the Court's decision in Chemical and Alkali Workers v. Pittsburgh Plate Glass, 404 U.S. 157 (1971), that retirees are not "employees" who are properly the concern of the union under the Act.

20. The nature and significance of these trends have been documented in detail by a number of scholars (interestingly, all writing from Cambridge, Massachusetts) who are sympathetic to union representation but concerned about the need for major adjustments in the direction of the union movement in the face of current fundamental shifts in the American economy and its work force. See Charles F. Sabel, *Work and Politics: The Division of Labor in Industry* (New York: Cambridge University Press, 1982); Robert B. Reich, *The Next American Frontier* (New York: Times Books, 1983); Piore and Sabel, *The Second Industrial Divide:* Thomas A. Kochan, Harry C. Katz, and Robert B. McKersie, *The Transformation of American Industrial Relations* (New York: Basic Books, 1986); Charles C. Heckscher, *The New Unionism: Employee Involvement in the Changing Corporation* (New York: Basic Books, 1988); and Paul Osterman, *Employment Futures: Reorganization, Dislocation and Public Policy* (New York: Oxford University Press, 1988).

quires a stable, high-volume customer base to justify the high fixed capital cost of the factories and equipment dedicated to such uses.

Two related trends have eroded this comfortable position of American business. One is the shrinkage in the available market relative to the supply, as many underdeveloped countries have been able to build modern steel mills and automobile plants, for example, which can use much lower-paid labor to perform the necessary routine tasks and thus undercut the price of higher-paying American producers. And the remaining market has become more volatile, partly because of a number of macroeconomic shocks to overall demand in recent years, and partly because the typical life cycle of products seems to be shortening as the richer nations become saturated with most standardized goods, such as certain household appliances.

The challenge posed to American industry today is to redirect its resources and energies into higher-value-added manufacturing and related producer services, which will utilize sophisticated computerized production techniques to make custom tailored goods for the smaller, constantly changing, but more expensive speciality markets. These goods consist not simply of high style consumer products such as fashions or computer software, but even more prominently of the technology and expertise that must be purchased and used by firms which will do the routine mass production of standard goods. In turn, this new form of "flexible specialization"[21] will place a premium on human rather than only physical capital, on a work force that is better educated, highly skilled, more adaptable, and capable of continuous innovation and improvements in production techniques. In other words, American firms have to be able to use high-quality workers who are worth the attractive and rising income that our political economy must be able to provide to the bulk of its labor force, not just to its elite.

But over and above good wages, what these employees will want (and what their employers will need) is a more horizontal, collegial, problem-solving relationship between the firm's leadership and its ordinary workers. We can no longer afford the traditional vertical relationship between manager and subordinate, in which the manager carefully and "scientifically" specifies what the subordinate must do. The new organization of the workplace will entail major changes in the way work is done and paid for. In many respects these trends incorporate some elements of the old craft model, with its emphasis on the

---

21. The meaning of this term is elaborated in Piore and Sabel, *The Second Industrial Divide*.

experience and responsibility of the skilled journeymen. However, most employees in the new setting will still have a career relationship with a single, often large firm, rather than the episodic relationships found in construction, for example. Thus a more apt characterization is that blue-collar production work will be treated by the firm according to the salaried model originally developed for the white-collar professional, administrative, and other workers in the front office.[22]

How might one summarize the elements of this evolving employment relationship? Rather than each individual worker's being assigned to a particular job in which he specializes in a single, predetermined function—a small cog in a large bureaucratic machine, employees are being grouped in teams that are assigned responsibility for a broader area of the operation. The members of these teams expect regularly to rotate from job to job, even from function to function, and to decide among themselves when and how they will rotate. Rather than pay the worker the exact rate specified for each job function he happens to be performing at any one time, more and more employees are being paid on the basis of their accumulated knowledge and skills, which equip them to fill a wider variety of roles on the team.[23] Rather than being imposed by a pattern-setting contract negotiated for the overall industry, the pay scale is designed more specifically for the individual firm, which must operate in its own niche in a product market that varies sharply in the type and profitability of goods and services being supplied. Indeed, compensation may well be divided into a basic guaranteed portion (which might equal two-thirds of the total expected pay) and another segment to be derived from the revenues or profits of the firm as they rise and fall.[24] Rather than a single set of fringe benefits designed to meet the needs of a mythical "national average" employee,

22. See Osterman, *Employment Futures*, pp. 60–91; compare Piore and Sabel, *The Second Industrial Divide*, pp. 115–124 and 205–220, on the "craft" model.

23. See U.S. Department of Labor, *Exploratory Investigations of Pay-For-Knowledge Systems* (Washington, D.C.: U.S. Department of Labor, 1986).

24. For an analytical account of the macroeconomic advantages of this particular compensation system, see Martin L. Weitzman, *The Share Economy: Conquering Stagflation* (Cambridge, Mass.: Harvard University Press, 1984). Richard B. Freeman and Martin L. Weitzman, in "Bonuses and Employment in Japan," 1 *Journal of Japanese & International Economics* 168 (1987), examine the effects of the Japanese version of the share economy on Japan's ability to enhance employment without exacerbating inflation. Ronald G. Ehrenberg and George T. Milkovich, in "Compensation and Firm Performance," in Morris Kleiner, Richard Block, Myron Roomkin, and Sidney Salsburg, eds., *Human Resources and the Performance of the Firm* (Madison, Wis.: Industrial Relations Research Association, 1987), examine what little we know about the impact of this or other compensation models on the productivity and performance of individual firms.

this part of the compensation package is being used to provide a "cafeteria-style" array of benefits: each worker can choose from a menu of options that enables him to tailor decisions about benefits such as medical insurance to his own individual situation, which likely includes the fact that his spouse is also employed by a firm with a benefit package, which the family would like to dovetail with his.

One obvious theme running through these workplace developments is flexibility: current arrangements allow for a much higher degree of flexibility than was typically available to production workers in the traditional nonunion plant, let alone under the standard industrial agreement. Rather than focus attention on a detailed set of personnel regulations designed to protect workers from a variety of employment harms that they might suffer at the hands of management, the aim is to create an environment in which each side can gain greater positive benefits from the relationship. The firm then enjoys much more leeway in the use of its work force to meet changing technological and market conditions. Employees are invited to become involved in a wider range of decisions about how their work is to be done; they are asked to display their own ingenuity in figuring out newer and more efficient ways of producing better, higher-quality products. But while this salaried model offers more flexibility for the firm in its ongoing deployment of the work force, it also entails a crucial commitment by the firm in its employment of the work force governed by this model.[25] Unlike hourly-paid, blue-collar production workers, the white-collar salaried employee has always expected a strong guarantee against the loss of his job, even in the face of a falloff in the employer's business. At a minimum, the expectation is that a layoff would be utilized as a last resort, only after the employer has tried to avoid it by such expensive measures as paid furloughs, retraining and transfers, early retirement on a pension, or buyouts of the employees' stake with generous severance benefits.

I am attracted to the arguments of those who discern and advocate an expansion of the salaried model to cover a much broader spectrum of the work force, including employees whose working life has been governed and improved by the traditional industrial union contract. But this new conception of the employment relationship does not eliminate the need for a device to fill the vacuum in employee representation that has emerged in the American workplace.

In that regard, let me emphasize that the foregoing description of

---

25. See Osterman, *Employment Futures*, pp. 65–67.

workplace trends presents a somewhat romanticized view of much that is going on in American industry. For example, the images of autonomy and collegiality are much less applicable to the computer chip assembler than to the product designer in the high technology plants in the Silicon Valley; there is a similar sharp contrast in the treatment of professional or administrative employees and of the vast number of clerical workers who toil in the factory-like atmosphere of typing pools or data processing units in the same head offices.[26] Even for the better educated, highly skilled knowledge workers, there is a price to be paid for greater flexibility in the conditions of employment: increased potential for opportunistic behavior by their employers. Workers whose salary is based in significant part on a share in the variable earnings of the firm must place a great deal of trust in management to provide them with a proper accounting at year's end.[27]

Even worse, the salaried model is now threatened at its root premise, its implicit promise of job security to white-collar employees in return for broad managerial flexibility in the use of the employees' services. As office labor and staff functions represent an increasingly prominent share of the firm's costs, they can no longer be treated as a fixed overhead item. In the face of growing pressures from product and capital markets to cut costs (often to fend off a hostile takeover or to pay interest on the debt incurred in a leveraged buyout), a natural inclination of the firm is to pare excess staff, especially higher-paid managerial and professional employees who never imagined that they

26. See generally Robert Howard, *Brave New Workplace* (New York: Viking, 1985).

27. For an analysis of reasons for concern about such arrangements, see Oliver Williamson's review of Martin Weitzman's book on the macroeconomic virtues of the share economy in "A Microanalytic Assessment of 'The Share Economy,' " 95 *Yale Law Journal* 627 (1986). Some corroboration for Williamson's qualms can be found in the stories of movie and television stars who have experienced great difficulty in obtaining a fair share of the proceeds of successful productions, even though these stars can employ high-priced accountants and lawyers to scrutinize the studio's books. If "workers" such as these have difficulty in appraising and securing fair performance by their employers of complex contractual arrangements, how can the ordinary employees in a plant or office job evaluate comparably arcane employer decisions—such as the decision to liquidate what is often an artificial inflation-generated surplus in the company pension plan and to use the proceeds for its own purposes, perhaps even to finance a leveraged buyout of the company for the benefit of top management? Indeed, examples like these demonstrate that as modern enterprise becomes more fluid, more flexible, and more complicated, workers will be even more in need of independent, professional, and forceful representation to monitor management decisions that can have a drastic impact on the employees' stake in the firm. If workers are systematically denied access to such representation to protect this stake, they may not make the type of commitment to the enterprise that, as we saw earlier, is indispensable for a productive and dynamic economy (see Robert B. Reich, *Tales of a New America*, pp. 130–151 (New York: Times Books, 1987)).

would be laid off late in their career with their employer. Thus, just as many unionized airline pilots and steelworkers have lost their jobs because of the straitened circumstances of their industries, so also have numerous department store managers and computer software designers been laid off when the retail and software business sectors experienced similarly wrenching economic change.

But having entered these caveats, I still believe that we should anticipate and welcome the emergence in the next several decades of a model of the employment relationship that will look very different from the one existing in the typical industrial plant or collective agreement that has evolved over the last half-century.

The question, however, remains: what precisely are the public policy implications of encouraging the new style of employment relationship? Does it mean that unionism as such has become an entirely outmoded instrument for the still indispensable role of representing the interests of employees when their interests conflict with the aims of the employer, even in the new salaried relationship? Surely that inference is no more logical now that it would have been at a time when the industrial model of unionism was beginning to emerge in a form very different from its predecessor, the trade model. (And recall that this transformation in American unionism was taking place in the late thirties, just when the key policy judgments about the shape of our labor laws were being made by the Congress, the NLRB, and the Supreme Court.) There is absolutely no reason why workers in the United States should not exercise significant influence (through their union representatives and bargaining leverage) on the contours of the newly emerging flexible employment relationship.

That such a worker voice is a real possibility may be readily corroborated by a look beyond the American borders, at countries like West Germany and Japan, which pioneered in the development and use of the salaried model for production workers in a format that was significantly shaped and influenced by representatives of the employees. Indeed, there are a number of illustrations of that connection in this country, perhaps the most prominent being the UAW-General Motors agreement for the forthcoming Saturn Project. This contract fills only about twenty-five rather than 500 typed pages; it is far more a statement of general principles and policies than of detailed rules and regulations; production employees are to be salaried rather than paid by the hour, and their salary will incorporate a substantial bonus component that will vary with the earnings of the project. The major thrust of the contract is to establish a team system of production, with joint worker-management committees to resolve problems before they occur, rather than to confer on management the authority to run the plant subject only to union negotiation and litigation over explicit restraints imposed on managerial prerogatives. Substantial commitments have been made by General Motors to the employment security of the workers once they become full-fledged members of the production team.

This novel contract was arrived at only after a great deal of soul searching within the UAW, and the debate over its future value continues.[28] A particular reason for concern is that such a profound reshaping of the workplace will clearly require a correspondingly major reorganization of the union as well. Far more authority will have to be lodged in the local union members and officials who participate on the joint committees, and much less control will be exercised by the national union body with which the local is affiliated. Just as the distinctive technological and organizational demands of the new product market will require novel kinds of employment arrangements through which workers will offer their services and secure remuneration, so also, if employees are to have an organized voice in the shaping of new employment relationships, will they require a novel form of union representation—one might call this the model of *enterprise* unionism—to secure and implement the new form of collective contract. The style of representation that workers look for and receive is always a function of the broader economic and industrial structure through which a nation grapples with its economic environment. But as illustrated by the Saturn contract and other examples,[29] in which we can now glimpse a

28. For a description of the debate now going on in the UAW about the specifics of Saturn and what it portends for the future of union representation in the auto industry, see Harry C. Katz, "Automobiles," in David B. Lipsky and Clifford B. Donn, eds., *Collective Bargaining in American Industry: Contemporary Perspectives and Future Directions*, pp. 13, 41–48 (Lexington, Mass.: Lexington Books, 1987). Note that from the entirely different perspective of the National Right To Work Committee there is also considerable distaste for the Saturn agreement; see Jeffrey L. Hall, "UAW-GM Saturn Contract: 'Sweetheart Deal' or Novel Labor-Management Agreement," 17 *Memphis State Law Review* 69 (1986).

29. There is an extended description in Heckscher, *The New Unionism*, pp. 249–264, of an agreement between Shell Oil and the Energy and Chemical Workers Union covering a newly constructed refinery in Sarnia, Ontario. Not only did this agreement precede Saturn with its sharply different approach to the employer-employee-union relationships, but the Shell contract has actually been in operation for the past decade. One should not assume, however, that the enterprise model exemplified by the Shell and Saturn agreements is unique. Analogous worker organizations and workplace arrangements exist in Japan and West Germany, and the model is quite similar to what is now standard practice in North American university faculty bargaining. The typical contract between a faculty association and a university administration focuses on the economic package, and simply establishes and reinforces the ground rules for the traditional collegial form of university governance for determining what work is to be done (the curriculum and research pro-

possible shift from the industrial to the enterprise model of union representation, the core feature of unionization—an independent organization of workers that negotiates a collective contract on their behalf—is entirely compatible with the brave new world of "flexible specialization," if that is indeed the setting in which more and more Americans are destined to work in the future.

Employee Involvement and Independent Unionism

While the concept of unionism is compatible with this vision of the new workplace, it is by no means inevitable that much, let alone most, of the American union movement will evolve toward this enterprise model, which seems better attuned to the salaried system of employment. Still lurking beneath the surface of the debate in the human resources community about the ideal nature and content of the employment relationship is the fundamental question of what is to be the preferred mode of governance of the workplace of the future.

When I addressed that question in Chapter 4 at a rather abstract level, I concluded that simply to assign such authority to the management of the firm would not adequately serve the interests of employees in acquiring a satisfactory level of participation in and protection from the decisions of the firm. That was why the law had to provide employees with some kind of organized representation to voice their needs and concerns. But here I acknowledge that the specific shape taken by industrial unionism and its labor contracts has often been too rigid and adversarial vis-à-vis the employer and too bureaucratic and alien vis-à-vis the employees. Hence even granted that the more flexible work arr ngements of the future will require a meaningful employee voice in the enterprise, is such a voice not a fair characterization of the variety of EIPs now burgeoning in the more innovative nonunion companies?

The premise of my argument, after all, has been that the aim of the law at work is to give employees the influence they need in the affairs of the enterprise, not to protect the union movement as it happened to

---

gram) and who is to do it (hiring and promotion with tenure). The key decisions about these matters are made by the faculty within the university's committee structure. Unfortunately, by a 5–4 margin the Supreme Court held, in NLRB v. Yeshiva University, 444 U.S. 672 (1980), that such involvement of faculty members in the decisions of the university enterprise would cost them their status as nonmanagerial employees entitled under the NLRA to organize for a collective voice in the affairs of their employer. That decision has especially concerned the Department of Labor in its analysis of the treatment by present-day labor law of innovations in employee participation; see U.S. Department of Labor, *Future of Labor-Management Cooperation*, pp. 66–68.

evolve to this stage. Many people would argue that whatever its historic contributions to the civilization of American working life, the adversarial and confrontational model of labor-management relations has outlived its utility. The traditional union movement has undoubtedly improved the lives of the blue-collar work force in the mass production industries, workers whose fate would otherwise have been dictated by the drive system, or scientific management, or both. However, unionization is no longer well suited to the needs and aspirations of the new knowledge workers, who see themselves as enjoying the flexible but secure environment of salaried employment. What these people need, and what the law should now encourage and endorse as the model for worker participation, is a more cooperative model of direct employee involvement through structures devised by human resource managers, who realize that this is the best way to maximize the firm's investment in its valuable human capital.

To respond to that challenge one should start with a clear sense of how union representation and nonunion employee involvement differ as alternative models for worker participation. Of course, each of these models exists in a fairly broad range of institutional formats. EIPs may take the form of a work team put in charge of a specific operation, a quality circle that covers a broader production division, a plant-wide, quality-of-life working committee, or even a company-wide ESOP. Similarly, a union may be confined to a specific enterprise (such as a university faculty association), it may represent workers in a single occupational category (teachers, for example) or industry (garment manufacturing), or it may have become a vast, two-million-member conglomerate, such as the Teamsters. But even with these qualifications, one can single out several characteristic differences in the two basic models.

Independence. An EIP is almost invariably created by the employer. Management originates the idea, drafts the working document and the constitution, if there is one, explains the EIP's purpose and *modus operandi*, and provides the facilities and resources needed for its operation. There is nothing sinister about this arrangement, taken by itself. Even if there has been an initial expression of interest from some of the employees, it is highly unlikely that an unorganized collection of nonunion workers will have the resources or the inclination to develop such a program on their own and to persuade management to cooperate and other workers to participate; all this to establish a vehicle for improving conditions in a workplace of which these workers are only a small part, and in which they may remain for only a brief period of time. If there is to be ongoing employee participation in a nonunion plant, management has to be the source and the implementor of this benefit, just as it is for a variety of other collective benefits and procedures in the enterprise.

By contrast, union organizations are created by workers, or by people accountable to workers, rather than by employers. Of course, most existing unions were established long ago; they now represent themselves to any new unit of employees as an existing fact of life, to be accepted or rejected as is. Yet it is still the immediate group of employees that makes the fundamental choice about whether there will be (or continue to be) union representation in their plant; in addition, they choose their own shop stewards, committee members, and local officers; they largely determine the rules, practices, and policies of their local organization (within constraints set by the national constitution or the national executive); and they vote for the national officers or the delegates who will go to a convention to choose the national executive and to revise the national constitution.

Admittedly, there is wide variation in the amount of immediate worker influence on the affairs of different unions and with respect to different decisions (for example, the acceptance of the national contract as contrasted with a decision to take a local grievance to arbitration). In no sizable union is there currently the degree of democratic membership control over the decisions of the organization that was celebrated in much of the rhetoric of the Wagner Act.[30] But there is a qualitative difference between the type of control exercised by members over their union and the control wielded by nonunion employees over the existence, the design, and the reach of an EIP. Unlike an EIP, a union is supposed to be independent of employer influence. The *raison d'être* of union representation is to advance the interests of workers in dealing with a management team that is ultimately accountable to the shareholders. People object to any blurring of the line between the two organizations for many of the same reasons that they would object to a public defender's office that was established, funded, and staffed by the District Attorney.

Size and Resources. Membership and participation in an EIP is confined to the employees in the specific production area of the firm that is covered by the plan. This limited scope flows from the very idea of direct employee involvement: the aim is to tap the knowledge of employees who actually work in the plant about how to improve both the quality of their production and the quality of life in their particular area of operation. To the extent that a program (such as a plant-wide QWL com-

---

30. See Summers, "Democracy in a One-Party State," and Alan S. Hyde, "Democracy in Collective Bargaining," 93 *Yale Law Journal* 793 (1984).

mittee) is representative rather than directly participatory, there is often regular rotation of the employee members of the committee to broaden the extent of worker involvement. The implication of such restricted coverage, though, is that the EIP will have few or no independent resources. The employee members develop only a limited degree of organizational expertise beyond what they already know from their training and work in their job, and no EIP that I know of accumulates funds for hiring outside experts to advise employees about esoteric issues such as toxic exposure on the job—not to mention funds to support a strike.

The reason that almost every union is significantly bigger and stronger than virtually any EIP is that a union must be in a position from which it can mount a serious challenge to the existing prerogatives and predilections of management. Typically such an effort requires the expertise of trained and specialized union officials, the financial resources that accumulate from the regular collection of membership dues, and the group action—collective withdrawal of labor in a strike—that is the result of cohesive organization and decisionmaking. While it is easy to imagine that the resources needed to deal effectively with corporate management can be derived from an organization whose membership is limited to the employees of a sizable firm (such as the several unions which separately represent the employees of the major Japanese auto manufacturers), such resources are hardly likely to be amassed by a body whose coverage is restricted to a single workplace, much less one department of a single firm. Of course, unions also feel the urge to expand to cover a broad product market, and thereby to reduce the pressures against wage and benefit gains that flow from consumer choice rather than management resistance.[31] But whatever the socially optimal size and reach of union representation, there is no doubt that any union organization worthy of the name would be significantly larger than the typical EIP.

Product. The ultimate reason for the differences in size and resources is the significant difference in the product that each model aims to achieve. EIPs make recommendations; unions make contracts. EIPs usually have only a formal recommending role with respect to, for example, changes in production or in the plant environment. Manage-

---

31. Note that broad-based union organizations may be attractive in industries like construction, which are composed of very small firms, because a union is particularly well suited in those circumstances for solving such "public good" problems as establishing substantial apprenticeship programs, pension plans, and the like, which help attract and retain a qualified labor force.

ment clearly reserves the power to accept or to reject the EIP's suggestions. In some situations the committee may be given formal decisionmaking authority over certain issues defined by the management-authored document. Whatever legal difference this may make,[32] in practice this authority is *not* binding on the employer. The employer that unilaterally conferred authority on the employee committee may unilaterally withdraw it, either with respect to any particular decision or more generally, if management decides that the benefits of doing so would outweigh the costs.

By contrast, the resources of an independent union are marshaled to win a binding contract from the employer. The contract may take the form of the typical agreement in the industrial model—detailed regulation of the way management may treat the workers, with ultimate enforcement by a neutral arbitrator. Alternatively, the contract may concentrate on the creation of a joint decisionmaking process with respect to a range of workplace decisions, as illustrated in the Saturn Project example of the emerging enterprise model. In either case, the tacit assumption of the collective bargaining process is that the workers, through the union, will deal with management and the shareholders on a somewhat more equal plane with respect to the employment relationship. Rather than workers simply making suggestions for management's approval, the union aspires to something closer to bilateral governance of the workplace, the product of which will be legal entitlements for the employees.

It is often supposed that employee involvement programs elicit more direct and immediate participation in the affairs of the workplace by employees who are actually affected, whereas union representation provides only indirect participation through the negotiation of a collective agreement by a distant union official. That contrast is overblown. Although many EIPs focus on more immediate issues at the job level, as EIPs get broader in scope or jurisdiction, such as plant-wide committees or company-wide ESOPs, the actual work is increasingly handled by employee representatives selected for the committees—though usually the representatives are full-time employees and only

---

32. The implication of the NLRB decisions in *Spark's Nugget Inc.*, 230 NLRB 275 (1977) and *Mercy-Memorial Hospital*, 231 NLRB 1108 (1977), is that employee groups that are authorized to make decisions on behalf of the employer are *not* "labor organizations" within the meaning of Section 2(5) of the NLRA, because they do not act in a representative capacity on behalf of the employees. Thus such programs are not caught by the strictures in Section 8(a)(2) against any management involvement in a labor organization. See pp. 211–218 for an extended review of Sections 2(5) and 8(a)(2).

part-time committee members. Union representation, on the other hand, provides a considerable degree of direct participation on the part of the employees, both in the collective bargaining process (deciding, for example, whether to ratify or to strike over a new contract, or whether to press or drop a grievance) and also in joint employer-employee committees (for example, the long-established practice of joint health and safety committees, or the more recent illustration of union QWLs). I have argued at several points in this book that traditional industrial unionism had too limited a vision of the need for direct employee participation and the potential scope of a direct employee voice in the life of the firm. It took a number of pioneering nonunion managers to show that such employee involvement could enhance both worker satisfaction and firm productivity. But I am confident that at the present time, if the management of a company felt that an EIP would be such a good idea in its plant or office that it would unilaterally introduce the program in an unorganized setting, few American unions would resist (though many might not actively pursue) the introduction of such an EIP in their bargaining units.

Indeed, another characteristic difference between the two types of worker representation may be more significant at this time. Only a minority of nonunion workplaces now have any direct employee involvement. If workers are interested in participation, but their managers are against it, then union representation is a means by which employees can secure and define a *right* to employee involvement. The collective agreement may entitle the employees to a certain form of participation, even in situations in which management has not been interested in worker participation or has become disgruntled with the experience (as might happen, for example, to a health and safety committee that has decided to shut down a coal mining operation as too hazardous). The agreement may also limit the authority of a particular EIP to tamper with other contract rights that have been won by a different constituency in the work force (such as a local QWL committee which might be inclined to cut certain benefits in a company or industry agreement in order to enlarge its share of a declining amount of business). The point is that although union representation and nonunion EIPs are both designed to give workers a greater degree of participation in the decisions of the firm that affect them, union representation provides such participation from a base of independent power; the EIP does not. Indeed, a term often used for the activities I have been calling employee involvement is "participatory management," a label that reflects the fact that in a nonunion firm this involvement is really a distinctive style of *managing* the work force. The employer devises procedures for learning from its employees and for motivating them in their jobs for the benefit of both. Ultimately, though, management alone *decides* what to do with what it has learned from the workers, and the employees have no independent organizational base from which to insist that management heed their wishes.

From one philosophical perspective this absence of power is not necessarily a deficiency in the EIP mode of worker participation. If employees are viewed as an integral part of the common enterprise, sharing a fundamental community of interests with the shareholders in the success of the business, it might seem natural to assign management the role of consulting with the employees through a variety of EIPs and then developing programs for the common good of everyone. Certainly there is a good deal of truth to this image. The contest between workers and shareholders is not a zero sum game in which what one side gains the other, perforce, must lose. There is ample room for cooperative arrangements to the mutual advantage of both, and extensive communication and collaboration is likely to be the best way to fashion these arrangements.

Perhaps, though, there is in fact an inherent conflict of interest between the employees and the other constituencies of the enterprise about precisely where to draw the line between work and leisure, investment and consumption, hierarchy and collegiality. Because management is ultimately accountable to the suppliers of capital to the enterprise, and is also inclined to protect its own prerogatives, a purely cooperative form of EIP may not be sufficient for the constituency that supplies labor to the firm. Many workers will want skilled and effective representation of their own to deal with management from an independent and arm's-length (though preferably not *antagonistic*) position at the crucial point in the relationship where the contractual ground rules for the daily life of the enterprise, including the extent and manner of employee participation, are defined.

"Company Unions" and the Managerial Exclusion

The National Labor Relations Act rests on the assumption that there is an intrinsic divergence of interest between labor and capital, and that workers therefore need forceful representation to secure a meaningful level of influence over their enterprise as well as a fair share of the firm's profits. Indeed, the Wagner act went even further than merely protecting and encouraging independent union representation as the preferred mode of employee participation: the Act specifically prohibited the alternative mode of employer-sponsored worker involvement as an illusory substitute for the real thing.[33]

In the current climate of widespread experimentation with a variety of modes of participatory management, a number of judges and scholars now chafe under this legal restraint. Their assumption is either that the Act was directed only at a pernicious form of company unionism, or that it was a misguided paternalistic effort to allow workers only the anachronistic adversarial style of employer-employee relationship, even if they might freely prefer a more contemporary cooperative form of relationship. Several circuit courts have begun to whittle away at Section 8(a)(2) and Section 2(5) of the Act,[34] to the

33. Section (8)(a)(2) makes it an unfair labor practice for an employer "to *dominate* or *interfere* with the formation or administration of any labor organization or to *contribute financial* or other *support* to it" [emphasis added]. In turn, a labor organization is defined by Section 2(5) as including "any organization of *any kind* or . . . *employee representation committee or plan*, in which employees participate and which exist for the purpose, in whole or in part, of *dealing* with employers concerning . . . *conditions of work*" [emphasis added]. The breadth of this statutory language was no accident: many of the words italicized here were deliberately added to the original version of the Wagner Act to make sure that the combination of the two provisions would catch all possible incidents of employer involvement in the representation of employee interests. In its key decisions interpreting the ambit of both provisions, the Supreme Court reinforced the meaning originally intended by the authors. Thus, in NLRB v. Cabot Carbon, 360 U.S. 203 (1959), the Court held that an employee committee that presented the workers' concerns and proposals to change employment conditions was a "labor organization" under Section 2(5), because even though the committee did not *bargain* with the employer, it did *deal* with the latter concerning conditions at work. Similarly, in NLRB v. Newport News Shipbuilding and Drydock Co., 308 U.S. 241 (1939), the Court held that an employee representation plan was "dominated" or "interfered with" by the employer, even though the plan had been overwhelmingly endorsed in a secret ballot referendum of all the employees, who had seemed satisfied with the plan's performance during the previous decade. So whether or not employees appear to want the immediate benefits of a particular representation scheme, the policy of the Act and the Supreme Court has been to prohibit any procedure for representing employee views concerning working conditions unless the arrangement was devised and run by the employees *alone*, without any intrusion by their employer.

34. The most prominent of these circuit decisions are Hertzka & Knowles v. NLRB, 503 F.2d 625 (9th Cir. 1974), on Section 8(a)(2); and NLRB v. Scott and Fetzer, 691 F.2d 288 (6th Cir. 1982), on Section 2(5). In *Scott and Fetzer*, the Sixth Circuit confronted an employer-created committee composed of managers and workers who regularly discussed problems of working conditions and employee grievances. Although the program looked very much like the arrangement that the Supreme Court had struck down in *Cabot Carbon*, the Circuit Court said that this committee was not really designed to engage in a prohibited "course of dealings" between employer and employees, but rather to give the employees a vehicle for "communication of ideas" about their job conditions: thus it was not a "labor organization" under Section 2(5) of the Act. In *Hertzka & Knowles*, the Ninth Circuit held that whether or not the program in question amounted to a labor organization, one could not say that the employer had exercised illegal "domination"

applause of a number of scholarly critics of collective bargaining.[35]

Even though I ultimately agree that there is no longer any sufficient reason to prohibit the typical nonunion EIP, I consider most of the arguments leading to this conclusion to be spurious. Present-day EIPs are not fundamentally different in nature or purpose from the initial employee representation plans developed in the era of "welfare capitalism" in the early twentieth century.[36] Congress heard exactly the same kinds of arguments for allowing employer and employees the freedom to choose this alternative to full-fledged union representation, and it decisively rejected that position.[37]

Of course, as I observed earlier, the fact that Congress passed a law in the thirties is no reason in the nineties to subscribe unthinkingly to the initial policy judgment. However, freedom of choice is not an especially persuasive argument for repealing Section 8(a)(2) of the Act. Nonunion employees do not usually have the freedom to choose to have an EIP (if their employer does not want one) or to abstain from an EIP (if the employer does institute one). Participatory management is developed and instituted by the employer when it appears to be to the firm's advantage—whether the advantage consists in an immediate improvement in worker satisfaction, motivation, and productivity, or in the longer-range avoidance of unionization. Once the employer has established an EIP for whatever reason, its employees must accept the

---

over or "interference" with its formation and administration. Instead, the employer had merely "cooperated" with a procedure freely chosen by the employees (in a meeting with management) as a means for expressing their workplace concerns. In both cases, the judges strove mightily to formulate verbal glosses on the sweeping language of the original Wagner Act, because they perceived the "adversarial model of labor relations" to be an anachronism and wanted to permit employers to develop increasingly "cooperative relations" as part of a more "enlightened personnel policy"—as long as the arrangements appeared to be freely accepted by the employees immediately involved.

35. See Jackson, "An Alternative to Unionization"; Richard A. Epstein, "A Common Law for Labor Relations: A Critique of the New Deal Labor Legislation," 92 *Yale Law Journal* 1357, 1391–92 (1983); and Charles Fried, "Individual and Collective Rights in Work Relations: Reflections on the Current State of Labor Law and Its Prospects," 51 *University of Chicago Law Review* 1012, 1026–27, 1038–39 (1984). The last two articles deal with this topic as aspects of the respective authors' broad-ranging critiques of contemporary labor law.

36. See, e.g., Daniel Nelson, "The Company Union Movement, 1900–37: A Reexamination," 56 *Business History Review* 335 (1982). For an influential revisionist look at the welfare capitalism movement, written by a historian committed to the values of independent unionism, see David Brody, *Workers in Industrial America: Essays on the Twentieth Century Struggle* (New York: Oxford University Press, 1980), especially Chapter 2, "The Rise and Decline of Welfare Capitalism," pp. 48–81.

37. See Kohler, "Models of Worker Participation," pp. 518–534. As I observed in note 33, this congressional verdict was accepted by the Supreme Court in its first decisions interpreting and applying these provisions.

program and whatever role they may have in it (in a quality circle, for example), just as they must participate in a contributory insurance or pension plan adopted by the company. Unlike the decision about union representation, the only choice that workers have in this situation is to keep or to leave their jobs, whether these be with or without an EIP.

However, even recognizing an EIP for what it is—a management-instituted program analogous to a pension plan—the case for legally banning EIPs is still not convincing. Instituting an EIP is likely to be an effort of the same sophisticated and benign human resource management that produces generous wages and benefits, seniority preferences in layoffs and promotions, appeal procedures in cases of discipline and discharge, and occasionally even guarantees of life-time employment. These benefits or programs are often inspired by the mixed motivation of satisfying employees and avoiding unions. None will be deemed illegal unless adopted in the immediate context of a union campaign with the specific intent of influencing its outcome.[38] I do not consider an EIP to be a benefit so qualitatively different that it should be singled out for a blanket legal ban, on the theory that this kind of program is peculiarly likely to divert workers from the collective bargaining alternative. EIPs seem no more threatening to collective bargaining than, say, the practice of a nonunion firm to match regularly the wage and benefit gains paid by the unionized firms in the same industry. Whatever might have been the case in the thirties when union representation was almost entirely absent from the mass production industries, American workers in the nineties seem perfectly capable of recognizing the difference between a union contract and a nonunion QWL program.

Although I believe, then, that Section 8(a)(2) should be cut back sharply,[39] the proper route to that end is not the one taken by circuit courts, which have been eviscerating this section through a variety of artificial interpretive devices. Even leaving aside general qualms about the legitimacy of a court's ignoring the clear language and unmistakable intent of Congress when it authored the statute, there remains a serious practical problem in piecemeal judicial renovation of the national

38. As was the case, for example, in NLRB v. Exchange Parts, 375 U.S. 405 (1964), applying Section 8(a)(1) of the NLRA.

39. In other words, I would favor repeal of Section 8(a)(2) as such, allowing the most egregious antiunion uses of this device to be appraised under Section 8(a)(1), just like other personnel policies of the employer. Thus, if an employer deliberately adopted an EIP in the midst of an organizational campaign in order to subvert the union drive, the tactic would still be illegal under *Exchange Parts*.

labor law. The consequence is likely to be the same as the aftermath of Boys Markets v. Retail Clerks Local 770,[40] in which the Supreme Court took it upon itself to relax what it considered to be the anachronistic ban by the Norris-LaGuardia Act of injunctions against strikes in order to give employers the benefit of a more effective means of enforcing the no-strike clause in collective agreements (a remedy that I think employers should enjoy, by the way). In the early seventies *Boys Markets* removed a major bargaining chip that might well have been used to secure from Congress a more balanced and bipartisan Labor Reform Act in the late seventies; the Act would also have provided some effective enforcement (including injunctive relief) of the statutory obligations of employers during union representation campaigns.[41]

Even if we ignore these important political connections in the evolution and reform of different components of our labor law system, we find an inherent functional relationship between Section 8(a)(2) and another essential feature of present-day labor laws: the exclusion of all managerial employees from the rights and protections of the NLRA.[42]

The original Wagner Act contained no such exception from its all-encompassing definition of "employee." When in 1947 the Supreme Court narrowly upheld the certification of a separate unit of foremen in a Packard Motors automobile plant,[43] the Court explained that although the employer needed the "wholehearted loyalty" on the job of the people who were responsible for immediate direction of the work force, these foremen also had the right to organize themselves to seek better terms and conditions than the firm was inclined to offer for their jobs. Shortly thereafter the Taft-Hartley Act amended the NLRA so as to specifically exclude (by Section 2(11)) from the Act any *supervisors*—people who exercised direct employment authority over the ordinary workers. Interestingly, Taft-Hartley inserted a provision in the NLRA immediately following the supervisory exclusion (Section 2(12)) which granted *professional* employees the right to organize into a unit for collective bar-

---

40. 398 U.S. 235 (1970).

41. For a detailed description of the pitched congressional battle over the Labor Reform Act of 1978, see Gerald E. Rosen, "Labor Law Reform: Dead or Alive?", 57 *University of Detroit Journal of Urban Law* 1 (1979); and Barbara Townley, *Labor Law Reform in U.S. Industrial Relations* (Brookfield, Vt.: Gower, 1986).

42. The best general discussion of this issue is by Stone, "Labor and the Corporate Structure," pp. 120–161. A devastating critique of the *Yeshiva* decision itself is Karl E. Klare's, "The Bitter and the Sweet: Reflections on the Supreme Court's *Yeshiva* Decision," 13 *Socialist Review* 99 (Sept.–Oct. 1983).

43. NLRB v. Packard Motor Co., 330 U.S. 485 (1947).

gaining of their own, with such professional status resting in part on "the consistent exercise of discretion and judgment in the performance of their work." But twenty-five years later, a closely divided Supreme Court held that all *managerial* employees—"those who formulate and effectuate management policies by expressing and making operative the decisions of their employer" (including, in this case, a group of employees whose job it was to buy and procure parts and other materials for the firm)—were impliedly excluded from the scope of the NLRA.[44] Only a few years later another 5–4 Court majority concluded that, notwithstanding their apparent status as professionals under the Act, university teachers were excluded from union representation because of their *collective* managerial role in influencing the university curriculum, course content, faculty hiring and tenure decisions, and the like.[45] The tacit assumption of this unfolding Taft-Hartley policy is that under our labor laws the employer must have a right to the undiluted loyalty of all employees whose job it is to exercise any kind of policy judgment on behalf of the enterprise; thus the allegiance of managers must not be divided in any way between the employer and a union.

Even considering that policy in its own right, the lengths to which the Supreme Court has taken it are troubling. Certainly such an exclusion seems persuasive in the case of senior executives, for example; not simply because of the degree to which the firm must rely on their decisions, but also because the position of the individual executive leaves him sufficiently able to protect himself without collective organization and bargaining. But the Court has, in effect, reasoned that in order to exclude the president and vice-presidents of Bell Aerospace from a union, they must interpret the law in a way that would also exclude the buyers and purchasing agents of the firm; in order to exclude the president and deans of Yeshiva University, they had to prohibit unionization of the entire university faculty. When these legal decisions are placed side by side with the vast expansion of the managerial structure in American enterprise, with the proliferation of staff positions in the head office, the result is that growing numbers of American workers are denied any access to the NLRA and forced to rely on their attenuated bargaining power as individuals in the open market.

The more interesting tension here concerns the initial premise of the

44. NLRB v. Bell Aerospace Co., 416 U.S. 267 (1974).
45. NLRB v. Yeshiva University, 444 U.S. 672 (1980).

Supreme Court's position—the importance of ensuring that the allegiance of every manager adheres to the enterprise he serves, rather than to a union which might be serving him. Again, this sentiment is most plausible in the case of the traditional hierarchical firm, in which there is assumedly a major conflict of interest between labor on one side and capital on the other. The premise is much less plausible, though, in situations in which contemporary collegial approaches to production have been adopted, and in which the firm seeks in effect to involve all employees in at least some aspect of management of the enterprise. Indeed, there is a serious question as to whether the employer's initiation of autonomous work teams might itself generate a further quantum leap in the management exclusion: will all the employee members of these teams—individuals who collectively may decide the organization of production, the allocation of tasks, and the ordering and scheduling of parts and materials, and who may even deal with customers in connection with product specifications and quality—thereby be excluded from the NLRA as members of management?[46] More fundamentally, it is difficult to square the position favoring the relaxation of Section 8(a)(2)—on the grounds that there is no divided loyalty problem when senior managers are allowed to be deeply involved in procedures and committees through which employees express their workplace concerns—with the position that demands rigid adherence to a managerial exclusion from the scope of the Act, on the grounds that the firm will face a severe risk if employees who wish to have a union are allowed to play any role in even lower-level management decisionmaking.

My inclination is to favor the first course, to remove the original statutory ban on the growing number of employee involvement plans designed and sponsored by more progressive and enlightened personnel. I would favor such deregulation not on the assumption that this type of worker participation is on a par with full-blown union representation (especially not if the union has itself negotiated an employee right to such involvement under its collective agreement), but because this kind

46. This legal issue might have been addressed in the recent case of *Anamag*, 284 NLRB No. 72 (1987), but in that case the Board was asked to decide only whether the team leaders were excluded as *supervisors*. The Board concluded that the team leaders were not excluded, because their role was simply to coordinate the activities of the team, which itself made all the key decisions as a group. But this conclusion simply poses the tougher question of whether all employees are thereby excluded from the Act as members of a collective *management* team analogous to the faculty members in *Yeshiva*, 444 U.S. 672 (1980).

of worker involvement is an attractive option to numerous nonunion firms and their employees, it does no harm to anyone else, and the law should not use its limited resources to stamp the practice out.

I also believe, however, that any effort to bring existing labor law into line with employer practice[47] should be made only as part of a broader legislative review of the entire NLRA. In that review, not only must Congress rethink the specific problem of the expanding management exclusion, but it should reaffirm the value of collective bargaining for all employees, and include in its reform package the kinds of statutory measures necessary to bring business reactions to union representation of their employees into line with the legal policy of fostering collective bargaining. It is only in an environment where workers may enjoy the kind of representation offered by unions as easily as they now enjoy the kind of direct involvement offered by certain employers that we can legitimately say that employee selection of an EIP evidences a true preference.

Employee Involvement and Enterprise Unionism

As my last comment implies, I do not believe that my earlier analytical conclusion—that collective bargaining is a mode of workplace governance well worth saving—has been undermined by the emergence of a variety of innovative forms of direct employee involvement on the job. But reflection on the nature of such EI programs and the broader trends in the world of work that helped inspire them gives us a much richer appreciation of the contemporary challenges faced by American unions, employers, and policymakers.

The growing recognition that American industry needs a healthy dose of worker participation underscores my verdict in Chapter 4 about the insufficiency of such institutions as the labor market, managerialism, and legal regulation. None of these systems adequately responds to the distinctive character of *labor* as a factor of production. Workers need not only direct benefits from and protection against the firm, but also a substantial voice in the workplace where they spend so much of their daily lives. In the longer run it is in the interests of both the firm and the economy that we figure out better ways to elicit from the labor

47. My impression is that nonunion EIPs have become so widespread in firms and sectors of the economy from which unions are remote, with no charges ever being laid against employers for instituting them, that fair and systematic enforcement of the original intent of Section 8(a)(2) seems now impossible.

force a greater commitment and contribution to better quality and higher productivity.

Assume, then, that the aim of labor law must be to enhance labor participation as much as worker protection. Again, both analytically and empirically, union representation and employee involvement are not mutually exclusive paths to that long-range goal.

American workers traditionally have influenced the shape of their employment package through collective bargaining. While collective bargaining is responsible for a multitude of valuable achievements for the labor force, it has given workers only a very limited voice in the operation of the firm. Employees do select and advise their union representatives about how to negotiate and enforce a variety of contract provisions that regulate management's authority to direct employees about what to do on the job and to decide how much workers will be paid for their services. The contractual guarantee against wrongful dismissal is as good an illustration as any of the important differences that collective bargaining can make in the lives of employees. I have argued that the characteristic *industrial* slant that collective bargaining gives to the employment relationship should be transformed into a *salaried* model, which is better suited to a postindustrial world. But whether or not that conclusion is correct, it is clear that more and more American workers want something beyond just a package of rights and benefits in return for agreeing to do what they are told. Employees also want the chance to exercise their own judgment about the work they are doing; they want to face the challenge of making a difference in the quality of their services and the success of the enterprise.

For a long time the American union movement shied away from any such role for itself or its members, partly because it was evident that the ideology of American management made managers extremely unwilling to give up any prerogatives on the shop floor, let alone in the executive suite. Now more and more business executives realize that they have something to gain by sharing the responsibility for production and quality with their employees. In addition, union leaders increasingly recognize that carving out such responsibility for their membership must be a key feature of any program to revive the union movement in the years ahead. Given such a conjunction of interests, it is plausible that collective bargaining may again play a major part in the evolution of worker participation. After all, it will require a procedure like collective negotiation by an independent union to win a contractual *right* to a participatory role for employees when management may be reluctant to share its prerogatives with people whom it is accustomed to regarding as subordinates.

Indeed, the special contribution of an organized voice for the work force will likely become more apparent as the appetite for employee involvement continues to broaden.[48] In their initial phase EIPs focused primarily on enrichment of the worker's immediate job and communication of his views about improving the quality of the firm's product and the amenities of life on the job. But once they experience having a limited influence on their surroundings, many workers chafe at the stringent restraints that remain on their ability to make workplace decisions. This leads to the second phase of employee involvement—the team system of production. Workers as a group exercise a much greater degree of autonomy in determining how they will carry out their part of the firm's operation and how they will deal with group members as well as with external relationships (not only inside the firm, but with outside customers and suppliers as well). This mode of workplace organization fits comfortably with the broader trends of flexible specialization of the firm, and a salaried employment relationship that dispenses with much of the job control apparatus of industrial bargaining, such as fixed wage rates and carefully defined job classifications or career ladders based on seniority rights. But when such historic sources of job protection and security are dismantled, employees will feel the need to have a significant voice in such key decisions as technological change or the division of firm revenues between investment and distribution, decisions that will have an even sharper impact on workers in the new industrial climate.

As one progresses along the path toward increasingly significant employee involvement in the affairs of the enterprise, one will probably encounter both growing reluctance on the part of managers to permit such participation and declining ability of the ordinary worker to play a meaningful role, even where the opportunity to do so might be formally available. This central challenge to the movement for worker participation is not likely to be satisfactorily solved by a human resource management team, ultimately accountable only to the shareholders. Meeting the challenge will require organizing workers into an independent body that can deploy the kind of leverage and sophisti-

---

48. On this topic I rely on the detailed account of the several phases of employee involvement by Kochan, Katz and McKersie, *Transformation*, pp. 148–162.

cation needed to secure employee involvement in the stronger senses of the term.

To the extent the foregoing analysis is valid, the need for labor law reform appears even more urgent as a necessary step for saving the kind of independent worker organization that can bring employee involvement closer to its full expression. I do not mean to imply that unions are indispensable for meaningful worker participation in the affairs of the employer. For many workers—especially the more skilled, mobile professionals—and many employers—especially some of the smaller, newer, science-based firms—this kind of autonomy and participation is a natural outgrowth of the collegial problem-solving atmosphere that exists in their labor and product markets. It is often the case that the organization of these workers into a union—in particular, a union of the still dominant industrial model—is an obstacle rather than a bridge to achieving the kind of direct, ongoing involvement to which the employees aspire and which their employers want them to have.

There is an inevitable tension, then, between the goal of enlarging workers' influence over what happens to them in their daily lives on the job and the delegation of the representation role to a large external union organization, in which the individual member or local unit has only limited influence. To a considerable extent, the expansion of union size and bureaucracy, with the resulting diminution of the effective voice of particular constituencies in the organization, was a consequence of the perceived need to increase the power of workers vis-à-vis their even larger, more powerful corporate employers. Only when their unions grew large and powerful were employees able to secure tangible substantive benefits, the prime reason for the pooling of their collective bargaining resources. But it is undeniably characteristic of this style of union representation that although the process may well be achieving many good things *for* workers, it is not doing so *through* the workers.

I do not mean to overplay the image of the union as an alien entity, separate and distant from its worker members. Those who have regular personal experience with union operation[49] are familiar with the considerable degree of worker activism, politicking, and challenging of the union leadership that goes on inside the organization, especially at the local level. At the crucial point where the union must display its

---

49. I have had such experience with the UAW as a member of its Public Review Board, a body that ultimately resolves disputes between the union's members and its officials.

power to the employer—in mounting a strike to win a better offer at the bargaining table—the union leadership is directly dependent on the commitment and support of the members immediately involved in the dispute. For example, when the Hotel and Restaurant Employees Union, which represented Yale University's office workers, called a strike in order to win a first contract, this large conglomerate union, with units scattered in hotels, restaurants, and other operations throughout the country, could provide remarkably little assistance to the university employees. So the decisions whether to accept or reject the university's offer, to go on strike, to return to work, and ultimately to ratify the final contract settlement, were all made by the single unit of employees whose fate was riding on their own judgment.

As we have seen, a growing number of scholarly observers believe that in the future American industry and work will be channeled into smaller, more flexible organizations. If that forecast holds true, the further consequence for unionism will be the unraveling of the traditional pattern of centralized bargaining for hundreds of thousands of auto workers, steel workers, long-distance truckers, and the like. Unions in these sectors will be forced to negotiate agreements that will be responsive to the special features not simply of individual firms, but of individual plants and locations within a firm. This pluralistic character of collective bargaining—a phenomenon of which we can already see many harbingers—will have a corresponding impact on layers of influence within the union. Much more responsibility and authority will inevitably be exercised at the local level, by officers and committees subject to direct influence from the members with whom they are in immediate contact. The current national union structure will likely evolve toward a looser confederation of member locals: the central body will provide a variety of important services and expertise, while the locals will enjoy a high degree of autonomy in shaping their relationship with particular employers or even local plant management.[50]

50. This is the standard for union representation of school teachers. Although teaching is a highly unionized profession, and although most teachers are members of two large national organizations, the National Education Association and the American Federation of Teachers (see Michael S. Finch and Trevor W. Nagel, "Collective Bargaining in the Public Schools: Reassessing Labor Policy in an Era of Reform," 1984 *Wisconsin Law Review* 1573, 1580–81), control over the conduct and the outcome of negotiations in individual school districts basically occurs at the local level. My impression is that there is very little difference in authority between a local affiliate of the NEA or the AFT in the affiliate's own negotiations, and a local teachers' association confined to the teachers in a single school district. I doubt that the unions which represent the employees of an auto man-

This emerging model of *enterprise* unionism will be far more conducive to direct worker involvement in the life of the plant or office, carried on in the looser framework of the salaried model of labor contracts like the one negotiated for the Saturn Project.

This rosy projection of a possible future course for worker participation is subject to one large caveat. As we saw in Chapter 3, determined business opposition has made it terribly difficult for American workers to join together in unions that can negotiate collective contracts with employers—including contracts that might establish a *right* to direct employee involvement in the enterprise. In that unfavorable climate for worker voice, an essential role that must be played by the large outside union organization is to provide the resources and backing needed by groups of nonunion workers to overcome the vigorous, often intimidating campaigns waged by firms determined to maintain a union-free environment in their plants and offices. In other words, the greater the employer resistance, and the higher the odds against the employees' winning NLRB certification and a first contract, the larger and more powerful must be the union organization capable of surmounting these obstacles. But the problem is that a great many American workers who might like to have a meaningful voice in the affairs of their employers, want to do so only through a smaller organization of their own, in which they would feel comfortable and in control. The last thing these employees want is to commit their destinies to a giant entity like the Teamsters union, with its intimidating reputation, even though they suspect that it would take a union that powerful to actually force their employer to allow them any influence over the terms and conditions of their employment. The result is that these workers now settle either for no voice at all or for the limited participation that the employer is prepared to concede in a program designed by its human resource manager.

If this diagnosis is valid, it provides another important reason for undertaking major surgery on current labor legislation, to make it nearly as easy for workers to have independent representation by a union of their own choosing as it now is for them to accept the sub-

---

ufacturer or a steel company will ever become as decentralized as the teachers' unions, if only because organization and control on the employer's side in the heavy manufacturing industries will always be radically different from organization and control in local school districts. However, as the auto industry and its constituent firms evolve toward a looser, more flexible network of managerial relationships, by the next century the UAW will likely resemble the NEA more than would have seemed possible only a decade ago.

stitute version of an employer-made EI program. Only in that atmosphere is there hope for a gradual transformation of unionism into something much closer to its original conception — not a service to be purchased from an external organization, but an activity in which workers themselves engage, a movement through which employees collectively reshape their role in the enterprise. It goes without saying that unless existing unions and their leadership more actively undertake this type of transformation, there will never be the political support needed to win the changes that could help save the union movement and make possible such a future for worker participation.

6 · A Future Course for American Labor Law

The Need for Labor Law Reform

Up to this point this book has traced and appraised the important trends that have been transforming the governance of our workplaces. The inquiry was triggered in particular by those who are challenging—in their writings or their actions—the initial premise of our labor laws that workers should have a realistic right to collective bargaining through independent unions of their own choosing. We must face squarely the question whether this half-century-old component of our national labor policy has been rendered outmoded by the emergence of programs for direct worker protection through legal rights and regulation—such as wrongful dismissal laws—as well as of programs for direct worker participation and influence in the workplace—such as management-sponsored employee involvement programs.

I believe that each of these institutions exhibits real virtues when measured against admitted limitations in collective bargaining. The level of contractual protection enjoyed by different groups of workers is inevitably erratic and uneven when employees are asked to deploy their unequal levels of bargaining power in negotiating such rights from their employers. The extent of worker participation is narrowed and diluted when the emphasis is placed on bargaining, through union representatives, for a set of contract restraints on management power. That is why I suggested in Chapter 5 that we should relax the apparent barrier in Section 8(a)(2) of the NLRA against certain popular forms of management-sponsored employee involvement, and why in Chapter 2 I advocated adopting a specific form of legal protection against unwarranted discharges, as part of the minimum safety net that the community should require for all its workplaces.

Still, we should be under no illusion about the sufficiency of a legal regime under which two such vital functions are severed from each other and allocated to two different governance mechanisms, each of which lacks the support of any independent employee organization inside the workplace. Even the benevolent manager or legislator cannot provide truly meaningful participation and protection to employees who have no real capacity to take advantage of such an offer. Equally important, effective representation and bargaining leverage is indispensable for enlarging the reach of these programs beyond what can be expected from such unilateral initiatives in the current economic and political climate.[1]

That is why we should now be contemplating a major overhaul of our labor laws. Such a program would endeavor to make good on the statutory promise made by Senator Wagner and his congressional colleagues a half-century ago. But that promise should not be confined to the single format of collective bargaining through union representatives. As I made clear at the outset and have reiterated throughout this work, the value of unionism consists in its capacity to meld and discharge the dual roles of participation and protection. A new labor law should expand beyond traditional unionism the range of choices available to American workers to satisfy these needs.

In that new environment, unionism as we know it now would likely reveal considerable flaws as well as attractions. The American trade union movement must therefore undertake an equally fundamental transformation of its own structures and practices to suit itself better to the new work force, the new economic climate, and, ideally, a new legal framework. In the last chapter I sketched one aspect of a possible evolution toward a more decentralized, enterprise-like unionism that would permit employees themselves to exercise a greater share of their union's influence and authority in the workplace. I believe as well that American unions will have to establish more effective protection for their members against the union's own organizational hierarchy— stronger individual rights to challenge unfair and arbitrary treatment

---

1. A textbook illustration of this proposition is the highly diluted version of the plant closing bill which eventually became the Worker Adjustment and Retraining Notification Act of 1988. For a brief description of WARNA which makes clear how limited its protections and remedies are, see Neil N. Bernstein, "The Plant Closing Bill Creates a New Set of Legal Restrictions," 11 National Law Journal (Oct. 31, 1988, p. 15, col. 1). However, as is made clear in the BNA Special Report, Plant Closings: The Complete Resource Guide (1988), WARNA's bare 60-day notice requirement gains significance for unionized workers when placed side-by-side with their right to bargain collectively about the effect of plant closings and their de facto ability to negotiate even about the employer's decision to close the facility.

by union officers, ideally enforceable through an independent authority, such as the Public Review Board which has long existed for the UAW. Measures like these would be required to make the idea of unionism more attractive to the vast number of unorganized workers even in a more propitious legal environment. Such measures are equally indispensable for rendering politically tolerable the searching labor law reform that we need to produce the new legal setting.

The major aim of this work has been to develop the social, economic, and philosophical reasons for making the political effort to change our labor laws. But guiding any such political effort must also be a clear understanding of how the new labor law structure would be designed. That distinctively legal inquiry is the subject of the remainder of the book.

I do not intend to provide a detailed blueprint for labor law reform, reviewing all the issues and options now on the table and expressing my views about each of them. I have undertaken elsewhere[2] a canvass of the problems now apparent in the representation campaign and the negotiation of the first union contract, the historic core of the Wagner Act and the areas most urgently in need of renovation. What I shall develop here is a map of some broader strategies for labor law reform, highlighting the special sore spots and the most promising proposals, which should have priority position on the reform agenda.

There are two dimensions to this selection process. The first is pragmatic. How significant is the particular problem? How likely is the proposed reform measure to ameliorate our concerns? How much leverage would success at this pressure point exert on the performance of the entire system? The second dimension is one of principle. How does any specific proposal accord with the values that animate the general body of labor law and the objectives that led us to adopt a system of labor law in the first place? Only if we can make a reasonable argument for the fit of our favored reforms with these larger values and principles do we have any chance of securing the adoption of measures that might be effective in achieving our goals.

Given these preliminary observations, then, what are the real deficiencies in the existing legal framework for the representation process? We

2. See Paul C. Weiler, "Promises to Keep: Securing Workers' Rights to Self-Organization Under the NLRA," 96 *Harvard Law Review* 1769 (1983): and Paul C. Weiler, "Striking a New Balance: Freedom of Contract and the Prospects for Union Representation," 98 *Harvard Law Review* 351 (1984). In Paul C. Weiler, "Milestone or Tombstone: The Wagner Act at Fifty," 23 *Harvard Journal on Legislation* 1 (1986), I summarize the arguments and update some of the statistics in the earlier, more extensive pieces.

must be clear-sighted in our judgments, because we are likely to have only limited political capital for this reform effort, and these scarce resources must be invested where they will have the highest payoff.

As illustration, many officials and supporters of the labor movement have been wont to blame the old Reagan and now the Bush Labor Boards for the plight of the unions: the feeling is that merely substituting a Dukakis Board would have markedly improved the situation. Admittedly, the Dotson-led Reagan Board came to office with an aggressive pro-employer program, determined to roll back a large number of NLRB doctrines favorable to unions and workers. But whatever one's opinion of the Reagan Board's jurisprudence—I myself find some aspects of it attractive; many others, deplorable—its decisions have made only a marginal contribution to the present straits of union organizing. The steep rise in employer resistance and the steady decline in union success under the NLRA began twenty-five years before President Reagan was even elected, and became especially evident during President Carter's tenure, notwithstanding the generally pro-union tilt of the Carter Board. The lesson from this history is that the flaws in our national labor laws are buried deep within the structure of the statute, and they will continue to take their toll regardless of the political complexion of the Board.

Turning next to examine the Act and its interpretation, we find a few explicitly one-sided restraints on union organizing efforts, most of these traceable to the Taft-Hartley amendments of 1947. By and large the important obstacles (including much of Taft-Hartley) reflect enduring and neutral values of the American political economy; but the interaction of these principles with the disparate tactical advantages of the parties at this stage in the relationship gives our labor law system its pronounced tilt against employee attraction to union representation.

Actually, that tilt has its roots in the common law background of the NLRA: the tacit legal assumption that the "natural" status for a workplace is nonunion, with management exercising on behalf of the shareholder-owners the prerogatives of property and contract law to establish the firm's terms and conditions of employment, constrained only by the parameters of an unorganized and unfettered labor market. This nonunion setting is what new employees encounter when they arrive on the job, and it is the standard experience throughout the working lives of most employees in nonunion occupations and industries.

With that legal and economic premise as a backdrop, the original Wagner Act created (by Section 7) a right of employees to change the status quo if they so desired and to organize themselves into a union that would represent them in collective bargaining and give the work force as a group more influence on their employment conditions. Section 9 of the NLRA set up the administrative machinery for determining and certifying the employee decision on unionization, and Section 8 created a network of legal restraints on management interference with the employees' exercise of their Section 7 rights—the most important target being discriminatory discharges of union supporters. Section 10 of the Act provided the enforcement mechanisms for the new unfair labor practice provisions. Implicit in the Wagner Act was the assumption that if the employees did not want a union, they were not obliged to have one. That assumption was made explicit by Taft-Hartley, which inserted in Section 7 a parallel right of employees to be free of union representation if that was their preference. In tandem with this employee right a new Section 8(b) was created, establishing a number of restraints on union coercion of nonunion adherents, the most important target of which is the secondary organizational boycott.

Within that statutory framework the majority employee verdict for or against union representation is supposed to be the decisive factor in setting the future course of the workplace. So elaborate procedures and administrative machinery have been developed to determine and certify that verdict. The process begins with a union organizing drive, which must produce signed cards from at least 30 percent—now usually 60 to 70 percent—of the employees authorizing the union to petition for representation rights for them. Then the Board investigates the union petition to determine its validity and to establish the scope of the unit and the voting constituency. Next comes an election campaign that lasts for several weeks until the actual vote; and finally the Board reviews any post-election objections before it certifies the results one way or the other. Either side is entitled to ask for a hearing on any disputed issue either before or after the election, a prerogative that can greatly extend the length of time required for certification.

More subtly, this entire body of NLRB election law and practice drives home to employees that the move from a nonunion to a union environment that they are contemplating is a truly momentous step which will have major and perhaps unforeseeable consequences for both workers and management of the enterprise. That mood is considered appropriate because the NLRA confers "exclusive bargaining authority" on the union that wins majority support from the employees, and this authority gives the union significant legal rights as against both the employer and the employees themselves.[3] As a result, the Act tacitly invites management to play a prominent role in the certification process:[4] not only to defend the employer's interests in the definition of the appropriate unit and the exclusion of managers and supervisors, but also to carry on a campaign against the union for the hearts and minds of the employees. The employer is assumed to have legitimate interests of its own in fending off any alteration of its common law prerogatives by the certification of a union bargaining agent; and management is considered to be best suited for explaining to the employee electorate why union representation might not be good for them.

But whatever the law's illusions about the significance of the election campaign and the majority's vote, the protagonists are fully aware that the union's winning certification from the Board does not in itself make representation and collective bargaining a real presence inside the workplace. That will come only after successful negotiation of the first contract, whereby the employees have their wishes and concerns reflected in new conditions of employment, a grievance arbitration procedure is created for challenging the actions of management, and local officers, committees, and shop stewards are selected to represent the workers in their day-to-day lives.

3. Once a union has established its bargaining authority, the employer is prohibited from dealing directly with individual employees without the union's consent, not even to offer the employees additional wages and benefits over and above the contract levels (see J. I. Case Co. v. NLRB, 321 U.S. 332 (1944)); moreover, dissident groups of employees also lose their statutory right to engage in "concerted activities . . . for purposes of mutual aid and protection" if they act contrary to the union's position (see Emporium Capwell Co. v. Western Addition Community Organization, 420 U.S. 50 (1975)).

4. In NLRB v. Virginia Electric & Power Co., 314 U.S. 469 (1941), the Supreme Court held that an employer has a constitutionally protected right to try to persuade (though not to coerce) its employees to reject the union during a representation campaign; in 1947 this principle was explicitly incorporated in Section 8(c) of the NLRA by the Taft-Hartley Act. This bill also guaranteed (Section 9(c)(1)) that there would be a campaign leading up to a secret ballot election before a union could be certified by the Board as the employees' representative. In 1974 the Supreme Court completed the circle by holding that the employer was entitled to force the union to proceed down the certification path (in an often lengthy and usually vigorous campaign) before the employer would be obligated to bargain with the union, no matter how large and unquestionable was the support that the union had amassed in its original organizing and card-signing drive: see Linden Lumber Division, Summer & Co. v. NLRB, 419 U.S. 301 (1974). The merits of the employer's role in the campaign are analyzed in Weiler, "Promises to Keep," pp. 1804-22. I will return to this issue later in this chapter.

Certification under Section 9(a) of the Act merely gives the successful union a license to try to negotiate such a contract on behalf of all the employees in the unit, and imposes (under Section 8(a)(5)) an obligation on the employer to come to the bargaining table with the good faith intention of settling a contract. But the NLRA—specifically Section 8(d), again enacted by Taft-Hartley—makes it clear that the employer is not required to agree to any particular union proposal or to make any concession that might produce a material change in the way the firm runs its business.[5] If the employees want to extract a favorable contract settlement from a recalcitrant employer, they must go out on strike, or at least mount a credible threat of a strike.

Although Section 7 of the Act creates a protected right of employees to engage in "concerted action," the employer is entitled in turn to resist such strike pressure by continuing to operate with permanent replacements in the strikers' jobs.[6] Within those legal boundaries (and also within the restraints imposed by Section 8(b)(4) on union exertion of "secondary" pressures on the employer),[7] the market serves as the acid test of whether there will be a contract and an enduring bargaining relationship in this unit. What are the relative costs to the employer and its management on the one hand, and to the employees and their union on the other, of agreeing to the terms sought by the other side, or of failing to agree and suffering the immediate longer-term losses of a work stoppage? In many cases either the employees who originally voted for union representation are unwilling to take these serious risks at the bargaining stage, or their strike is unsuccessful and their jobs are lost to replacements. In either instance the employer will eventually withdraw its recognition from the union, and an eventual Board decertification order simply provides formal ratification of this denouement of the entire proceeding.

5. See NLRB v. American National Insurance Co., 343 U.S. 395 (1952). Indeed, the principle of freedom of contract is so dominant under the Act that it precludes the Board from ordering an employer to alter its bargaining position even on an issue that the Board has already found to have been illegally adopted by the employer, in bad faith and solely to frustrate any possibility of agreement. See H. K. Porter Co. v. NLRB, 397 U.S. 99 (1970). For an extended appraisal and defense of this principle, see Weiler, "Striking a New Balance," pp. 357–382.

6. This was the conclusion of the U.S. Supreme Court in its crucial early decision in NLRB v. Mackay Radio and Telegraph Co., 304 U.S. 333 (1938). I have criticized this legal rule in detail in Weiler, "Striking a New Balance," pp. 387–394, and will summarize my arguments against it at pp. 264–269.

7. For a detailed analysis of the history and current status of the statutory ban on secondary boycotts, see Weiler, "Striking a New Balance," pp. 397–404 and 415–419.

When one steps back from these specifics, the picture that emerges is one of a determined struggle between employer and union every step of the way. During the election campaign each side vigorously argues its case to the employee electorate about the pros and cons of the union and nonunion alternatives. At the bargaining table each side fights hard to secure its contract position at the least cost. The role of labor law is to set the ground rules for that heated contest by outlawing a number of especially harmful and unacceptable tactics.

For example, while the employer may offer rather bleak *predictions* of the consequences of union representation, it may not convey any *threats* of reprisal against the employees if they choose that course. Additionally, while the employer may engage in *hard* bargaining to obtain a contract most favorable to its financial and managerial position, it may not engage in *surface* bargaining with no intention of settling any contract at all with the union. And while the employer is free to make the various personnel decisions which it considers necessary for *efficient* operations—discipline, discharge, promotion, demotion, and layoff—it must not *discriminate* against union supporters in order to discourage the appeal of union representation among the employees as a whole.

The role of the NLRB is to act as the umpire in this protracted contest, charged with the responsibility for interpreting as well as enforcing these ground rules. The Board inevitably encounters serious difficulties in both endeavors.

The interpretation problem stems from our inevitable ambivalence about where the line should be drawn between the labor law rights of the employees and other important values and interests with which labor law may come into conflict. As I observed above, during the campaign the employer is invited to speak freely by predicting, though not threatening, the possible unhappy consequences of unionization; but in fact many of them, such as the loss of employees' pay and perhaps even jobs if they must go out on strike for a decent contract offer and are then permanently replaced, depend on actions that the employer can legally take. Similarly, during negotiations the employer is free to insist on a contract as favorable as possible to its market situation but cannot take a negotiation position designed simply to avoid any collective agreement at all; however, if the employer's stance is that it will not agree with the union to any meaningful changes or improvements in employment conditions, the result will likely be that no contract will be signed, and collective bargaining will become a dead letter. Finally, throughout the representation contest the law leaves the employer free to manage the business and the work force in ways that enhance efficiency and reduce costs; however, the harmful consequences of many of these decisions will be visited on union adherents and will leave an impression among the employees as a whole that they must be extremely cautious in their support of the union. But these and other apparent contradictions are inevitable in a system of labor law which, even as it places its legal imprimatur on the importance of collective employee action, must also respect the values of free speech, free markets, and managerial efficiency that are prevalent in our political and legal culture and incorporated in the NLRA itself.

Of course this sense of ambivalence and contradiction is greatly reduced when one closely examines actual individual cases and can assess the motives of the parties in context. But even when an employer has been especially hamhanded in its antiunion position, it is very difficult for the Board to enforce the statutory prohibitions and to prevent the occurrence of such behavior. The source of this problem is the weakness and delay inherent in current Board remedies and sanctions.

In that respect, the NLRA is simply another illustration of the broader syndrome I described earlier. External administrative regulation can exert only limited leverage over the practices of employers that remain in charge of their workplaces, determined to resist the government's policies and directives. If there is anything unique about labor law, it is the strength of the management incentive to flout the NLRA and the weakness of the disincentives that the Board can bring to bear against that employer inclination.

I need not rehearse here all the reasons that employers would just as soon not have a union in their operations, even if fending off a union requires some fairly drastic resistance tactics.[8] I will focus instead on

8. The intuitive reaction of most people is that any employer would naturally want to fend off the organization of its employees into a union which might wield bargaining power capable of extracting compensation gains of 15 percent, the average size of the union effect on wages and benefits, or even more. As this union wage premium rose steadily throughout the seventies, it was predictable that employer opposition (legal and illegal) to new certification would rise accordingly; see Robert J. Flanagan, *Labor Relations and the Litigation Explosion*, pp. 66–71 (Washington, D.C.: Brookings Institution, 1987). Interestingly, however, Richard B. Freeman and Morris M. Kleiner, "The Impact of New Unionization on Wages and Working Conditions: A Longitudinal Study of Establishments under NLRB Elections," 8 *Journal of Labor Economics* S8 (January 1990), report that newly organized firms initially experienced only a very modest wage gain over comparable nonunion operations. In contrast, Freeman and Kleiner found that even the first contract substantially alters the firm's personnel practices by successfully imposing a variety of restraints on employer disciplinary decisions, work assignments, and the like.

the nature of the NLRB response to those tactics. Take, for example, the no longer unusual case of the employer that hears of an organizing drive in its plant, discovers who the key union supporters are, and immediately fires them on some pretext. What are the statutory sanctions against that behavior, the procedural mechanisms for administering them, and the results of the interplay between sanctions and procedures?

To most outside observers, the legal consequences of such a deliberate and egregious violation of the Act will appear quite mild. There are no criminal consequences whatsoever, not even monetary fines. The victimized employees have a right to civil compensation, but only for the net back pay they lost, after deducting any amounts that were or should have been earned in other jobs in the interim. So workers who are fired in violation of this half-century-old policy have no right to sue for general damages for consequential economic losses or emotional trauma, let alone to collect punitive damages. Such limited back pay awards now average only about $2,000 per fired employee,[9] hardly a meaningful deterrent to an employer determined to keep a union out of its plant by fair means or foul.

This feature of the law is no accident. The emphasis in our national labor policy has always been on repairing the harm to the victim rather than imposing punitive sanctions on the violator.[10] Even more important, it is assumed that such reparations will normally be in kind rather than in cash; that is, when a key union supporter is fired, the primary relief offered by the Board is reinstatement in the former job rather than a large lump sum for permanent loss of the job, in direct contrast to the common law approach to wrongful dismissal suits.[11]

But whether it is because of these immediate intrusions on managerial prerogatives, the union's possible long-term effects on relative employee compensation, or simply a fundamental ideological tenet of American business (on the latter see Sanford M. Jacoby, "American Exceptionalism Revisited: The Importance of Management," in Sanford M. Jacoby, ed., *Historical and Comparative Perspectives on American Employers* (forthcoming, New York: Columbia University Press, 1990)), the undeniable fact is that virtually every employer now fights hard to preserve its union-free environment.

9. See Table II in Weiler, "Promises to Keep," p. 1780, for the trend in back pay awards from 1950 (when the average award was $479) to 1980 (when it was $2,054). The NLRB's Annual Report for 1985 puts the figure for back pay awards in that year at $1,926 (see 50 *NLRB Annual Report*, Table 4).

10. This special cast to the remedial philosophy of the NLRA is primarily derived from the Supreme Court's decision in Republic Steel Corp. v. NLRB, 311 U.S. 7 (1940); see Weiler, "Promises to Keep," pp. 1787–89.

11. As I described in Chapter 2.

Even if in principle that line of attack were best suited to the general aims of the NLRA, in practice this in-kind remedy is fatally flawed by the other characteristic weakness of this remedial regime—delay in the implementation of remedies.

The Act establishes an elaborate four-stage administrative process. First, the fired employee (or the union) must file a charge at a regional office of the Board. The Board staff investigates the circumstances, and if it judges the charge to be meritorious, issues a formal complaint against the employer. Next, a full trial-type hearing is conducted near the site in front of an Administrative Law Judge, who makes findings about what actually occurred and proposes a remedy for the incident. Then the NLRB itself, located in Washington, reviews written submissions about the ALJ's tentative findings and recommended disposition before the Board issues its formal decision and order. But even this final Board ruling becomes legally enforceable only after it has been reviewed and incorporated in an order from one of the circuit courts of appeal. A discriminatory discharge case that goes through this entire procedure from start to finish will take an average of one thousand days to do so.[12]

This painstaking process was designed to provide full due process to the parties and thereby to guard against any serious error in the administrative judgments. Such care might seem especially appropriate in the context of labor law, where delicate lines must often be drawn between a firing for cause and a firing because of antiunion animus, or between protected free speech and illegal threats. But the price of the additional quality vested in the legal verdict by multiple reviews of the same incident is that little efficacy remains in the ultimate order. An employer willing to invest the legal fees necessary to secure all the process that is its due can postpone the legal day of reckoning to a time when the victim's right of reinstatement to a job lost years earlier will have become meaningless.

I should point out immediately that only a small proportion of all the charges filed against employers actually do complete this entire legal journey. The vast majority of even meritorious charges are settled well

12. See Table III in Weiler, "Promises to Keep," p. 1796, for the situation from 1950 to 1980. In 1980 unfair labor practice charges took a median of 484 days to get a decision from the Board and another 369 days to get a judgment from a court of appeals. By 1985 the situation inside the Board had deteriorated markedly: the median time there had risen to 720 days (see Table 23 in 50 NLRB Annual Report 202 (1985)). In "Promises to Keep," pp. 1795–98, I elaborate on the sources and reasons for such extensive delays in processing unfair labor practice charges.

early in the process, usually just before or after the issuance of the formal complaint by the NLRB's regional office.

That fact does not, however, undo the impact of procedural delay on effective statutory remedies. First, any settlement prior to completion of the full legal process requires voluntary acquiescence by the employer. Often there will be consent to a full settlement by firms that respect the labor laws yet find themselves responding to an unfair labor practice charge, perhaps because of the actions of an overzealous manager at a particular location. But if a firm has consciously chosen to violate the NLRA in order to undermine an organizing drive and preserve its union-free environment, it will voluntarily consent only to limited relief that will not frustrate its strategy. Typically such a settlement will pay the dismissed employee his lost wages in return for his dropping any claim for reinstatement in the shop, thus avoiding whatever encouragement the employee might give to the efforts of the pro-union employees. A large and growing number of discriminatory discharge complaints now produce only such a monetary slap on the wrist from the Board.[13]

Suppose that the employee and the union were to hold out for full remedies. Even then, an employer strategy of digging its heels in for only the early (and less expensive) stages of Board proceedings would probably prove successful, because the employer needs only weeks or months, not years, to win the representation struggle on the job. If the firm and its legal counsel spin the process out for as little as four or five months, the employees involved are likely to have found other jobs to support themselves, and they will be reluctant to exchange these new jobs for an unpleasant reception in the prior workplace under management that fired them for their union sympathies.[14] Meanwhile, the momentum of the union's organizing drive will have subsided, the election will have been lost or postponed, the work force will gradually

13. The actual ratios vary from year to year. Thus in 1980 10,033 employees secured a right of reinstatement and 15,064 received back pay (including those who had been reinstated), but in 1981 there were 26,091 back pay recipients versus 6,463 reinstatees. More recently, in 1984 there were fully 34,863 back pay recipients versus 5,363 reinstatees, but in 1985 this ratio moved closer to the 1980 level, with 10,905 employees winning the right of reinstatement and 18,482 receiving back pay. These figures are presented each year in Table 4 of the *NLRB Annual Report*.

14. In Weiler, "Promises to Keep," pp. 1791–93, I review two empirical studies which found that only about 40 percent of employees fired in violation of the Act who secured a right of reinstatement through NLRB procedures actually went back to their old jobs; and of those who did go back, four out of five left within a year, most blaming their departure on harassment and vindictive treatment by the employer.

turn over under the watchful eye of management alerted to this threat, and the union will remain on the outside looking in. To appreciate how easy it is for the employer to win the breathing space it needs, it is sufficient to observe that the first hearing date for the complaint will be scheduled some six months or more after the dismissal occurred.

The implications of this scenario are evident. The reason we use *legal,* rather than rely simply on *moral,* obligations is that we sense the need to create a tangible disincentive against actions that otherwise would be in someone's immediate self-interest. But our labor law deploys terribly weak sanctions to counterbalance the strong incentives employers have to preserve their union-free environment so as to maintain the profitability of the firm and the prerogatives of management.

I have focused on the standard remedy of reinstatement with back pay for discriminatory discharge of union supporters, the most common unfair labor practice dealt with by the Board. The analysis applies equally to the so-called extraordinary remedy of a *Gissel* bargaining order, issued in favor of a union that loses an election apparently because of management intimidation.[15] If the Board, situated on the outside and acting some considerable time after the fact, finds it difficult to re-establish a discharged employee in his original job, then, *a fortiori,* it will have even less success at inserting the union for the first time as a bargaining agent, trying to deal with a recalcitrant employer on behalf of a constantly changing work force. A number of empirical studies have now corroborated these intuitive appraisals of the inefficacy of such in-kind Board remedies.[16] And as American employers have gradually come to realize how little sting there is in Board sanctions, it is not surprising that the number of employer unfair labor practices has spiraled upward.

The dimensions of the increases in unfair labor practices are quite astounding. I have depicted and analyzed elsewhere the trends visible

15. In NLRB v. Gissel Packing Co., 395 U.S. 575 (1969), the Supreme Court held that as a remedy the NLRB could direct an employer to bargain with a union which had earlier signed up a majority of the employees, but which had then been unable to win a certification election because of the employer's unfair labor practices, at least if the Board believed that the employer's behavior had made it unlikely that a fair and free election could be held in the future.

16. Findings about the inefficacy of Board-ordered reinstatement are similar to the findings about the impact of *Gissel* bargaining orders. Only one in three of these orders actually results in a first contract, and most of these contracts do not produce gains for the employees meaningful enough to make it likely that they will be renewed. See the studies in Weiler, "Promises to Keep," p. 1795, and Weiler, "Striking a New Balance," pp. 361, 410–412.

in NLRB statistics from the early fifties to the early eighties; here I shall just sketch and update the highlights.[17]

1. The number of unfair labor practice charges of all kinds against employers rose from under 4,400 in 1955 to over 31,000 in 1980, a seven-fold increase, before declining to 22,500 in 1985.

2. Many of the unfair labor practice charges under Section 8(a)(1) involved less damaging behavior such as verbal threats, interrogation, and the offer of benefits and inducements. But if we focus only on tangible reprisals against union supporters, such Section 8(a)(3) charges rose from under 3,100 to over 18,300 between 1955 and 1980, a six-fold increase, before dropping to 11,800 in 1985.[18]

3. As I emphasized earlier, employer resistance to union representation occurs not only before the Board election, but also when the newly certified union attempts to negotiate its first contract. Charges of employer violations of the Section 8(a)(5) duty to bargain in good faith rose from 1,200 in 1955 to nearly 10,000 in 1980, more than an eight-fold increase.

4. It should be emphasized, however, that these statistics represent charges, not violations; so these increases might be interpreted as simply reflecting an increased propensity of workers to file NLRB charges, not of employers to commit unfair labor practices. However, the proportion of such charges found by the Board to have merit nearly doubled in that twenty-five-year period, from just over 20 percent to nearly 40 percent of the far higher absolute number of cases in the early eighties.

5. Perhaps the best index of this phenomenon is the fact that through either settlement or order, in both 1980 and 1985 the Board secured rights of reinstatement (rather than simply back pay) for more than 10,000 workers who had been dismissed in violation of Section 8(a)(3),

17. In both "Promises to Keep" and "Striking a New Balance" I present the data from NLRB annual reports at five-year intervals from 1955 through 1980. Here I shall also include figures from the 1985 *NLRB Annual Report*, the most recent report I had received at the time of this writing.

18. Although there was a substantial drop in the crucial Section 8(a)(3) rate from 1980 to 1985 (though not, as we will see, in the number of employees needing back pay and reinstatement), the drop in absolute numbers is misleading. The reason is that the number of union petitions for certification, the baseline activity that creates the opportunity and incentive for the illegal employer resistance, had dropped even more sharply during that period, from 7,296 elections held in 1980 to 3,749 elections in 1985. Thus the key ratio, the number of Section 8(a)(3) charges to the number of elections held, which had been 2.5 charges per election in 1980, actually rose to 3.15 charges per election in 1985. There was an even larger increase in the comparable ratio for Section 8(a)(5) charges of bad faith bargaining, referred to in the next paragraph in the text.

most of whom were union supporters fired during representation campaigns. This figure, the most tangible measure of all, was up more than ten-fold from the number of workers reinstated in the mid-fifties. When one puts the total of those reinstated side by side with the total of 200,000 employees who voted for the union in representation elections in 1980 and the 100,000 pro-union voters in 1985, the current level of employer lawlessness is dismaying indeed.[19]

In the same time frame unions experienced a stark decline in securing representation rights under the Act. The most revealing measure describes the fate of units in which the union had already overcome whatever natural inhibition or disinclination the employees felt about collective bargaining, and had signed up enough workers to file for certification with the Board. Even though at that point the union might have enjoyed widespread support within the unit, two further obstacles remained to be overcome—the certification election and negotiation of the first contract. What was the trend in union success in these areas from the fifties to the eighties?

In the earlier period unions were able to win certification for units comprising 75 to 80 percent of the total number of employees involved

19. I should add a caveat lest anyone assume too close a connection between these last figures. Not all Section 8(a)(3) charges involve employer reprisals during the workers' representation campaign. In 1978 the NLRB estimated that 90 percent of the Section 8(a)(3) cases arose out of representation campaigns (see Weiler, "Promises to Keep," p. 1781, n.35), whereas in 1982 the GAO found this proportion had dropped to 60 percent (see Weiler, "Striking a New Balance," p. 356, n.13). More recently, though, the contribution of the representation campaign to the Section 8(a)(3) caseload is again increasing, because certain key Reagan Board decisions cut back sharply both on the ability of nonunion workers to claim that their dismissal was for "concerted" activities (see *Meyers Industries, Inc.,* 268 NLRB 493 (1984)), and on the ability of union workers covered by collective agreements to bring Section 8(a)(3) claims instead of relying on the grievance arbitration procedure in the labor contract (see *United Technologies Corp.,* 268 NLRB 557 (1984), and *Olin Corp.,* 268 NLRB 573 (1984)); see also Patricia Greenfield, "The NLRB's Deferral to Arbitration Before and After *Olin:* An Empirical Analysis," 42 *Industrial and Labor Relations Review* 34 (1988)). But while the overall Section 8(a)(3) figure in Board statistics involves some overcount of organizational discharges, the reinstatee rate involves a potentially significant *undercount.* Some unknowable number of employees who were fired for supporting the union during the representation campaign did not file or were not able to substantiate Section 8(a)(3) charges; and many of those who did file and prove their claim settled for the remedy of back pay, without reinstatement into what had become the inhospitable environment of their old job. Some sense of the dimensions of this phenomenon is evidenced by the fact that in 1985 there were 18,482 recipients of back pay versus "only" 10,905 reinstatees. Thus it is clear that at least some of the employees who received only back pay were fired during the representation campaign, and that their numbers offset a portion of the overcount that results from assuming that all 11,000 or so reinstatees were fired under those circumstances.

in certification campaigns, and were then able to obtain first contracts for 85 to 90 percent of the units that had been certified. But by the early eighties American unions were winning certification covering less than 40 percent of potential unit members, then translating these certifications into first contracts barely more than half the time. Thus the current NLRA procedures, which were designed to protect and encourage collective employee action, now yield representation rights for little more than a fifth of the workers who enter the process, even though the unions had conducted apparently successful organizing drives just a few months earlier.[20]

I do not mean to suggest that all or even nearly all such union losses are attributable to unfair labor practices committed by employers during the campaign. Despite the evident weakness in Board sanctions, serious unfair labor practices—defined as meritorious Section 8(a)(3) charges producing a right of reinstatement for one or more employees—now occur in approximately one-third of Board elections.[21] While that number is far too high in light of the federal labor law policy adopted a half-century ago, the fact remains that a substantial majority of American employers do comply voluntarily with the essential principle of the Wagner Act and conduct their fight with the union on a somewhat higher plane.

But as I observed much earlier, the antiunion campaigns of the "good" law-abiding employers are the beneficiaries of the wave of unfair labor practices by the "bad" employers, who are willing to flout the labor laws if that suits their purposes. Given the inertial effect of the existing nonunion character to the employment relationship, a significant level of dissatisfaction with their working conditions is necessary before a group of employees will venture into the uncharted waters of collective bargaining. Add to that natural hurdle the fact that American workers now realize that their employer will determinedly resist unionization: that at best the campaign will be heated and decisive, and that at worst there is a strong possibility that identified union activists will suffer reprisals.[22] There is nothing paranoid in these em-

20. See Table I and the accompanying text in Weiler, "Striking a New Balance," pp. 353–357, for the sources of these statistics and the statistical trend.

21. See Weiler, "Milestone or Tombstone," p. 11, n.17.

22. Recall the figures cited earlier from the Lou Harris poll of 1984. In a national sample of nonunion, nonmanagerial employees, 59 percent of the respondents said that they expected there would be trouble and tension during a representation campaign in their workplace, and 43 percent believed that their employer would fire, demote, or take retaliatory measures against people who visibly supported the union. A more recent

ployee fears. The statistics we have seen confirm that most nonunion firms strongly oppose unionization, and that a sizable minority of employers will resort to dirty tactics if they feel they must. Suppose, though, that a group of employees happens to work for an employer who would, if faced with a union campaign, religiously respect their free choice under the Act. These employees would still feel inhibited about exploring the idea of union representation in the first place, and during the campaign they would probably read ominous overtones into even the most scrupulous management predictions about the possibly dire consequences of collective bargaining. In my opinion, this subtler spillover effect of the remarkable rise in unfair labor practices is an equally important barrier to employees' exercising the legal option promised them by the Wagner Act.

At the same time, we must recognize that to the extent the law is responsible for permitting this phenomenon to emerge, it is largely due to attractive features of the overall legal regime—respect for free speech in the campaign and for the free market in negotiations; deference to managerial judgments about the selection and assignment of personnel and the operations of the firm; a reparative rather than a punitive cast to Board remedies; and meticulous attention to due process in administration. These important values in our political economy and legal culture inevitably limit our wholehearted pursuit of the specific aims and policies of our labor laws. The problem is that the cumulative result of all these constraining principles, applied in a setting in which management is inside the workplace fighting to preserve the firm's nonunion status against a union on the outside, is that the Act and the Board now offer little effective assistance to employees who would entertain the union option. It will require a searching reexamination of our basic policies and some imaginative redesign of our legal instruments if we hope to alter that equation.

The Regulatory Model for Labor Law Reform

The many changes that have been or might be proposed for this substantive area of our labor law can be distributed among three basic models of labor law reform. What I call the "regulatory" model accepts

Gallup Poll found in 1988 that fully 69 percent of Americans believe that corporations sometimes harass, intimidate, or fire employees who openly speak out for a union (only 21 percent disagreed with that statement).

the current legal conception of a contest between union and employer over whether the employees will choose collective bargaining, and then tries to provide more effective legal disincentives to the employer's violating the rules of that contest. A second approach, the "reconstructive" model, would substantially change the nature of the contest by altering the underlying environment in ways that would reduce the employer's initial opportunity and incentive to improperly influence employee choice. The third, or "constitutive" model, rejects the idea that there must be a choice and thus that there will be a contest; it would have the law mandate, instead, a minimum degree of employee participation in the affairs of the workplace. In the next three sections I shall develop the meaning and implication of each of these strategies for labor law reform. Let us begin with the more traditional regulatory model, of which many suggested reforms were reflected in the proposed Labor Reform Act of 1978, which came within an eyelash of enactment.

Union Access?

Labor law, like any form of legal regulation, is made up of substantive rights and rules and remedial sanctions and procedures. A pet proposal of labor law reformers of the regulatory persuasion is the creation of a new right for the union of equal access to the employees during the campaign. If the employer chooses to use its premises to argue the case against union representation, it would be obligated to give the union equal time and facilities for a rebuttal.

In principle this idea is reasonable. Common sense tells us that the employer has a far greater opportunity to campaign among employees who are available at work than does the union, which must try to get the employees to the union hall for a meeting. Empirical research has shown that such disparities in access can make a significant difference in the vote of employees who are wavering.[23] Whether our concern is

23. Julius G. Getman, Stephen B. Goldberg, and Jeanne M. Herman, *Union Representation Elections: Law and Reality*, pp. 156–158 (New York: Russell Sage Foundation, 1976), found that while employers were easily able to reach almost all their employees in meetings held on the job, unions were able to get only about a third of the work force to attend meetings held away from the plant and outside working hours. At the same time, interviews with employees disclosed that attendance at a union meeting was a crucial factor in determining whether an initially uncommitted or antiunion employee would eventually switch to the union cause. Thus Getman et al. were the most prominent scholarly exponents of the provision in the proposed Labor Reform Act of 1978 that

the enlightenment of the employee electorate or fairness to the union campaign, a simple solution would be to offer the union the same access to the employees on the job as the employer has.

After reflecting on the practical problems, though, I am skeptical that this proposal should be high on our list of priorities. As the 1978 congressional debates made clear, the issue of access is controversial and likely to be hotly contested, because employers feel abused by having to invite an outside union organizer onto their premises, perhaps even to take up employee time that the employer has paid for. Enactment of such a measure would require, then, a sizable investment of scarce political resources. Worse, even if this right were enacted, it would encounter severe difficulties in administration. After all, we still have not even figured out how to enforce a fifty-year-old ban on discriminatory discharges, the general validity of which is rarely challenged. I predict that enactment of such a controversial and difficult-to-apply right of union access would simply add another labor law doctrine that many employers would feel free to ignore or obstruct with impunity.

Interim Injunctions

Rather than add new pieces to the elaborate mosaic of rights and duties of labor law, we should tackle instead the weakness and delay in Board remedies that undermine the effectiveness of *all* the existing rules—particularly Section 8(a)(3), which bars discriminatory reprisals against union supporters. As I outlined in the prior section, the problem with the in-cash remedy of back pay is that it is too small, and the problem with the in-kind remedy of reinstatement is that it is too slow. What measures could we use and what arguments could we make to add more bite to these sanctions against discriminatory discharges, thereby giving greater pause to employers who might be tempted down that path?

Probably the most attractive proposal from the regulatory point of view would be a significant speed-up in the reinstatement of illegally discharged union supporters. If such a reinstatement order were to become legally available in no more than one or two months, the exercise of that right would be a much more viable option than it is

would have guaranteed unions the same right of access to employees on the job as was exercised by the employer. The battle over that proposal and the fate of the entire bill is described in detail in Barbara Townley, *Labor Law Reform in U.S. Industrial Relations* (Brookfield, Vt.: Gower, 1986).

now, when many cases take one to two years or even longer. An immediate return to the job in which the employee has invested years of his working life is the best way to contain and repair the financial losses and personal dislocation suffered by the fired worker. Moreover, the return of a key union supporter to the plant would occur at a time when it would inflict a major setback on the employer in its ongoing struggle with the union. The unit of employees would have tangible proof that the hitherto near absolute sway of management in the plant or office could be successfully challenged through the power of group action and labor law protection. The prospect of this legal denouement would be a highly effective deterrent to any employer choosing to make violation of Section 8(a)(3) a part of its antiunion strategy.

It is easy to appreciate the virtues of speedy in-kind remedies; it is much harder to devise procedures that would achieve them. One cannot realistically secure this goal within the NLRB itself, by tinkering with different components of its four-stage process.[24] The most dramatic and controversial measure would be to give binding effect to the decisions of the ALJ who conducts the first trial of a case, only sparingly granting stays of his orders pending subsequent review by the Board and the courts. This sensible idea has been around for three decades, but there seems to be little prospect that it will be adopted. Our political and legal culture is simply not prepared to give such authority to a mere "administrative" official. Not only is such an idea politically untenable; it is likely to be ineffective as well. The problem is that it now takes an average of ten months or more to obtain the first ALJ decision, while *effective* reinstatement usually requires an order in one or two months. In the entire history of the Board, nothing has ever been able to galvanize its corps of ALJs into that kind of "instant" response.

Recognizing this fact of administrative life, the regulatory reformers have taken a different tack. They would outflank this cumbersome NLRB process by providing interim judicial relief for discriminatory discharges committed during the representation contest.[25] The present NLRA authorizes, though it does not require, the use of such an expedited procedure. Section 10(j) empowers the Board to petition a federal district judge for an interim order in connection with any unfair labor practice, pending the Board's own leisurely proceeding toward a

24. For an extended discussion of why this is so, see Weiler, "Promises to Keep," pp. 1795–98.
25. See ibid., pp. 1798–1803, and Catherine H. Helm, "The Practicality of Increasing the Use of NLRA Section 10(j) Injunctions," 7 *Industrial Relations Law Journal* 599 (1985).

final verdict. In practice, however, Section 10(j) is rarely used: in the early eighties it was invoked in only about fifty of the annual total of 30,000 unfair labor practice charges, and in only ten of the 18,000 Section 8(a)(3) cases. Perhaps the single most important proposal in the entire Labor Reform Act of 1978 would have required an immediate NLRB investigation and petition for injunctive relief for any discriminatory discharge occurring during an organizational campaign or first contract negotiation.

While there are compelling reasons of principle for giving union members this kind of relief against employer reprisals—for example, as I shall note shortly, employers now enjoy such protection from analogous tactics employed by unions—there would be major institutional difficulties in its implementation. The number, the complexity, and the stakes in Section 8(a)(3) cases make it hard even to imagine shifting the front-line responsibility for their administration from the NLRB to the federal district courts.

The most obvious problem is the sheer number of such cases. In 1978 the Board estimated to Congress that on the basis solely of the 1978 claims of discriminatory discharges during the organizational phase of the relationship, approximately 3,500 petitions for injunctions would have been filed.[26] Most such cases would present complex issues of fact and judgments about the employer's true motive for the dismissal. A composite of circumstantial evidence would have to be developed and weighed regarding the employee's involvement in the union campaign and the likelihood of the employer's knowing about it, the kind of infraction for which the employee was dismissed and the way comparable incidents had been handled when no union was on the scene, the degree of employer opposition to the union, and so on. Because so much would ride on the outcome of the injunction hearing, one would expect the employer to invest all its legal resources in fully litigating this "interim" proceeding in order to avoid a sharp rebuff of its managerial authority just when it would most likely boost the union's odds in the upcoming election. It is not surprising, then, that an empirical study found that in the tiny handful of Section 10(j) petitions brought in the early eighties, weeks of work time was required from the Board attorneys and federal judges involved, and it took nearly four months on average to dispose of those cases.[27] There are simply not enough Board agents available to give priority investigation to more than 10,000

26. See Weiler, "Promises to Keep," p. 1802.
27. This was the finding of the study done by Helm, "Section 10(j) Injunctions," pp. 615–617.

such discharge cases, nor federal judges to hear and dispose of a couple of thousand injunction petitions, let alone to do so in the two-to-three-month time frame required to make effective use of the reinstatement remedy and thereby insure the fairness of the representation process.

Those concerns about the viability of a broad right to injunctive relief under the NLRA are not meant to deny the value of this remedy in situations in which it can effectively be utilized.[28] Rather, this measure must be just one component of a larger package of labor law reform that is designed to reduce the Board's caseload to more manageable proportions, and thus to permit injunctive reinstatement to be reserved for those cases in which it would prove most useful.

Indeed, in the longer run the availability of such injunctions would itself make a contribution to lightening the NLRB caseload, because as employers realized that such reprisals could backfire in this way, many would eventually be deterred from deploying them. In the short run, though, the availability of more attractive injunctive relief would surely expand the Board's caseload even above the current numbers: more employees could be expected to file charges, and fewer charges would

---

28. My own inclination would be toward a program that could be put into operation without the need for legislative reform of the existing statutory framework. I would establish a fast-track procedure that would be available for a limited number of discriminatory discharge claims (perhaps 500 cases a year) that were declared crucial to an organizing drive within a unit. The union would be required to attach to its initial charge document extensive affidavits and a detailed submission explaining why the particular case warranted expedited processing. The case would be assigned to an NLRB regional attorney for priority investigation and mediation, and at the same time the employer and union would be alerted to a hearing date, tentatively scheduled for two weeks later before an Administrative Law Judge whose time had been cleared for that purpose. If after a brief investigation the matter appeared to be meritorious but incapable of being settled voluntarily, a formal complaint would issue and the trial hearing would be held at the time fixed earlier. The ALJ would be instructed to prepare quickly a memorandum of decision recording his key findings of fact and his recommended order. If the ALJ concluded that there had been an illegal firing requiring reinstatement of the employee, the enforcement office of the Board would ask for immediate authorization to petition for a Section 10(j) injunction from a federal district judge. With the benefit of a full transcript of an evidentiary hearing and a set of findings by an experienced ALJ, I expect that federal judges would be far more likely to respond quickly and favorably to such Board requests for interim relief. Not only would such a fast-track process provide much more meaningful relief to the individual victim in a particular case, but the prospect of expedited and effective reinstatement would likely be a strong disincentive to employers to risk such a rebuff in the midst of a campaign against the union. However, the key to the possible success of any such procedure is that the Board itself take responsibility for channeling its own scarce administrative resources toward cases where more effective enforcement of the Act would have a broader payoff.

be settled only on the basis of immediate back pay. So enactment of a general right to injunctive reinstatement in this large category of Section 8(a)(3) cases could swamp the system with petitions and discredit this reform idea when the Board and the federal courts proved unable to cope with the new demands.

Tort Damages

The last observation implies that we must simultaneously tackle the related problem of the weak sanctions now imposed on employers before or in lieu of reinstatement. The present formula of awarding only the net back pay lost by the discharged employee produces far too little financial exposure to worry more than a handful of firms.

Again, the authors of the Labor Reform Act did address this aspect of the problem. Borrowing from the Fair Labor Standards Act, they proposed to award the discharged employee *double* the back pay lost *before* deducting any amounts earned in other jobs. The new provision would have eliminated the credit now received by the guilty employer under the *net* loss principle for all earnings that the employee-victim was able to make up in the interim. However, even the proposed formula would have produced far too small and too easily calculable a penalty to deter many employers who were serious about fending off a union organizing drive. I suggest a rather different approach to the problem of how to define and compensate the losses actually suffered by the illegally fired employee, an approach that would also sharply increase the risks to employers of taking such action.

One reason these Board awards are so low is because they are confined to *back* pay, that is, the net earnings lost between the time the employee was fired and the time the Board secured a right of reinstatement. The assumption is that returning to the old job is a viable option for the worker, so that he has no grounds for further complaint and compensation if he chooses not to take the offer.

In many cases, reinstatement is a sufficient remedy, or at least it would be if it were offered more promptly under the new procedure just discussed. However, in many other cases even a speedy offer of reinstatement (perhaps made by an employer seeking to limit its financial exposure) is not so attractive to the employee, who understandably worries about an unpleasant reception back at work, and about continuing harassment by supervisors whose dismissal decision may have been overturned, but who continue to exercise control over daily life on the job, far from any realistic scrutiny and control by the Board. Recognizing this problem in another context, recent age discrimination litigation has developed the concept of "front pay." If this were adopted under the NLRA, an employee who was illegally fired and who chose not to go back to the old job would be compensated for the tangible *future* consequences of losing years of service invested in the firm and having to start over at the bottom of the seniority ladder with a new employer. Both in its assessment of the real harms suffered by the employee and in its deterrent impact on the employer, a right to front pay is a much more appropriate remedy than an arbitrarily selected multiple of an award which was itself artificially confined to back pay.

But there is no reason to stop here in this critical re-examination of the net back pay formula. Why not recognize and compensate for all the losses produced by an illegal discharge, over and above the immediate loss of *pay* for the job?

When the NLRA was enacted in the mid-thirties, employment at will was the prevailing common law regime, so it seemed reasonable to confine the scope of the new legislative intervention within the strict compass of contract remedies (in fact, the range was even narrower). A half-century later, the legal environment has been transformed. Statutory and judicial regulation of employment and its termination is now commonplace. More importantly, as we saw in Chapter 2, most states now recognize a tort action for the individual employee who has been fired in contravention of some identifiable public policy, such as for exercising the right to file for workers' compensation benefits. Indeed, in the case with which this book began, when Barbara Luck was fired for exercising her somewhat amorphous right of privacy against mandatory drug testing, she received nearly a half million dollars in damages.

The cognizable losses in wrongful dismissal cases include not only past and future losses of wages and benefits, but other consequential economic harms—such as repossession of one's car or foreclosure of one's mortgage due to the cutoff of regular earnings—as well as the nonpecuniary psychological distress created by such treatment. In addition, the employee may win substantial punitive damages when the jury responds to the deliberate wrongful conduct of the defendant. But if Barbara Luck had been fired for exercising her long-established rights to join a union (perhaps to help her fight against the employer's drug testing program), the NLRB's calculation of her losses would have amounted to no more than a few thousand dollars in net back pay lost. There is no possible justification for this stark disparity in the law's treatment of these two kinds of cases. The simplest way to put teeth in Section 8(a)(3) would be to remove the present preemptive effect of the NLRA on a state court's authority to include the right to join a union among the categories of public policy protected by its wrongful dismissal laws.[29] I suspect that it would not take long for a burst of tort litigation brought by topflight attorneys seeking the kinds of damages which juries are now disposed to award to produce a marked difference in the attitude of American employers toward their obligations under the national labor laws.

First Contract Arbitration

My focus in the prior section has been on the reinstatement and compensation of illegally discharged employees. That focus might convey the mistaken impression that the sole problem of labor law is the protection of the individual employee. Certainly that *is* a major problem, but it is not our exclusive concern. Section 8(a)(3) was enacted as part of a statute that sought to establish the right of employees as a group to organize for purposes of collective dealings with their employer. Although providing effective protection and remedies for individual workers who suffer reprisals for their participation in collective activity is an essential means of securing the underlying rights of the employee group, we must also apply our legal imagination to devising better ways of protecting the group's activity in its own right.

As good a case study as any is the rise of bad faith bargaining by employers once the employees' union has won certification for the unit. That tactic itself poses a major threat to the decision by the majority of employees to make representation in collective bargaining a real presence in their working lives. But in the absence of any reprisals against

29. Recently the Supreme Court held, in Lingle v. Norge Division of Magic Chef, Inc., 486 U.S. 399 (1988), that a unionized worker covered by a collective agreement was entitled to bring a tort action which contended that his wrongful dismissal—allegedly motivated by his filing for workers' compensation benefits—contravened the state's public policy under the workers' compensation program; the Court upheld the right to sue even though Lingle, the employee, also had the right under federal labor law to challenge the validity of his firing in front of an arbitrator under the labor contract. After *Lingle* there is no longer any good reason for denying the same jury relief and protection to union members who are fired in contravention of the national labor policy establishing their right to join and organize on behalf of a union, simply because these employees may also use the additional, but often ineffective, administrative procedures of the NLRB.

individual employees, there is now no tangible response at all to employer violations of Section 8(a)(5) of the Act. After the customary lengthy proceedings, the standard Board remedy is an order specifically directing the employer to bargain in good faith, just as the Act itself had already directed in more general terms. But by the time the Board order has been issued, the composition and sentiments of the workforce may have changed markedly, and much of the union's support may have melted away. Consequently, when the employer returns to the bargaining table prepared to negotiate seriously but only on its own "hard" terms, there is little chance it will be forced to sign a contract that offers any real improvement in working conditions and that the employees would press to have renewed. As more and more firms appreciate the lack of force in their obligation to recognize and deal with a certified union, the incidence of bad faith bargaining has risen even faster in the last three decades than has the rate of discriminatory discharges.[30]

A possible tangible remedy for violations of Section 8(a)(5) has been devised under the comparable labor law system in Canada: arbitration of the first contract for a newly certified unit.[31] Such an imposed collective agreement would not only improve the wages and benefits of the employees, but would install the union in the firm and give the employees a chance to experience life under a union contract with terms likely to be favorable enough that the employees would seek to have it renewed. The logic of this remedy tracks the rationale sketched earlier for the *Gissel* bargaining order. The employer that sets out on a course of illegal action to avoid a union agreement will find itself saddled with a union contract precisely because of its behavior.

The immediate reaction in the United States to even diluted versions of this idea is that it flouts the fundamental principle of freedom of contract and collective bargaining. I have argued elsewhere that such criticism is misconceived, at least in connection with a provision that is carefully designed as an exceptional remedy for egregious bad faith bargaining, rather than as an automatic right that either party could use to break a deadlock in good faith negotiations. I shall not develop that argument here, because I doubt the practical feasibility of this remedy in the American labor law system. First contract arbitration is

---

30. See the figures presented at pp. 237–240 and developed in more detail in Weiler, "Striking a New Balance," pp. 353–357, where I explain how and why the Board remedies for bad faith bargaining have become so weak, and also review empirical studies which demonstrate how little help the standard Board order gives to unions seeking a first contract (pp. 360–361 and 406, n.188).

31. This notion is discussed in detail in ibid., with extensive references to the Canadian experience and literature.

the quintessential in-kind remedy, one that requires difficult judgments about whether the statutory violations that authorize its use have in fact occurred; but unlike either reinstatement or bargaining orders, first contract arbitration would require the Board to write, on a clean slate, a brand new contract for the parties. The last thing our overburdened NLRB needs is the addition of such an onerous, time-consuming, and error-prone responsibility.

Yet if we want to address rather than just ignore the underlying problem, there is a less ambitious remedy of the kind that American law does utilize rather successfully—the requirement that a violator pay money to a victim. In this context, an independent right of action could be conferred on the unit of employees if their employer illegally denies them their statutory right to meaningful collective bargaining. A jury would hear all the evidence about the situation of the employees and the tactics used by the employer to frustrate the workers' aspirations, and then express the community's judgment about the value of what the employees lost because of the unacceptable behavior of the employer. The capacity of this remedy to satisfy the compensatory and preventive functions of legal regulation certainly stands in stark contrast to the cease-and-desist order, which is now standard fare under Section 8(a)(5) and much of the rest of the NLRA.

Reciprocity in Remedies

Admittedly, defining and implementing a rather amorphous group right to sue for the loss of meaningful bargaining rights poses much greater difficulties than does giving an individual union member the same right to sue for wrongful dismissal as nonunion workers have in other contexts. The priority in labor law reform should certainly be placed on the second proposal, not the first. But when one steps back and looks at the wrongful dismissal proposal, along with its companion piece of a right to expedited injunctive reinstatement of fired union supporters, some important observations can be made about both.

First, this particular strategy for reform of labor law regulation tacitly concedes the defeat of the New Deal commitment to the *administrative* process in place of the *judicial* process. Both expedited reinstatement and at-large monetary damages would be available only through proceedings in the courts. Rightly or wrongly, even fifty years after we created the NLRB, we are simply not prepared to entrust to such an administrative agency the procedures that are essential for enforcing the substantive requirements of our labor laws.

Next, it will be asked, how can one justify giving unions such favored access to the courts in the face of the contrary principle apparently embodied in the Act? The simple answer is that we would not be giving unions anything special. Indeed, unions and their employee supporters would finally be getting what Congress provided for employers long ago.

When Taft-Hartley was enacted in 1947, a major focus of concern was the secondary boycott weapon used by unions for organizational purposes.[32] If a group of employees chose not to vote for the union, the union would often cut off the employer's business dealings with other unionized firms in order to force the employer to sign a union contract that would then sweep the dissident employees under the union's umbrella. Section 8(b)(4) was inserted in the NLRA primarily in order to prevent unions from engaging in such "top-down" organizing and thereby overriding the wishes of the employees. When Congress imposed this substantive restraint on union behavior, the enforcement procedure it adopted included both mandatory interim injunctions under Section 10(1) and an employer right to sue the union for general damages under Section 303 of the Labor Management Relations Act (LMRA). The availability and the threat of such a stiff judicial response to this activity has proved remarkably successful in reducing the incidence of this union tactic and consequently the effect it would have on employee free choice.[33] But I can imagine no reason for treating the legal prohibition on employer intimidation of the choice *for* collective bargaining as less important, less in need of effective enforcement, than the comparable prohibition in the same Act of union intimidation of the choice *against* collective bargaining. The NLRA principle governing this analogous problem demands comparable expansion of the legal remedies available for violation of Section 8(a)(3).

The Reconstructive Model

One should not feel entirely comfortable with the regulatory program of labor law reform, at least not if it is proposed as a sufficient response to the problem. The source of these qualms is implicit in the analysis earlier in this book.

A disturbing tension between ends and means pervades both the ex-

---

32. See ibid., pp. 397–404.
33. See, e.g., the statistics in Weiler, "Promises to Keep," p. 1801, n.123, on the starkly different rates and trends in union violations of Section 8(b)(4) and employer violations of Section 8(a)(3).

isting labor law and the foregoing proposals for its reform. Recall that the *raison d'être* of the Act is to facilitate union organization of workers precisely because it is believed that employees can better pursue their interests through private voluntary bargaining with their employers, rather than through public mandatory regulation by the government. But achieving such a reconstruction of the individualistic labor market required creating a system of labor laws to protect the basic right of union representation from the actions of employers, which typically prefer that their employees not wield such group leverage in the workplace. Fifty years of legislative, administrative, and judicial elaboration of the NLRA has produced a complex legal regime characterized by most of the weaknesses of external regulation of the employment relationship. I have just proposed stronger doses of judicial medicine to replace or supplement the weak and ineffective enforcement of Section 8(a)(3), the core provision in the NLRA. But my earlier criticisms of the often costly, erratic, and inequitable character of judicial regulation of employment through ad hoc, *ex post* wrongful dismissal suits would also apply in considerable measure to litigation for injunctions or damages against this particular form of wrongful dismissal.

That is why I believe that any such regulatory reform should be pursued in tandem with a quite different strategy. We must reconstruct the background labor law so as to lessen our sole reliance on external NLRB or judicial regulation, and enlist more effort and resources of the workers themselves to secure their fundamental Section 7 rights. This "reconstructive" program has two major components. The first, within the initial election process, would shorten the length of the campaign so as to reduce the initial opportunity and incentive of employers to resist unions through the use of improper tactics. The second component, directed at negotiation of the first contract, would enhance the ability of employees to take effective strike action so as to counteract the employer's attempt to abort collective bargaining at a later stage.

Instant Elections[34]

The logic of this strategy is evident when we review the case for eliminating the representation campaign. What is it about the existing process that makes it so prone to unfair labor practices?

34. In this section I develop an argument I first made in Paul C. Weiler, *Reconcilable Differences: New Directions in Canadian Labour Law* 37–49 (Toronto: Carswell, 1980), and which I then elaborated for the American context in Weiler, "Promises to Keep," pp. 1804–22.

The union must do its initial organizing work among the employees, signing up a substantial number of them. But even if the union can produce cards signed by an overwhelming majority of the work force authorizing representation for purposes of collective bargaining, the employer is not required to recognize and deal with the union simply on that informal showing. Instead, the union must petition the Board for a certification election to test its majority support. The petition alerts the employer to the organizing effort inside its work force and invites management to mount a vigorous campaign to turn employee sentiments around before the vote. The actual length of the campaign will depend on whether the employer exercises its right to insist on a hearing before the vote on a variety of questions pertaining to the appropriateness of the unit or the exclusion of certain persons as managers or supervisors. Alternatively, if the employer believes that the usual four-week campaign period without a hearing will give it sufficient time, it can waive its hearing rights in return for favorable concessions from the union about the scope of the voting constituency. Given the opportunity they have to do so and the high stakes of the campaign, many employers are tempted to use a variety of illegitimate tactics to win the vote if they can.

The standard regulatory approach by the NLRB is to announce and enforce a host of legal standards that are supposed to insure "laboratory" conditions for a free and rational choice by the employees.[35] As we saw in the previous section, that aspiration has been largely frustrated by the weaknesses of the legal counterincentives that the Board can deploy against the initial temptation by the parties to contaminate the experiment. The alternative reconstructive approach would operate on the background legal environment by simply eliminating the campaign, so as to remove the opportunity and thence the inclination to use and profit from these tactics.

The viability of this strategy is vividly demonstrated by the comparative example of Canadian labor law. Canada has a far lower incidence of employer unfair labor practices, in particular discriminatory discharges, a much higher rate of union success in obtaining certification

---

35. This ambitious aim was first articulated by the Truman-appointed NLRB in the case of *General Shoe Corp.*, 77 NLRB 123 (1948), then substantially expanded by the Kennedy Board, in particular in its 1962 trilogy laying down the boundaries for legitimate campaign propaganda: *Dal-Tex Optical Co.*, 137 NLRB 1782 (1962) (threatening speech); *Hollywood Ceramics Co.*, 140 NLRB 221 (1962) (inaccurate speech); and *Sewell Manufacturing Co.*, 138 NLRB 66 (1962) (inflammatory speech).

under its legislation, and a union density ratio that has moved, for the last quarter-century, in the opposite direction from the trend we have observed in the United States.[36] While there are a number of intervening factors affecting the difference in aggregate union representation, these do not account for the stark contrast in the rates of employer unfair labor practices and union certification success in the two countries. The unions, the employers, the attitudes of the work force, and the legal and collective bargaining systems are all remarkably similar. Nor does Canadian labor law train significantly greater deterrents on employer unfair labor practices: the same net back pay formula is used to measure compensation, and reinstatement or other in-kind remedies can easily be delayed by the employer for long enough to remove their sting. What is different about Canadian labor law is that it has largely eliminated the pitched representation campaign and the invitation this extends to the employer to use illegal tactics if doing so seems the best way to win the crucial contest.[37]

Most Canadian jurisdictions continue to rely simply on the union's authorization cards for certification. The labor board just checks to see whether a majority of the employees were signed up ás of the date the union applied. Recently two provinces—Nova Scotia and British Columbia—introduced the notion of an instant election, which is my preference for the United States as well as for Canada.

Under that system the union would still have to have more than a bare majority (say, 55 or 60 percent) of the employees sign cards clearly authorizing the union to represent them and, in addition, pay a minimum membership fee (on the order of $5.00) to impress on them that signing up was a serious matter, not simply the casual addition of their signature to a petition. The Board would then conduct an immediate election in five days or so, postponing any significant questions about unit inclusions or exclusions until after the vote (any ballot in dispute

36. On various trends in the Canadian representation process through 1980, see Weiler, "Promises to Keep," pp. 1816–19, and sources cited therein. For later analyses that update the Canadian-American comparisons and that are largely in accord with my earlier judgments, see Christopher Huxley, David Kettler, and James Struthers, "Is Canada's Experience 'Especially Instructive'?" in Seymour M. Lipset, ed., *Unions in Transition*, p. 133 (San Francisco: ICS Press, 1986); and Gary N. Chaison and Joseph B. Rose, "Continental Divide: The Direction and Fate of North American Unions," forthcoming in *Advances in Industrial and Labor Relations*, vol. 5 (Greenwich, Conn.: JAI Press, 1989). There are some qualifications one would want to make about recent trends in union density (though not unfair labor practices) in the Canadian private sector, to which I will return at pp. 280–281.

37. See sources cited in Weiler, "Promises to Keep," and *Reconcilable Differences*.

would be sealed pending that decision). The vote would give the employees some opportunity to have second thoughts on the matter and, in any event, to express their final views in the secrecy of the voting booth. If the union were to win the vote, it would have the mandate and legitimacy that derive from an election. But because the vote would be conducted so close to the time the union surfaced from its organizational drive, the die would largely be cast as far as the employer was concerned. There would be no extended campaign during which management could try either to persuade or to pressure its employees to change their minds. Thus the law would accomplish its aim of reducing the incidence of unfair labor practices, but by making such tactics fruitless rather than by trying to mount sanctions designed to make the tactics legally risky.

Two arguments can be directed against my proposal. One concerns the efficacy of this approach. If the employer does not have adequate time to campaign against the union after it petitions for certification, won't it simply do so beforehand, during the union's card-signing drive?

My answer to that objection is that a serious, antiunion reaction by an employer is feasible only during lengthy campaigns in sizable units, where, of necessity, much of the union's effort would be carried on in the open. In those situations the union's organizational drive would give the employers so inclined the time and opportunity to engage in the kind of massive resistance which is now usually reserved for the subsequent election campaign. But such situations comprise only a small proportion of the Board's certification work.[38] In smaller units the union's card-signing effort is fast and discreet; often it is simply a reaction to calls from the employees. The major value of the instant election proposal is that it would sharply reduce the incidence of unfair labor practices in this much larger category of cases, thereby enhancing the Board's ability to deal effectively with the problems presented by the large strategic units (which can be troublesome under Canadian labor law as well). The kinds of injunctions and damage remedies I advocated earlier would still be required for effective enforcement of the law in the remaining unfair labor practice caseload. The reconstruc-

38. Fully 50 percent of NLRB certification elections are held in units of 20 or fewer employees, 75 percent in units of 50 or fewer, 95 percent in units of 250 or fewer, and only 1 percent in units of 1,000 employees or more; see Myron Roomkin and Richard N. Block, "Case Processing Time and the Outcome of Representation Elections: Some Empirical Evidence," 1981 *University of Illinois Law Review* 75, 85–86.

tive and regulatory models for labor law reform should be viewed as complementary to, not exclusive of, each other.

Even if one concedes that instant elections would do a better job of protecting the workers' right to have union representation if they want it, the tougher challenge will come from proponents of the second argument, who say that this procedure would deprive both the employer and the employees of their equally important right to have a meaningful campaign before the vote.

After all, it will be argued, the union had its chance to persuade the employees of the virtues of collective bargaining when it undertook the initial organizing drive. The employer should have an equal opportunity to make the case against unionization, and perhaps persuade its employees that they would fare better under the existing regime of individual employment relationships. And the employees themselves will benefit from the employer's playing this role in the election process, because by hearing the arguments against union representation they will be able to make a more informed choice. It would be unthinkable to structure an electoral system in such a way that one political party, having carefully nurtured its support among the electorate, could unilaterally trigger a snap election at a favorable moment and thereby rob the other party of any chance to compete in the race. For precisely the same reasons, many would decry instant elections in the labor context.

That argument brings me face to face with what I believe to be the single most important assumption underlying the entire NLRA model of the representation process: since certification confers on the trade union a quasi-governmental authority over the employees, we must have an election procedure comparable to the one by which our political governors are chosen. A corollary of this assumption is that the employer is legitimately entitled to play the same role in a campaign leading up to a certification election as the Republican party plays in a political campaign against the Democrats.

Admittedly there are legal indicia of government-type authority wielded by the union over the employees once the union secures exclusive representation rights for the entire unit, from which it can be dislodged only at specific points in its mandate.[39] Even vis-à-vis the

---

39. Section 9(a) of the NLRA gives a union selected by the majority of the employees the exclusive right to bargain collectively with the employer, which in turn precludes the employer from dealing directly with individual employees, whether to obtain a waiver of any of the terms of the union contract (see Railroad Telegraphers v. Railway Express

employees, as I shall explain shortly, this legal image disguises more than it discloses about the true character of the relationship between the union and a newly certified unit. But the analogy breaks down entirely when we consider the position of the employer.

A political campaign produces a verdict about who is to govern the entire jurisdiction, voters and nonvoters alike. But an NLRB certification gives the union no authority at all over the employer. The firm remains free to pursue its own interests and priorities, to determine its own personnel and compensation policies, and to refuse to make any significant changes in its current practices and prerogatives.[40] The fact

---

Agency, Inc., 321 U.S. 342 (1944)), or even to negotiate improved terms for these employees (see J. I. Case Co. v. NLRB, 321 U.S. 332 (1944)). Once this legal authority has been conferred upon the union, even the majority of the employees cannot then repudiate their representative and deal directly with the employer (see Medo Photo Supply Corp. v. NLRB, 321 U.S. 678 (1944)), at least until the union has had a minimum mandate of at least one year (see Brooks v. NLRB, 348 U.S. 96 (1954)). This means that once the majority has selected its preferred bargaining agent, dissident employees have lost their protected statutory right to take concerted action on their own behalf (see Emporium Capwell Co. v. Western Addition Community Organization, 420 U.S. 50 (1975)); however, the Supreme Court has fashioned a legal duty of fair representation which the union owes to all its constituents, whether members and supporters or not, a duty which is expressly analogous to the obligation that the Constitution imposes on the legislature (see Steele v. Louisville & Nashville Railway Co., 323 U.S. 192 (1944)).

40. It is the case that once a union has been certified as exclusive bargaining agent for the employees, a corresponding legal obligation is imposed upon the employer. Sections 8(a)(5) and 8(d) of the NLRA require the employer to bargain with the union in a good faith effort to arrive at a collective agreement. The initial bare requirement of the Wagner Act that the employer recognize and sit down to talk with the bargaining agent of the employees does not seem like the kind of intrusion on employer prerogatives that should entitle the employer to a role in the campaign leading eventually to such contract talks. However, given the continual Board and judicial expansion of the content of the duty to bargain, perhaps the balance has shifted too far in the direction of such intrusion: the employer is now prohibited from taking unilateral action to alter any terms or conditions of employment without first having bargained to an impasse with the union about that "mandatory" subject; see NLRB v. Katz, 369 U.S. 736 (1962). I have never been a great fan of *Katz*, nor of much of the other paraphernalia of Section 8(a)(5) jurisprudence. In fact, in my earlier incarnation as chairman of a Canadian Labor Relations Board, I wrote a decision which held that so long as the employer was genuinely prepared to negotiate an agreement with the union covering some terms of employment, it had no obligation even to discuss any one particular topic, let alone to refrain from acting on it until discussions had proved fruitless: see Pulp & Paper Industrial Relations Bureau & Canadian Paperworkers' Union, [1978] 1 Canadian Labor Relations Board Reporter 60, 65–66; see also Weiler, "Striking a New Balance," pp. 379–380, n.92. Thus I would be quite comfortable with a package of labor law reforms that would sharply reduce the length of, and the employer's role in, the representation campaign, while also cutting back on Section 8(a)(5) obligations (including overruling *Katz*) imposed on the employer when the union wins an "instant" election.

that the presence of a union may make it more difficult for the employer to run its business as it chooses, because the employees will be more cohesive, more determined, and better equipped to pursue their own aims regarding working conditions, hardly gives the employer an independent right to play a significant role in the procedure by which employees decide whether or not they would like the net advantages of collective bargaining with the employer.

A more apt picture of the NLRA's role is that it is protecting a group activity of the employees, an activity that begins with the fundamental decision about whether the employees will organize themselves for purposes of collective dealings with their employer, and, if so, who will be their union representative. The activity continues with the formulation of negotiating positions, acceptance or rejection of contract offers, the decision to strike or not, and administration of the agreement through settlement or grievance arbitration. If the employees in a particular unit are so inclined, then the union organization (through its officials elected by the employees) is the entity through which that group activity will be carried on. But the employer is a distinct party, with management selected by and beholden to the shareholders; and these two groups often have interests contrary to those of the employees. Of course the outcome of the election will affect the interests of the managers and shareholders. But that is no more a reason for letting the employer play a role in the employees' decision about union representation than is the fact that a particular management decision has a powerful impact on the employees a reason for giving them a right to a major voice in that corporate decision.

To complete the political comparison, the more apt political analog to the employer in the representation election is the role of a foreign government in an American election. Canada, for example, has a significant interest in who will be elected to govern the United States: selection of a particular party or president may make life considerably easier or more difficult for Canadians in negotiations over trade, natural resources, energy, and defense. Yet no one would seriously claim that agencies of the Canadian government should therefore have a formal right to participate in U.S election campaigns, to try to persuade American citizens to vote for a party more favorable to Canadian interests. We recognize that it is the job of the United States government to advance the interests of its own citizens when those interests conflict with the interests of Canadians; Canadians in turn have the government of Canada to defend their position, irrespective of the election verdict in the United States. Because there is precisely the same potential conflict of interest between worker and employer about terms and conditions of employment, the employer can claim no independent right to a campaign lengthy enough to permit its management team to influence the worker decision about how and by what means the employees will deal with management.

Admittedly there is an abstract flavor to the foregoing argument, which focuses on the supposed independent right of the employer itself to participate in the representation campaign. It is important to confront and respond to such a case for fair treatment of the employer, because that sentiment (especially with respect to small businesses) definitely lurks beneath the surface of the heated debate over shortening the length of the representation campaign. But a more plausible argument is centered on the needs of the employees, not the rights of the employer. The contention is that employees need to have the employer participate in the campaign to assure that the nonunion side of the issues will be adequately presented to the employee electorate.

Indeed, that is the obvious problem in the analogy I drew earlier to the role of a foreign government in a domestic election contest between two or more political parties. My analogy would fit the case in which two unions were competing for the right to represent employees who had already decided to have collective bargaining through one union or another. Even conceding that the preferred course for the employer is to stay out of that kind of contest (as well as out of union elections in which two candidates are competing for office), the standard representation election poses quite a different choice—between a particular union and no union at all. In such a contest, employees who support collective bargaining have the resources and expertise of a large union to make the case for its side. By contrast, individual employees favoring the nonunion option will likely be disorganized and unsophisticated about the issue. Such an unequal contest seems incompatible with Section 7 of the NLRA, which grants employees the equal right to decide *not* to engage in collective bargaining. If that right is to have any real meaning, employees opposing unionization need the support of the employer, which, in pursuit of its own interest in fending off union representation, will perform the function of deflating the promises of the union proponents and pointing out the risks for the employees in taking the path of collective bargaining. In sum, this argument for designing a representation procedure that invites extensive employer participation rests not on a principle of fairness to employers as such, but rather on the practical judgment that only the employer and its management can defend the statutory rights of the antiunion employees.

In my view, this is the best case that can be made for the American-style representation campaign. One cannot respond to it at the level of abstract principle. Rather, one must examine the empirical assumptions in the argument and appraise the tangible benefits and costs of the election procedure it supposedly justifies.

My reading of the evidence about how the current lengthy representation campaign has actually operated in practice leaves me quite unpersuaded of its net social value. After all, the employer that hired and has managed all its employees for a considerable time before the union even appeared on the scene has had ample opportunity to demonstrate the advantages of the individual employment relationship. Nor are American workers typically unsophisticated about the pros and cons of union representation. Research has disclosed how little employees actually learn from their employer that they did not already know about the costs of unionization, in terms of union dues, strikes, possible job losses, and the like.[41]

Of course, the champions of fully informed choice will still insist on designing our labor laws to achieve even such incremental enlightenment of a few employees. While I agree that all other things being equal, a more informed employee choice would be a freer one, the problem is that when we extend an opportunity to the law-abiding employer to illuminate the issues for its employees, we inevitably create both the opportunity and the incentive for the law-violating employer to intimidate its workers in their decision, with relative impunity from meaningful NLRB response. The data I summarized earlier about the trends and current levels of employer unfair labor practices in this country make it clear that we need a major restructuring of the current representation system to reduce the current degree of intimidation of employees, even if doing so requires some marginal sacrifice in their illumination.

Protecting the Right to Strike

There is a more fundamental reason why I lean the way I do in my appraisal of the net values of the current representation system. The

41. The interviews conducted by Getman et al., *Union Representation Elections*, disclosed a surprising degree of experience and knowledge of unions among currently nonunion employees, and showed that few of these workers became much better informed as a result of the employer's campaign (pp. 140–144).

proponents of a vigorous campaign prior to the certification vote seriously overestimate the significance of that decision. They rely too heavily on the legal image of NLRB certification as conferring on the union quasi-governmental authority over the employees, with the union supposedly displacing management from the same role in the nonunion employment context. If that image were valid, one could understand the perceived need to establish in labor law the same kind of extended campaign contest we use when we choose our political leaders. In fact, though, that image is quite misleading.

A trade union does *not* govern the employees in the bargaining unit. Unlike an elected legislature, the union does not have the authority to prescribe legally required conditions for the workplace. Unlike the firm's management, the union does not even have the power to set terms of employment within the broad leeway left by actual labor markets. All that the union can do is negotiate with the employer to try to obtain some of the improvements it promised the employees during its campaign. The mere fact of certification, even after the most painstaking of representation procedures, in no way guarantees that the union will obtain an agreement and a real presence in the life of the workplace.

The reason is that once the union has navigated its way past the shoals of the certification process, it faces the equally daunting challenge of life in the world of freedom of (collective) contract. The employer is under no obligation to offer any tangible benefits to the union and its members. The NLRA provides the facilities through which the employees can organize themselves into a union to deal more effectively with their employers, but it promises these employees no particular gains as a result of that choice. Those gains the workers must win through their own efforts.

Unions can extract concessions and secure contracts from employers only with the lever of pressure from the employees, by the use or the threat of strike action. Thus to achieve any degree of real authority over the bargaining unit and to win a favorable contract that will give collective action a reasonable prospect of survival, the union must obtain a strike mandate from the employees. The tacit campaign that goes on in the workplace before the strike vote, during which time the employees must consider how necessary are their union's contract proposals and how reasonable are the employer's counteroffers, furnishes what I consider to be the true laboratory test of whether or not the unit actually wants to have collective bargaining. Only if the union wins such a mandate—and in practice it must come from a solid, not just a bare, majority of the employees—is the message driven home to the employer not only that its workers were prepared to vote for union representation in the abstract, but that they are now prepared to put their livelihood on the line to obtain such group influence on their working conditions. Essentially, all that the initial decision about certification accomplishes is to authorize the union to represent the employees and force the employer to come to the negotiating table and expose its true position about what improvements, if any, it is prepared to make in the employees' situation.

This established principle of freedom of contract in collective bargaining itself evokes criticism from the left, from those who deplore the power it gives certain employers to engage in hard bargaining and thereby force workers out on strike in an often fruitless effort to win minimally decent employment conditions. I have argued elsewhere[42] that despite the discomfort we feel about certain egregious cases, the broader institution of free collective bargaining—with its key corollary that employees may have to strike to win a better offer from their employer—is better than the alternatives. One must acknowledge that such collective bargaining produces real inequalities in employee gains from the process, favoring those who start from a better market position because of their special skills or their employer's insulated product market. But overall, the strategy of group reconstruction rather than legal regulation of the labor market produces a significant improvement in both the absolute levels and the more equal distribution of employment terms, while preserving much of the flexibility and innovative potential of the market.[43]

There is a deeper problem, however. The outcome of this economic contest is not simply a product of private resources. It is also deeply influenced by the legal framework that determines what resources the parties start out with. Much of that legal framework—the laws of property, inheritance, incorporation, and the like—is far beyond the reach of labor law and its reform. But the same labor statute that facilitates organization of the employees and sends them to the table to negotiate with their employer under the umbrella of freedom of contract also places significant legal limits on the economic weapons that can be

42. See Weiler, "Striking a New Balance," pp. 364–384.
43. I should note the recent forceful argument to the contrary made by Brian A. Langille and Patrick Macklem, "Beyond Belief: Labour Law's Duty to Bargain," 13 *Queen's Law Journal* 62 (1988).

deployed by either side.[44] American labor law as it has evolved now exhibits a serious imbalance in its treatment of the crucial component in the bargaining struggle, the strike weapon. The employer is permitted to continue operating during a strike by hiring permanent replacements, but the strikers and their union are prohibited from asking other unionized workers to stop assisting their own employers in carrying on business as usual with the struck employer. That particular tilt in our labor law comes into play primarily in settings in which striking workers are already disadvantaged in the labor market, which is especially likely to be so in the case of newly organized units trying not merely to win appreciable economic gains, but also to secure a meaningful voice in the affairs of their workplace.

American labor law affirmatively promises workers the right to strike. Section 7 of the NLRA establishes not only the initial right of worker self-organization but also the further right "to engage in . . . concerted activities for the purposes of collective bargaining or other mutual aid and protection." In turn, this employee right is explicitly protected from employer interference, restraint, or coercion, and from "discrimination in regard to hire or tenure." Thus rather than force American workers to secure the right to strike through their own efforts, the reconstructive strategy of our labor laws defines and protects this crucial component of the entire system of collective employee action.

It is one thing for the law to tell workers they may strike without fear of employer reprisal. It would be quite another for it to cushion strikers against the consequences of action taken by their employer to defend its position in the bargaining dispute. Indeed, the fact that the employees themselves will suffer the financial pain of no longer receiving a paycheck from their employer is an intrinsic feature of the two-edged sword of strike action.

For over half a century, labor law jurisprudence has tried to demarcate the appropriate boundary line between protected employee action and legitimate employer response. But the most important principle of all was laid down almost offhandedly, when the Supreme Court decided the case of NLRB v. Mackay Radio and Telegraph Co.[45] fifty years ago. In *Mackay Radio,* its first pronouncement on the scope of the

44. Ibid., pp. 385ff.

45. 304 U.S. 333 (1938). For a valuable description and critique of *Mackay Radio,* see James B. Atleson, *Values and Assumptions in American Labor Law,* pp. 19–34 (Amherst: University of Massachusetts Press, 1983).

right to strike, the Court was actually faced with quite a different employee complaint and legal question. But in the course of arriving at its conclusion on the issues under contention, the Court's opinion stated that a struck employer has not "lost the right to protect and continue its business by supplying places left vacant by the strikers," and that it was therefore not illegal "to replace the striking employees with others in an effort to carry on the business." More important, the Court remarked that the employer "is not bound to discharge those hired to fill the place of strikers upon the election of the latter to resume their employment, in order to create places for them." These almost casual dicta, endorsing the legality of what has become the most important economic weapon in the employer's arsenal, remain virtually unchanged to this day.

Analytically, this judicially fashioned managerial prerogative has two distinct facets: the freedom to continue operating during the strike, and the power to grant permanent priority to strike replacements. Although the law assumes the latter right to be implicit in the former, in reality there is no automatic connection between the two. And it is the threat of *permanent* replacement that is most damaging to the exercise by employees of their rights under Section 7 of the Act.

The employer's immediate objective is to keep its business operating despite the collective cessation of work by its present employees. Clearly, such continued operation will "interfere" with the effective exercise of the right to strike, because although the striking employees forego their paychecks, the employer suffers correspondingly little loss in net revenues. That puts the union under much greater pressure to compromise at the bargaining table, and this imbalance has evident consequences for the terms of settlement. The prospect of such a costly yet fruitless venture will likely restrain the employees from going on strike in the first place. Nonetheless, the employer certainly has a legitimate reason for behaving this way—it wants to maintain its labor costs at what it believes to be a reasonable level. Though the issue is not as clear-cut as is usually assumed in the American political economy,[46] I believe this is a substantial enough reason for struck

46. The labor laws in the province of Quebec prohibit the use of almost any form of temporary replacement of lawful strikers, without any especially distressing consequences for its business and economic activity. For a brief description and critique of the Quebec law, see Weiler, "Striking a New Balance," pp. 202–204. A more extended treatment of the legislation and experience under it is to be found in L. Garant, *Les Briseurs de grève et le code du travail* (Quebec City: Gouvernement du Québec, 1982).

employers to have the freedom to continue operating if they can. But it does not necessarily follow that the employer should also be able to grant permanent tenure to the replacements it hires. That facet of *Mackay Radio* poses an entirely different set of issues in terms of its impact on the employees' statutory rights and on the employer's business needs.

First, the NLRA's unmistakable intent is that an employer may not *discharge* an employee as a reprisal for going on strike. But as we have just seen, the Court has interpreted the law as allowing the *permanent replacement* of the striker. The law may draw its own fine distinction between these two actions in terms of the subjective intent of the employer, but employees may be excused if they do not perceive much practical difference as far as their Section 7 rights are concerned. The bleak prospect of permanently losing his job is obviously likely to chill an employee's willingness to exercise his statutory right to engage in "concerted activities."

Second, although continued operation of the business during the strike has an immediate effect on the terms of the particular bargain between the parties, hiring permanent replacements puts in doubt the future of the collective bargaining relationship itself. Because the employer can successfully fend off any financial threat simply by maintaining its operations during the strike, the ultimate settlement will almost certainly be unfavorable to the employees. But when the employees return to their jobs, they know there will be another round of bargaining at a different phase in the business cycle; the ground they have lost this time may be made up then.

Contrast what happens if the employer has hired a group of workers as permanent replacements. These workers are almost certain to be hostile to union representation, if only because the union will insist that they be dismissed in favor of the strikers as a condition of any settlement. Yet the NLRA gives the permanent replacements full voting rights in any future decertification proceeding, while limiting the strikers' eligibility to a period of twelve months from the beginning of the strike. Thus if an employer succeeds in frustrating the economic impact of the work stoppage by hiring a sizable cadre of permanent replacements, it can also look forward to a possible end to the whole struggle through an NLRB-sponsored vote that will eliminate the union altogether. Indeed, the employer does not even have to wait for the results of a formal decertification petition and vote by its employees. After one year the employer is entitled to withdraw recognition from a certified union if the employer has a bona fide and reasonable doubt about whether the union has majority support. If the majority of the workforce consists of strike replacements, the employer may well be entitled to conclude that such derecognition of the union is legitimate. One need not belabor the significance of these labor law principles in the first contract setting.

For these reasons we should be seriously concerned about the present-day effect of permanent replacement of strikers on the exercise of American workers of any of their Section 7 rights. The evident rejoinder, of course, is that if one concedes (as I do) that employers should have the right to continue operating during a strike if they can, the employer needs the freedom to offer permanent status to the replacements it will try to recruit for that purpose. This supposed economic connection is always offered as the justification for a narrow definition of the scope of the Section 7 rights of the employees. On closer examination, though, that time-honored argument turns out to be largely spurious.

First, even if it were true that *some* employers on *some* occasions have to promise permanent jobs in order to recruit the people they need to operate their plant, the current rule is overinclusive because it allows *all* employers to do so. Experience in a variety of contexts has demonstrated that employers can quite comfortably make do with temporary replacements, be they supervisors, personnel drawn from other locations or job classifications, or casual help hired for the duration of the strike.[47] But *Mackay Radio* creates an irrebuttable presumption that all strike replacements should enjoy permanent status, whatever the actual recruiting difficulties of the employer. At a minimum, then, the law should be changed to require an employer to prove that it actually needed to promise permanent tenure to replacements in order to maintain its operations before permitting such a serious inroad on the Section 7 rights of striking employees.

Few if any employers would be able to discharge that burden, for a

---

47. For a number of case studies which document this claim, see Charles R. Perry, Andrew M. Kramer, and Thomas J. Schneider, *Operating During Strikes: Company Experience, NLRB Policies, and Governmental Regulations* (Philadelphia: Industrial Research Unit, Wharton School, University of Pennsylvania, 1982). In fact, while employers are free to continue operating during a lockout of their employees (see NLRB v. Brown, 380 U.S. 278 (1965); and Operating Engineers v. NLRB (Harter Equipment), 829 F.2d 458 (3d Cir. 1987)), so far they have been legally permitted to use only temporary replacements for that purpose, and many American employers have found this to be a perfectly viable option.

more fundamental reason. Recall that the nonunion replacements typically are able to enjoy only the status of employment at will.[48] In that status, they are exposed not only to the loss of their jobs for business reasons, but also to individual dismissal largely at the employer's discretion. What employers actually promise replacements is most accurately characterized not as *permanent* tenure in their jobs, but only *priority* over the strikers in the allocation of available jobs at the end of the strike.

And in reality, the employer cannot and does not guarantee even this limited a priority. If the strike was in any way attributable to the employer's unfair labor practice, the law itself guarantees strikers the right to get their jobs back. Moreover, if the union manages to bring to bear on the employer enough strike pressure to win a decent settlement, the agreement will almost invariably provide for rehiring the strikers and dislodging the replacements. So all the employer really offers its replacements is the *chance* that they will retain their jobs at the end of the strike. While I agree that even this tenuous a hope could occasionally assist employers in recruiting replacements in tight labor markets, the advantage derived in those few cases is simply too small to justify the seriously chilling effect that the prospect of permanent loss of a job has generally on the exercise of employees' Section 7 rights.

My conclusion, then, is that the judicially created permanent replacement doctrine should be a major target of labor law reform. The type of alternative rule that I favor [49] exists already in Ontario labor law, which grants lawful strikers a right to return to their jobs for a period of up to six months after the beginning of the work stoppage, even if their return will dislodge newly hired replacements. Ontario firms are free to operate to try to withstand the pressure of the work stoppage and thereby obtain better contract settlements. But the employees are given a reasonable opportunity to test their union's resources and the employer's bargaining resolve. If that effort is not successful in securing the terms desired in the current round of negotiations, the employees can return to work and try collective bargaining again at a future and more auspicious time. But workers should not be

---

48. In Belknap, Inc. v. Hale, 463 U.S. 491 (1983), the Supreme Court made it clear that the employer was entitled to offer replacements a guarantee of a job that was conditional on the employer's future willingness and ability to retain these workers, and that this contingent status was sufficiently "permanent" under *Mackay Radio* to override any legal claim by the unsuccessful strikers to their old positions, in which they may have invested much of their working lives.

49. See Weiler, "Striking a New Balance," pp. 393–394.

forced to gamble their very jobs when they utilize the procedure pre-
scribed by the national labor laws to break deadlocks in the process of
free collective bargaining.

Boycotting the Struck Product

Contrary to the expectations of many legal critics of *Mackay Radio*,
overturning the permanent replacement doctrine would only partially
ameliorate the problems of a newly organized unit struggling to win a
first contract from an employer determined not to give the union any
foothold in its business. The employer would still be legally entitled to
operate during a strike. Experience under the Ontario legislation corroborates my earlier conclusion that hiring temporary replacements is
usually a viable means of securing the work force necessary to stay
open. That option is especially feasible in the case of small units of
relatively unskilled employees, often primarily composed of female or
minority workers, who are most in need of legal help to overcome their
adverse economic circumstances.

I do not favor adoption of the recent response of Quebec labor law to
this problem:[50] the government effectively requires employers to shut
down at least the bulk of their operations because they are legally
prohibited from using any nonmanagerial personnel to replace strikers. But I believe we must confront another key feature of our labor
laws that denies strikers a self-help tactic they would naturally want to
use to try to shut down their employer—an appeal to fellow workers
and unionists at other firms to stop performing the services necessary
to maintain normal, uninterrupted business relations with the struck
employer.

The existing legal obstacle to the use of that tactic is found in Section
8(b)(4) of the NLRA, the so-called secondary boycott provision.[51] The
Congress that enacted this feature of Taft-Hartley was motivated by its
distaste for coercive top-down organizing, which too often was the reason why unions used that boycott tactic. But the language of Section
8(b)(4) focused on the impact of boycotts on outside firms rather than
on the context and motivation of the union action. Indeed, the apparent
blanket ban on any secondary impact of union pressures posed a severe

50. See the references in note 36.
51. For an extended discussion of the secondary boycott issue with extensive references to the major cases and the literature, see Weiler, "Striking a New Balance," pp.
397–404 and 415–419.

threat to every form of strike action, no matter how much it was focused on the primary employer. As a result, the NLRB and the courts have spent over forty years grappling with the question of when union action constitutes permissible primary or prohibited secondary pressure.

At first glance the common law jurisprudence of the secondary boycott appears to be a legal swamp. For example, unions are entitled to picket the premises of the struck employer even if the real object of the picketing is to induce employees of other businesses not to make deliveries or pickups or do other work at the primary site.[52] To counter this tactic, however, the third-party employer can simply substitute non-union employees (perhaps supervisors or replacements) for the limited purpose of crossing such a picket line. The union, in turn, will want to respond by moving its pickets to the site of the secondary employer's business in order to follow the primary product coming out of the struck plant. The Supreme Court has said that the union may legally use this tactic to induce *consumers* not to buy the secondary product,[53] at least if the primary product's share of the secondary employer's business is not so large that the pickets would "threaten neutral parties with ruin or substantial loss."[54] The problem is that picketing in front of the store aimed at consumers is likely to have only a marginal impact in the vast majority of cases. Thus the single most important feature of current secondary boycott law is that the union is not entitled to position its pickets behind the store in an effort to induce unionized *workers* not to unload the trucks carrying the struck goods, or move these goods through the warehouse, or stock them on the shelves.[55]

Is it unfair for labor law, having carved out an employer's right to operate during the strike, to ban the most effective tactic by which the

52. See NLRB v. International Rice Milling Co., 341 U.S. 665 (1951). In certain circumstances the union may also be permitted to make this appeal where there are both primary and secondary employers doing business at a common site; see *Sailors Union of the Pacific (Moore Dry Dock)*, 92 NLRB 547 (1950). To avoid this result, either employer may establish separate gates on the common site to be used by the separate groups of employees, but this tactic will be legally effective in insulating one group from picketing by the other only when the work done by the secondary employer is "unconnected to the normal operations of the striking employer"; see Local 761, International Union of Electrical Workers v. NLRB (General Electric), 366 U.S. 667 (1961).

53. See NLRB v. Fruit and Vegetable Packers, Local 760 (Tree Fruits), 377 U.S. 58 (1964).

54. This qualification on the legality of consumer picketing was developed by the Supreme Court in NLRB v. Retail Store Employees Union, Local 1001 (Safeco), 447 U.S. 607 (1980).

55. See Local 1796, United Brotherhood of Carpenters v. NLRB (Sand Door), 357 U.S. 93 (1958).

union could try to foil the employer's continuing to operate? The obvious response is that this is not one-sided legal intervention in favor of the employer against the union. The law, it is argued, is simply seeking to confine the conflict to the two warring parties, and to protect innocent outsiders from the harmful consequences of a dispute they did not cause and cannot settle.

However plausible this defense of Section 8(b)(4) law might seem initially, on closer inspection it contains more myth than truth. Protection of neutrals from the economic fallout of labor disputes is not and cannot be the basis of our labor policy.[56] If it were, the original language of Section 8(b)(4) would have been read literally so as to prohibit even primary strikes. Take, for example, a strike by auto workers against a company such as General Motors. Any concerted withdrawal of labor from GM inevitably inflicts substantial harm on outside suppliers of steel, rubber, or glass, as well as on the shippers, dealers, and advertising agencies involved in getting the finished cars into the hands of consumers. But as we have seen, the central premise of free collective bargaining is that a union must be able to shut down the firm's operation in order to break a deadlock at the negotiating table. The neutral outsider has no choice but to bear the cost and disruption produced by such action.

In the vast majority of strikes, then, including those causing the greatest external damage, our society recognizes and accepts the notion that harm to such innocent parties is the price that must be paid to maintain our system of free collective bargaining. Only in the secondary boycott situation—in which the employer has been able to operate during the strike—does the NLRB step in to protect ostensibly "innocent" parties. In this case, not only does the law intervene, but it goes out of its way to insure that the secondary employer does not suffer even the rather insignificant harm caused by its own workers' refusal to handle a single struck product that may constitute only a tiny share of its overall business. Whatever the manifest justification for Section 8(b)(4), its latent function and practical impact are to tilt the balance of power even further toward the employer in those disputes in which *Mackay Radio* makes a significant difference in the employer's arsenal: strikes involving small units of unskilled workers struggling for first

56. This argument was first made by Howard Lesnick, "The Gravamen of the Secondary Boycott," 62 *Columbia Law Review* 1363 (1962), and elaborated further by David M. Beatty, "Secondary Boycotts: A Functional Analysis," 52 *Canadian Bar Review* 388 (1974).

contracts in settings of low union density and high unemployment.

I suggest, then, a single change in the current scope of our antiboy-cott law. This law should characterize as *primary* activity a request by a striking union to other workers not to provide services to or handle products from the affected operations of a struck employer. Such a hands-off legal posture toward the efforts of striking workers would correspond to the similar stance the law now takes toward the employer's effort to continue operating during the strike.

I am aware that some people will be uneasy about such tinkering with Section 8(b)(4), because they will worry about the potential escalation of a dispute far beyond its initial location. A possible series of events like the following may evoke such concern: the union has struck a manufacturer, which continues nonetheless to operate. The union then approaches an outside retailer to try to have the struck product removed from its shelves. That outside retailer continues to do business with the primary employer, perhaps because its employees are not willing to stop handling the struck product. Should the union then be able to establish a general consumer boycott of all products sold by the retailer, thereby not only increasing pressure on the latter but also harming other manufacturers whose products it sells? Worse, should the union be entitled to approach and perhaps picket manufacturers doing business with this retailer in order to force them to stop? If so, this frightening explosion of what began as a localized labor dispute would harm not only the innocent outside businesses, but the employees who work in them as well.

I must underline, then, that no such scenario could unfold under the inherently limited expansion of boycott pressures that I suggest should be available to striking workers. Although a union ought to be entitled to ask outside employees not to perform services for, or handle bids from, the struck firm, it should not be entitled to call for a general sympathy strike against the entire line of business of the secondary firm in order to force that firm to sever relations with the primary employer.[57]

---

57. Justice Brennan's dissent in the *Safeco* case, 447 U.S. 621, explains further why the striking union should not be able to engage in consumer picketing that would escalate its dispute with the primary employer into a general attack on the sales of all outside firms doing business with that employer. Granting that premise, from an industrial relations perspective the recent decision by the Supreme Court (including Justice Brennan) in Edward J. DeBartolo Corp. v. Florida Gulf Coast Building and Construction Trades Council, 485 U.S. 568 (1988), is wrong insofar as it permitted the union to escalate its primary dispute with one contractor, which had erected one of the buildings in a shopping mall, into a call for a consumer boycott of all the stores in the mall, simply because

A boycott so limited would cause no more harm to uninvolved third parties than the harm that currently results when a primary strike successfully shuts down the employer, as it normally does. In practice, in such bellwether industries as auto, steel, coal, trucking, and rail, purely primary strikes do have a significant spillover effect on outside parties. Even in other industries there are not very many units in which employers are able to replace strikers, and these units typically are extremely small and have relatively few business relations that would be subject to such escalation. So the only time that outside parties are actually protected from the negative effects of a legal strike is when the struck employer is able to exercise its own freedom to continue operating. The true effect of this aspect of supposedly "secondary" boycott law is to protect the viability of that option for the primary employer, not to insulate outside neutrals from the normal consequences of most labor disputes.[58] It is high time we removed this special legal advantage enjoyed by employers, with its seriously damaging impact on precisely those employees who are least able to help themselves.

The Uses and Limits of NLRA Reform

The limited change I just proposed for Section 8(b)(4) law to permit more effective boycotts of the products of struck employers is one vital piece of a broader strategy for labor law reform. Along with guarantees against permanent replacement of legal strikers, this step would enhance the ability of workers themselves to counter an employer negotiation posture which, legal or not, is likely to foil the employee effort to secure a first collective agreement.[59] Put together with instant elec-

---

the union there used handbills rather than picket signs (although I recognize that this distinction in the means of communication may entail a legal distinction under the current wording of the NLRA and the Court's interpretation of "freedom of speech" in labor disputes).

58. This strange tilt in the actual operation of secondary boycott law is illustrated in the recent decision in Charvet v. International Longshoremen's Association, 736 F.2d 1572 (D.C. Cir. 1984), in which the D.C. Court of Appeals held that although the primary employer who was actually the party to a labor dispute with a striking union could sue the union when it extended its picketing to outside third parties, the need to protect the union from potentially crushing liability required that truly uninvolved tertiary parties whose business was interrupted by the picketing be denied standing to sue under the secondary boycott laws.

59. I would build a further feature and safeguard into those alterations in the legal framework that defines the rights of employees to bring economic pressure on the employer. Before any such strike action and primary product picketing would be legally

tions, such a reform package would place less reliance on legal sanctions imposed by an outside government agency to implement our public policy encouraging collective bargaining. Instead, through measures carefully designed to reconstruct the legal environment, our labor laws would try to achieve a different equilibrium between employer and employees themselves in these conflicts.

My argument is not that we should eschew all NLRB rules and sanctions. Not only is such regulation necessary, but it must be strengthened, by, for example, the kinds of injunctive and general damages relief that I outlined earlier. But our use of such regulatory resources must be more closely targeted at a much smaller set of the vital concerns of the parties. At this stage in the relationship, rather than fritter away the scarce time and energy of NLRB personnel on a host of complaints about what the employer (or the union) allegedly *said*[60] in the campaign or at the negotiating table, we must concentrate Board efforts on providing truly effective relief and meaningful deterrence in cases where workers suffer tangible injury because of what the employer (or the union) *did*—in particular, loss of a job due to discrim-

---

permitted, the strike would have to be authorized by a majority verdict in a secret ballot vote of all the employees in the unit. A legal guarantee of this kind of direct employee participation in such a key collective bargaining decision is intrinsically valuable (for reasons I set out in *Reconcilable Differences*, pp. 70–74). However, it plays a subtle but important role in the specific labor law reform package which I have been developing here. First, a secret ballot strike vote gives the employees in a unit that is newly certified after an instant election an opportunity, de facto, to change their mind about the virtues of collective bargaining as they come face to face with a concrete choice between their union's demands and their employer's offer. In addition, for any striking unit, such a vote adds moral force to the claim by the employees that their exercise of the legal right to strike should be protected against loss of jobs through permanent replacement.

60. While I am not persuaded by the arguments of Getman et al., *Union Representation Elections*, that discriminatory discharges of individual union supporters generate no chilling effect on the willingness of the overall unit of employees to vote for and support the union, I agree with them that the majority of current Board regulation of employer (and union) speech should be dismantled. Therefore I approve of the decision in *Midland National Life Insurance Co.*, 263 NLRB 127 (1982), where the Reagan Board retreated from any effort to control *inaccurate* campaign propaganda; I would overturn *Sewell Manufacturing Co.*, 138 NLRB 66 (1962), and its progeny, which have tried to penalize *inflammatory* propaganda; and I agree with the effort of Judge Posner in NLRB v. Village IX, Inc., 723 F.2d 1360 (7th Cir. 1983) to cut back sharply on the definition and prohibition of supposedly *threatening* employer speech. But I part company with Getman and his colleagues with respect to their advocacy of additional legal intervention to guarantee the union *equal access* to the employer's premises to campaign against the employer. As I said earlier, my feeling is that such an ambitious new form of Board regulation would prove just as fruitless as have been efforts to enforce laboratory election conditions under the doctrines just mentioned.

inatory discharge or permanent replacement. As a general matter, I am largely in agreement with those who suggest that we now rely far too much on the law for resolving labor problems, be it under the NLRB or in other contexts.[61] But in my case that attitude does not presume that there are no real problems in the workplace: I am merely doubtful that the law can provide worthwhile solutions very often. The result: my recommendation that we redeploy our legal resources to better protect the core of Section 7 rights of workers against the most harmful features of the broad employer onslaught of the last several decades.

What might we expect from such a revamped legal policy? Even those who are highly sympathetic to the union movement express considerable skepticism that any more than a marginal payoff would result from even the most searching type of labor law reform.[62] Like the current one, a revised labor statute would inevitably focus on the process by which unions win certification elections and negotiate first contracts. However, a close look at the pronounced decline in private-sector union representation over the last three decades reveals that the drop in union success in winning NLRB elections (and consequently first contracts) turns out to make much less of a contribution to this decline than do changes in industrial structure, worker demography, and the inability of union organizers to tap latent employee demand for what they have to offer.[63] From this perspective, then, rather than blame the existing law for their present plight, union leaders would be better advised to concentrate their energies on rethinking their traditional ways of operating, in the hope that they will then be able to

61. That is why at a number of points in this book I recommend major retrenchment in the reach of our current labor laws. In Chapter 5 I propose the repeal of the current absolute ban on employer creation of employee representation plans (pp. 211–215); earlier in this Chapter I urge the repeal of the ban on unilateral changes by employers in working conditions prior to an impasse in bargaining with the union (see note 40); and in the previous note I propose deregulating campaign propaganda. While I favor the development of certain minimum legal guarantees for workers against unjust discharges, in Chapter 2 I also propose a sharp cutback in potential wrongful dismissal litigation (see pp. 99–100).

62. Thus Thomas A. Kochan, Harry C. Katz, and Robert B. McKersie, *The Transformation of American Industrial Relations* (New York: Basic Books, 1986), and Charles C. Heckscher, *The New York Unionism: Employee Involvement in the Changing Corporation* (New York: Basic Books, 1988), although favoring reform of the NLRA as a matter of principle, are skeptical that such reform would make a substantial practical difference in the future prospects for union representation in this country.

63. See the calculations in William T. Dickens and Jonathan S. Leonard, "Accounting for the Decline in Union Membership, 1950–1980," 38 *Industrial and Labor Relations Review* 323 (1985).

spark considerably more interest among unorganized workers and enable unions to establish the required showing before the NLRA apparatus is ever set in motion.

Anyone reading a piece written by a law professor should allow for the tendency of the labor lawyer and law reformer to emphasize the importance of his own specialty. I recognize that the law is only one feature of a larger picture, which will have to include a profound adjustment by the union movement to the socioeconomic trends that I outlined earlier. Having acknowledged that, I still believe that if private-sector unionism is to be revived, reform of the NLRA representation process will have to play a central role.

This part of the legal framework becomes significant at a number of points. First, the design of the representation process is the one area where public policy can make an important difference in the outcome. Labor law reform could make the representation procedure something less of an obstacle course, freighted with the threatening overtones that now typically characterize it. If one accepts the premise that workers have a fundamental right to deal collectively with their employers if they so wish, making it easier for employees to try the institution out to see whether they can benefit from the experience would seem to be a sufficient reason to justify the reform effort. And if after such an effort has been made it turns out that the new breed of American worker really does not want union representation, even when it is readily available, the institution could then be given a decent burial and we could turn our attention to alternatives.

It is a mistake, though, to assume that NLRA procedures have an impact only with respect to situations in which they happen to come into play and in which, by counting up *ex post* the number of potential members lost in unsuccessful petitions, one can estimate the significance of that variable in the larger picture. In truth, our perception of how well the NLRA performs when it is actually utilized has a further important influence, *ex ante,* on the incentives and actions of the protagonists outside the legal procedure—unions, employers, and workers.

As an illustration, consider the incentive structure that the various actors in an organizing drive face under the current NLRA representation procedures, from which about one in five workers involved in elections emerges covered by a collective agreement.

The Union. Even ignoring the fact that losses in some elections mean that the union will not thereby generate new members and dues payments that could be used to finance further organizational efforts, the union leader who considers whether to undertake a new drive realizes that the investment of the union's resources offers only a small potential yield, even if the drive were successful in developing initial interest in collective bargaining among the employees. As I stated, on average just over 20 percent of the workers in units where there was such a showing of interest will end up as union members. So there is naturally some reluctance to spend the current membership's dues money in the more difficult organizing situations, those which involve largely nonunion industries, occupations, or regions.[64]

The Employer. The other side of the coin is that the nonunion employer that sees its counterparts successfully fending off unionization through a variety of tactics and expenditures (on consultants or lawyers, for example) will be encouraged to follow the same tack. Indeed, unionized employers face competitive pressures to de-unionize their own operations. That strategy is likely to be pursued not so much through decertification of presently unionized plants[65] as through the

64. This is one of the major reasons why there has been such a marked decline in union organizing efforts during the past decade, with less than half the number of new certification elections conducted in 1985 (3,498) as in 1975 (8,061). After years of beating their heads (and throwing their members' money) against a legal wall, union leaders are simply unwilling to invest increasingly scarce union resources in fighting nonunion employers in front of a much less hospitable Labor Board. And in what I believe is one of the most preposterous decisions ever rendered under our labor laws, a *unanimous* Supreme Court held, in Ellis v. Brotherhood of Railway Clerks, 466 U.S. 435 (1984), that a union was forbidden from expending dues monies collected from dissident nonunion employees under an agency shop clause for purposes of organizing new workers. The Court's theory was that such outside organizing was not significantly connected to the interests of the employees in the presently represented unit. This almost casual holding by the Court reflected either unawareness of or unwillingness to look at the overwhelming analytical and empirical support for the proposition that economic gains by a union for the employees at one location or in one firm depend heavily on the degree to which the union has organized (and thus reduced the competition from) other nonunion locations and firms in that market. See Richard B. Freeman and James L. Medoff, "The Impact of the Percent Organized on Union and Nonunion Wages," 63 *Review of Economics and Statistics* 561 (1981). The point is that the generally unsympathetic attitude of the law toward union organizing as exhibited in *Ellis* and a host of other legal doctrines, has helped produce a situation in which unions bring before the Board fewer and fewer such cases which turn up in the Board's statistics, and thus help demonstrate again what a difference the law makes to the fate of unions.

65. Though decertification petitions have increased sharply over the last two decades, the absolute number of workers included in decertified units is still very small; see Richard B. Freeman and James E. Medoff, *What Do Unions Do?* p. 240 (New York: Basic Books, 1984). This accords with surveys that indicate broad satisfaction of union members with the performance of their unions (Freeman and Medoff, *What Do Unions Do?* pp. 143–145), and marked reluctance on the part of workers who are now covered by collective agreements to dispense with that protection; see, e.g., Stephen M. Hills, "The Attitudes of Union and Nonunion Male Workers Toward Union Representation," 38 *Industrial and Labor Relations Review* 179 (1985) (finding that 87 percent of current union

deliberate channeling of new capital investments into smaller plants in nonunion locations, rather than into expansion of existing, more convenient, but unionized operations.[66] Again, though, this investment strategy makes sense only if it is fairly certain that these new plants are unlikely to be organized under the current NLRA procedures.[67]

The Employee. Workers in nonunion plants or offices realize that to become involved in an organizing drive is a somewhat risky step, especially if one is a visible leader of such an effort.[68] Even if there is no immediate risk of dismissal by an employer that is ready to honor the requirements of the law, such employee action is not likely to enhance the prospects for later promotion by management, which will feel, rightly or wrongly, that an employee involved in a union organizing effort has exhibited considerable dissatisfaction with and disloyalty to the firm. Taking such a risk is sensible only if the employees believe that there is a good chance that their union will win the election and secure a collective agreement, particularly a contract with terms generous enough to make all the effort worthwhile. However, it is evident to even the casual onlooker that the odds are quite low that any of these aims will be achieved under the current legal regime, especially in occupations, industries, and locations where there is now little union presence. In this setting, the natural step for the nonunion worker is either to accept the current working arrangements as reasonably satisfactory,[69] even though they may not be quite as good as what

members would now vote for union representation, and, indeed, that 82 percent of the employees who are covered by collective agreements but have chosen not to join the union would also vote for collective bargaining in their workplace).

66. See Anil Verma, "Relative Flow of Capital to Union and Nonunion Plants Within a Firm," 24 *Industrial Relations* 395 (1985); Anil Verma and Thomas A. Kochan, "The Growth and Nature of the Nonunion Sector Within a Firm," in Thomas A. Kochan, ed., *Challenges and Choices Facing American Labor*, p. 89 (Cambridge, Mass.: MIT Press, 1985); and Kochan, Katz, and McKersie, *Transformation*, pp. 65–76.

67. Crucial to this deunionization strategy is the legal premise I noted earlier (in Chapter 3, pp. 114–117) that the natural state for a new plant is nonunion, even in a firm as broadly unionized as General Electric. The current law assumes that such a principle gives the workers at each appropriate location freedom of choice to have or not to have union representation. From a formal perspective the employees would have precisely the same freedom to embrace or reject union representation if the law directed that they start out *with* a union. From a practical perspective, however, the current starting point produces a pronounced tilt against the prospect of the work force in new plants ever having collective bargaining, whatever their personal inclinations might be.

68. Recall the figures presented at pp. 238–241 regarding both the actual and the perceived risk of employer reprisal against union supporters during the campaign.

69. In the psychological literature this tack is referred to as adaptive preferences or cognitive dissonance: a phenomenon whereby an individual who knows that a particular option is not realistically available to him feels that the best way to enhance his welfare

might have been obtained through organized group action; or, if the employees are really dissatisfied, to exit from the firm one by one, in search of better conditions elsewhere.

My judgment, then, is that searching reform of our labor laws would make a significant difference in the prospects for union representation and collective bargaining. That difference would be felt not only in those cases that now embark on the NLRA procedures and fail, but also in cases that would have entered the system in the first place had it not been for the current high risks of failure and reprisal. Over an extended period of time, a new labor law would help produce an indeterminate but appreciable change in the statistical trend lines that I traced earlier.

One reason I am confident about that is that I am sure that labor law reform could not be achieved in isolation. The existing intense employer opposition to such congressional action could only be overcome if our political leaders were to display much greater appreciation for the virtues of collective bargaining than they have in recent years. Such a political reaction would likely be forthcoming only if the union movement itself undertook a thoroughgoing reorientation of its own organization and programs. But if such political and institutional shifts were to occur, they would be accompanied by corresponding changes in worker attitudes: employees would probably display much more receptivity to a process that could give them a meaningful voice and influence in their workplaces. Thus any serious statutory reform must go hand in hand with the social and institutional changes that, in turn, could make these legal revisions fruitful.

I insist that even with a favorable shift in the appeal of union representation, labor law reform would still be indispensable. We have to ease the existing legal endurance contest that American managers regularly put their workers through in order to stifle any awakening interest in collective bargaining. If we believe that the functions performed by that institution are worth saving, then investing the necessary political resources to thoroughly revamp our labor laws is a worthwhile endeavor.

---

in that case is to adapt his attitudes to the circumstances and to no longer remain especially interested in pursuing the unattainable option. See Cass R. Sunstein, "Legal Interference With Private Preferences," 53 *University of Chicago Law Review* 1129, 1147–50 (1986), for a discussion of this phenomenon with extensive references to the scholarly literature. This mode of psychological adjustment helps explain the decline in interest in collective bargaining among nonunion workers even when collective bargaining has been producing bigger and bigger gains for their unionized counterparts, who generally display substantial satisfaction with the performance of their union representative; see sources cited in note 65.

However, we must be equally realistic about the limited leverage that the law can offer in this regard. Even with a new brand of unionism, one which enjoyed much greater popular and political appeal and eventually even produced a drastic revision in our labor legislation (and this is only partially, if at all, foreseeable), we should still expect that only a minority of American workers would have union representation for decades to come.

Indeed, one can get a good sense of the outer limits of such legislative action by returning to the Canadian example from which I earlier drew some of my proposals and rationales. In a legal environment that is about as favorable as one could imagine, under labor legislation that has successfully contained much of the kind of employer resistance that is rampant in the United States, still only about 45 percent of Canadian nonagricultural, nonmanagerial workers now have union representation.[70] That is roughly the level one would project that American unionism would have reached by now had it been able to maintain its earlier rate of success in the similarly shifting industrial and occupational environment.[71] And the Canadian union share of the private sector, especially in the fast growing private service industries, is significantly smaller than such aggregate union density figures might suggest.[72] But it is unrealistic to suppose that American unions could now aspire to anything near that level, even if the Canadian labor law system were delivered to them in the nineties.

There are a number of reasons why that is so. To many, the most likely explanation for the slackened drive to unionize is that most American workers are fully satisfied with their present job situation and with the treatment voluntarily provided to them by their employers under the spur of a loosely competitive labor market. These workers therefore feel no need for the protective and participatory functions performed by collective bargaining.

While that claim is probably valid for many nonunion employees, I doubt that it holds true for even close to all of them. It does not square

70. See Pradeep Kumar, "Union Growth in Canada: Retrospect and Prospect," in W. Craig Riddell, ed., *Canadian Labour Relations*, pp. 95, 97 (Toronto: University of Toronto Press, 1986).

71. See Dickens and Leonard, "Accounting for the Decline," pp. 331–332.

72. The most recent analysis of Canadian trends in an unpublished paper by Noah M. Meltz, "Unionism in the Private Service Sector: A Canada–U.S. Comparison" (University of Toronto, 1989), shows that while the present situation of Canadian unions is far better than that of their U.S. counterparts, the prospects for collective bargaining in the Canadian private sector are not particularly rosy, despite the more favorable legal framework.

with the fact that as the effective reach of collective bargaining has declined so sharply over the last few decades, the vacuum left has had to be filled by a variety of forms of outside government protection and inside participatory management, with all the inadequacies characteristic of such programs when employees have no cohesive base from which to take full advantage of them. The more likely explanation is that although a large number of American workers feel the need for the kinds of functions traditionally performed by collective bargaining, they are not prepared to adopt either that process or the union organization through which it is carried out.

The nature of the union bargaining process, shaped as it has been by our labor laws, helps explain this lack of worker interest. I do not suggest that the somewhat narrow focus of traditional collective bargaining on only the negotiation and administration of wages, benefits, and employment protections is cast in stone. As we have seen earlier, in a growing number of labor-management relationships—such as the UAW with GM or the Communication Workers of America with AT&T—the parties have devised elaborate programs through which the employees themselves become directly involved in many of the decisions about their jobs and the employer's operations. But to achieve that measure of worker participation, let alone the generous compensation and elaborate protections which were once secured by collective bargaining, American unions have had to become tightly knit, hierarchical organizations that can wield the kind of countervailing power necessary to wrest a fair share of the fruits of the enterprise from capital and its managerial organizations.

Worse, just to gain a foothold in the firm sufficient to give workers even a modicum of influence in dealing with their employer, the unit of employees must run an arduous obstacle course under the NLRA if their employer chooses to resist their effort. A constantly shifting group of ordinary workers simply does not have the resources, the experience, and the cohesion to make that certification effort on its own. If the inertial force of the nonunion status quo is to be overcome, employees will require another already existing organization, the union, to fight on their behalf against the employer throughout the representation process. But as I said earlier, the problem with that option is that while many workers would like a good deal more participation and protection than their employer will unilaterally concede to them, many of these workers do not want the kind of union organization that is necessary to take advantage of the right to such a voice apparently offered by the NLRA.

The Constitutive Model

Perhaps, then, we should take a sharply different approach to this problem. When we look for the true underlying source of the heated contest that worker representation has become, we find it in the fact that our labor law gives the employees a choice about the matter. It is precisely because there *is* a formal procedure for making this choice that it has become worthwhile for American employers to pour so much effort, legal and illegal, into winning the contest for a favorable employee verdict. Labor law reforms of the kind outlined above could help even up the struggle and thereby increase the odds that the majority would vote for collective bargaining.

But there would still be a vigorous contest over such employee choice, if not before the certification then afterward, and thus a large and powerful union would be an indispensable counterweight to the employer. My own pessimistic judgment is that if we are ever to provide American workers meaningful involvement and influence in their workplaces, unmediated by the kind of hierarchical union organization that a good many workers would rather not have, it is necessary to take away from the employees (and also the employer) the choice about whether such a participatory mechanism will be present.

That is the thrust of the third strategy of labor law reform, the "constitutive" model, to which I alluded earlier. Public policy would require not collective bargaining, secured with great difficulty, unit by unit, but a guarantee to all employees of easy access to a basic level of internal participation in a specified range of decisions in all enterprises.

The initial reaction of most people to that idea is that it would be even more unthinkable, more unAmerican, than instant elections. How could one possibly justify taking away employee freedom of choice about an issue as vital as this one?

Upon reflection, however, the idea should be at least thinkable. Our emerging employment law has, after all, removed worker choice about an increasing variety of issues—whether to work for less than the minimum wage, for example, or whether to expose oneself to a variety of unsafe or toxic working conditions, or whether to allow the employer to fire an employee in violation of some public policy. As I pointed out in my detailed analysis of the wrongful dismissal problem, such laws assume a social judgment that these crucial interests of workers deserve a degree of protection that an imperfect labor market will not supply on its own. Instead, such protection must be guaranteed as a matter of moral right and legal principle, rather than be left to individual workers to struggle for by themselves, with the inevitable disparities and gaps left by that process. Suppose, then, that the community is also convinced that some meaningful employee voice in the governance of the workplace would be good for its workers and for its broader political economy. That premise could readily justify a law that would mandate some such participatory procedure, rather than leave this issue to the vagaries of employee choice and the invitable employer reaction.

The proposal is more plausible when one considers the problem from a political rather than simply an economic vantage point. The economic view supposes that collective employee action is no more than a technique through which workers can pool their bargaining power to extract better wages and benefits from their employer. On that premise, it would make sense to leave it to the workers immediately affected to decide whether they are sufficiently dissatisfied with the status quo to organize themselves to extract a better financial deal from their employer. Certainly the economic factor has been a prime motivation for both union representation and legal regulation. But a theme that runs throughout this book is that there is much more to life in the workplace than these bread-and-butter concerns. In the contemporary employment relationship, management is able to wield real power about a host of issues in the workers' lives. Those issues are often more significant than many that are addressed by municipal councils or school boards, for example. Just as is true in the school context, in which a dissatisfied citizen cannot easily move to a different community or school system, the worker who has committed himself to a career with a particular firm can advance a strong moral claim to some meaningful voice about the exercise of managerial power, with its far-reaching impact on his stake in the firm. The deeper political values served by employee participation are not reducible to nor are they necessarily exhausted by a one-time majority vote about a specific mode of employee representation, whatever may be the result.

Employee Participation

This argument is comparatively easy to make at such a high level of abstraction. It is more difficult to specify a particular mode of employee participation that would be so attractive across the board that one could reasonably require its adoption in virtually all firms as a matter of public policy. Certainly one could not make that claim for union representation and collective bargaining, which now appeal to only a minority of nonunion workers, let alone to employers and the general public.

The specific model I have in mind is the West German *Betriebsrat*, or Works Council—an in-house procedure through which the employees at local work sites address and help resolve a range of employment issues. By all accounts, such mandatory Works Councils have played a valuable role in the evolution of West German human resource policy. So we can draw upon this quite successful experience for at least some of the ingredients of a proposal that must still be tailored to fit the current trends and needs in the American employment relationship.[73]

Assume, then, that one favors a public policy that would require the adoption of what I shall call Employee Participation Committees (EPCs). A variety of legal footholds can be imagined for such a policy— a broad-ranging statutory mandate, or a more limited Executive Order targeted at certain kinds of employer-contractors that work with the

73. There is a growing English-language literature on the German Works Council and how this institution fits into the broader industrial relations system in West Germany. I have found a number of pieces especially useful in connecting the German experience to the North American context: in Canada, Roy Adams has been the major exponent of the works council idea: see Roy J. Adams and C. H. Rummell, "Workers' Participation in Management in West Germany: Impact on the Worker, the Enterprise and the Trade Union," 8 *Industrial Relations Journal* 4 (1977); Roy J. Adams, "Should Works Councils Be Used As Industrial Relations Policy?" *Monthly Labor Review* 25 (July 1985); and Roy J. Adams, "Two Policy Approaches to Labour–Management Decision Making at the Level of the Enterprise," in W. Craig Riddell, ed., *Labour-Management Cooperation in Canada*, p. 87 (Toronto: University of Toronto Press, 1986). Recently David M. Beatty has proposed in his *Putting the Charter to Work: Designing a Constitutional Labour Code* (Kingston: McGill-Queen's University Press, 1987) the adoption of the works council model to replace the current system of union as exclusive bargaining agent. In the United States, Clyde Summers has described and appraised the West German model as part of his decade-long exploration of the relevance of European industrial relations experience to the limitations of American labor laws: see Clyde W. Summers, "Worker Participation in the U.S. and West Germany: A Comparative Study from an American Perspective," 28 *American Journal of Comparative Law* 367 (1980); Clyde W. Summers, "The Usefulness of Unions in a Major Industrial Society," 58 *Tulane Law Review* 1409 (1984); and Clyde W. Summers, "An American Perspective on the German Model of Worker Participation," *Comparative Labor Law Journal* 333 (1987). Kirsten Wever has recently written a very useful paper that connects the works council idea to recent innovations in the organization of work in the United States: see Kirsten R. Wever, "Works Councils in the U.S.? Exploring a Public Policy Solution to Private Sector Problems" (March 1988). Finally, I should mention a valuable case study of the manner in which the German Works Council has responded to much the same kinds of economic and industrial changes which I traced in the American workplace in Chapter 5: see Kathleen Thelen, "The Dilemmas of Dualism: Works Council Politics in the Crisis" (working paper, 1986).

government, defined by size, industry, and so on. I shall make some observations later about the appropriate legal format, but a variety of crucial issues must first be worked out in the design of this representation model. These issues include, respectively, the *structure* of the EPC, its *responsibilities*, its *resources* and its *relations* with other workplace governance systems—in particular, with union representation for purposes of collective bargaining.

Structure. In every workplace above a certain minimum size—perhaps twenty-five workers—the employees would elect at least one of their fellow employees as a representative to the EPC. As the size of the workplace grew larger, so also would the number of elected representatives (though not necessarily in proportion to the body of workers). Excluded from the employee constituency would be only the senior executive team and those working in the human resource and industrial relations departments. All other employees—ordinary workers in the plant and office, supervisors, professionals, lower-echelon managers—would be eligible to vote and to run for office as a representative. In firms of medium to larger size, a proportional electoral system would be designed to insure specific representation of each of the different employee constituencies. In the case of larger, multi-site enterprises, each of which would have its own EPC, there would also be a broader firm-wide committee to coordinate the exercise of employee influence inside the firm. The aim of this entire structure would be to develop an in-house, bottom-up system of employee representation which acknowledged that the work force as a whole had a common stake in the human resource policies and other programs of the employer, whatever the specific responsibilities and status enjoyed by any one occupational category.

Responsibilities. The primary responsibility of this committee structure would be to address and react to the broad spectrum of resource policies of the firm. The employer would be required to inform and consult with the EPC about changes in its criteria for wages, benefits, hiring, training, and work assignments; about policies and grievances regarding dismissal, discipline, promotion, demotion, and layoff; regarding manpower adjustments to plant closings, relocations, technological and organizational innovation, and other such changes in the firm's economic environment. I assume that the range of subject matter appropriate for direct employer-employee discussion in such an in-house procedure would be even broader than that which is now required by the NLRA for employers engaged in full-fledged bargaining with a national union. And the discussions would occur on a regular basis as each new problem arose and had to be dealt with, rather than be confined to a triennial round of negotiations like a comprehensive union agreement.

The EPC would also take major initial responsibility for the administration of the broad array of legal policies that now shape and control the employment practices of individual firms. Among the programs I have in mind are the following:

(1) *Occupational Health and Safety.* Through their elected representatives, American workers themselves would play the front-line role in implementing and enforcing OSHA regulations, rather than having to rely on the tiny handful of inspectors now available to monitor hundreds of thousands of work sites across the country.[74] The EPC would have the same kind of implementation and enforcement responsibility for pension security regulation under ERISA and a variety of other protective employment laws.

(2) *Plant Closings.* Now that a statute has been enacted mandating prior notification of plant closings and mass layoffs, the EPC would be an employee organization already in place to receive the notice and to do something constructive with it, whether that be through job banks, work sharing, retraining, early retirement with expedited pensions, or perhaps even an employee buyout of the endangered plant.

(3) *Equal Employment Policy.* The same committee structure would be available to implement the widening array of antidiscrimination laws, affirmative action requirements, programs for securing pay equity or for eliminating sexual harrassment, and so on. Needless to say, care would have to be taken to ensure that the EPC itself had appropriate representation from the affected employee constituencies.

(4) *Wrongful Dismissal.* My proposal for a stripped-down guarantee of basic protection against unjustified dismissal, under which only

74. The most significant illustration in North America of the use of employee participation committees to implement statutory programs is the mandatory health and safety committee required under the occupational health and safety legislation of a number of Canadian provinces. I describe that idea briefly in Paul C. Weiler, *Protecting the Worker from Disability: Challenges for the Eighties*, pp. 108–111 (Toronto: Government of Ontario, 1983). More extended descriptions and sharply contrasting appraisals can be found in Katherine E. Swinton, "Enforcement of Occupational Health and Safety Legislation: The Role of the Internal Responsibility System," in Kenneth P. Swan and Katherine E. Swinton, eds., *Studies in Labour Law* p. 143 (Toronto: Butterworths, 1983); and in Eric Tucker, "The Persistence of Market Regulation of Occupational Health and Safety: The Stillbirth of Voluntarism," in Geoffrey J. England, ed., *Essays in Labour Relations Law* (Don Mills, Ont.: CCH Canadian, 1986).

limited compensation would be offered through the rather rough administrative justice of state UI boards, rested on the assumption that there would be no employee base in the typical nonunion workplace. However, if there were a committee structure capable of representing employees in internal grievance and arbitration procedures, one could envisage the viability of broader legal protections against unjust dismissal, culminating in reinstatement on the job as a standard remedy.

(5) *Employee Stock Ownership Plan.* As I described earlier, over the last fifteen years ESOP legislation has provided American firms with nearly $20 billion in publicly financed tax expenditures to encourage worker ownership of their employers. In practice, though, ESOPs have been designed and utilized primarily as tools of corporate finance and liquidity, and more recently as antitakeover buffers for incumbent management. There has been no guaranteed role for workers in the adoption, let alone the exercise, of any apparent ownership rights over the actual decisions of the firm. The development of an elected employee committee structure might give Congress the vehicle it needs to ensure that ESOP tax benefits are spent in ways that really enhance the employees' stake in and commitment to the firm.

As a general matter, then, one would want all existing and future employment laws adapted to the new mode of employee organization that would now exist in even nonunion workplaces. The presence of such a worker base in the firm would give affected employees a better chance to take advantage of their legal rights, and would thus improve the prospects that the broader aims of such legal programs would be systematically implemented.

There might be some interest in going even further with channeling the primary administration of employment regulation through an EPC structure. Perhaps some power of decision should also be conferred on the EPC about the application of particular statutes inside individual workplaces. One could imagine, for example, an EPC's being able to waive a general OSHA standard as unnecessary and unduly onerous in its own operations, or being entitled to settle and compromise a wrongful dismissal claim on the grounds that the employer's policy under attack (mandatory random drug testing, for example) was acceptable to the majority of the employees. Those decisions of the EPC would govern despite the contrary views of the affected individual workers (and their lawyers) who sought to pursue the legal claim in an outside forum.

Of course, any authority of a privately elected EPC over public laws and rights would have to be subject to a corresponding duty to represent the employees fairly and on a rational basis, a duty analogous to the DFR now imposed on unions concerning the rights created by collective agreements. One might also want to exempt from any such internal authority certain minority rights—rights addressed by the core of antidiscrimination laws—which we would be no more willing to expose to the prejudices of the work force than to the predilections of management. But with those caveats, any reasonably ambitious model of employee representation in the firm would have to involve some significant displacement of the government, as well as the union, as guarantor of the rights of the employees.

Resources. An obvious concern about a more ambitious role for the EPC is that the committee would be too weak and ineffectual a counterweight to management to permit any reduction in external legal enforcement at the behest of affected individuals or groups. It is clear that an EPC would probably be significantly weaker than the typical union, and as yet we have not countenanced any transfer even to unions of authority over the government's legal programs. But however far we feel we can safely proceed with the EPC idea, I believe it could manage and should have more resources and influence than might appear reasonable at first blush.

One such resource would be *information.*[75] The employer should be required to provide the EPC with regular and detailed information not only about its personnel policies, but also about the broader financial, investment, and profit situation of the firm. The employees, through their elected representative, should be just as entitled as are the shareholders and their Board of Directors to the kind of information that is necessary to assess and defend their stake in the enterprise. Such a measure would at the least enhance the operation of labor market incentives and constraints on the firm, as currently happens in the more smoothly operating capital markets.

Along with information goes *access:* once management has supplied the data regarding its plans, it must then sit down and talk with the EPC about the implications of and the alternatives to these plans. That

75. Leslie K. Shedlin, "Regulation of Disclosure of Economic and Financial Data and the Impact on the American System of Labor-Management Relations," 41 *Ohio State Law Journal* 441 (1980), shows how limited is the current legal entitlement of unionized (let alone nonunion) workers to information they need about their employer's situation and plans, an information gap in this country that is especially pronounced by comparison with the situation in Germany and other European countries.

format would provide employees as a group with far more influence than is now exerted by the disconnected and uninformed individual worker, whose only realistic recourse is to exit the firm if he is dissatisfied.

But to maximize the values of its information and access, the EPC will need to draw upon expertise to analyze the issues and the data. Procuring that expertise might involve training EPC members (about OSHA standards, for example) or hiring professional advisors (about more esoteric issues such as ERISA). In either case, the EPC will need adequate *finances* for its activities. Any public policy favoring the EPC model, therefore, must include some provision for financial support by the employer—not simply in relief time from work, but also in money for hiring lawyers, scientists, economists, and so on. In a sense, then, a small but defined part of the firm's revenues would be channeled for the support of an effective EPC component of the human resource function, just as a portion of firm revenues is now regularly expended on its personnel department. I would also require that the employees themselves make some financial contribution, which the employer would have to match according to a specified multiple.

This combination of guaranteed information, access, and financing would markedly increase the importance of the employee voice in the workplace. An EPC would go far beyond the typical EI program in even the more sophisticated and benevolent nonunion firms, let alone what is available from employers who demonstrate no such inclination to share decisionmaking with their employees. When elected, informed, trained, and well advised representatives of the employees meet regularly with their opposite numbers in the senior management team to address a continuing series of employment issues, one can expect the employees eventually to develop considerable persuasive influence on the ultimate policies and practices of the firm.

At the same time, one would also expect that with respect to a number of matters, especially issues that run counter to major conflicting interests of either shareholder equity or managerial prerogative, such persuasive influence will not be enough. In such cases, under West German law the Works Council is given another lever to put it on a more equal plane vis-à-vis management. At least in regard to specifically human resource questions—which include measures to deal with the impact of plant closings or technological change—the German Works Council must give its prior consent to any management action. When mutual consent is not achieved through the parties' discussions, an appeal may be taken by either side to binding outside arbitration.

I do *not* favor the arbitration option for the United States. In West Germany the Works Council has the responsibility for administering and enforcing both the collective agreement negotiated by the union for the industry and a much more extensive body of employment standards law. Thus arbitration, in lieu of a right to strike, evolved as a natural method for resolving what is often a disagreement about the application of these general standards to particular cases. Under American labor policy, at least in the private sector, we have decided for good reasons not to give unions a regime of binding interest arbitration to help them bargain for protective employment standards.[76] It would be incongruous and unwise to reverse that course and provide this too-easy mechanism in a new EPC procedure, which is after all designed primarily for employees who do not have (and may not want) full-fledged collective bargaining.

That judgment would not, however, leave the employees represented by an EPC with no power to move an intransigent employer. Those employees would still enjoy precisely the same right to strike under Section 7 of the NLRA—"to take concerted action . . . for their mutual aid or protection"—as is now used by union members engaged in collective bargaining.[77] The immediate rejoinder, of course, is that a small group of nonunion workers with the limited resources and lack of tradition of an EPC would probably be too timid and inhibited to actually exercise the legal right to strike without the backing and support of a large union. But if it is the case, as I am sure it usually would be, that the purely persuasive efforts of the EPC were not sufficient to move the employer to improve working conditions, then that is a reason for these employees to exercise their further Section 7 legal right— to join a real union.

Relations. That brings me to a final issue: what is the appropriate relationship between the EPC model and union representation itself?

76. For a detailed critique of binding arbitration as the standard procedure for resolving negotiating disputes, see Weiler, "Striking a New Balance," pp. 371–380.

77. Under the current labor law, nonunion workers have the same statutory right as union members to strike in protest against their working conditions: see NLRB v. Washington Aluminum Co., 370 U.S. 9 (1962). Indeed, from a formal point of view nonunion employees may have even broader legal rights, because their statutory protection is not limited by the prerogatives of a majority-selected union bargaining agent (see *Emporium Capwell*, 420 U.S. 50), nor by the extensive regulation under Taft-Hartley of strike action authorized by the union.

One fundamental objection to the EPC is that American workers will be bewitched by the false allure of in-house representation without real power, and thus will not consider and will not choose the real thing—organization into unions that engage in full-scale bargaining and that will strike if necessary.

In a sense, that argument is a reprise of what I tussled with when I considered the question of whether we should continue or reverse the current step-by-step dismantling of the Section 8(a)(2) ban on company unions.[78] My answer here is simply an elaboration of what I said in that context.

First, direct employee involvement in a range of on-the-job decisions and responsibilities is a good thing, something that more and more workers genuinely want. Conventional collective bargaining by union officials only partially responds to that felt need. It is true that a growing number of union contracts contain extensive and attractive EI programs. But many American workers—in particular, managers and supervisors—are now legally excluded from any right to collective bargaining, and many others do not feel comfortable with representation by the types of unions they see around them. As I have argued throughout this book, the primary aim of the law must be to satisfy the employee need for meaningful protection and participation in the workplace, rather than simply to preserve the institutional formats through which those functions have traditionally been performed. If, as I believe to be the case, a large number of nonunion employees would prefer to cast their lot with the new EPC version of worker representation, they should not be confined to the traditional model of "true" unionism.

Nor should one lightly assume that the supposedly "not as good" EPC procedure is actually the enemy of the "very good" union version. After all, a company union is not a quasi-totalitarian state from which the employees can never extricate themselves in favor of a different governance mechanism. Even in those historical situations in which management was actually the sponsor of an employee representation plan, many such programs eventually did evolve into independent unions.[79] That transformation tends to happen when a group of work-

78. See Chapter 5.
79. An excellent recent study of this evolution at Thompson Products (now TRW Ltd.) is Sanford M. Jacoby's "Reckoning with Company Unions: The Case of Thompson Products, 1934–1964, 42 *Industrial and Labor Relations Review* (1989), and Sanford M. Jacoby and Anil Verna, "Enterprise Unions in the United States: A Case Study of Cor-

ers has had the experience of trying to voice their concerns directly to management but eventually feels the need to ally themselves with a broader organization to make real progress in dealing with the employer.

My assessment is that such a scenario would be much more likely to unfold within the broader legal framework I envisage for the EPC. First, there would be a reformed NLRA that would give the option of full-fledged collective bargaining a much better chance of being utilized. Second, the EPC in-house representation procedure would rest not on unilateral and carefully controlled initiatives of management, but on an independent legal directive. Such a guarantee of an organized employee voice is a better launching pad from which employees could expand their influence. But if many American workers were able to use the tools that an EPC program could give them to make satisfactory progress in improving their employment conditions, I see absolutely no public policy reason for lamenting the fact that these employees have chosen not to join a union.

Assuming, as I do, that there would continue to be a substantial union movement even after the adoption of a new public policy that required in-house EPCs, the next question concerns the relationship between these two institutions. That question actually has two parts. First, what connection would the union movement have with workplaces in which there was an EPC but no union bargaining agent? Second, in workplaces where there was a union with bargaining rights under the NLRA, what should happen to the general EPC requirement?

Regarding presently nonunion plants that do not have or develop full-fledged union bargaining agents, I envisage the possibility that there might still be a substantial connection between the in-house EPC procedure and the outside labor movement. In a sense, American unions are already laying the foundation for such a possibility through the new AFL-CIO-sponsored idea of associate union membership.[80]

An associate member is someone who joins a union not necessarily for purposes of collective bargaining, but rather to take advantage of a variety of attractive union services that workers can use, short of the negotiation of a collective agreement. Some of these services (volume

---

porate Compensation and Industrial Relations Strategies," forthcoming, 30 *Industrial Relations* (1990).

80. See AFL-CIO Committee on the Evolution of Work, *The Changing Situation of Workers and Their Unions* (February 1985).

consumer discounts, for example) are not work-related at all. Others are explicitly tailored to the variety of workplace trends that I have been tracing, especially the rise of employment rights. I have reiterated a number of times that for ordinary workers, at least, real access to regulatory programs (such as workers' compensation) depends to a considerable extent on their ability to draw on the resources, expertise, and backing of a broader organization of workers. Associate membership (at a somewhat lower dues level) offers unorganized workers the opportunity to avail themselves of the representation resources of the union movement in enforcing the broad array of new employment rights.

If the EPC idea were to be adopted in a form something like what I have suggested, especially with some guaranteed level of financial resources, this procedure would dovetail quite nicely with the AFL-CIO associate membership program. The EPC could enter into a relationship with a union, in which the union would provide the in-house EPC with the kinds of expert advice and assistance it might need in dealing with a variety of complex problems such as pension reversions, toxic exposures, new technology, or comparable worth revaluation of female-dominated jobs.

Of course, EPCs would and should draw on similar assistance from a variety of other groups—the NAACP, NOW, AARP, the Public Citizen Group and so on—depending on their specific issues and needs. But I doubt that any other source could provide *workers* as such with the breadth and depth of assistance that the union movement can. And if the union movement were thus able to prove its tangible value to workers across the country who were regularly grappling with problems of real importance to them, that might serve as an entree for a union's tapping latent employee interest in full-scale bargaining.

If employees already have a union for bargaining purposes, would there be any need for an EPC as well? In West Germany that is not a problem, because unions there concentrate their efforts on the negotiation of industry-wide agreements and on political action to secure government-imposed employment standards that together set the basic floor of employment terms for all firms. Inside the individual enterprise the Works Council is the body that actually deals directly with management about both the application and the improvement of the standards contained in the basic union agreement and in the law. By contrast, the United States industrial relations system consists of national unions which have a strong base in local entities that negotiate and enforce agreements specifying all the relevant terms of the employment relationship. Given this presence of established local unions and contracts, there is a real risk of confusion and conflict if a new and somewhat mismatched EPC procedure were to be superimposed on them. Would it not make sense, then, simply to exclude present and future unionized establishments from the scope of any EPC policy?

In my view, such a blanket exclusion would be a mistake. It is inconsistent with our present approach to the variety of existing employment rights.[81] For example, although unions negotiated over workplace safety and health long before OSHA was enacted, it seemed unfair and unwise to exclude unionized plants from the new legal standards contained in that act. Although an EPC policy would create a new right to workplace participation rather than new substantive protection, EPC-like participation implies a number of specific rights that unionized employees have not necessarily enjoyed even when they have selected a bargaining agent under the NLRA. Thus under the EPC program the employees would be entitled to receive from the employer specific information, access, and financial support; and from the union, the right to elect from their own numbers the people who would represent them in dealing with management on a broad range of topics. If we believe that these participatory rights are valuable enough to justify public policy support, then they should not be withheld from workers who happen to be union members.

My preferred method of dealing with this problem would be as follows. In those cases in which the union bargaining agent satisfied certain key EPC conditions for direct employee member elections and representatives, the employees in that bargaining unit would be entitled to designate, by a majority vote, their local union as the committee that would represent them in the EPC program. Elected employee officials of the union local would then exercise the variety of rights and duties conferred on EPCs. Another EPC would have to be created for the benefit of the nonunion employees at that work site, but the rela-

81. An exception to this generalization is the recent Montana wrongful dismissal legislation which excludes employees covered by collective agreements from its coverage. Given my critical appraisal of the limitations of this statute (see Chapter 2, pp. 96–99), the exclusion may well be a blessing in disguise for union members. But assuming that a better law was developed guaranteeing adequate protection to employees against wrongful dismissal, there is absolutely no justification for excluding unionized employees from its substantive rights and benefits (though one could imagine a requirement that union members utilize the private arbitration procedure established under the labor contract to enforce the new substantive protections against dismissal).

tions between the two bodies would be coordinated in essentially the same way as they would be handled for EPCs at different plants or office sites of the same nonunion firm.

The Challenge of Implementation

Serious thinking about both the design and the rationale of the EPC concept helps put labor law reform in a broader perspective. The *raison d'être* of such legislative action would not be to help unions as such. Rather, the aim would be to secure for workers the protective and participatory functions traditionally performed by trade unions—sometimes well, sometimes not so well. We must acknowledge that representation by a national union for purposes of collective bargaining with one's employer is only one vehicle through which these vital functions can be performed. What we need now is a multifaceted strategy that will provide American employees with a variety of institutional options through which they can play a meaningful role in the governance of their workplaces.

The legal starting point would be a guarantee to all employees that wherever they work, they will find a structure for elected and informed representation of their interests in the firm. I believe that many workers would find that this procedure alone will give them the kind of voice that they need and want. Ideally, having provided employees with that mode of direct indigenous representation, we could at the same time reduce considerably the burden we are now placing on governmental resources to protect the interests of employees from outside the firm. It is also likely that a substantial number of employees who are not faring well in our new product, capital, and labor markets will feel the need for the additional leverage and influence that comes from membership in a larger union that can bargain for more advantageous contract benefits from the employer, and that can help enforce the basic social and legal safety net that the government will want to provide to all workers. And it will take a new National Labor Relations Act, thoroughly revamped along the lines I sketched earlier, to finally make good on the original promise of the Wagner Act that American workers can readily organize themselves into a union for their mutual aid and protection. But while I remain convinced that labor law reform is a necessary and important step toward filling the representation gap in the American workplace, I insist that it is not a sufficient response to the felt needs of the many workers who want a greater voice and influence than management has been ready to cede voluntarily, but who would rather not have a union for that purpose.

Of course, union representation and employee participation committees do not exhaust the possible modes of employee voice within the enterprise. One can imagine a national labor policy that would also seek to give workers a presence in the executive suite to help influence the key strategic decisions of the firm. In fact, if one goes to West Germany to learn about the operation of elected Works Councils in plants and offices, one will also find in that country a codetermination law that guarantees employees representation on the supervisory boards of the major corporations, a labor policy that has spread to a number of other European countries.[82] Why not make this idea a prominent part of the agenda for labor law reform in this country?

In principle, I have no doubt that a worker voice in the corporate boardroom would be a valuable component of the governance structure of the firm. After all, that is the place where many of the major decisions are made about the firm's product lines, investments, plant closings and relocations, mergers and acquisitions, and a host of other steps that dictate the economic parameters within which all other corporate decisions must be made. It has been suggested by some economists[83] that employees are not a constituency that must be represented in the boardroom. They argue that notwithstanding the inadequate protection that competitive labor markets provide for an employee's substantial investment in a particular firm, the employee's interests can be effectively defended through contracts negotiated by his union. The problem is that even if employees do have a union, both the legal framework and the historic dynamic of the American industrial relations system have almost entirely removed these decisions from the purview of the negotiating table,[84] and once the decisions are made they largely preempt the ability of a union to advance and secure the vital needs of its members in this area. And as we have seen, an

82. See Clyde Summers, "Worker Participation in the U.S. and West Germany: A Comparative Study from an American Perspective," 28 *American Journal of Comparative Law* 367 (1980); and John Crispo, *Industrial Democracy in Western Europe: A North American Perspective* (Toronto: McGraw-Hill Ryerson, 1978), especially Chapter 7, "Worker Representation on Corporate Boards."

83. Most prominently by Oliver E. Williamson in his "Corporate Governance," 93 *Yale Law Journal* 1197 (1984).

84. On the law see Katherine Van Wezel Stone, "Labor and the Corporate Structure," 55 *University of Chicago Law Review* 73, 152–161 (1988); on the industrial relations setting see Thomas A. Kochan et al., *Transformation*, pp. 178–197.

even bigger problem in the American workplace is that the vast majority of employees of private firms do not now enjoy union representation and have no realistic prospect of securing this right under the current law. If even an established union is typically unable to roll back a proposed corporate merger, for example, because of its harmful effects on employees, then, *a fortiori*, an EPC would be powerless to do so in any circumstances.

At a minimum, then, it is important that a comprehensive labor policy include measures that would clear away the numerous features of our present labor, corporate, and antitrust laws that are potential obstacles to firms' voluntarily agreeing to have employee representatives (say, union leaders) on corporate boards.[85] Having said that, I would give comparatively little political priority to establishing any such employee presence on the board. The problem is that the bare insertion on a corporate board of a director elected by or from among the employees is highly unlikely to make much real difference in the employees' lives, at least until there is established in the firm the type of organized employee base through which the workers could define their common concerns as guidance for "their" directors and to which those directors would be accountable for their decisions.

Indeed, that is precisely the ESOP problem that we observed earlier.[86] In form at least, the ESOP gives employees the even more significant influence in the firm that comes from *ownership*, but in practice such ownership has turned out to be a largely empty promise, at least for the vast majority of nonunion employees who participate in ESOPs. In West Germany, that problem has been addressed reasonably well through effective councils elected at each work site of the enterprise, and strong and resourceful national unions with a great deal of experience in the functioning of the codetermined corporate board in their respective industries. In seeking to fill the representation gap in the American workplace, I believe we must begin at the base, with the development of employee participation committees in all sizable firms, and with real protection of the right of employees to organize themselves into local unions that can affiliate with large national

---

85. Valuable analyses of these problems, with arrays of proposals to deal with them, appear in Clyde W. Summers, "Codetermination in the United States," 4 *Journal of Comparative Corporate Law and Securities Regulation* 155 (1982); and Michael C. Harper, "Reconciling Collective Bargaining With Employee Supervision of Management," 137 *University of Pennsylvania Law Review* 1 (1988).

86. See Chapter 4, pp. 169–173.

bodies for purposes of collective bargaining. Only after significant progress has been made in these areas will it be time to consider the headier atmosphere of corporate decision-making in the boardroom.[87]

From many readers the foregoing observation will evoke the response that we are as far away as ever from any serious prospect for this program of supposedly lower-level labor law reform. When I began writing this book, the Democratic contenders for the 1988 presidential nomination were just beginning to assemble their ideas and position papers. The problem of how to govern the workplace, of how best to represent the interests of employees in the enterprise, was conspicuous by its absence from the debates within the party. As I finished this manuscript, George Bush had been elected President, but I doubt that these concerns are what he had in mind when he spoke of a "kinder, gentler nation." And surely the reason that is so is that when one thinks of labor law reform, one immediately thinks of unions, and when one thinks of unions, one imagines a special interest group, an institution that was so unpopular that it hung like a millstone around the candidacy of Walter Mondale in 1984. Of course, it is not an argument against a scholarly work that its conclusions may be politically unpalatable. Still, having labored through writing (or reading) a book that has made the case for a fairly detailed package of substantial labor law reform, one would expect to find some attention paid to the question of whether these ideas might ever appear on the political agenda within any foreseeable time.

There is reason to believe that major changes in our labor and employment law—if properly presented and defended—would be considerably more appealing to the general public than one might initially suspect. I referred earlier to the 1988 Gallup Poll, which documents an appreciable rise in the net approval rating of labor unions over the last several years.[88] And when one penetrates beneath the surface of that

87. As was aptly concluded by Raymond Russell, "Using Ownership to Control: Making Workers Owners in the Contemporary United States," 14 *Politics and Society* 253–287 (1984), "not much more workers' power is likely come out of worker ownership [via ESOPs, for example] than goes into it at the start."

88. In 1981, 55 percent of a national sample of the general public said they approved of unions, versus 35 percent who said they disapproved. This net positive rating of 20 percent was the lowest in the fifty-year history of polling this issue. However, by 1988 the union positive rating had risen to 61 percent and the negative had dropped to 25 percent; so net union support was up to 36 percent, nearly double what it had been just a few years earlier.

popular sentiment about unions, one discovers a variety of more specific attitudes that are even more promising.[89]

It is clear that the single biggest drawback to the image of American unionism is the popular feeling that the union movement—Big Labor—is too powerful, especially in the political arena; and that union leaders wield this power for their own personal interests rather than for the good of their members or the community as a whole. If there is one silver lining in the series of major public defeats suffered by unions during the Reagan administration (ranging from the air traffic controller disaster to the NFL Players Association debacle), it is the growing realization that unions are once again the underdogs, and Americans tend to like an underdog.[90]

Even more important, there is strong public approval of the functions performed by unions. By significant margins the public believes that the standard of living of American workers has been seriously undermined by wage reductions and benefit cuts (73 percent to 23 percent); that when firms seek to cut their costs, it is workers who suffer, not managers (55 percent to 37 percent); and that unions are the best instrument with which to increase wages and job security (75 percent to 23 percent), to resolve complaints and grievances (82 percent to 15 percent), to defend and enforce laws that benefit employees (68 percent to 21 percent), to secure fair treatment for employees on the job (62 percent to 35 percent), and generally to protect employees from exploitation by their employers (56 percent to 38 percent). These feel-

89. The best review of polling data regarding unions and the workplace through the early eighties is by Seymour M. Lipset, "Labor Unions in the Public Mind," in Seymour M. Lipset, ed., *Unions in Transition* p. 287 (San Francisco, ICS Press, 1986). Since then there have been significant changes in popular attitude, as evidenced in the report of a detailed opinion poll by Lou Harris, *A Study on the Outlook for Trade Union Organizing* (1984); in the review of the Harris and other polling data by James L. Medoff, *The Public's Image of Labor and Labor's Response* (1984); in an AFL-CIO *Compendium of Survey Data* (1987), which collects data from polls taken by the *Washington Post* (1986), CBS News–*New York Times* (1986), the National Opinion Research Center (1986), the *Los Angeles Times* (1987) and others; and in a Gallup study, *Public Opinion and Knowledge Concerning the Labor Movement* (1988). I have drawn on these various sources for the assertions I make in the text about changing popular sentiment regarding unions and labor law reform.

90. By a 52 percent to 39 percent margin, respondents to the 1988 Gallup Poll agreed that unions have become too weak to protect their members. On the other hand, there remains a seriously inaccurate stereotype of the degree of power still left to the union movement. That same Gallup Poll asked for estimates of the current proportion of the work force which is unionized, and the mean estimate was 45 percent, or nearly three times the true figure.

ings are why most Americans (69 percent to 26 percent) agree that "labor unions are good for the nation as a whole," and say (by a margin of 58 percent to 36 percent) that they are "personally more sympathetic to labor than to business." And that in turn is why, by a resounding margin (81 percent to 11 percent), the American public strongly believes that workers should have the right to union representation if they want it.

The public also realizes that this worker right is in serious danger from corporate resistance in the past few years (73 percent to 15 percent), that "corporations sometimes harass, intimidate and fire employees who openly speak out for a union" (69 percent to 21 percent), and that if one's own employer learned of a union drive, active supporters could well be fired.[91] The vast majority of Americans (78 percent to 17 percent) believe "it is unfair for the employer to resist its employees' efforts to form a union or employee association," and agree (by 66 percent to 25 percent) that "existing American laws should be strengthened to prevent corporations from denying their workers' right to organize."

Of course, as supporters of gun control laws regularly learn, it is one thing to detect such popular sentiments in opinion polls, and it is quite another to pilot statutory reform through the reefs and shoals of the political process in Washington, which has been carefully designed to maximize the leverage of those who are strongly interested in preserving the legal status quo. After all, in 1978, a relatively modest package of labor law reform, one which was backed by a Democratic president and approved by a large margin in the House of Representatives, was foiled in the Senate when its supporters could not get the three-fifths margin to end a filibuster and put the measure to a final up-or-down vote. The somewhat farther-reaching ideas I propose here would attract even more intense opposition from the business community and its political action committees, and would arguably have even worse prospects for successful enactment.[92]

91. When questions about the last, more specific, risk of firing were posed by the Lou Harris Poll, the response was that 38 percent thought *their* employer would fire, demote, or otherwise make life difficult for a union supporter (versus 54 percent who did not think that, and 8 percent who were not sure). In a 1986 ABC News–*Washington Post* poll, 34 percent said they thought that they themselves would be in personal danger of being fired by their own employer for supporting a union (versus 60 percent who did not think that, and 4 percent who did not know).

92. On the declining success of the union movement in the current electoral and political environment, see Thomas Byrne Edsall, *The New Politics of Inequality* (New York:

If there is to be any hope of labor law reform some time in the next decade, one thing is certain: the package of reforms must be presented (and must be genuinely presentable) as responsive to certain vital needs of American workers, not of unions and their leaders.

Take, for example, the proposals I made for more effective remedies for discriminatory discharges and for prohibition of permanent replacement of strikers. It is vital that these ideas be seen as a form of protection for individual workers against loss of their jobs, in which they may have invested much of their working lives, at the hands of often powerful corporations seeking to deny their employees the free exercise of their fundamental rights. That aspect of the essential elements of my labor law reform package would be much more credible if it were incorporated in a broader statutory protection against the dismissal of an employee in violation of *any* public policy, a statute that would provide such remedies as at-large damages and expedited interim injunctions from the courts, with provisions for attorney fees and other means of legal assistance.

By the same token, the idea of "instant elections" would be more appealing if it were developed as part of a broader package designed to maximize worker participation in the firm, and which included the repeal of Section 8(a)(2) of the NLRA and substitution of the requirement of worker participation committees at sizable work sites. A very revealing question in the 1988 Gallup Poll asked Americans whether "employees should have an *organization* of coworkers to discuss and resolve legitimate concerns with their employers" [emphasis added]. The level of agreement was overwhelming (90 percent to 6 percent). I have argued throughout this book that we must be able to restore to the term "union" the sense that unionism is an *activity* of the employees, not an *entity* external to them, often even more remote from their lives than the corporation they work for. Collective bargaining is a process through which employees may voice their workplace concerns and wield group leverage to elicit favorable responses from their employer. Imagine a future environment in which the natural state of every workplace included an indigenous elected local organization, an Employee Participation Committee, to represent the employees. A group of employees decides that its in-plant or office EPC arrangement

---

W. W. Norton, 1984); Thomas Ferguson and Joel Rogers, *Right Turn: The Decline of the Democrats and the Future of American Politics* (New York: Hill and Wang, 1986); and Robert Kuttner, *The Life of the Party: Democratic Prospects in 1988 and Beyond* (New York: Viking, 1988).

would be even more effective if it could draw upon the knowledge, experience, and resources of a national union that had confronted the same kinds of problems in many other firms in the same industry. From that viewpoint it is easy to defend the proposition that these employees should have easy and "instant" access to such union affiliation, without allowing the employer the elaborate opportunities now offered by the NLRA to mount a scorched earth campaign against that employee choice. But the key is to make it clear that each of these legal reforms is part of a multifaceted strategy to give more meaningful participation and more effective protection to American workers, not to preserve and enhance the power of unions as such (as, rightly or wrongly, the purpose of 1978 Labor Reform Act was regarded).

Still, no matter how artfully such a package of worker rights might be designed in order to appeal to these latent public attitudes, there is no chance that President Bush would sign such a sweeping national reform of our labor and employment laws, and no realistic prospect that his veto could be overridden. That suggests that we should take a serious look at the possibility of action at the state level.

Earlier in this chapter, I referred to a number of substantive ideas from Canadian labor law that might be tailored for the American market. One reason why Canada's laws have been so much more innovative and progresssive is that in Canada the basic constitutional responsibility for the law at work resides at the provincial rather than the federal level.[93] It has been perfectly feasible for the Province of Ontario, for example, to govern through its labor legislation the relationship between the Canadian Auto Workers and General Motors at the GM plant in Oakville, and for the Province of Quebec to apply a somewhat different law to the GM plant at Ste. Thérèse. More important, the fact that each province has this responsibility for the major industries within its borders means that the provinces also have both the opportunity and the incentive to act, in Brandeis's phrase, as "laboratories for social experimentation." Almost all the significant advances in the Canadian law of the workplace first took hold in individual provinces (as did many of the pioneering efforts in health care, civil rights, and other policy fields) and then spread gradually through a natural process of emulation and competition to other jurisdictions across the country, including the federal government (Canadian federal labor and employment laws cover about 10 percent of the total work force).

---

93. See Weiler, *Reconcilable Differences,* pp. 1–11, for a more extended discussion and references.

Nor are these uses of federalism in labor relations inherently un-American. In fact, since the early sixties the states have engaged in much the same process of creative experimentation in their public sector labor laws that were (fortunately) excluded from the purview of the Wagner Act in 1935. But in the private sector, such state innovation has been blocked by the presence of the NLRA, which preempts almost this entire field.[94] Suppose, though, one were to experiment with a very different approach. The threshold for NLRB jurisdiction would be lifted to exclude all small businesses—defined, for example, as any firm with twenty-five or fewer employees. One political advantage of this step would be largely to remove the powerful small business lobby as a major obstacle to reform of the NLRA itself. As to the smaller firms and their employees, the several states would be free to devise their own more effective means of protecting their citizens' right to representation in the workplace, if that is what their voters want to do.

The reaction of most liberals and others who support workers' rights is that any such revival of states' rights is unthinkable, given what the more politically reactionary states—such as North Carolina or Utah—might do or not do for employees who often are exploited by small businesses.[95] Since the New Deal era, the assumption of the union movement and its supporters has been that the more liberal congressional delegations from states like Massachusetts and New York must be relied on to secure national legal standards that will guarantee equal rights and protections to those who work in the Carolinas or in the Rocky Mountain states, and, not incidentally, to protect those employed in the more progressive states from being politically whipsawed by mobile capital pursuing the lowest common denominator of labor legislation.

As to the concern about competition, the Canadian experience suggests that it is not inevitable that the terms of labor legislation will play a particularly prominent role in the decisions (as opposed to the rhetoric) of manufacturing firms choosing where to locate their plants and offices. Certainly the vast majority of businesses in the service, transportation, and construction sectors have no choice but to locate where

94. The one exception to that generalization stems from the exclusion of farm workers from the NLRA. This statutory exclusion gave California the opening in the seventies to enact an Agricultural Labor Relations Act, which pioneered a number of legal innovations that were eventually embodied in the abortive federal Labor Reform Act of 1978.

95. Firms that employ twenty-five or fewer workers comprise fully 35 percent of the private sector labor force, but only about 5 percent of the employees in such firms are unionized, and they receive almost uniformly lower wages and poorer benefits than do their counterparts working for big business.

their customers are. In any event, to allay that concern I have suggested only the very modest exclusion of smaller firms from the NLRA, because these are the employers that are the least capable of relocating from one region to another.

The simple answer to the other egalitarian objection—that workers in North Carolina and Utah would do worse than workers in Massachusetts and New York—is that it is precisely senators like Orrin Hatch from Utah and Jesse Helms from North Carolina who have been and will be in the vanguard of the battle against any labor law reform in Washington, against legal changes that might help employees wanting to organize in New York and Massachusetts. I think it is time to take a chance on what might emanate from state capitals like Boston and Albany, and hope that workers in other states will fight to send better and more responsive legislators to their own state capitals.

One signal virtue of the Employee Participation Committee idea is that it does not require federal statutory action to remove the preemptive effect of the National Labor Relations Act.[96] Recent judicial developments in the law of labor preemption have made it clear that when a state legislature[97] or a state court[98] adopts a general legal standard providing certain substantive benefits and protections to all its employees, union and nonunion alike, the collective bargaining regime fostered by the NLRA must simply accept this as the minimum floor for its contract negotiations. By the same token, then, if a state were to adopt a law mandating elected EPCs in all its workplaces, this requirement would serve only as a floor from which specific units of employees would still be able to opt for full-fledged union representation for purposes of collective bargaining under the NLRA.[99] That means that

96. It would be enjoyable, however, to watch a Republican President and congressmen try to devise arguments about why it is necessary to preserve the federal government's control of labor relations in the small business sector.

97. See Metropolitan Life Insurance v. Massachusetts, 471 U.S. 724 (1985), concerning a Massachusetts statute mandating psychiatric benefits in all employer-provided health insurance; and Fort Halifax Packing Co., Inc. v. Coyne, 482 U.S. 1 (1987), dealing with a Maine law presumptively requiring a severance payment to employees laid off as a result of a plant closing.

98. See Lingle v. Norge Division of Magic Chef, Inc., 486 U.S. 399 (1988), where the Illinois courts had adopted a general public policy doctrine protecting employees against wrongful discharge for claiming workers' compensation benefits.

99. The claim in the text assumes that if such an EPC were to be created by the employer, it would not be held to be an illegal employer-dominated labor organization under Section 8(a)(2) of the NLRA, because the Board and the courts would apply to such a program the rubrics of "communication" and "cooperation" which I depicted in

Governor Mario Cuomo, who chose not to run for President in 1988 but whose Commission authored a report calling for a healthy dose of employee participation as a solution to America's competitive problems,[100] is perfectly free to establish in New York State a legal framework that would help realize the Commissions's objective.[101] And if I am right in my impression that this is an idea whose time may be arriving, successful implementation of the EPC idea in New York could well mean that politicians elsewhere would compete to get the credit for implementing, rather than fighting, the idea in their own states.

While I believe, then, that there is some political hope for the kinds of serious change I am proposing in the law at work, I am under no illusion about how difficult a struggle bringing about such change will be. Even if there were significant reforms in our labor laws, there is no guarantee that American unions would then be able to strike a responsive enough chord among unorganized workers to take advantage of such a new law. A significant obstacle, one to which I have alluded a number of times, is that American workers often feel the same need for protection against arbitrary treatment by their union officials as by company managers, and the same lack of democratic participation in the decisions of their union as of their employer. And the existence of these feelings (especially among nonunion workers), fed by just a few well-publicized incidents, is important whether or not it represents a true picture of the typical experience of members with their unions.

If these observations are valid, American unions must think seriously about making substantial changes in their own mode of gover-

---

Chapter 5, pp. 212–218. It is of course possible that the Supreme Court might reverse this evolving interpretation and return to the original understanding of Section 8(a)(2) as a blanket prohibition on any employee involvement in firm decisions outside the ambit of collective bargaining with independent unions. In that (unlikely) event, a state law which required employers to establish programs that are illegal under the NLRA would be nullified by the federal law and by the Supremacy Clause of the Constitution. But assuming the continuation and expansion of the current "liberal" interpretation of Section 8(a)(2) as permitting employers to adopt unilaterally a variety of EI programs without running afoul of the NLRA, current preemption doctrine allows a state to require employers within its borders to give workers the EPC version of this workplace benefit.

100. See Cuomo Commission on Trade and Competitiveness, *The Cuomo Commission Report: A New American Formula for a Strong Economy* (New York: Simon and Schuster, 1988).

101. Recall that my own prescription in Chapter 6 assumes that such an EPC structure would assume the primary responsibility for asserting and resolving much of the array of direct government regulation of the workplace, and thus relieve business of some of the burden of dealing with increasing statutory and judicial intervention in connection with problems such as wrongful dismissal.

nance at the same time as they are busy advocating changes in the governance of the workplace itself. An example of the kind of governance device that could be adopted, one to which I am partial, is the Public Review Board of the United Auto Workers: an internal UAW procedure that guarantees to each member of the union a right of appeal to an independent neutral body of any constitutional grievance the member may have against the UAW and its national or local officials. Why should we ask that unions alone adopt far-reaching, self-limiting measures like this (and that they also guarantee secret ballots for strike votes, contract ratifications, and a host of other decisions that will be made by the membership directly), when we do not dream of asking this much of the corporation, or the university, or other powerful institutions in our society? To my mind we are justified in asking more of unions, because we have a right to expect the highest level of membership protection and participation in an institution whose *raison d'être*, after all, is to pursue exactly that kind of employee treatment and voice in the workplace. In any event, dramatic steps such as these are going to be necessary to persuade the American people and the politicians whom they elect that the institution of unionism is sufficiently worthwhile in our political economy that it warrants once again the kind of legal lifeline that it received from the Wagner Act over a half-century ago.

7 · Conclusion

Closing the Representation Gap

My argument in this book has followed a long and winding road. I have addressed a considerable number of workplace problems—from wrongful dismissal to occupational safety, from pay equity to pension security—and have reviewed the capacity and performance of several institutional alternatives through which we now address these problems—competitive markets and government regulation, human resource management and collective bargaining. In appraising these institutions and their characteristic ways of addressing workplace issues, I have drawn upon scholarly analyses from law, economics, industrial relations, and critical theory. Looking back on my argument, the following are some of the crucial claims I have made.

First, the workplace poses a more vital challenge to public policy than has been generally acknowledged in recent public debates. It is equally if not more important than the family, the school, the farm, the stock market, or the other settings in our domestic life that have figured much more prominently in recent political debates. What goes on in the employment relationship makes a huge difference in the economic and social fate of the vast majority of American citizens, as well as in the productivity and competitiveness of American enterprise. And as we have seen in previous chapters, the allocation of authority over the terms of that employment relationship has undergone a fundamental transformation over the last quarter century, with little national attention being paid to the nature and direction of the changes.

My assumption, then, is that the governance of the workplace requires the exercise of real authority. Although competitive labor markets set significant outer bounds to the terms and conditions of employment, a distinctive feature of the modern labor market is the special commitment made by both worker and firm to the existing employment relationship. This commitment satisfies the reciprocal interests of the employee in security and stability in his working (and consequently his personal) life, and of the firm in retaining a trained, experienced, and cohesive work team. But because these special mutual advantages cannot readily be duplicated elsewhere, the process of competitive outside bidding for jobs and workers does not easily and effectively restrain one party from exploiting a particular situation in order to reap most of the net advantage from the bilateral relationship. Whether and to what extent such exploitation occurs is heavily influenced by the forms of governance that predominate in a nation's economy.

From the point of view of the American worker, the risk has been exacerbated by a number of coincident trends in our economy. Stiffer competition in product markets means that many American firms face strong pressures to reduce their labor costs. The potential for hostile takeovers and leveraged buyouts in the new capital markets has made American management much more inclined to increase the immediate value of the shareholders' equity, even if doing so would produce a sharp decrease in the relative value of the employees' stake in the firm, which in turn would produce a decline in long-term employee morale and in the commitment of the work force to the success of the enterprise. The pension reversion phenomenon described in Chapter 4 is a textbook illustration of this syndrome. Finally, the stark decline of collective bargaining in the private sector labor market has eroded this historic bulwark of the employee's interests, both in firms that once were unionized and in many others than traditionally followed the lead set by collective bargaining when it came to devising solutions to similar workplace problems.

But the labor market, like nature, abhors a vacuum. So we have observed the evolution of two phenomena: the first, a proliferation of legal regulation to protect employee interests in certain vital aspects of employment, with government bureaucrats and private lawyers seeking to represent and defend the interests of workers; the second, the emergence of human resource programs that involve employees in a variety of decisions concerning their jobs and the employer's operations, with many personnel departments interpreting their role as representing the work force in the deliberations of management.

These institutional alternatives have admitted virtues relative to collective bargaining. Government regulation guarantees more equal protection to the vital interests of all employees than can be produced by a market reconstructed through collective bargaining. Similarly, employee involvement programs offer workers a more immediate and often broader degree of direct employee participation in the judgments which are made in their day-to-day working lives. But I believe that both of these models of workplace governance suffer from a fundamental flaw. Neither provides a base of organization of and by workers inside the firm which would enable ordinary employees to take advantage of the legal rights promised by the government from the outside, and which would give employees real power to fulfill their other needs, including the desire for broader participation, when such preferences conflict with the prerogatives of management or appear to threaten larger financial returns for the shareholders.

Yet those who believe that collective bargaining through unions has major comparative advantages as a device for addressing workplace problems must acknowledge the shortcomings of union representation as it has evolved in America. On the one hand, collective agreements negotiated by national unions have imposed rigid restraints on the sensible operation of individual enterprises, thereby fueling the latent resistance of management to any intrusions on its powers. On the other hand, the actual bargaining process often provides such an attenuated version of workplace participation for the employees themselves that this mode of involvement has become less attractive to workers. Indeed, these all too human flaws in collective bargaining themselves reflect the historic tendency of the union movement to shift power from the local body with roots in the immediate workplace to the more remote national union organization and its leadership.

I have argued that the kind of worker organization that is attuned to the needs of the changing work force and marketplace will be more oriented toward the individual enterprise and its employees, with a central organization whose role is confined to providing resources and assistance to constituent units of a loose union confederation. But we have seen how our current labor laws pose a major obstacle to such a reconfiguration of authority within the union. Many employees would like to associate with their fellow workers to secure a meaningful voice in what happens to them inside the firm. But in order to overcome the typically fierce resistance by management to *any* employee organization and to secure a contract that will give them enforceable rights on the job, workers are obliged to rely on the leadership and resources of large, powerful bureaucratic unions, to which many employees are unwilling to commit their destinies.

This dilemma is a major source of the yawning representation gap in the American workplace. In Chapter 6 I outlined a detailed program for overcoming the quandary. One part of the program involves searching labor law reform, which will be necessary to give full-fledged union representation a fighting chance to revive and to survive into the next century. But I am convinced that we need to do more, that we must go beyond the fundamental assumption of the NLRA that American workers must choose unionized collective bargaining as the sole alternative to the nonunion status quo they experience when they go to work in the millions of offices and plants in this country. The labor policy for the next century must include a third option: a guarantee of a minimum level of indigenous worker organization and representation for employees in every sizable workplace in the country. This should be the new "natural" state, in which employees may or may not feel the need to exercise their right—a more accessible right—to collective bargaining under a reformed NLRA.

I am all too aware of the uphill political struggle that would be required to establish such an independent worker voice in the American corporate enterprise. There appear to be no immediate prospects for even modest versions of conventional labor law reform, let alone the more fundamental constitution of a system of employee participation that I propose in this book. Even so, I still believe that it is preferable to aim for the more ambitious program of mandatory employee participation committees. In fact, because this program is more directly responsive to an evident need of all employees, it would actually impart a more appealing aura to related revisions of the NLRA that might otherwise be attacked as advancing only the special interests of organized labor.

Perhaps enactment of such a program is just a fond hope, but I take comfort in the thought that the problem of workplace governance now occupies a position analogous to that of tax reform in the seventies. In that decade a variety of tax scholars were exploring the myriad ways in which the tax laws frustrated the underlying values that the tax system was supposed to be bolstering. Once the careful intellectual spadework had been done, the way was clear for several prominent political leaders to embrace the cause of tax reform, to educate the general public about the huge gap between the promise and reality of the tax laws, and to lead the battle (and take the credit) for the major reconstruction of the Internal Revenue Code that took place in the mid-eighties.[1]

1. The story of the tax code overhaul is grippingly narrated in Jeffrey H. Birnbaum and Alan S. Murray, *Showdown At Gucci Gulch: Lawmakers, Lobbyists, and the Unlikely Triumph of the Tax Reform* (New York: Random House, 1987).

Together with the many other industrial relations scholars on whose work I have relied in writing this book, my focus has been on the battle of ideas now being waged about the world of work. What is needed is systematic exploration of the nature and consequences of the widening representation gap in our plants and offices, and explanations of why and how an effective organizational base should be restored to employees in the governance of the workplace. If I am correct in concluding that it is not just the American worker, but the American political economy as well that will benefit from an independent employee voice in the business firm, I am confident that there will be political leaders who will make this quest their cause for the nineties.

Index of Cases

General Index